W9-CAU-817

EDUCATING EVERYBODY'S CHILDREN

Diverse Teaching Strategies for Diverse Learners

Revised and Expanded 2nd Edition

Mixed Sources

Product group from well-managed
forests and other controlled sources

www.fsc.org Cert no. SW-COC-1530
© 1996 Forest Stewardship Council

ASCD cares about Planet Earth. This book has been
printed on environmentally friendly paper.

EDUCATING EVERYBODY'S CHILDREN

Diverse Teaching Strategies for Diverse Learners

Revised and Expanded 2nd Edition

Robert W. Cole, Editor

Association for Supervision and Curriculum Development

Alexandria, Virginia USA

Association for Supervision and Curriculum Development
1703 N. Beauregard St. • Alexandria, VA 22311-1714 USA
Phone: 800-933-2723 or 703-578-9600 • Fax: 703-575-5400
Web site: www.ascd.org • E-mail: member@ascd.org
Author guidelines: www.ascd.org/write

Gene R. Carter, *Executive Director*; Nancy Modrak, *Publisher*; Julie Houtz, *Director of Book Editing & Production*; Miriam Goldstein, *Project Manager*; Catherine Guyer, *Senior Graphic Designer*; Mike Kalyan, *Production Manager*; Keith Demmons, *Desktop Publishing Specialist*

Copyright © 2008 by the Association for Supervision and Curriculum Development (ASCD). All rights reserved. No part of this publication may be reproduced or transmitted in any form or by any means, electronic or mechanical, including photocopy, recording, or any information storage and retrieval system, without permission from ASCD. Readers who wish to duplicate material copyrighted by ASCD may do so for a small fee by contacting the Copyright Clearance Center (CCC), 222 Rosewood Dr., Danvers, MA 01923, USA (phone: 978-750-8400; fax: 978-646-8600; Web: www.copyright.com). For requests to reprint rather than photocopy, contact ASCD's permissions office: 703-578-9600 or permissions@ascd.org. Translation inquiries: translations@ascd.org.

Material in this book includes updated and adapted content from *Educating Everybody's Children*, by Robert W. Cole (Ed.), 1995, Alexandria, VA: Association for Supervision and Curriculum Development and from *More Strategies for Educating Everybody's Children*, by Robert W. Cole (Ed.), 2001, Alexandria, VA: Association for Supervision and Curriculum Development.

Printed in the United States of America. Cover art copyright © 2008 by ASCD. ASCD publications present a variety of viewpoints. The views expressed or implied in this book should not be interpreted as official positions of the Association.

All Web links in this book are correct as of the publication date below but may have become inactive or otherwise modified since that time. If you notice a deactivated or changed link, please e-mail books@ascd.org with the words "Link Update" in the subject line. In your message, please specify the Web link, the book title, and the page number on which the link appears.

PAPERBACK ISBN-13: 978-1-4166-0674-1   ASCD product #107003   s6/08
Also available as an e-book through ebrary, netLibrary, and many online booksellers (see Books in Print for the ISBNs).

Quantity discounts for the paperback edition only: 10–49 copies, 10%; 50+ copies, 15%; for 1,000 or more copies, call 800-933-2723, ext. 5634, or 703-575-5634. For desk copies: member@ascd.org.

Library of Congress Cataloging-in-Publication Data
Educating everybody's children : diverse teaching strategies for diverse learners / Robert W. Cole, editor. — Rev. and expanded 2nd ed.
     p. cm.
  Earlier ed. entered under: ASCD Improving Student Achievement Research Panel.
  Includes bibliographical references and index.
  ISBN 978-1-4166-0674-1 (pbk. : alk. paper) 1. Education—United States—Experimental methods. 2. Educational equalization—United States. 3. Minorities—Education—United States. 4. Children with social disabilities—Education—United States. 5. Academic achievement—United States. 6. Multicultural education—United States. I. Cole, Robert W., 1945- II. ASCD Improving Student Achievement Research Panel. Educating everybody's children.

  LB1027.3.A73 2008
  371.39—dc22
                                                            2008008528

17 16 15 14 13 12 11 10 09 08   1 2 3 4 5 6 7 8 9 10 11 12

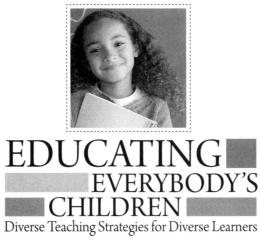

EDUCATING EVERYBODY'S CHILDREN

Diverse Teaching Strategies for Diverse Learners

Revised and Expanded 2nd Edition

Preface:

Educating Everybody's Children: We Know What We Need to Do

Robert W. Cole

In the spring of 1991, ASCD convened a special Advisory Panel on Improving Student Achievement. The panel's aim was to develop school improvement plans that made use of the knowledge base of best practices in teaching and learning. The panel was also charged with identifying the degree to which young people's demographic profiles and social conditions (including gender, socioeconomic status, and cultural, ethnic, and linguistic heritage) influenced their performance in school. The panel members found that good teaching—teaching that is engaging, relevant, multicultural, and appealing to a variety of learning styles—works well with *all* students, but that students from diverse backgrounds may have additional educational needs. To meet the educational needs of all students, the panel concluded, educators need an extensive repertoire of effective instructional tools. Those tools and the knowledge base behind them, gleaned from an extensive review of both basic and applied research, serve as the foundation of this book, just as they did for the two previous volumes in the *Educating Everybody's Children* series.

In 1992, as part of this same effort to make the knowledge base on effective teaching available to practitioners, ASCD convened the Improving Student Achievement

Research Panel, composed of 18 distinguished researchers representing diverse fields and disciplines. The charges to that panel:

1. Produce a publication conveying what research and practice reveal about enhancing the achievement of all students.

2. Identify principles and strategies shown to be effective in meeting the needs of a broad base of our student population.

3. Explore what research has revealed about successfully addressing the needs of students from economically, ethnically, racially, culturally, and linguistically diverse groups.

In dealing with diverse student populations, it is crucial to consider language, heritage, culture, and other contextual factors that may influence academic achievement. Practitioners need to focus on the knowledge and abilities that diverse learners bring to the education setting. Culture and social circumstances profoundly shape learners' interactions with their environment and influence the ways in which they respond to classroom activities.

The differences in achievement between students of mainstream backgrounds and students of nonmainstream backgrounds are not the result of differences in their ability to learn, but rather of discrepancies in the quality of instruction they have received in school. For too long, these students have been poorly served by U.S. schools, and meeting the needs of students from diverse backgrounds continues to be a challenge for many practitioners in the field. Often, teachers have low expectations of poor or minority students that are shaped by inaccurate assumptions about innate ability and a lack of knowledge about students' different cultural backgrounds, including the rules of social interaction between adults and children. In addition, the conditions of schooling in high-poverty areas often include dilapidated buildings, faulty or nonexistent equipment, low wages for teachers, teachers with minimal teaching skills, fragmented families, and deteriorated and demoralized neighborhoods.

Rapidly Changing Demographics

Despite these problems, pockets of educational excellence have emerged in which schools have reversed low achievement. But we need more than pockets of excellence. The demographic makeup of the United States continues to change at a rate scarcely imagined when the first volume of *Educating Everybody's Children* was published more than a decade ago. According to *The Condition of Education 2006* (Rooney et al., 2006), minority students now make up roughly 43 percent of U.S. public school enrollment. And in 2000, almost 20 percent of the country's 58 million preK–12 students were children of immigrants (Capps et al., 2005). Public schools are at the heart of efforts to incorporate these immigrants into U.S. society, and the number of immigrant students grows daily. Children who speak a language other than English are the fastest-growing segment of the U.S. school-age population.

Let us examine some of the specific demographic changes that are overtaking the United States and its schools, with the aim of considering their implications for classroom instruction. (The following statistics were drawn from the U.S. Census Bureau's Web site: http://www.census.gov/popest/estimates.php.)

• The U.S. Hispanic population has almost doubled between the 1990 census (22.4 million) and the U.S. Census Bureau's July 2005 population estimate (42.7 million). Twenty-two percent of the U.S. population under age 5 is Hispanic, and 31 million U.S. household residents ages 5 or older speak Spanish at home. In 2004, 21.9 percent of Hispanics were living in poverty, and 32.7 percent lacked health insurance.

• The African American population, once the largest U.S. minority group, is now estimated by the U.S. Census Bureau to be 39.2 million, making up 13.4 percent of the total population. Thirty-two percent of the black population was under age 18 as of July 1, 2004, and 24.7 percent of blacks were living in poverty. Eleven percent of black youngsters live in grandparent-headed households.

• The population of American Indians (or First Nation people) and Alaskan Natives is 4.4 million, or 1.5 percent of the U.S. population, according to the 2004 census estimates. Some 381,000 people ages 5 or older speak a native North American language at home. (The most prevalent is Navajo; there are 178,014 Navajo speakers.) Twenty-four percent of American Indians live in poverty, and 29 percent lack health insurance. Why focus on these three demographic groups? Because, on average, "African American, Latino, and American Indian children arrive at kindergarten or first grade with lower levels of oral language, prereading, and premathematics skills, as well as lesser general knowledge, than are possessed by White and Asian American children. African American, Latino, and American Indian children also display behaviors less well suited to the school's learning environment" (Farkas, 2003).

And a special *Education Week* online report noted that "while chances exist at every level of education—early-childhood, K–12, and postsecondary—to help break the cycle of poverty, a recent volume by the Washington-based Brookings Institution suggests that too often schools perpetuate rather than reduce class differences. That's in part because children from low-income families generally attend schools that by any measure—school resources, student achievement, qualified teachers—lag behind those of their more affluent peers" (Olson, 2007).

The National Commission on Teaching and America's Future noted that the Education Trust's 2006 report *Teaching Inequality* "unequivocally shows that low-income students and children of color continue to be disproportionately taught by inexperienced, under-qualified teachers" (2006). Indeed, the Education Trust reports that "a full 86% of math and science teachers in the nation's highest minority schools are teaching out of field" (2006).

Overcoming a Pedagogy of Poverty

In 1999, UNESCO declared that every child has the right to high-quality educational experiences. It has become increasingly clear, however, that an enormous gap yawns between that high-minded declaration and the reality of schooling for too many of our children. The good news is that worldwide efforts continue in the push to educate *everybody's* children. The bad news, of course, is that so much remains to be accomplished.

Research shows an ever-widening achievement gap between low-income children and children in more fortunate circumstances. Researchers are examining the barriers that some students face in our schools—barriers too often grounded in class and race—that systematically exclude them from any chance of success in school and in society.

It is no mystery why some students fail. Our education system was designed in the early 1900s as a convenient means of sorting and labeling young people. But labels brand and stifle students rather than encourage them to succeed. Labels identify some students as being less worthy of high-quality school experiences.

The result of such systemic labeling is what Martin Haberman (1991) calls a "pedagogy of poverty," in which low-level tasks become the norm for the less fortunate. Haberman identified the heart of this all-too-common approach to instruction as a set of activities that some teachers use "to the exclusion of nearly everything else." These tasks include "giving information, asking questions, giving directions, making assignments, monitoring seat work, reviewing assignments, giving tests, reviewing tests, assigning homework, reviewing homework, settling disputes, publishing non-compliance, marking papers, and giving grades" (p. 291).

Every one of these activities can be beneficial, admits Haberman. But, he notes, "taken together and performed to the systematic exclusion of other acts, they have become the pedagogical coin of the realm in urban schools. They constitute the pedagogy of poverty—not merely what teachers do and what youngsters expect, but, for different reasons, what parents, the community, and the general public assume teaching to be" (p. 291).

As Eleanor Dougherty and Patte Barth (1997) have observed, "poor and minority children are systematically bludgeoned into low academic performance with a steady dose of low-level, boring, if not downright silly assignments and curricula" (pp. 40–44). In such settings, students do not learn how to think critically and are thus unable to use what they already know to help them understand their world. The willful failure to provide a high-quality education can be a death sentence for these students' futures. Yet we allow some youngsters to languish in such settings during their entire academic careers. A pedagogy of poverty contradicts what we have learned of best teaching and learning practices; it is a subtle, pernicious form of racism.

All too frequently, the young people who need our help the most—children of color who attend high-poverty urban schools—are taught by teachers who "often do not realize that they are setting such low expectations" (Dougherty & Barth, 1997, p. 40). Like many teachers in diverse settings, they have few opportunities to interact with their colleagues or to pursue enriched professional development opportunities—opportunities that should be a part of the professional experience of all teachers, regardless of where or whom they teach. Teaching and learning are complex processes, best supported by research-based practices. These practices cannot be learned and implemented in a vacuum. They must be learned and used within the context of high-quality professional development experiences.

Naturally, most teachers do not intentionally deliver poor instruction. But some most certainly are guilty of doing so, and we cannot afford to ignore that fact. Students cannot learn when they are intellectually starved. Dougherty and Barth (1997) believe that "schools would be far better off ensuring that every activity in every classroom challenges students and guides them toward achieving mastery of core academic content and skills. The best way to do this is by making every assignment worth doing" (p. 40). More often than not in this era of high-stakes testing, and particularly in the case of diverse learners, not every assignment is worth doing.

This unrelenting exposure to a pedagogy of poverty continues to be a pervasive problem in high-poverty schools. Mary Metz (1998/1999) found glaring differences in the educational experiences offered to youngsters in high-poverty areas:

When analyzing the differences in teachers' work in . . . schools across communities differing in social class . . . everything was different . . . the teachers' concerns, and, most strikingly, the rhythm and content of classes—even when they had the same title and used the same textbook. American schools are supposed to be similar, in order to provide equal opportunity to all children. . . . There are, increasingly, . . . distressing circumstances that hinder education in schools in poverty areas, especially those in central cities. These differences between schools [differing in social class] are informal and unofficial, however. These differences in student achievement . . . and the differing expectations that teachers . . . hold for their future accomplishments powerfully affect . . . teachers' . . . motivation to pour resources into academic effort. It is painful and politically delicate to look too closely at the separation among schools created by housing and school district lines in metropolitan areas. To look too closely, to admit that this separation has profound educational consequences, is to admit that we are not offering equality of opportunity to the nation's children. (p. 6)

Although the differences Metz describes fall along income lines, it is important to note that they also fall along color lines. When it comes to academic achievement, a disproportionate number of students of color finish at the bottom. Racism permits some youngsters access to the very best that U.S. society has to offer, while barring others from an equal chance for success in life. Changing this nation's deeply entrenched attitudes toward children of color will take courage—and time.

Can we hope to change the outlook of an entire nation, working person by person? One thing is certain: we can work to ensure that each student, regardless of background and racial characteristics, receives a high-quality education. The most vital fact we have learned as a result of the education reform movement is this: *student achievement stands or falls on the motivation and skills of teachers.* We can begin by certifying that all teachers are capable of delivering a standards-based curriculum that describes what all students should know and be able to do by the time they reach specified grade levels. Then we must ensure that these standards are delivered by means of a "pedagogy of plenty." By these two acts alone we can help to ensure that all schools will be ready and able to educate everybody's children.

No Child Left Behind

There is another topic that cannot be ignored: the No Child Left Behind Act (NCLB). As Monty Neill noted, the fundamental promise of NCLB when it was signed into law in 2002 was that it would "bring new levels of attention and achievement to students traditionally underserved by schools" (quoted in Meier & Wood, 2004, p. 102)—in other words, exactly those young people for whom this book was created.

Unfortunately, according to Linda Darling-Hammond, "the biggest problem with the NCLB Act is that it mistakes measuring schools with fixing them" (quoted in Meier & Wood, 2004, p. 9). In addition, it does not "acknowledge or effectively address . . . the enormous inequality in the provision of education offered in the United States. Unlike most countries that fund schools centrally and equally, the wealthiest U.S. public schools spend at least ten times more than the poorest schools—ranging from over $30,000 per pupil at the wealthy schools to only $3,000 at the poorest. These disparities contribute to a wider achievement gap in this country than in virtually any other industrialized country in the world" (Meier & Wood, 2004, p. 6).

In the end, Neill finds, "NCLB's promises are undermined by its realities. The accountability measures . . . are fundamentally insufficient and counterproductive to the goals of educating all students well and of serving well the underserved" (quoted in Meier & Wood, 2004, p. 104). And educating *all* students well—with special attention to the underserved—is the aim of this book.

A Pedagogy of Plenty:
Addressing the Achievement Gap

Just as we can pinpoint reasons why some of our children seem doomed to failure, we can also identify concrete solutions that offer all students greater opportunities to succeed in school. These solutions constitute a pedagogy of plenty.

A pedagogy of plenty is teaching at its best. When we integrate proven, research-based strategies into daily classroom practice and use them to help children transcend their situations outside school, we enable students to reach their highest potential and, in the process, to acquire a range of resilient behaviors that lead to success both in school and in life. What might all children attempt if they knew they could not fail? We know that the stronger children's self-esteem is, the more likely they are to capitalize on their strengths. This is why some children do well despite the many obstacles in their lives.

A pedagogy of plenty

- Offers authentic tasks that give students real purposes for schoolwork and real audiences for that work.
- Provides a literacy-rich learning environment containing a wide variety of high-quality resources.
- Helps students make connections between their learning and their day-to-day experiences in their homes and communities.
- Offers experiential, problem-based, active learning opportunities.
- Engages students in working collaboratively on issues of deep concern to them.
- Exposes students to an inquiry-based approach to instruction that emphasizes making meaning, not just getting the right answer.
- Engages students in substantive dialogue, discussion, and debate to help them learn, understand, and apply the content of a given subject area.
- Allows students to have their home and community cultures, language heritages, and experiences acknowledged and incorporated into their schooling.
- Presents students with cognitive and metacognitive problems within the context of purposeful activities.

Teachers who succeed in bringing diverse learners to high levels of achievement have a considerable degree of expertise in subject-specific learning strategies. Yet they also recognize the importance of using a set of universal, research-proven teaching and learning practices that provide students with multiple avenues for academic success. These practices help teachers successfully implement content-specific strategies and, more important, are adaptable and proven to work with a broad range of students with varied backgrounds, abilities, and perspectives.

The first edition of *Educating Everybody's Children* identified 13 universal practices that had been found to be key in bridging the achievement gap. Five years later, in *More Strategies for Educating Everybody's Children*, three more such practices were added to the list, for a total of 16. These practices, which are examined in detail in Chapter 1, include the following:

Strategy 1.1: Provide opportunities for students to work in a variety of social configurations and settings.

Strategy 1.2: Use reality-based learning approaches.

Strategy 1.3: Encourage interdisciplinary teaching.

Strategy 1.4: Involve students actively.

Strategy 1.5: Analyze students' learning and reading styles.

Strategy 1.6: Actively model behaviors.

Strategy 1.7: Explore the fullest dimensions of thought.

Strategy 1.8: Use a multicultural teaching approach.

Strategy 1.9: Use alternative assessments.

Strategy 1.10: Promote home/school partnerships.

Strategy 1.11: Use accelerated learning techniques.

Strategy 1.12: Foster strategies in questioning.

Strategy 1.13: Emphasize brain-compatible instruction.

Strategy 1.14: Activate students' prior knowledge.

Strategy 1.15: Use a constructivist approach to teaching.

Strategy 1.16: Organize instructionally effective classroom environments.

To help practitioners systematically apply a range of powerful teaching methods, Helené Hodges, formerly director of collaborative ventures at ASCD, developed an organizing framework for these 16 universal strategies. Strategies founded in a common philosophical base and best implemented in context with one another are grouped together under a broader instructional objective. By applying complementary strategies in tandem, teachers can offer their students increased instructional support.

Organizing Framework for Universal Strategies

- *Capitalize on Students' Strengths* (Strategies 1.5 and 1.13)
- *Match Instructional Methods to Students' Instructional Needs* (Strategies 1.2, 1.4, 1.6, and 1.11)
- *Increase Interest, Motivation, and Engagement* (Strategies 1.12, 1.14, and 1.15)
- *Create Varied Learning Configurations* (Strategies 1.1 and 1.16)
- *Make Connections for Understanding* (Strategies 1.3, 1.7, 1.8, 1.9, and 1.10)

continued on p. xvi

continued from p. xv

> This framework affords practitioners an opportunity to improve each student's performance. By capitalizing on students' individual learning strengths (strategies 1.5 and 1.13), teachers are in a better position to match appropriate instructional methods to students' instructional needs (strategies 1.2, 1.4, 1.6, and 1.11). Once teachers have begun to teach to youngsters' strengths and multiple intelligences, they can further increase students' interest, motivation, and engagement in learning (strategies 1.12, 1.14, and 1.15) by creating varied learning configurations (strategies 1.1 and 1.16) that enable students to make connections for understanding (strategies 1.3, 1.7, 1.8, 1.9, and 1.10).

Teachers will find this framework helpful for delivering not only the 16 universal practices but also content-specific teaching strategies. The heart of this book, in fact, is devoted to updated, in-depth examinations of strategies to improve achievement in specific content areas. The authors of the content-area chapters in this volume discuss a number of effective cross-disciplinary instructional strategies that are validated by research and classroom application. Common themes that appear throughout the book include

- Cooperative learning and collaborative problem solving.
- Integration across areas of the curriculum.
- Augmentation and application of students' prior knowledge and experiences.
- Recognition and application of students' cultural capital.
- Use of conceptual frameworks.
- Organization of instruction around themes.
- Problem-based learning, real-world applications of instruction, and student involvement and exploration.
- Use of technology, as well as reading and writing across the curriculum.

Chapter 2 and Chapter 8, the bookends of the five content-specific chapters, address teaching strategies to assist the diverse learners and immigrant and refugee children whose numbers continue to increase in U.S. classrooms. These chapters place special emphasis on establishing a climate of high expectations. In Chapter 2, Marietta Saravia-Shore notes the importance of "high expectations for the success of all students and a belief that all students can succeed" (p. 45). Elsewhere in her chapter, she warns that "teachers may have low expectations for students of diverse backgrounds and thus fail to present them with challenging and interesting lessons" (p. 47). And JoAnn Crandall and colleagues assert in Chapter 8 that "students need opportunities to identify and celebrate their strengths, not focus on their weaknesses. Fortunately, there are many ways to accomplish this. Perhaps the most important is to have high expectations of these students and to provide opportunities that allow them to live up to those expectations" (p. 263).

Doing the Possible

I have come to understand that some of the fundamental elements of schooling in the United States, for good and for ill, persist no matter how much we might prefer to believe otherwise. As I worked on the final stages of this volume, it occurred to me to look back at the editorials I wrote for *Phi Delta Kappan* magazine. It was a sobering task.

In October 1981, during my first year as *Kappan* editor in chief, I wrote of "surprise that our schools are performing as well as they are when American children spend more time attending to TV than to teachers, when they return to badly troubled homes in neighborhoods that ignore the young, when schooling is not a national priority, when educators themselves cannot speak with one convincing and effective voice."

The following year, in October 1982, I wrote,

> Time rules teaching. Do not recent studies show that time on task is one of the most crucial of alterable variables in the learning process? Time. Is the mission of the schools crippled by an overcrowded, inflexible curriculum and competing demands for class time that leave teachers and administrators confused and rudderless? Time. Is it not true that the average student spends more time in front of the television than in the classroom? Time. Are not the number of single-parent homes—and the number of families in which both parents (if there are two) must work—at an all-time high, reducing the amount of time spent with the children? Time again. Time takes an awful toll on the work of the schools.

In March 1983, I quoted John Goodlad's *A Study of Schooling*, a monumental report that examined more than 1,000 classrooms in 38 enormously diverse schools. Goodlad's findings? Monotony. Lack of interest and cooperation. Low-level cognitive demands. Reliance on simple recall of facts—not on exploration or independent thinking or discovery. "The cards are stacked against innovation," Goodlad said then, adding that to continue on the same course would only widen the gap between what was and what could be.

In March 1987, I wrote of children who live in pain, and of "today's test-driven, competency-based, tightly scheduled, reform-conscious schools."

The next month, I wrote that "educating our children for the 21st century means creating greater flexibility, not limiting it."

And during my final few months as *Kappan* editor, I quoted Bob Saunders, who once said, "We need to do the possible while we're waiting for perfection."

So, a couple of decades later, here we all are: well into the 21st century, still painfully hobbled by new versions of what I wrote about all those years ago. We have a new generation of "test-driven, competency-based, tightly scheduled, reform-conscious schools." We have new laws that limit rather than release teachers' creativity and flexibility. We work with a new generation of students—very likely the children of the students I wrote about then—who face the very same demons that plagued their parents.

More than ever, we need to "do the possible." And what's immediately possible lives in the pages of this book: tested instructional strategies that have given life and hope to real students of all abilities and backgrounds in real classrooms. Research shows plainly, repeatedly, that teachers who succeed at bringing diverse learners to high levels of achievement possess a wide array of research-based teaching and learning strategies. As our students become more and more diverse, so must our ways of teaching them. It is the quality of instruction, not a youngster's life circumstances, that determines performance in school.

All too often, the young people in our classrooms live lives on the ragged edges of viability. Homelessness, discrimination, starvation, abuse—the everyday conditions of their lives defy our convenient attempts to compartmentalize their experiences and our prescriptions for dealing with them. Too often, they and their barely subsistent families (if they have families at all) are voiceless. We have the power to give them a voice, to give them power, to give them the keys to a better life.

Bibliography

Capps, R., Fix, M., Murray, J., Ost, J., Passel, J., & Herwantoro, S. (2005). *The new demography of America's schools: Immigration and the No Child Left Behind Act.* Washington, DC: Urban Institute.

Cole, R. W. (1981, October). *Phi Delta Kappan, 63*(2).

Cole, R. W. (1982, October). *Phi Delta Kappan, 64*(2).

Cole, R. W. (1987, March). Education's role in preventing teenage suicide. *Phi Delta Kappan, 68*(7), 490.

Cole, R. W. (1995). *Educating everybody's children: Diverse teaching strategies for diverse learners.* Alexandria, VA: Association for Supervision and Curriculum Development.

Cole, R. W. (2001). *More strategies for educating everybody's children.* Alexandria, VA: Association for Supervision and Curriculum Development.

Dougherty, E., & Barth, P. (1997, April 2). How to close the achievement gap. *Education Week*, pp. 40, 44.

Education Trust. (2006, April 11). Testimony of Russlynn Ali, Director, Education Trust-West, before the Commission on No Child Left Behind [Online]. Available: http://www2.edtrust.org/EdTrust/ETW/RAtestimony_April06.htm

Farkas, G. (2003, August). Racial disparities and discrimination in education: What do we know, how do we know it, and why do we need to know? *Teachers College Record, 105*(6), 1140.

Haberman, M. (1991). The pedagogy of poverty versus good teaching. *Phi Delta Kappan, 73*(4), 290–294.

Meier, D., & Wood, G. (2004). *Many children left behind: How the No Child Left Behind Act is damaging our children and our schools.* Boston: Beacon Press.

Metz, M. (1998/1999, Winter). Community social class affects teachers' perspectives and practices. *Wisconsin Center for Education Research Highlights, 10*(4), 6.

National Commission on Teaching and America's Future. (2006, June 15). Teaching inequality: How poor and minority students are shortchanged on teacher quality. *NCTAF Weekly News Digest.*

Olson, L. (2007, January 4). Breaking the cycle of poverty [Online article]. *Education Week, 26*(17). Available: http://www.edweek.org/ew/articles/2007/01/04/17wellbeing.h26.html

Rooney, P., Hussar, W., Planty, M., Choy, S., Hampden-Thompson, G., Provasnik, S., & Fox, M. (2006). *The condition of education 2006* (NCES 2006-071). Washington, DC: U.S. Department of Education, National Center for Education Statistics.

1

Educating Everybody's Children: We Know What Works—And What Doesn't

Robert W. Cole

Children know how to learn in more ways than we know how to teach them.
—Ronald Edmonds (1991)

Good instruction is good instruction, regardless of students' racial, ethnic, or socioeconomic backgrounds. To a large extent, good teaching—teaching that is engaging, relevant, multicultural, and appealing to a variety of modalities and learning styles—works well with all children.

The instructional strategies outlined in this chapter reflect a sampling of the most exciting and determined efforts to change the way the United States educates its citizens. These "ideas at work" range in complexity and magnitude. They represent concepts that cut across content areas. They overlap so comfortably that they sometimes look like separate facets of a single gem. They are as much about attitude and general approach as about specific pedagogical techniques and classroom application. They have a few characteristics in common:

- They tend to be inclusive, not exclusive.
- They work best in context with other ideas and concepts, not in isolation.
- They often focus on students working within social situations rather than alone.
- Their activities, techniques, and goals are interactive and interdisciplinary, realistic rather than esoteric.
- Possibly most important, they empower students to be actively involved in the processes of their own learning, rather than passively receptive.

None of the ideas in this chapter is new. Although some of them tend to be identified with specific programs, individuals, or locations, they are presented here as generic—that is, as applicable in virtually any classroom, in any subject area. All are adaptable.

Why ideas *at* work rather than ideas *that* work? Because "ideas that work" implies a kind of guarantee of effectiveness. In the real world of the schools, however, nothing works every time, everywhere, for everyone. No single strategy, approach, or technique works with all students. But the concepts in this chapter have proven themselves over time, with a multitude of students of diverse backgrounds and widely ranging abilities.

Unfortunately, numerous barriers can prevent poor and minority students from receiving good instruction. Some of these barriers are caused by educators' attitudes and beliefs; others are the result of institutional practices. The intent of the listing that follows is not to provide a thorough cataloguing of every barrier to

sound instruction, but rather to place educators on alert.

Attitudes and Beliefs

Racism and Prejudice

Despite much progress during the past few decades, racism and prejudice are still ugly realities in all sectors of life in the United States, including education. Today, racism may be less overt and virulent than in the past, but its effects can still greatly harm minority students. In fact, subtle, insidious forms of racism may be even more harmful to young people than more blatant forms.

Prejudice against the poor, of whatever race or ethnicity, is another force that works against the academic achievement of disadvantaged students. For example, some teachers of poor students don't let them take materials home, out of fear that the materials will never be returned. Yet these same students tend to be proud to have the responsibility for taking materials home and are generally exceedingly careful to return them.

Obviously teachers must avoid discriminating, consciously or unconsciously, against students because of their racial, ethnic, or socio-economic backgrounds. Such discrimination can be as blatant as imposing harsher discipline on minority students or as subtle as lowering expectations for poor children because they have "difficult" home lives. Teachers must be aware that they see students' behavior through the lens of their own culture. They must carefully examine their own attitudes and behaviors to be sure that they are not imposing a double standard. Most important, they must believe sincerely and completely that all children can learn.

Expectations

Educators must hold equally high expectations for affluent white students and poor and minority students—despite the disparity in students' backgrounds. Under the right conditions, low-income and minority students can learn just as well as any other children. One necessary condition, of course, is that the teacher hold expectations of high performance for *all* students.

Both high and low expectations can create self-fulfilling prophecies. Students must believe that they can achieve before they will risk trying, and young people are astute at sensing whether their teachers believe they can succeed. By the same token, teachers must truly believe their students can achieve before they will put forth their best effort to teach them. The teacher's beliefs must be translated into instructional practices if students are to benefit: actions speak louder than attitudes.

Teachers must also be sensitive to the subtle ways in which low expectations can be conveyed. According to researcher Sandra Graham of the University of California–Los Angeles, when a teacher expresses sympathy over failure, students typically infer that the teacher thinks they are incapable of succeeding, not that they simply may not have tried hard enough. Similarly, when a teacher gives students lavish praise for completing a simple task or offers help before being asked for it, students infer that the teacher thinks they are stupid. In other words,

holding high expectations is not simply a matter of cheerleading; it requires insight into how students may interpret a teacher's words and behaviors.

Teachers must also resist the temptation to attribute student failure to lack of ability ("I've taught this concept and they didn't understand it; they must not be smart enough"). Failure to learn can stem from many other causes, such as inadequate prior knowledge, insufficient effort or motivation, lack of the right learning strategy, or inappropriate teaching. The bottom line is this: if students are not learning, the teacher needs to change the approach to teaching them.

Teachers are not the only ones who need to examine their expectations for students, however. Administrators who decide what courses their schools offer should ask themselves whether they are providing too few challenging courses. And counselors must consider whether they are steering students into undemanding courses because the students are poor, minority, or female. The expectation that all students can achieve at high levels, under the right circumstances, should be the guiding principle of every school.

Lack of Understanding of Cultural Differences

Teachers sometimes misinterpret the behaviors of poor and minority students because they do not understand the cultures they come from. White teachers can easily misread the behaviors of black students, for example. In *Black Students and School Failure*, Jacqueline Jordan Irvine (1990) writes:

Because the culture of black children is different and often misunderstood, ignored, or discounted, black students are likely to experience cultural discontinuity in schools.... This lack of cultural sync becomes evident in instructional situations in which teachers misinterpret, denigrate, and dismiss black students' language, nonverbal cues, physical movements, learning styles, cognitive approaches, and worldview. When teachers and students are out of sync, they clash and confront each other, both consciously and unconsciously.... (p. xix)

Only when teachers understand their students' cultural backgrounds can they avoid this kind of culture clash. In the meantime, the ways in which teachers comprehend and react to students' culture, language, and behaviors may create problems (Erickson, 1987). In too many schools, students are, in effect, required to leave their family and cultural backgrounds at the schoolhouse door and live in a kind of "hybrid culture" composed of the community of fellow learners (Au & Kawakami, 1991).

Especially in the early grades, teachers and students may differ in their expectations for the classroom setting; each may act in ways that the other misinterprets. In addition, those teachers (and they are legion) who insist on a single pedagogical style and who see other styles as being out of step, may be refusing to allow students to work to their strengths.

As Knapp and Shields (1990a) suggest, the so-called "deficit" or "disadvantage" model has

two serious problems: (1) teachers are likely to set low standards for certain children "because their patterns of behavior, language use, and values do not match those required in the school setting"; and (2) over time a cycle of failure and despair is created that culminates "in students' turning their backs on school and dropping out . . . because teachers and administrators fail to adapt to and take advantage of the strengths that these students do possess" (p. 755).

Institutional Practices

Tracking

The most notorious of the harmful institutional practices is tracking, which dooms children in the low tracks to a second-rate education by failing to provide them with the support they need to move to a higher track. As a result, they fall further and further behind their peers. Students in low tracks are stigmatized and lose self-esteem and motivation, while expectations for their performance plummet.

In *Keeping Track*, researcher Jeannie Oakes (1985) says, "We can be quite certain that the deficiencies of slower students are not more easily remediated when they are grouped together" (p. 12). Yet even now the practice of tracking persists, despite the negative effects on students documented by Oakes and many other researchers. Tracking is especially harmful to poor and minority students because these students are more likely to end up in the low tracks.

Effective alternatives to tracking have included the Accelerated Schools Project, developed by Henry Levin of Stanford University, which includes accelerated programs to bring at-risk students into the mainstream by the end of elementary school and results in faster learning because students receive engaging, active, interdisciplinary instruction; and the Higher Order Thinking Skills (HOTS) program, developed by Stanley Pogrow of the University of Arizona–Tucson, which works to enhance the general thinking skills of remedial students by showing them how to work with ideas. These programs and others are aimed at helping students get up to speed, rather than permanently segregating them and feeding them a dumbed-down curriculum.

Inappropriate Instruction

Inappropriate instruction harms poor and minority students. Instead of being presented in a variety of modes, instruction in too many U.S. schools tends to be abstract, devoid of application, overly sequential, and redundant. Bits of knowledge are emphasized, not the big picture, thus handicapping global thinkers. Moreover, the largely Eurocentric curriculum downplays the experiences and contributions of minorities.

For teachers of diverse students, it is especially important to use a broad repertoire of strategies. Some children may be global thinkers; others, more analytical. Some children may learn best from lecture and reading; others, through manipulatives and other hands-on experiences. Some children may thrive on competition; others may achieve far more in cooperative groups.

Differential Access

Poor and minority students are often denied access to challenging coursework. Counselors place them in remedial or undemanding courses, and because more challenging courses often require students to have taken specific introductory courses, students can never switch to a more demanding track. Irvine (1990) cites data showing that "black students, particularly black male students, are three times as likely to be in a class for the educable mentally retarded as are white students, but only one-half as likely to be in a class for the gifted and talented" (p. xiv). In addition, the pull-out programs intended to help many of these students end up fragmenting their school day. And after pull-out programs end, students are given little support for reentering the regular classroom, so they tend to backslide when they rejoin their peers.

Lack of Consequences

Unfortunately, there are few consequences for students and teachers if poor and minority students do not learn. So long as students put in the required seat time, they will receive a diploma; so long as teachers go through the motions, they will have a job. In many cases, nobody—not the education establishment, not the parents or guardians, not the politicians—protests a status quo that is woefully deficient.

Schools that have had success in teaching poor and minority students do not keep ineffective teachers on the faculty; in these schools, teachers are held responsible if their students do not learn. These schools also collaborate with parents or guardians to ensure that students who come to school and strive to achieve are rewarded.

Disciplinary Practices

Teachers sometimes punish poor and minority children more harshly than they do other children for the same offenses. Moreover, suspension is often the punishment of choice, causing students to miss valuable class time. According to Irvine (1990), "one factor related to the nonachievement of black students is the disproportionate use of severe disciplinary practices, which leads to black students' exclusion from classes, their perceptions of mistreatment, and feelings of alienation and rejection, which result ultimately in their misbehaving more and/or leaving school" (p. 16).

On the other hand, some teachers are more lenient with poor or minority students, because they believe these children have been socialized differently than mainstream children. For example, teachers might overlook boisterous or aggressive behavior among poor or minority students while chastising mainstream students for similar behavior. Teachers need to establish a clear, reasonable discipline policy and require all students to abide by it.

Involvement of Parents or Guardians

Poor and minority parents or guardians often have no opportunities to create an ongoing relationship with their children's schools; in fact, they often have no communication with the schools at all. In turn, schools tend to make few efforts to develop a relationship with poor and minority parents or guardians, who may be too intimidated or hard-pressed to initiate contact themselves. For parents who don't speak English, the language barrier can pose another formidable obstacle.

James Comer of the Yale Child Study Center has developed a process to foster good relationships among children, teachers, and parents or guardians. Parents or guardians are encouraged to be an active presence in the school. Social activities bring families and school staff together, helping parents or guardians gain trust in the school. The program has reportedly helped to lower dropout rates, among other benefits.

Unequal Access to Resources

Unequal access to resources further reduces poor and minority students' chances of receiving equal opportunities to learn. Poor and minority students typically attend schools that receive less funding than those attended by mainstream students. As a result, they are taught with inferior materials and equipment and have fewer manipulatives, laboratories, and facilities. Teachers in such schools receive less staff development, must cope with larger classes, and have less free time.

The Negative Impact of Testing

Standardized tests can be seen as one way in which a meritocratic society reorders a widely disparate populace into hierarchies of abilities, achievement, and opportunity. In fact, the power of tests to translate difference into disadvantage is felt at many points in the world of education, most notably in the decision to place low-income and language-minority students into compensatory or bilingual education classes, where a watered-down, fragmented, and rote curriculum reinforces the disadvantages presumably diagnosed by the tests.

More than ever before, it would seem, multiple-choice tests are being used inappropriately as the ultimate measure of students' learning and capabilities—despite a wealth of evidence that undermines the wisdom of using them in this manner. Decisions that significantly affect students' academic destinies are often made on the basis of a single test score. Moreover, norm-referenced tests reinforce the attitude that some students should be *expected* to do poorly. To be fair to all students, assessment should be primarily criterion-referenced and, as far as possible, based on actual performances. Perhaps most important, a variety of measures should be used to assess student learning.

Lack of Bilingual Instruction

Not surprisingly, many students who do not speak English fall behind in their studies early, because they are not taught content in their native language. When they eventually learn English, they have lost so much ground in their schoolwork that they find it difficult (and sometimes impossible) to catch up with their peers. In far too many cases, these students become discouraged and drop out of school.

Overall, there is the too-common problem of organizational inertia and resistance to change: reluctance to accept bilingual programs, to hire bilingual personnel, to upgrade the status of teachers of English as a second language (ESL), to support the acquisition and development of primary-language materials, to monitor and assess the progress of language-minority students, and to deal with the unique problems facing newcomers, including their need for counseling.

The number of bilingual teachers in U.S. schools is woefully insufficient, and the use of existing bilingual teachers is far from satisfactory. Schools do not use bilingual teachers to the best advantage—that is, to take maximum advantage of their dual-language abilities. The training and staffing of ESL and "sheltered English" classes remain inadequate. Beyond staffing, there is a dearth of primary-language materials, especially for languages other than Spanish, and bilingual educators regard even those materials as inadequate.

Students who speak a language other than English need to be taught content, for a time, in their native language, while they are also given intensive training in English. When they rejoin their English-speaking peers, they will be up to speed in their studies.

Universal Teaching Strategies

Naming the barriers to the kind of schooling we want for all of our children is at least a beginning. Naming the problem allows the challenging process of treating it to begin. The next section of this chapter will outline 16 generic instructional strategies that are intended to provide assistance in treatment.

Strategy 1.1:

Provide opportunities for students to work in a variety of social configurations and settings.

Susie, Ron, Tasha, Jamal, and Juan have a lot in common. They are roughly the same age, sit in the same classroom, have the same teacher, and enjoy many of the same foods, games, and interests. As learners, however, they differ in critical ways. Susie is one of the 13 percent of youngsters in grades K–12 who learn best working alone; Ron, one of the 28 percent strongly oriented to working with a peer; and Tasha and Jamal, two of the 28 percent who learn best with adults (Tasha, by the way, with a collegial adult; Jamal, with an authoritative adult).

Of the five children, only Juan seems to learn reasonably well in any or all of those social configurations. In that respect, he represents fewer than one-third of the youngsters in a typical K–12 classroom. Of the five, only Susie and Juan are reasonably well served in the traditional teacher-oriented, teacher-directed classroom. Most of the time, the other three would be much better off in a different kind of learning situation—one far more diverse in its activities, curricular organization, and social configurations.

Few individuals in today's work world think of trying to solve a problem or launch a product or service without massive and persistent teamwork, including open discussion, fact gathering, consideration and argument, trial-and-error experimentation, research, and development. Typically, they not only depend on working with other individuals in their place of business, but also frequently call on outside consultants. Only in U.S. classrooms are individuals expected to find every answer, solve every problem, complete every task, and pass every test by relying solely on their own efforts and abilities.

The concept of cooperative/collaborative learning seeks to tap the potential that group interaction offers for learning and development. In its most formal manifestation, it places students—usually of varying levels of performance—into small groups in which they work together toward common goals. At the other end of the continuum is the more informal arrangement of peer tutoring, which has gained legitimacy as an effective form of cooperative/collaborative learning.

Those who advocate attending to students' varying learning styles note that some young people work best alone; others work most successfully with authority figures such as parents or teachers. In planning the use of various teaching strategies, teachers must be prepared to make adjustments according to the needs and learning styles of their students (Carbo, Dunn, & Dunn, 1986).

"So often teachers tell students to 'get along' or 'cooperate' but spend little time on skill practice and discussion of this basic human need," writes Robert Slavin (1986, p. 24). "Cooperative learning provides the teacher with a model to improve academic performance and socialization skills, and to instill democratic values. A wealth of research supports the idea that the consistent use of this technique improves students' academic performance and helps them become more caring." Slavin cites positive effects in such diverse areas as student achievement at various grade levels and subjects, intergroup relations, relationships between mainstreamed and normal-progress students, and student self-esteem.

David Johnson and Roger Johnson (1990), two veteran advocates of cooperation and collaboration in the classroom, note that people in general do not know instinctively how to interact effectively with others. If cooperative efforts in the classroom are to succeed, students must get to know and trust one another, communicate accurately and unambiguously, accept and support one another, and resolve conflicts constructively.

Some advocates of cooperative/collaborative learning suggest that students be periodically regrouped within heterogeneous classes. They also recognize the value of flexible grouping—that is, regrouping at various times by varying criteria for varying purposes, based on immediate needs. Their reasoning is as follows:

• Small-group participation in various contexts for various purposes helps students recognize and learn to function effectively in a variety of social configurations.

• Forming teams of students who perform at different levels of achievement not only encourages self-esteem and group pride, but also engenders general appreciation and understanding of how individuals differ from each other in attitudes, abilities, points of view, and approaches to problem solving.

Cooperative/collaborative learning has been incorporated in a variety of classrooms for a variety of purposes. Those applications have involved student-selected activities, apportioning specific elements of classroom projects or lessons, brainstorming, role playing, problem solving, developing awareness of thinking strategies used by oneself or by one's peers, common interests, group analyses, and team learning.

To implement a technique known as a circle of knowledge, for instance, a teacher organizes a class into small groups (circles) of four or five students each, appoints a recorder/reporter in each, poses to all a single question to which there are many possible answers, sets a time limit, expects each group member to contribute at least one answer, and then, after facilitating whole-class sharing and challenges, announces a winning group.

Another technique, the jigsaw, allows a teacher to assign specific components of a major learning project to small task-oriented groups; each group has only a piece of the larger picture under consideration. When all the groups have reported their findings to the entire class, every student has the opportunity to grasp the entire picture.

Peer conferencing and peer collaboration are two techniques that are particularly useful for teaching writing. They offer student writers the critical response of firsthand, face-to-face comments, help them discover what it is to write for an audience, and provide them with opportunities to improve their writing ability as they work on assignments and interact with their peers (Herrmann, 1989).

Cross-age and peer tutoring are other forms of student-to-student interaction. The age-old idea of tutoring has helped countless students. Many students identify with peers more easily than with adults, especially adult authority figures, and find it easier to model the behaviors of their peers than of their adult teachers. Finally, the one-to-one nature of peer tutoring offers immediate feedback, clarification, extension, and modification—usually in a nonthreatening social relationship (Webb, 1988).

Resources

Adams, 1990; Carbo, Dunn, & Dunn, 1986; Dunn & Dunn, 1993; Edmonds, 1991; Herrmann, 1989; Johnson & Johnson, 1986, 1990; Kilman & Richards, 1990; Knapp & Shields, 1990a, 1990b; Lehr & Harris, 1988; Slavin, 1986, 1987; Stevens, Madden, Slavin, & Farnish, 1987; Stover, 1993; Webb, 1988.

Strategy 1.2:

Use reality-based learning approaches.

Jim had trouble writing effectively. To be sure, his sentences were complete and grammatical, the words in them spelled correctly, the syntax straightforward if prosaic. There was one overriding problem with Jim's writing: what he wrote didn't say much of anything. His content and purpose were not specific, precise, or clear. That fact led to a more personal problem for Jim: he had ceased to trust his teacher's judgments of his work. When the teacher observed that his writing wasn't clear, Jim balked. "You're just saying that," he blurted out. "What have you got against me?"

"I'll tell you what, Jim," said the teacher. "Write to me about something you know that I don't know anything about."

After considering two or three possibilities, Jim named a card game his teacher had never heard of.

"OK," the teacher agreed. "Write step-by-step instructions on how to play the game and bring them to me. I'll follow the instructions, and you can tell me whenever I make a mistake."

"Fair enough!" Jim said.

Jim wrote in his typical style, and his teacher followed the instructions as earnestly as possible. Step by frustrated step, Jim saw the game fall to pieces. He stopped the exercise midway through.

"Give me time for a rewrite," he said, determined as ever. This time, however, he was convinced that he had a problem with his writing, and he was armed with a clearer perception of what to do about it.

Provide students with real purposes and real audiences for their speaking and writing, and you offer them valuable feedback as well as increased motivation. Writing an essay on a topic assigned by the teacher to every member of the entire class lacks the punch and the credibility of writing a personal letter to an editor, a local politician, or a community activist to express a heartfelt compliment, complain about an injustice, or inquire about an important issue. Students derive no satisfaction from succeeding with a mindless, silly activity such as circling the silent *E* in a list of words. Such an activity has no relation to real reading and no link to real life.

Communicating with real people about real issues, feelings, and beliefs is further enhanced when the content and style of that writing are grounded in the outside reality that the student brings to school. No matter how gilded or gutted its location—in city, suburb, or countryside—the student's community and personal experiences are valuable resources to be explored. They are grounds for inquiry and learning—things that count most in any classroom!

Schema theory firmly undergirds the strategy of reality-based learning. It outlines the belief that individual facts and phenomena are best perceived, learned, and understood within the larger contexts of structure or process. The value of reality-based learning has been firmly documented in the language arts—in reading and writing as well as in the understanding and appreciation of literature. It bridges school and home, classroom and clubhouse, hallway and street.

Extending the recognition and use of authentic purposes, materials, and content into any subject area helps ensure that learning experiences are meaningful and satisfying. Thus maps, directions, brochures, and directories find a comfortable home in English classes, and community surveys in math classes.

Ideas proliferate in every school—real problems to solve, real issues to resolve: how to manage recycling in the school cafeteria; how to make hallways safer and more hospitable; what to do about truancy or dropouts; whether to lock school doors and when. Problems awaiting study lie just outside the walls of virtually any school in the United States: traffic patterns; paths for bicyclists, joggers, or rollerbladers; recreational needs and resources for young people; the needs of and services for an aging population.

The combined processes of analyzing real problems and then suggesting solutions to them not only motivate learners, but also enable them to range in their thinking processes from recognizing information they need in the resources available to them, to gathering relevant information, to summarizing ideas, to generating potential solutions, and finally to analyzing the consequences and effectiveness of their solutions.

Reality-based learning counters the common notion that many students suffer from "cultural deprivation" and bring no educationally worthwhile experiences to school. "A more worthwhile approach . . . might be to examine the relationship between what particular groups of children know or how they learn and pedagogical practices," suggests Etta Ruth Hollins (1993, p. 93). "An improvement in teachers' understanding of how to build on and extend the knowledge and skills these children bring to school, rather than attempting to force the children to fit existing school practices, might get better results."

Resources

Bloome, 1976, 1985; Danehower, 1993; Hall, 1989; Hollins, 1993; Knapp & Turnbull, 1990; Lozanov & Gateva, 1988; Marzano et al., 1988; Marzano et al., 1992; Palincsar & Klenk, 1991; Palincsar, Ransom, & Derber, 1989/1990; Resnick, 1987; Richardson, 1988; Rowan, Guthrie, Lee, & Guthrie, 1986; U.S. Department of Labor, 1992; Walmsley & Walp, 1990.

Strategy 1.3:
Encourage interdisciplinary teaching.

Lynn Cherkasky-Davis (1993) described a collaborative project at the Foundations School (part of the Chicago Public Schools): an original version of the opera *Aida*, written, produced, costumed, rehearsed, and staged by students. What did that culminating event represent? It represented what the students had learned about the history, geography, sociology, culture, and drama of ancient Egypt, topics that over preceding weeks both nourished and fed on every subject area in the curriculum.

How useful might it be for a student to know something about the economics and the technology of 19th century New England whaling before reading *Moby-Dick*—and what better opportunity to merge the talents and interests inherent in the respective teachers of social studies, science, and language arts?

How might a thoughtful reading of Aldous Huxley's *Brave New World* illuminate issues, arguments, and ideas as diverse as eugenics, Malthusian economics, and the perceived amorality of modern mores and technology—again using convergent elements of separate disciplines?

Rarely, if ever, do we live our lives outside of school according to academic pigeonholes. We don't switch to a different frame of reference or way of doing things every 20 or 40 or 60 minutes. Even a well-executed shopping trip to the supermarket is an interdisciplinary experience! Scheduling, timing, planning, measuring, counting, reading, identifying, describing,

comparing, assessing, affording, budgeting—not to mention spatial orientation, nutrition, and considerations of quality of life—all come into play within a single trip. Consciously or unconsciously, by the time we have negotiated our way from home through traffic to parking lot, then aisle to aisle to the checkout lane and home again, we have routinely called on the skills and content of every basic academic discipline that schools have to offer.

Most interdisciplinary teaching is not nearly so eclectic nor so involved. Just the same, such teaching does cross traditional subject-area lines and typically involves professional teamwork. It can incorporate into a social studies unit samples of literature and art produced during a given period or by a particular society. Ask students to interpret the samples in light of a specific social context, or to infer specific characteristics of the society from their observations and interpretations. Then let them compare their interpretations with those of their peers, and finally with written records from that period or society.

As another example, how about having students study the social impact of a given scientific or technological development at the same time they are becoming acquainted with the science or technology itself? Mathematics is a natural for interdisciplinary learning. Solving its problems can depend heavily on reading skills. Not only is math an integral component in scientific processes; it also plays an appealing role in creating puzzles, music, and architecture.

Interdisciplinary projects promote thinking strategies that cross content areas and transfer solidly into real-life applications—analytical observation, for instance, or critical thinking, comparison and contrast, evaluation, perspective, and judgment. The teacher's role includes supporting those processes and helping students, through practice, to become aware of them and comfortable in using them.

Probably no other interdisciplinary approach has won greater acceptance, especially in the earlier grades, than that which has integrated five "basic skills"—reading, writing, listening, speaking, and mathematics—into one holistic classroom enterprise. Dorothy Strickland (1985) has itemized how simply and obviously such integration can be attained. Reading, for instance, can serve as model and motivation for writing that classmates can share by listening to such spoken activities as storytelling, reporting, oral composition, poetry, and dramatic readings. Reading skills also give a student access to information required in solving mathematical problems, and they play a major role in the interpretation of tables, charts, and graphs.

The "whole language" approach to instruction in reading and the language arts is a salutary example of how "disciplines" once viewed and taught as essentially discrete and separate from each other—that is, reading, writing, speaking, and listening—can easily be explored as interwoven threads in a single, unified tapestry of individual development.

Resources

Cherkasky-Davis, 1993; Jacobs, 1991; Marzano et al., 1988; Paris, Wasik, & Turner, 1991; Strickland, 1985; U.S. Department of Labor, 1992.

Strategy 1.4:
Involve students actively.

In collecting lunch money, the 1st grade teacher discovered that 8 of her 20 students had apparently brought their lunches to school with them. Rather than simply filing that observation mentally under "classroom administrivia," she posed a question to her class: "Twelve of you brought lunch money today. Knowing that, how many of you apparently brought your own lunches to school with you?"

"Some got out blocks," Mary Lindquist reported. "Some got out toy figures, some used number lines, some used their fingers, and some just thought through it. There were 10 or 12 different solutions, and each child wanted to explain his or her own way."

Students passively memorizing a single arithmetic procedure? Not at all. Instead, students actively involved in problem solving, whether or not they agreed on their methods and results.

"Most of us can remember sitting in a math class at one time or another thinking, 'When in the world am I ever going to use this?'" Lindquist commented. Mary Lindquist, then president of the National Council of Teachers of Mathematics, recounted the anecdote during an interview for an article that appeared in *Better Homes and Gardens* (Atkins, 1993). "Rote memorization is not preparing our children for the future. Kids need to use and understand math."

"By far, the highest percentage of students are tactile/kinesthetic," writes Angela Bruno (1982), "and when these youngsters manipulate hands-on materials they tend to remember more of the required information than through the use of any other sense."

There are several other reasons why students should be allowed to construct their own understandings, generate their own analyses, and create their own solutions to problems:

• It is neither engaging nor authentic to understand a fact or a situation exactly as someone else understands it. In real life, we build our own understandings to supplement, change, or confirm for ourselves what we already think we know or what others offer us in knowledge or ideas.

• Teachers promote interest and engagement when they let students address problems for which answers do not exist or are not readily apparent. Students then have real purposes for discovering and applying information and for using all the strategies that might possibly apply and that are available to them.

• Students who are intrinsically motivated and substantially engaged because of interest in meaningful learning activities are more likely to achieve high levels of performance than those for whom the completion of learning activities is simply a means of avoiding punishment.

Integrated throughout the school day and in every area of the curriculum, the range of active learning experiences includes games, simulations, role playing, creative dramatics, pantomime, storytelling, drawing, and contests that demonstrate integration of concepts and allow students to experience the ways in which concepts relate to each other in the world outside school. Other hands-on, tactile materials and activities include Cuisenaire rods, measuring cups, blocks and cubes, task cards, flip charts, field trips, and laboratory experiences. Many advocates suggest strongly that students be allowed to select for themselves those activities in which they will become involved.

Resources

Atkins, 1993; Brown, 1990; Bruno, 1982; Cohen, 1992; Hartshorn & Boren, 1990; Hodges, 1994; Joyner, 1990; National Council of Teachers of Mathematics, 1989; Roser, 1987; Strickland & Morrow, 1989.

Strategy 1.5:

Analyze students' learning and reading styles.

Everyone knows that there are all kinds of people: thinkers and doers, audiences and actors, readers and viewers, athletes and couch potatoes. (At least one venerated 6th grade music teacher routinely divided her class into singers and listeners.) Probably no other approach attempts to accommodate differences among individual students in greater detail than does that body of thought given the general rubric of learning styles.

David Kolb (Boyatzis & Kolb, 1991) identifies four predominant learning styles. *Imaginative* learners, he says, excel in watching, sensing, and feeling; *analytic* learners, in watching and thinking; *common-sense* learners, in thinking and doing; and *dynamic* learners, in doing, sensing, and feeling.

Anthony Gregorc (1982, 1985a, 1985b) identifies four basic processes by which individuals differ in their learning patterns: (1) a *concrete-sequential* process characterized as structured, practical, predictable, and thorough; (2) an *abstract-sequential* process—logical, analytical, conceptual, and studious; (3) an *abstract-random* process—sensitive, sociable, imaginative, and expressive; and (4) a *concrete-random* process—intuitive, original, investigative, and able to solve problems.

In his highly regarded theory of multiple intelligences, Howard Gardner (1999) outlined eight different aspects by which individuals can come to know the world: linguistic, logical/mathematical, musical, spatial, bodily/kinesthetic, interpersonal, intrapersonal, and naturalist.

Addressing perennial debates about the best approach to teaching reading—phonics, whole language, sight vocabulary, and so forth—Marie Carbo (1987) writes that "any one of a dozen reading methods is 'best' if it enables a child to learn to read with facility and enjoyment" (p. 56).

No matter how much they echo or differ from each other, all descriptions of learning styles are simply attempts to define and accommodate the manner in which a given student learns most readily. The theory holds that learning styles develop through the unique interactions of biology, experience, personal interests, talents, and energy. A task force commissioned by the National Association of Secondary School Principals considered the many factors that can significantly shape an individual's learning style and selected 24 for further study; these range from "perceptual responses," "field dependence/independence," and "successive/simultaneous processing" to "persistence," "environmental elements," and "need for mobility."

Whatever the ultimate taxonomy of learning styles, it seems obvious that although all children can learn, each concentrates, processes, absorbs, and remembers new and difficult information differently. According to Rita and Kenneth Dunn (1993), the factors involved include the following:

- Immediate environment—for example, noise level, temperature, amount of light, furniture type, and room design.
- Emotional profile—for example, degree of motivation, persistence, responsibility, and need for structure and feedback.
- Sociological needs—for example, learning alone or with peers, learning with adults present, learning in groups.
- Physical characteristics—for example, perceptual strengths (auditory, visual, tactile, kinesthetic), best time of day for learning, potential need for periodic nourishment and mobility.
- Psychological inclination—for example, global and analytic strengths.

In the most formal model of matching instruction to learning style, teachers first identify each individual student's style through observation, interview, or questionnaire. They share their observations individually with students and parents, and then plan and carry out an appropriate learning program for that child. The program includes compatible instructional practices and management strategies appropriate to what has been observed about the child's learning style. A less formal approach is to emphasize strategies that capitalize on the styles of most students, while accommodating those whose style differs markedly from the group.

Thus, instruction that attends to learning or reading styles capitalizes on an individual student's strengths and preferences while simultaneously removing barriers to learning. Instructional planning extends to such complementary methods, materials, and techniques as floor games, choices among reading materials and ways of receiving or presenting information, and participation in given activities (that is, with the entire class, in a small group, or alone). No one learning style is considered better or worse than any other (Carbo & Hodges, 1988; Hodges, 1994).

Research in learning styles and reading styles indicates that teaching academic underachievers in ways that complement their strengths in style has significantly increased their standardized test scores in reading and across subject areas.

Resources

Andrews, 1990, 1991; Bauer, 1991; Boyatzis & Kolb, 1991; Brunner & Majewski, 1990; Butler, 1984; Carbo, 1987; Carbo & Hodges, 1988; Dunn & Dunn, 1993; Gardner, 1999; Gardner & Hatch, 1989; Garrett, 1991; Gregorc, 1982, 1985a, 1985b; Hodges, 1994; Lewis & Steinberger, 1991; Orsak, 1990; Perrin, 1990.

Strategy 1.6:
Actively model behaviors.

Dorothy had tried for weeks to get her 6th graders to open up in class discussions. After years of traditional teaching, however (that is, the teacher asking the questions and one or two students offering "right" or "wrong" answers), her students were predictably passive. They consistently resisted all her attempts to open up her classroom. On the rare occasions when an intrepid student asked a question in return or dared to offer a comment, the eyes of every student in the room swung immediately and automatically to Dorothy for her verdict: right or wrong?

Then, quite by chance, Dorothy happened on a life-sized human figure made of cardboard. She realized at once that it was the very thing she needed to make her point. The following day, she launched a classroom discussion and popped a direct question to see if any of her students would volunteer a response.

Kathy did volunteer—tentatively, of course, and with just a word or two—but her response seemed to the class to merit a judgment from the teacher. All eyes fell in silence on Dorothy. Without saying a word, Dorothy walked to her closet, pulled out the cardboard figure, and set it in the chair behind her desk. With every eye following her in amazement, she sat down beside Kathy and stared silently at the cardboard figure, waiting like her students for its response.

Dorothy was modeling the behavior she saw in her students—behavior she was hoping they would overcome. They got the point! The humor in the situation engaged their trust, demonstrated Dorothy's sincerity as a teacher, and dramatized their responsibility as participants in their own learning. Class discussions began to pick up, and Dorothy found fewer and fewer occasions to pull her cardboard counterpart out of the closet.

Most modeling, of course, is intended to work the other way around—that is, teachers usually behave as they would have their students behave. Learners gain when teachers practice what they preach, try out ideas in front of the class, or even participate actively in projects or tasks with the class.

When modeling, teachers—regardless of their subject area—follow the same assignments or suggestions that they give their students: they write on the same topics, figure out the same problems, play the same games, and ask themselves the same questions. And they do so in full view and hearing of their students, often as coparticipants in small-group activities, or one-to-one with a student.

The practice is neither demeaning nor condescending. Instead, it dramatizes desired behavior, one of the surest means available to demonstrate process, motivate and guide students, and help develop perspective on a given task or concept. As a teacher, let your students hear you think aloud. Teachers who share thoughts on how they have completed a certain task or arrived at a particular conclusion help students become aware of their own thinking strategies.

Modeling enables teachers to furnish appropriate cues and reminders that help students apply particular problem-solving processes or complete specific tasks—in storytelling, for instance, or inquiry, or evaluation. Among such techniques, scaffolding is one of the most generic and useful approaches. Scaffolding is a device by which the teacher builds on the point of reference at which a student hesitates or leaves off—in telling a story, in explaining a process, in seeking an answer, in any moment of discourse, analysis, or explanation. In scaffolding, the teacher simply suggests the next step, both reinforcing what the student has already achieved and guiding the student to greater understanding or accomplishment.

More generally, Costa and Marzano (1987) identify seven starting points by which teachers can create a classroom "language of cognition":

- Using precise vocabulary.
- Posing critical and interpretive questions, rather than simple recall.
- Providing data, not solutions.
- Giving directions.
- Probing for specificity.
- Modeling metacognitive processes.
- Analyzing the logic of language.

"Most teachers put too much emphasis on facts and right answers and too little attention on how to interpret those facts," writes school administrator Robert Burroughs (1993), commenting specifically on the teaching of literature. "The result has been growth in basic literacy at the expense of thoughtfulness . . . ."

Burroughs outlines specific preferred techniques among those he has seen teachers use to guide learning processes and thus structure growth in understanding and appreciation. The techniques are adaptable to discourse, inquiry, or discussion in any subject area:

• Focusing—refocusing students' efforts at refining their own responses if, for instance, they begin wandering from the specific content at hand.

• Modifying or shaping—rephrasing a student's idea in slightly different language; for instance, if a student suggests that a character in a novel is resisting change, the teacher might add a word or two to encourage consideration of other explanations for the character's behavior.

• Hinting—calling attention to a passage in the text that challenges a student's view.

• Summarizing—restating ideas to bring them to everyone's attention and to spur discussion, or summarizing various positions students have taken along the way (1993, pp. 27–29).

Resources

Burroughs, 1993; Costa & Marzano, 1987; Langer, 1991; Marzano et al., 1988; Paris, Wasik, & Turner, 1991; Rosenshine & Meister, 1992; Vygotsky, 1962, 1978.

Strategy 1.7:

Explore the fullest dimensions of thought.

"What a beautiful horse!" said the city-bred dude. "How much is it worth?"

"Depends if you're buyin' or sellin'," answered the cowhand.

"Thinking cannot be divorced from content," writes Carr (1988). "In fact, thinking is a way of learning content. In every course, and especially in content subjects, students should be taught to think logically, analyze and compare, question and evaluate. Skills taught in isolation do little more than prepare students for tests of isolated skills."

If any of the ideas at work described in this chapter challenges the conventional wisdom of classroom practice, it is this notion: students, regardless of their performance levels, are capable of using higher-order thinking skills. This concept contrasts sharply with the attitude and practice of the high school English teacher who, on the first day of school, gave all 125 of her seniors a writing assignment. She collected and corrected their papers; pointed out the various lapses in spelling, grammar, and punctuation; and then used those errors to justify an unproductive, unchallenging year spent reviewing the same sterile exercises in spelling, grammar, and punctuation that her students had seen countless times before.

No one condones faulty grammar and inaccurate spelling, of course. At the same time, however (and far more important), teachers need not wait until students have mastered basic skills before they introduce the more complex skills of analysis, synthesis, criticism, and metacognition into their classroom routines. The process of gathering information, evaluating it critically, drawing inferences, and arriving at logical conclusions is based on evidence, and evidence can be expressed and recognized by many different means and in many different formats. Yes, every student should learn to spell accurately, but it is not necessary to know that *I* comes before *E* except after *C* in order to test fairness or bias in an editorial statement or to detect straightforwardness or ambiguity in a politician's promise.

Wiggins (1992) notes that tests typically overassess students' knowledge and underassess their know-how. Onosko (1992) reports measurable "climates of thoughtfulness" in the classrooms of social studies teachers who reflect on their own practices, who value thinking, and who emphasize depth over breadth in content coverage.

Carr (1988) and others suggest various ways by which to introduce and pursue higher-order thinking skills in the classroom. For example, using all major news media—newspapers, magazines, television, and radio—motivates students, and comparing different accounts of the same story helps them develop questioning attitudes. "In the process," writes Carr, "they become more discriminating consumers of news media, advertising, and entertainment."

"All classification tasks," she notes, "require identification of attributes and sorting into categories according to some rule. While sorting concrete objects is an appropriate activity for the young child, verbal analogies (for example, 'How are a diamond and an egg alike?') are appropriate for learners of any age. . . . Applications to mathematics and science, especially the inquiry approach to science, are readily apparent."

"Schema theory," she continues, "holds that information, if it is to be retained, must be categorized with something already stored in memory. Brainstorming techniques that

aid comprehension . . . help students to access their prior knowledge about a topic to be introduced, and thus to classify and retain the new information."

Children's literature becomes its own powerful tool, Carr concludes, citing Somers and Worthington (1979): "Literature offers children more opportunities than any other area of the curriculum to consider ideas, values, and ethical questions."

Just how seriously should Chicken Little's neighbors have taken her complaint that the sky was falling? Why? Why not? Was it fair for the Little Red Hen to keep all the bread she had baked for herself? How true is it that sticks and stones can break your bones, but names will never hurt you? Why does a rolling stone gather no moss? If water is heavier than air, how do raindrops get up in the sky? How does science differ from art, music from noise, wisdom from fact?

What is truth?

Resources

Adams, 1986; Bransford, Sherwood, Vye, & Rieser, 1986; Carr, 1988; Chi, Bassok, Lewis, Reimann, & Glaser, 1989; Lambert, 1990; Onosko, 1992; Paul, 1984; Rosenshine & Meister, 1992; Somers & Worthington, 1979; Wiggins, 1992.

Strategy 1.8:
Use a multicultural teaching approach.

Multiculturalism doesn't mean what it used to mean in education in the United States. Adding a speech by Martin Luther King Jr. to the literature anthology and offering parental instructions in Spanish—both good ideas in their own right—simply do not go far enough anymore. Teaching multiculturally throughout the curriculum is more than simply an attempt to combat racism. The more important aim of studying human cultures in all their diversity is to understand what it is to be human.

Unfortunately, such study has too often been skewed to a single perspective while more inclusive perspectives have been labeled as somehow disloyal to the American tradition. The fact that racism is so prevalent in American society has until recently led many theorists to concentrate primarily on the study of specific ethnic groups, on their characteristics and unique contributions to the more general culture—usually described from a Euro-American or Anglo-American point of view.

By contrast, the history of the United States is actually the history of all the cultures that it comprises. Until recently, multicultural education has focused mostly on minority groups, even though Euro-Americans and Anglo-Americans also spring from a culture that was not originally and purely "American." Such skewing sets up the fallacy that Euro- and Anglo-American descendants are the "real" Americans while all others, particularly people of color, are culturally "different."

Classroom instruction in a multicultural context is enhanced when it involves students in learning about *themselves* first—through oral history projects, for example, in which children involve their parents, grandparents, and other older, living adults who can relate information about family backgrounds and histories. Shared in the classroom, such information becomes a powerful tool both for identifying similarities among students and for highlighting how they differ from one another in positive rather than negative ways.

In short, teaching multiculturally cultivates a school culture that celebrates diversity; supports mutual acceptance of, respect for, and understanding of all human differences; and provides a balanced viewpoint on key issues involved in such teaching. It provides students with a global, international perspective on the world in which they live. It seeks to eliminate racial, ethnic, cultural, and gender stereotypes and to resolve or ameliorate problems associated with racism and prejudice. And it underscores the importance of teaching ethics, values, and citizenship in promoting the democratic heritage of the United States.

Resources
Au & Kawakami, 1985; Banks, 1990; Bennett, 1986; Bloom, 1985; Collins, 1988; Dillon, 1989; Fullinwider, 1993; Hall, 1989; Hollins, 1993; Kendall, 1983; Quellmalz & Hoskyn, 1988; Taylor & Dorsey-Gaines, 1988; Tiedt & Tiedt, 1986.

Strategy 1.9:
Use alternative assessments.

The student report card is no longer the primary measure of success in schooling. The general vocabulary of education in the United States now includes a whole range of assessment terms: adequate yearly progress, SAT, standardized tests, norms, criterion references, outcomes, portfolios, and on and on. Little wonder that teachers and administrators feel pressured by the demands of "assessment" and harried by the clamor and misunderstanding that surround the term today.

Various modes of assessment yield critical and useful information to inform and shape tools and methods that promise to improve academic achievement. "Why do we evaluate students?" ask Rasbow and Hernandez (1988). Among the answers are to determine the following:

- If objectives have been achieved.
- The knowledge and skills that students have acquired.
- Areas in which the curriculum needs improvement.
- The effectiveness of a teaching process or methodology.
- Student responses to specific aspects of the curriculum.
- Students' ability to use knowledge and skills.

Evaluations are also used to do the following:

- Design instruction for individuals, groups, or entire classes.
- Diagnose a student's level of understanding before recommending further instruction on a given topic.
- Gather information on the quality of the learning environment.
- Guide the direction of future study.
- Summarize an activity, topic, or unit of work.
- Provide a basis for extra help where needed.
- Identify the most useful information to communicate to students and parents.

Traditional assessment techniques and instruments for filling one or another of those roles are as familiar to most teachers as they are widespread in use: the National Assessment of Educational Progress, the SAT, norm- and criterion-referenced tests (some mandated by state legislatures, and even by the federal government), standardized tests in specific subject areas (the Stanford, the California, and the Metropolitan, among others), performance scales, and checklists. And, of course, among teacher-made instruments, examples include the essay exam and the ubiquitous multiple-choice test.

Researchers and curriculum specialists have emphasized the power of various alternative methods of assessment, such as the following:

- Exhibitions or demonstrations that serve as culminating activities in a student's learning experience.
- Observation and analysis of hands-on or open-ended experiences.

• Portfolios (collections of records, letters of reference, samples of work, sometimes even including videotapes of student performance or task accomplishment—in fact, any evidence that appropriately documents a student's skills, capabilities, and past experiences).

If two of the primary purposes of assessment are to determine whether the goals of education are being met and to inform various stakeholders of the progress of education, then assessment techniques should be sufficiently varied to perform these functions as appropriately and accurately as possible. Those goals vary, after all, from broad national goals to the individual teacher's lesson plan. They encompass diagnoses of ability or style in teaching and learning, measurements of proficiency and achievement of individual students or entire classes, and the effectiveness of entire schools, districts, state systems, or national programs. The audiences for assessments may include students, teachers, parents, policymakers, colleges, and businesses. Some assessments serve gatekeeping roles—college admission tests, for instance.

Some assessment methods reflect some of what we have come to realize are preferred teaching practices; consequently, they contain activities that are congruent with and that support good instruction. They tend to invite diverse responses and to promote a range of thinking—hands-on science and mathematics problem-solving activities, for example. In some cases, assessment tasks may extend over several days, allowing students to reflect on their work, to polish and revise it. Some assessments give students the opportunity to respond in any of several ways, including writing, drawing, and making charts or graphic organizers.

In general, trends indicate that alternative assessment tends to do the following:

• Use a variety of progress indicators, such as projects, writing samples, interviews, and observations.
• Focus on an individual's progress over time rather than on one-time performance within a group.
• Bring teachers into conference with students about their work and progress, helping students to evaluate themselves by perceiving the results of their own work.

Resources

Association for Supervision and Curriculum Development, 1992; Buechler, 1992; Grace, 1992; Hewitt, 1993; Johnson, 1993; Lockwood, 1991; Marzano et al., 1992; Marzano, Pickering, & McTighe, 1993; Perrone, 1991; Rasbow & Hernandez, 1988; Schnitzer, 1993; Sweet & Zimmerman, 1992; Worthen, 1993.

Strategy 1.10:
Promote home/school partnerships.

Years ago, the professionals at Harlem Park Middle School in Baltimore realized the vital importance of taking parental involvement seriously. They added three parent coordinators to their staff and located them full-time in the neighborhoods the school serves rather than in the school building itself. Living and working in those neighborhoods, the coordinators helped to fight a steady rise in the school's dropout rate by teaching parents how to keep their children in school, help with homework, keep track of progress, and work with school representatives before a crisis develops.

In Mesa, Arizona, school officials recognized that parenthood is 18 years of on-the-job training. So they organized a "Parent University," filling a Saturday schedule with 40 workshops ranging from creative art activities for preschoolers, to helping young people survive junior high, to financing a college education. More than 800 people attended (Education Leaders Consortium, 1989).

The list of ways in which school people have come to grips with the need to bring home and school together for the good of the children varies widely across the United States, limited only by the resourcefulness and imagination of the people in each school and district.

Epstein (1989) outlines several broad avenues by which parents and schools can share in a child's development. Parents have the basic obligation to provide food, clothing, and shelter; to ensure a child's general health and safety; and to provide child rearing and home training. But parents can also provide school supplies, a place for schoolwork at home, and positive home conditions for learning. The school, in turn, is obliged to communicate to the home such important information as school calendars; schedules; notices of special events, school goals, programs, and services; school rules, codes, and policies; report cards, grades, test scores, and informal evaluations; and the availability of parent/teacher conferences.

Parents can be directly involved in the work of the school: assisting teachers and students with lessons; chaperoning class trips; participating in classroom activities; aiding administrators, teachers, and school staff in the school cafeteria, library, laboratories, and workshops; organizing parent groups in fund-raising, community relations, political awareness, and program development; attending student assemblies, sports events, and special presentations; and participating in workshops, discussion groups, and training sessions. Parents can involve themselves in learning activities at home by developing a child's social and personal skills and by contributing to basic-skills education, development of advanced skills, and enrichment.

In governance and advocacy, parents can assume decision-making roles in parent-teacher organizations, on advisory councils, or through other committees and groups at the school, district, or state levels. They can become activists in monitoring schools and by working for school improvement.

Among private philanthropic organizations, the Rockefeller Foundation funded a $3 million effort to launch a project that incorporated the pioneering practices of James Comer, a child psychiatrist at Yale University. The Comer Model is based on the belief that parental involvement is the cornerstone of effective and responsible school change. Comer maintains that one cannot separate academic development from the child's social and cultural background. Thus one of several programs within the project has emphasized a school's obligation to work cooperatively with parents and mental health professionals in meeting the needs of children.

Williams and Chavkin (1989) report that successful home/school programs tend to share seven characteristics: (1) they are guided by written policies; (2) they enjoy administrative support; (3) they include training of staff, parents, or both; (4) they take a partnership approach; (5) they maintain two-way communications; (6) they encourage networking; and (7) they are constantly informed and reshaped by project evaluation.

Having abstracted and reviewed nearly 50 studies of home/school cooperation, Henderson (1987) reached the following conclusions:

• The family provides the primary educational environment.

• Involving parents in their children's formal education improves student achievement.

• Parent involvement is most effective when it is comprehensive, long-lasting, and well planned.

The benefits of family involvement are not confined to early childhood or the elementary levels of schooling; strong effects result from involving parents continuously throughout high school. Henderson also concluded that involving parents in their own children's education at home is not enough. To ensure the quality of schools as institutions serving the community, parents must be involved at all levels of schooling. Moreover, children from low-income and minority families have the most to gain when schools involve parents. Parents can help, regardless of their level of formal education.

We cannot look at the school and the home in isolation from one another. We must see how they interconnect with each other and with the world at large.

Resources

Becher, 1984; Comer, 1980; Education Leaders Consortium, 1989; Epstein, 1987, 1989; Epstein & Dauber, 1991; Goodson & Hess, 1975; Henderson, 1987; Leler, 1983; Steinberg, 1988; U.S. Department of Education, 1990; Williams & Chavkin, 1989.

Strategy 1.11:
Use accelerated learning techniques.

In *Empowering the Spectrum of Your Mind*, Colin Rose (1985) declares that most of us are probably using only 4 percent of the enormous potential of our brains. "The more you use your brain," he maintains, "and the more facts and experience you store, the more associations and connections you make. Therefore, the easier it is to remember and learn yet more new material."

Once considered appropriate for use almost exclusively with students identified as gifted and talented, accelerated learning has come to be regarded as effective with students of any level of performance or ability. How does one "accelerate learning"? What is the theory behind the phrase? Rose (1985) begins with a seemingly obvious fact: no learning can take place without memory. How does one best encode things into memory? By creating concrete images of sights, sounds, and feelings, and by the strong association of one image with another. The stronger the original encoding, the better the ultimate recall.

"To achieve good memory," Rose writes, "you need to link a series of facts or ideas together, so that when one is remembered, it triggers recall for a whole series of others."

Thus, an ideal learning pattern involves the following steps:

- Immediate rehearsal of new facts in the short term.
- Repetition or testing of the facts a few minutes later.
- Review of the facts an hour later.
- A short recap of them after a night's rest. (Sleep appears to help memorization; new information is reviewed during REM—rapid eye movement—sleep.)
- Short review a week later.
- Short review a month later.

Rose claims that such a schedule of learning can enable the recall of up to 88 percent of the new information an individual receives—four times better than the usual rate of recall.

Among techniques recommended by advocates of accelerated learning are the following:

- Chunking, that is, reducing new information to manageable bits—a chunk no longer than seven words or seven digits, for instance.
- Use of music and rhyme as aids to memory.
- Peripheral learning and the use of memory maps to encourage association, and thus recall.
- Encoding as specifically as possible by principles rather than through isolated examples by rote.

- Psychiatrist Georgi Lozanov (Lozanov & Gateva, 1988) urges maintaining an upbeat classroom presentation at all times, with constant attention to physical surroundings, self-esteem, goals and outcomes, competition, right and wrong answers, and individual learning styles, expectations, and outcomes.

Resources

Galyean, 1983; Levin, 1988a, 1988b, 1991a, 1991b; Lozanov & Gateva, 1988; Means & Knapp, 1991; Pritchard & Taylor, 1980; Richardson, 1988; Rose, 1985; Russell, 1975; Schuster, 1985.

Strategy 1.12:
Foster strategies in questioning.

The classroom "discussion" dragged on. Predictably, the teacher asked one factual-recall question after another about the short story at hand. Each question invariably elicited a right-or-wrong answer from one, and sometimes two, student volunteers. Then the teacher reached that point in the story where the main character faced what seemed like a life-or-death personal dilemma. "I wonder how many of you have ever faced such a situation," the teacher remarked offhandedly. Hands shot up all around the room, some flapping in urgency. "Oh, my! I'm afraid I've touched some raw nerves," the teacher exclaimed. "Let me withdraw the question." All the raised hands dropped. So did the students' attention to the topic.

That teacher couldn't have read Lehr and Harris's *At-Risk, Low-Achieving Students in the Classroom* (1988). The authors suggest (and their suggestions are well supported by research) how even the timeless classroom practice of questions from the teacher can be adapted to elicit individual involvement rather than passive response. They also show how to follow through for even greater student participation and response. Their advice, in part, includes the following suggestions (pp. 43–44):

• Structure questions so that students can succeed.

• Encourage students to respond. (Most teachers answer two-thirds of their own questions.)

• Ask questions in all modes. (Most questions are asked at the level of basic recall or recognition. Questioning that is more complex increases student achievement.)

• Pause. The number and quality of student answers increase when teachers provide wait time of three to five seconds after asking a question. Appropriate wait time is particularly important in teaching low achievers. Some higher-level questions might require as much as 15 to 20 seconds of wait time.

• Call on students randomly, but be sure not to forget the low achiever.

• If a student's response is vague, call for clarification or elaboration—for example, "Tell me more." Probe students to encourage higher levels of thinking.

• Encourage students to develop and ask their own questions, thus increasing their opportunities for thinking.

• Use techniques that require students to pose their own questions and to make discoveries on their own. For example, ask students in a science class to make predictions, based on their own experiences, before a demonstration or an experiment. The processes of observing, comparing, and describing are as important as the product.

Other studies of questioning techniques suggest that teachers break the total content of their questioning into bits small enough so that students are assured of being able to answer at least three-quarters of the questions correctly. They urge a high proportion of questions that are well beyond mere factual recall—questions that encourage interpretation or that challenge critical thinking.

Questioning need not simply follow a lesson or an assignment as a means of checking to see if students have completed or understood it. Reading specialists, for instance, have long advocated the use of prereading questioning techniques, using teacher- or student-generated questions to develop background knowledge, to preview key concepts, and to set purposes for the reading. Questioning after reading should provide students with opportunities to practice or rehearse what they have learned from the text, as well as increase associations between textual information and their own background knowledge ("Questioning Promotes," 1987).

To stimulate student discussions, Dillon (1984) suggests a three-step process:

• Carefully formulate one or two questions to get the discussion going.

• From then on, ask questions only when perplexed and genuinely in need of more information.

• Then make more statements that present facts or opinions, reflect students' opinions to them, register confusion, or invite elaboration and student-to-student exchanges.

Student-generated questions and student-led discussions give students a higher stake and interest in their classroom activities and learning. Framing their own questions requires young people to interact with the meaning of content or text from a variety of perspectives. Generating their own questions, they support and challenge each other and recognize the social aspects of exploring the meaning of what they encounter in reading or in other learning activities.

Teachers need to model effective questioning and discussion strategies, including how to interact with others as well as how to think about and discuss text or content. Touch a raw nerve now and then—not to aggravate, but to stimulate!

Resources

Adams, 1986; Carlsen, 1991; Dillon, 1984; Goatley & Raphael, 1992; Lehr & Harris, 1988; "Questioning Promotes," 1987; Roberts & Zody, 1989; "Teachers' Questions," 1987.

Strategy 1.13:

Emphasize brain-compatible instruction.

Think of your most recent drink of water. Exactly what steps did you follow in taking it? What facts, what prior experiences, what understandings did you call on? It's been estimated that you performed 50 or so actions while taking that drink of water. Did you think of all 50—that is, did you bring any of them, in isolation, to the forefront of your consciousness while drinking?

Probably not. Your brain handled all the necessary steps for you! At the same time, your brain was probably helping you consider your plans for the weekend, reminding you of the slight soreness in your left thumb, telling you it was a warm afternoon, and juggling countless other "programs"—chains of thought needed to accomplish some foreseen goal, whether soaking your thumb or quenching your thirst (Della Neve et al., 1986).

Brain-compatible instruction builds on the notion that the human brain operates as an incredibly powerful parallel processor, always doing many different things simultaneously (Caine & Caine, 1991). The brain is capable of such a vast number and array of functions that its functioning can be visualized most easily only in terms of programs and patterns—one program, perhaps, for getting a glass of water at the kitchen sink, a different program for sipping from the water fountain outside your classroom door.

How does the brain differentiate among the vast array of programs it stores? By recognizing an apparently endless number and variety of patterns among them. Thus "brain-compatible instruction defines learning as the acquisition of useful programs," write Della Neve and her colleagues (1986). "The human brain is exceedingly intricate. For educational purposes, however, what counts is a broad, holistic understanding of what the brain is for (it did not evolve to pass tests or fill in worksheets), its principal architecture, its main drives, and its way of relating to the real world."

Carnine (1990) describes some of the misunderstandings that can result in teachers, students, or both after "brain-antagonistic" instruction:

> Very young children know that the name of an object stays the same even after the orientation of the object has changed. For example, when a chair is turned to face the opposite direction, it remains a chair.
>
> Consequently, in preschool, when a *b* is flipped to face the opposite direction, children often assume that it still goes by the name of *b*. Making this error doesn't necessarily imply that a student's visual brain function is weak or that the student would benefit from a kinesthetic approach to learning lowercase letters. Extensive research has shown that students are more likely to confuse objects and symbols that share visual or auditory sameness, such as *b* and *d*.
>
> In solving simple computation problems, such as 24 + 13, 1st graders learn that they can start with the bottom number in the units column or with the top number: 4 + 3 equals 7, and so does 3 + 4. The sameness they note is that these problems can be worked in either direction, from top to bottom or the reverse.
>
> Soon thereafter come subtraction problems, such as 24 − 13. Students can still apply the sameness learned in addition, thinking of the difference between 4 and 3 or between 3 and 4 and always subtracting the smaller number from the larger. However, when students encounter a problem such as 74 − 15, applying the sameness noted earlier leads them to subtract the smaller from the larger number and come up with the answer 61. Such a mistake is a sensible application of a mislearned sameness. . . .

"The brain's search for samenesses," Carnine concludes, "has little regard for the intentions of educators." At the same time, he notes that although the brain's relentless search for patterns helps explain certain common student misconceptions, it can also help educators develop more effective classroom activities.

Della Neve and her colleagues at Drew Elementary School developed their own seven principles, which serve as focal points to guide teachers in designing and implementing brain-compatible instruction:

1. Create a nonthreatening climate.

2. Input lots of raw material from which students can extract patterns—a vast array of activities, aided by an ample supply of materials, equipment, and print and audiovisual resources.

3. Emphasize genuine communication in talking, listening, writing, and reading as ways to interact with other people.

4. Encourage lots of manipulation of materials. Students need to be in command and able to push things around, encouraging them to work toward goals and explore a range of means.

5. Emphasize reality. By using problems, examples, and contacts drawn from the "real world" rather than contrived exercises, texts, worksheets, and basal readers, students can see the real value of their own learning.

6. Address learning activities to actual, productive uses.

7. Respect natural thinking, including intuitive leaps, a grasp of patterns (as in number tables or good writing), and aesthetic and nonverbal interests and activities.

"Brain-based instruction," Caine and Caine (1991) warn us, "stems from recognizing that the brain does not take logical steps down one path like an analog computer, but can go down a hundred different paths simultaneously like an enormously powerful digital computer." They add, "Each brain is unique. Teaching should be multifaceted to allow all students to express visual, tactile, emotional, and auditory preferences. Providing choices that are variable enough to attract individual interests may require the reshaping of schools so that they exhibit the complexity found in life."

Resources

Bateson, 1980; Caine & Caine, 1991; Campbell, 1989; Carnine, 1990; Cousins, 1989; Della Neve, Hart, & Thomas, 1986; Hart, 1983, 1986; Vygotsky, 1962, 1978.

Strategy 1.14:
Activate students' prior knowledge.

Activating students' prior knowledge—through the use of schema theory, for example—helps youngsters integrate new knowledge and skills with their own experiences. By doing so, teachers acknowledge that all students, regardless of their background, bring a wealth of knowledge to learning. The kind and amount "of knowledge one has before encountering a given topic in a discipline affects how one constructs meaning," writes Gaea Leinhardt (1992). "The impact of prior knowledge is not a matter of 'readiness,' component skills, or exhaustiveness; it is an issue of depth, interconnectedness, and access. Outcomes are determined jointly by what was known before and by the content of the instruction" (pp. 51–56).

Consequently, it just makes sense for teachers to begin by learning what students already know about a topic, thus preventing youngsters from having to repeat what they already know or trying to build on knowledge they do not yet possess. Connecting new knowledge to previous learning builds a strong foundation for future learning; it also gives teachers valuable opportunities to correct misperceptions. Modifying activities to suit learners' preferences helps them construct new understandings.

When tapping into students' prior knowledge, teachers recognize that the most effective means of learning is discovery, and the most effective means of teaching is modeling. Modeling by the teacher is one of many powerful tools

29

for activating prior knowledge. Depending on the task, the teacher decides what prior knowledge needs to be activated and asks students to develop and answer questions that cause them to activate it. The teacher then proceeds to model appropriate questioning processes. Activating students' prior knowledge engages them more actively in learning, in generating their own questions, and in leading their own discussions.

Another strategy that effectively activates students' prior knowledge, allowing them to explore what they already know about a topic, is the K-W-L activity, first developed by Donna Ogle. This strategy asks students to identify what they already *know* about a topic, *w*hat they would like to learn, and, at the conclusion of the unit, what they actually did *learn*.

Teachers can encourage students to develop a list of questions they would like to answer. (Teacher modeling helps students form these questions.) Teachers can then assist students in clustering similar questions and in deciding which questions to answer by further explaining the content to be learned. The teacher and students design a plan to find the answer for each question. Allowing students to work in cooperative and collaborative groups is effective because such groups encourage students to share their answers and the rationale behind the answers. During the sharing, the teacher has an opportunity to correct student misunderstandings.

In exploring new topics, students can experience a variety of active, experiential, or authentic assignments. Such assignments—for example, manipulating objects or concepts, engaging in product-oriented activities, and participating in real-life experiences that actively construct knowledge—allow youngsters to explore concepts in some depth and to make discoveries on their own. The opportunity to apply new learnings to real-life contexts that reflect the students' world helps them retain and effectively use new concepts and skills.

Strategy 1.15:
Use a constructivist approach to teaching.

Many of the approaches to teaching and learning that appear in this book challenge the traditional model of schooling, which demands that students receive knowledge solely from the teacher. In explaining the nature of the "pedagogy of poverty," Martin Haberman (1991) notes that teachers and students are engaged in fundamentally different activities: teachers teach and students learn. But what if teachers join students as fellow learners searching for answers to real-life problems or for ways to describe and generalize scientific phenomena?

Another means of creating what might be called a pedagogy of plenty is to embrace a constructivist approach to teaching. Constructivism emphasizes an understanding of how and why students (and adults) learn; it provides a way to combine good teaching and learning practices. These practices include activating students' prior knowledge; providing a variety of active learning resources; using a variety of hands-on, minds-on activities; engaging youngsters in a variety of cooperative learning experiences; allowing students to formulate questions and discover concepts that can guide future learnings; asking students to think aloud while approaching a task; modeling powerful thinking strategies; and providing students with opportunities to apply new learnings within the context of real-life activities.

Such an instructional setting honors the importance of hands-on and "heads-on" experiences in learning. For students to learn to reason about their world, they must be constantly encouraged to ask questions and to solve problems that have meaning to them. Teachers can provide a wide variety of activities to help students construct—and reconstruct—their new learning in their own terms, as they begin to realize that knowledge is created out of life experiences.

Constructivist theory suggests that the goal of schooling is not simply acquiring specific knowledge and expertise, but rather *building understanding*. Learning how to learn becomes the goal. Considered from a constructivist viewpoint, the learning environment is a laboratory that provides the tools to support learners in their quest for understanding. In this approach, teachers facilitate learning by providing appropriate activities such as modeling and questioning techniques in well-designed, well-organized, well-managed classroom environments that allow students to construct their own understandings of concepts.

Constructivist teaching is best facilitated though the use of varied learning configurations. Providing students with opportunities to work in collaborative or small-group learning activities helps them to construct their own knowledge. Students have the opportunity to listen to other points of view, debate, discuss, and form insights into new ideas while working collaboratively with their peers. Such activities must also activate students' prior knowledge to help them develop questioning skills.

Strategy 1.16:
Organize instructionally effective classroom environments.

When the classroom environment encourages growth and development, students will respond. Instructionally effective environments offer youngsters a wide variety of powerful experiences, which include ways of interacting with and learning from one another in instructional areas that support experiential, problem-based, active learning. Creating such environments calls for the teacher to construct and allow cooperative, collaborative strategies.

Classroom design simply means arranging the room to make the best use of space and to create a comfortable learning climate—both physically and psychologically. Classroom management reflects the ways in which the teacher orchestrates high-quality instructional activities that help children take charge of their learning and eliminate unwanted behavioral and discipline problems.

Classroom Design

Our school system was invented to provide a sit-and-learn process of education. In 1915, for

31

instance, John Dewey reportedly described the difficulties he encountered during an exhaustive search for furniture "suitable from all points of view—artistic . . . and educational—to the needs of children." According to the account, Dewey finally met one school-supply dealer who admitted, "I'm afraid we do not have what you want. You want something at which children may work; these are for listening."

Amazingly, little has changed in U.S. classrooms since Dewey's time. Regardless of individual differences, many, many children are still expected to sit on a hard seat, not move, and not speak—just listen and answer questions.

Research strongly supports the important role of environmental preferences in students' motivation and their ability to learn. The *quality* of the environment in which we live and work is vitally important. Individuals tend to respond to their physical environment first in terms of personal comfort. Harmony makes it easier to concentrate and remember information.

The proper use of space within a classroom generates student activity and learning. Room arrangement, for example, allows students to work at computer stations, engage in small-group work, engage in project-based learning, and use multimedia equipment for individual or group activities. Appropriate classroom design empowers teachers to create instructional areas, such as learning and interest centers and media centers, that offer students varied learning opportunities and accommodate individual learning needs and interests.

Well-designed classrooms display high levels of student cooperation, academic success, and task involvement. Teachers work to develop intrinsic motivation in students, which is essential to creating lifelong learners. Thus effective classroom environments create multiple learning situations capable of addressing students' diverse characteristics to enhance their satisfaction and academic performance. Such classes are child centered; they meet young people's instructional needs by exposing them to a variety of highly motivating, stimulating, multilevel instructional activities.

Current research in the functioning of the brain confirms that we learn best in a rich, multisensory environment. We learn more about people by interacting with them in real-life contexts. We learn more meaningfully when we are fully immersed in the learning experience. Therefore, we should provide students with active learning experiences that incorporate a wide variety of materials, including high-quality, well-written literature.

Powerful learning activities are most likely to occur in a highly organized learning environment. When orchestrating such a setting, it is important to keep in mind how instruction will be reinforced, reviewed, and enriched to extend youngsters' learning potential; how procedures for completing assignments, working, locating instructional resources, and acquiring assistance will be facilitated; and how students will evaluate their own performance and that of others.

Classroom Management

Making a classroom an effective educational tool depends on creating not only a physically comfortable environment that supports instructional goals but also one that is emotionally, socially, psychologically, and physically safe. Classrooms should be places where a child can think, discover, grow, and ultimately learn to work independently and cooperatively in a group setting, developing self-discipline and self-esteem. At the heart of an emotionally safe learning environment is cooperation—among staff, students, and other stakeholders.

Cooperation leads to ownership, involvement, and great opportunities for student self-discipline, says Jerome Freiberg (1996)—but first must come *trust*. Students learn to trust through opportunities to take ownership of and responsibility for their own actions and those of others. Strategies to promote cooperation include establishing rules and regulations (with the assistance of students) for codes of behavior and conduct; talking about consequences of behavior; offering youngsters training in peer mediation and conflict resolution; creating rotating classroom management positions, with clearly outlined responsibilities; and helping youngsters develop norms of collaboration and social skills to enable them to work effectively in groups.

When children are truly engaged in learning and the approach to discipline is an active one, teachers do not have to waste valuable time dealing with disciplinary issues. When learning becomes less meaningful to students' lives, less interactive, or less stimulating, teachers increasingly need to control their students; in the process, they unwittingly create opportunities for undesirable student behaviors.

Teachers who try to impose too many rules, too much rigidity, and too many uniform

activities quickly lose control. Teachers who can bring themselves to share power and confidence with their students gain more control. That is exactly why teachers should concentrate on creating conditions in which students can and will manage themselves.

Author's note: I would like to acknowledge the ASCD Advisory Panel on Improving Student Achievement and Lloyd W. Kline for their contributions to this chapter.

Bibliography

Adams, M. J. (1986, June 17–18). Teaching thinking to Chapter 1 students. In B. I. Williams et al. (Eds.), *Designs for compensatory education: Conference proceedings and papers.* Chapel Hill, NC: Research and Evaluation Associates, Inc.

Adams, M. J. (1990). *Beginning to read: Thinking and learning about print.* Cambridge, MA: Bradford Books/MIT Press.

Andrews, R. H. (1990, July–September). The development of a learning styles program in a low socioeconomic, underachieving, North Carolina elementary school. *Journal of Reading, Writing, and Learning Disability International, 6*(3), 307–314.

Andrews, R. H. (1991). Insights into education: An elementary principal's perspective. In R. S. Dunn (Ed.), *Hands-on approaches to learning styles: Practical approaches to successful schooling* (pp. 50–52). New Wilmington, PA: Association for the Advancement of International Education.

Ascher, C. (1990, March). *Testing students in urban schools: Current problems and new directions* (Urban Diversity Series No. 100). New York: ERIC Clearinghouse on Urban Education/Institute for Urban and Minority Education.

Association for Supervision and Curriculum Development. (1992). *Redesigning assessment* [Videotape]. Alexandria, VA: Author.

Atkins, A. (1993, February). New ways to learn. *Better Homes and Gardens, 71*(2), 35–36.

Au, K., & Kawakami, A. J. (1985). Research currents: Talk story and learning to read. *Language Arts, 62*(4), 406–411.

Au, K., & Kawakami, A. J. (1991). Culture and ownership: Schooling of minority students. *Childhood Education, 67*(5), 280–284.

Banks, J. A. (1990). *Preparing teachers and administrators in a multicultural society.* Austin, TX: Southwest Educational Development Laboratory.

Bateson, G. (1980). *Mind and nature: A necessary unity.* New York: Bantam.

Bauer, E. (1991). The relationships between and among learning styles, perceptual preferences, instructional strategies, mathematics achievement and attitude toward mathematics of learning disabled and emotionally handicapped students in a suburban junior high school. *Dissertation Abstracts International, 53*(6), 1378.

Becher, R. M. (1984). *Parent involvement: A review of research and principles of successful practice.* Washington, DC: National Institute of Education.

Bempechat, J., & Ginsberg, H. P. (1989, November). *Underachievement and educational disadvantage: The home and school experience of at-risk youth* (Urban Diversity Series No. 99). New York: ERIC Clearinghouse on Urban Education/Institute for Urban and Minority Education.

Benard, B. (1991, April). *Moving toward a "just and vital culture": Multiculturalism in our schools.* Portland, OR: Western Regional Center for Drug-Free Schools and Communities, Northwest Regional Educational Laboratory. (ERIC Document Reproduction Service No. ED336439)

Bennett, C. I. (1986). *Comprehensive multicultural education: Theory and practice.* Newton, MA: Allyn and Bacon.

Bloom, B. S. (1976). *Human characteristics and school learning.* New York: McGraw-Hill.

Bloome, D. (1985). Reading as a social process. *Language Arts, 62*(2), 134–142.

Boyatzis, R. E., & Kolb, D. A. (1991). Assessing individuality in learning: The learning skills profile. *Educational Psychology: An International Journal of Experimental Educational Psychology, 11*(34), 279–295.

Bransford, J. D., Sherwood, R. S., Vye, N. J., & Rieser, J. (1986, October). Teaching thinking and problem solving: Research foundations. *American Psychologist, 41*(10), 1078–1089.

Brown, S. (1990, October). Integrating manipulatives and computers in problem-solving experiences. *Arithmetic Teacher, 38*(2), 8–10.

Brunner, C. E., & Majewski, W. S. (1990, October). Mildly handicapped students can succeed with learning styles. *Educational Leadership, 48*(2), 21–23.

Bruno, A. (1982, October). Hands-on wins hands down. *Early Years, 13*(2), 60–67.

Buechler, M. (1992, April). *Performance assessment.* Policy Bulletin. Bloomington, IN: Indiana Education Policy Center.

Burroughs, R. (1993, July). The uses of literature. *Executive Educator, 15*(7), 27–29.

Butler, K. A. (1984). *Learning and teaching styles: In theory and practice.* Maynard, MA: Gabriel Systems.

Caine, R. N., & Caine, G. (1991). *Teaching and the human brain.* Alexandria, VA: Association for Supervision and Curriculum Development.

Campbell, J. (1989). *The improbable machine.* New York: Simon & Schuster.

Carbo, M. (1987, October). Matching reading styles: Correcting ineffective instruction. *Educational Leadership, 45*(2), 55–62.

Carbo, M., Dunn, R., & Dunn, K. (1986). *Teaching students to read through their individual learning styles.* Englewood Cliffs, NJ: Prentice-Hall.

Carbo, M., & Hodges, H. (1988, Summer). Learning styles strategies can help students at risk. *Teaching Exceptional Children, 20*(4), 55–58.

Carlsen, W. S. (1991, Summer). Questioning in classrooms: A sociolinguistic perspective. *Review of Educational Research, 61*(2), 157–178.

Carnine, D. (1990, January). New research on the brain: Implications for instruction. *Phi Delta Kappan, 71*(5), 372–377.

Carr, K. S. (1988, Winter). How can we teach critical thinking? *Childhood Education, 65*(2), 69–73.

Cherkasky-Davis, L. (1993, June 11). Presentation at the annual conference of the Educational Press Association of America, Philadelphia.

Chi, M. T. H., Bassok, M., Lewis, M. W., Reimann, P., & Glaser, R. (1989). Self-explanations: How students study and use examples in learning to solve problems. *Cognitive Science, 13*(2), 145–182.

Cohen, H. G. (1992, March). Two teaching strategies: Their effectiveness with students of varying cognitive abilities. *School, Science and Mathematics, 92*(3), 126–132.

Cole, M., & Griffin, P. (Eds.). (1987). *Improving science and mathematics education for minorities and women: Contextual factors in education.* Madison, WI: University of Wisconsin.

Collins, J. (1988, December). Language and class in minority education. *Anthropology in Education, 19*(4), 299–326.

Comer, J. P. (1980). *School power.* New York: Macmillan, The Free Press.

Connolly, L. H., & Tucker, S. M. (1982, March). *Motivating the Mexican American student.* Las Cruces, NM: ERIC Clearinghouse on Rural Education and Small Schools. (ERIC Document Reproduction Service No. ED287657)

Costa, A. L., & Marzano, R. (1987, October). Teaching the language of thinking. *Educational Leadership, 45*(2), 29–33.

Cousins, N. (1989). *Head first: The biology of hope.* New York: E. P. Dutton.

Danehower, V. F. (1993, Summer). Implementing whole language: Understanding the change process. *Schools in the Middle, 2*(4), 45–46.

Darling-Hammond, L., & Ascher, C. (1991, March). *Creating accountability in big city schools* (Urban Diversity Series No. 102). New York: ERIC Clearinghouse on Urban Education/ Institute on Urban and Minority Education, and the National Center for Restructuring Education, Schools and Teaching. (ERIC Document Reproduction Service No. ED334339)

Dash, R. (Ed.). (1988, September). *The challenge—Preparing teachers for diverse student populations* (Roundtable Report). San Francisco: Far West Laboratory for Educational Research and Development. (ERIC Document Reproduction Service No. ED334191)

Della Neve, C., Hart, L. A., & Thomas, E. C. (1986, October). Huge learning jumps show potency of brain-based instruction. *Phi Delta Kappan, 68*(2), 143–148.

Dillon, D. R. (1989). Showing them that I want them to learn and that I care about who they are: A microethnography of the social organization of a secondary low-track English-reading classroom. *American Educational Research Journal, 26*(2), 227–259.

Dillon, J. T. (1984, November). Research on questioning and discussion. *Educational Leadership, 42*(3), 50–56.

Dunn, R., & Dunn, K. (1993). *Teaching secondary students through their individual learning styles: Practical approaches for grades 7–12.* Boston: Allyn and Bacon.

Edmonds, R. (Program Consultant). (1991). *Effective schools for children at risk* [Videotape]. Alexandria, VA: Association for Supervision and Curriculum Development.

Education Leaders Consortium. (1989). *Schools, parents work best when they work together.* Washington, DC: Education Leaders Consortium.

Epstein, J. L. (1987). Toward a theory of family-school connections: Teacher practices and parent involvement. In K. Hurrelmann, F. X. Kaufmann, & F. Lösel (Eds.), *Social intervention: Potential and constraints.* New York: Walter de Gruyter.

Epstein, J. L. (1989). Effects on student achievement of teachers' practices of parental involvement. In S. Silvern (Ed.), *Literacy through family, community, and school.* Greenwich, CT: JAI Press.

Epstein, J. L., & Dauber, S. L. (1991, January). School programs and teacher practices of parent involvement in inner-city elementary and middle schools. *Elementary School Journal, 91*(3), 289–305.

Erickson, F. (1987). Transformation and school success: The politics and culture of educational attainment. *Anthropology and Education Quarterly, 18*(4), 335–356.

ETS Policy Information Center. (1990). *The education reform decade.* Princeton, NJ: Educational Testing Service.

Farr, M., & Daniels, H. (1986). *Language diversity and writing instruction.* New York: ERIC Clearinghouse on Urban Education/Institute for Urban and Minority Education, the ERIC Clearinghouse on Reading and Communication Skills, and the NCTE.

Flaxman, E., Ascher, C., & Harrington, C. (1988, December). *Youth mentoring: Programs and practices* (Urban Diversity Series No. 97). New York: ERIC Clearinghouse on Urban Education/Institute for Urban and Minority Education.

Freiberg, J. (1996, September). From tourists to citizens in the classroom. *Educational Leadership, 54*(1), 32–36.

Fullinwider, R. K. (1993, Spring). Multiculturalism: Themes and variations. *Perspective, 5*(2).

Galyean, B. C. (1983). *Mind sight: Learning through imaging.* Long Beach, CA: Center for Integrative Learning.

Gardner, H. (1999). *Intelligence reframed: Multiple intelligences for the 21st century.* New York: BasicBooks.

Gardner, H., & Hatch, T. (1989, November). Multiple intelligences go to school. *Educational Researcher, 18*(8), 4–9.

Garrett, S. L. (1991). The effects of perceptual preference and motivation on vocabulary and test scores among high school students. Unpublished doctoral dissertation, University of La Verne, California.

Goatley, V. J., & Raphael, T. E. (1992). Non-traditional learners' written and dialogic response to literature. In C. K. Kinzer & D. K. Leu (Eds.), *Literacy research, theory, and practice: Views from many perspectives.* Chicago: National Reading Conference.

Goodson, B. D., & Hess, R. D. (1975). *Parents as teachers of young children: An evaluative review of some contemporary concepts and programs.* Washington, DC: Bureau of Educational Personnel Development, DHEW, Office of Education.

Grace, C. (1992). *The portfolio and its use: Developmentally appropriate assessment of young children.* Urbana, IL: ERIC Clearinghouse on Elementary and Early Childhood Education.

Gregorc, A. E. (1982). *An adult's guide to style.* Columbia, CT: Gregorc Associates, Inc.

Gregorc, A. E. (1985a). *Inside styles: Beyond the basics.* Columbia, CT: Gregorc Associates, Inc.

Gregorc, A. E. (1985b). *Gregorc style delineator.* Columbia, CT: Gregorc Associates, Inc.

Haberman, M. (1987, November). *Recruiting and selecting teachers for urban schools.* New York: ERIC Clearinghouse on Urban Education/Institute for Urban and Minority Education and Association of Teacher Educators.

Haberman, M. (1991). The pedagogy of poverty versus good teaching. *Phi Delta Kappan, 73*(4), 290–294.

Hall, E. T. (1989, Fall). Unstated features of the cultural context of learning. *Educational Forum, 54*(1), 21–34.

Hart, L. (1983, January). A quick tour of the brain. *School Administrator, 40*(1), 13–15.

Hart, L. (1986, May). All "thinking" paths lead to the brain. *Educational Leadership, 43*(8), 45–48.

Hartshorn, R., & Boren, S. (1990, June). *Experiential learning of mathematics: Using manipulatives.* Charleston, WV: ERIC Clearinghouse on Rural Education and Small Schools. (ERIC Document Reproduction Service No. ED321967)

Henderson, A. T. (1987). *The evidence continues to grow: Parent involvement improves students' achievement.* Columbia, MD: National Committee for Citizens in Education.

Herrmann, A. W. (1989, May). *Teaching writing with peer response groups.* Bloomington, IN: ERIC

Clearinghouse on Reading and Communication Skills. (ERIC Document Reproduction Service No. ED307616)

Hewitt, G. (1993, May/June). Vermont's portfolio-based writing assessment program: A brief history. *Teachers & Writers, 24*(5), 1–6.

Hodges, H. (1994, January). A consumer's guide to learning styles programs: An expert's advice on selecting and implementing various models in the classroom. *School Administrator, 51*(1), 14–18.

Hollins, E. R. (1993, Spring). Assessing teacher competence for diverse populations. *Theory into Practice, 32*(1), 93–99.

Irvine, J. J. (1990). *Black students and school failure: Policies, practices, and prescriptions.* New York: Greenwood Press.

Jacobs, H. H. (1991, October). Planning for curriculum integration. *Educational Leadership, 49*(2), 27–28.

Johnson, D. W., & Johnson, R. T. (1986). *Learning together and alone* (2nd ed.). Englewood Cliffs, NJ: Prentice-Hall.

Johnson, D. W., & Johnson, R. T. (1990, December/January). Social skills for successful group work. *Educational Leadership, 47*(4), 29–33.

Johnson, N. J. (1993). *Celebrating growth over time: Classroom-based assessment in language arts* (Literacy Improvement Series for Elementary Educators). Washington, DC: Office of Educational Research and Improvement.

Joyner, J. M. (1990, October). Using manipulatives successfully. *Arithmetic Teacher, 38*(2), 6–7.

Kendall, F. E. (1983). *Diversity in the classroom: A multicultural approach to the education of young children.* New York: Teachers College Press.

Kilman, M., & Richards, J. (1990). *Now that we've done the calculation, how do we solve the problem? Writing, sharing, and discussing arithmetic stories.* Newton, MA: The Literacies Institute, Education Development Center, Inc.

Knapp, M. S., & Shields, P. M. (1990a, June). Reconceiving academic instruction for the children of poverty. *Phi Delta Kappan, 71*(10), 753–758.

Knapp, M. S., & Shields, P. M. (Eds.). (1990b, January). *Better schooling for the children of poverty: Alternatives to conventional wisdom.* Study of Academic Instruction for Disadvantaged Students. Volume II: Commissioned Papers and Literature Review. Washington, DC, and Menlo Park, CA: Policy Studies Associates and SRI International.

Knapp, M. S., & Turnbull, B. J. (1990, January). *Better schooling for the children of poverty: Alternatives to conventional wisdom.* Study of Academic Instruction for Disadvantaged Students. Volume I: Summary. Washington, DC, and Menlo Park, CA: Policy Studies Associates and SRI International.

Lambert, M. (1990). When the problem is not the question and the solution is not the answer: Mathematical knowing and teaching. *American Educational Research Journal, 27*(1), 29–63.

Langer, J. A. (1991). *Literary understanding and literature instruction* (Report Series 2.11). Albany, NY: National Research Center on Literature Teaching and Learning.

Lehr, J. B., & Harris, H. W. (1988). *At-risk, low-achieving students in the classroom.* Washington, DC: National Education Association.

Leinhardt, G. (1992, April). What research on learning tells us about teaching. *Educational Leadership, 49*(7), 51–56.

Leler, H. (1983). Parent education and involvement in relation to the schools and to parents of school-aged children. In R. Haskins & D. Adams (Eds.), *Parent education and public policy.* Norwood, NJ: Ablex.

Levin, H. M. (1988a). *Structuring schools for greater effectiveness with educationally disadvantaged or at-risk students.* Paper presented at the annual meeting of the American Educational Research Association, New Orleans.

Levin, H. M. (1988b, September). *Accelerated schools for at-risk students.* (CPRE Research Report Series RR-010). New Brunswick, NJ: Center for Policy Research in Education, Eagleton Institute of Politics, Rutgers, State University of New Jersey.

Levin, H. M. (1991a, January). Don't remediate: Accelerate. *Principal, 70*(3), 11–13.

Levin, H. M. (1991b). *Accelerating the progress of ALL students* (Rockefeller Institute Special Report, Number 31). Albany: State University of New York, Nelson A. Rockefeller Institute of Government.

Lewis, A., & Steinberger, E. (1991). *Learning styles: Putting research and common sense into practice.* Arlington, VA: American Association of School Administrators.

Lockwood, A. T. (1991, March). Authentic assessment. *Focus in Change, 3*(1). (Available from the National Center for Effective Schools, Madison, WI.)

Lozanov, G., & Gateva, E. (1988). *The foreign language teacher's suggestopedic manual.* New York: Gordon and Breach Science Publishers.

Maehr, M. L. (1980, April). *Cultural differences do not have to mean motivational inequality.* Paper presented at the annual meeting of the American Educational Research Association, Boston. (ERIC Document Reproduction Service No. ED199353)

Marzano, R. J., Brandt, R. S., Hughes, C. S., Jones, B. F., Presseisen, B. Z., Rankin, S. C., & Suhor, C. (1988). *Dimensions of thinking.* Alexandria, VA: Association for Supervision and Curriculum Development.

Marzano, R. J., Pickering, D., & McTighe, J. (1993). *Assessing student outcomes: Performance assessment using the Dimensions of Learning model.* Alexandria, VA: Association for Supervision and Curriculum Development.

Marzano, R. J., Pickering, D. J., Whisler, J., Kendall, J. S., Mayeski, F., & Paynter, D. E. (1992). *Toward a comprehensive model of assessment.* Aurora, CO: Mid-continent Regional Educational Laboratory.

Mathematical Sciences Education Board. (1993). *Making mathematics work for minorities: Framework for a national action plan.* Washington, DC: National Academy Press. (ERIC Document Reproduction Service No. ED373961)

Means, B., & Knapp, M. S. (1991). *Teaching advanced skills to educationally disadvantaged students.* (Final Report). Washington, DC: Prepared under contract by SRI International and Policy Studies Associates for the U.S. Department of Education, Office of Planning, Budget, and Evaluation.

Miller, S. K., & Crano, W. D. (1980, April). *Raising low-income/minority achievement by reducing student sense of academic futility: The underlying theoretical commonalities of suggested strategies.* Paper presented at the annual meeting of the American Educational Research Association, Boston. (ERIC Document Reproduction Service No. ED186575)

National Council of Teachers of Mathematics. (1989). *Curriculum and evaluation standards for school mathematics.* Reston, VA: Author.

Oakes, J. (1985). *Keeping track: How schools structure inequality.* New Haven, CT: Yale University Press.

Onosko, J. J. (1992, April). Exploring the thinking of thoughtful teachers. *Educational Leadership, 49*(7), 40–43.

Orsak, L. (1990, October). Learning styles versus the Rip Van Winkle syndrome. *Educational Leadership, 48*(2), 19–20.

Palincsar, A. S., Englert, C. S., Raphael, T. E., & Gavalek, J. R. (1991, May/June). Examining the context of strategy instruction. *Remedial and Special Education (RASE), 12*(3), 43–53.

Palincsar, A. S., & Klenk, L. J. (1991). Learning dialogues to promote text comprehension. In B. Means & M. S. Knapp (Eds.), *Teaching advanced skills to educationally disadvantaged students.* Washington, DC: U.S. Department of Education.

Palincsar, A. S., Ransom, K., & Derber, S. (1989/1990, December/January). Collaborative research and development of reciprocal teaching. *Educational Leadership, 46*(4), 37–40.

Paris, S. G., Wasik, B. A., & Turner, J. C. (1991). The development of strategic readers. In R. Barr, M. L. Kamil, P. B. Mosenthal, & P. D. Pearson (Eds.), *Handbook of reading research* (Vol. 2, pp. 609–640). New York: Longman.

Paul, R. W. (1984, September). Critical thinking: Fundamental to education for a free society. *Educational Leadership, 42*(1), 4–14.

Perrin, J. (1990, October). The learning styles project for potential dropouts. *Educational Leadership, 48*(2), 23–24.

Perrone, V. (1991). *Expanding student assessment.* Alexandria, VA: Association for Supervision and Curriculum Development.

Pritchard, A., & Taylor, J. (1980). *Accelerated learning: The use of suggestion in the classroom.* Novato, CA: Academic Therapy.

Quality Education for Minorities Project. (1990, January). *Education that works: An action plan for the education of minorities.* Cambridge: Massachusetts Institute of Technology.

Quellmalz, E. S., & Hoskyn, J. (1988, April). Making a difference in Arkansas: The multicultural reading and thinking project. *Educational Leadership, 46*(7), 52–55.

Questioning promotes active reader/text interaction. (1987, Spring). *IRT Communication Quarterly.*

Rasbow, J., & Hernandez, A. C. R. (1988, June). The price of the "GPA perspective": An empirical study of "making the grade." *Youth and Society, 19*(4), 363–377.

Resnick, L. B. (1987). Learning in school and out. *Educational Researcher, 16*(9), 13–20.

Richardson, R. B. (1988, March). *Active affective learning for accelerated schools.* Stanford, CA: Center for Educational Research at Stanford University.

Roberts, J., & Zody, M. (1989, March). Using the research for effective supervision: Measuring a teacher's questioning techniques. *NASSP Bulletin, 73*(515), 8–14.

Rose, C. (1985). *Empowering the spectrum of your mind.* Flushing, NY: Spectrum Educational Services, Inc.

Rosenshine, B., & Meister, C. (1992, April). The use of scaffolds for teaching higher-level cognitive strategies. *Educational Leadership, 49*(7), 26–33.

Roser, N. L. (1987). Research currents: Returning literature and literacy. *Language Arts, 64,* 90–97.

Rowan, B., Guthrie, L. F., Lee, G. V., & Guthrie, G. P. (1986). *The design and implementation of Chapter 1 instructional services: A study of 24 schools.* San Francisco: Far West Laboratory for Educational Research and Development.

Russell, A. (1990, Summer/Fall). In *Carnegie Quarterly 25,* 3–4. New York: Carnegie Corporation of New York.

Russell, P. (1975). *The brain book.* New York: E. P. Dutton.

Schnitzer, S. (1993, April). Designing an authentic assessment. *Educational Leadership, 50*(7), 32–35.

Schuster, D. H. (1985). *Suggestive accelerated learning and teaching: A manual of classroom procedures based on the Lozanov method.* Ames, IA: Society for Accelerated Learning and Teaching.

Secada, W. G., & Carey, D. A. (1990, October). *Teaching mathematics with understanding to limited English proficient students* (Urban Diversity Series, No. 101). New York: ERIC Clearinghouse on Urban Education/Institute on Urban and Minority Education.

Shulman, J. H., & Mesa-Bains, A. (Eds.). (1990, November). *Teaching diverse students: Cases and commentaries.* San Francisco: Far West Laboratory for Educational Research and Development.

Sinatra, R. (1983, May). Brain research sheds light on language learning. *Educational Leadership, 40*(8), 9–12.

Slavin, R. E. (1986). *Using student team learning* (3rd ed.). Baltimore: Johns Hopkins University Press.

Slavin, R. E. (1987, October). Making Chapter 1 make a difference. *Phi Delta Kappan, 69*(2), 110–119.

Somers, A. B., & Worthington, J. E. (1979). *Response guides for teaching children's books.* Urbana, IL: National Council of Teachers of English.

Steinberg, A. (1988, November/December). School-parent relationships that work: An interview with Dr. James Comer. *Harvard Education Letter, 4*(6), 4–6.

Stevens, R. J., Madden, N. A., Slavin, R. E., & Farnish, A. M. (1987). Cooperative integrated reading and composition: Two field experiments. *Reading Research Quarterly, 22*(4), 433–454.

Stover, D. (1993, May 25). School boards caught up in debate over tracking. *School Board News, 13*(9), 1, 8.

Strickland, D. S. (1985). *Integrating the basic skills through the content areas.* Workshop materials. New York: Teachers College, Columbia University.

Strickland, D. S., & Morrow, L. M. (1989). *Emerging literacy: Young children learn to read and write.* Newark, DE: International Reading Association.

Sweet, D., & Zimmerman, J. (Eds.). (1992, November). *Performance assessment.* Education Research Consumer Guide. Washington, DC: Office of Educational Research and Improvement. (ERIC Document Reproduction Service No. ED353329)

Taylor, D., & Dorsey-Gaines, C. (1988). *Growing up literate: Learning from inner-city families.* Portsmouth, NH: Heinemann.

Teachers' questions: Why do you ask? (May, 1987). *Harvard Education Letter, 3*(3), 1.

Tiedt, P. L., & Tiedt, I. M. (1986). *Multicultural teaching.* Newton, MA: Allyn and Bacon.

U.S. Department of Education, Office of Educational Research and Improvement. (1990, August). Parental involvement in education. *Issues in Education* (0-861-983). Washington, DC: Author.

U.S. Department of Labor. (1992). *Learning a living: A blueprint for high performance.* (A SCANS Report for America 2000). Washington, DC: Secretary's Commission on Achieving Necessary Skills, U.S. Department of Labor.

Vygotsky, L. S. (1962). *Thought and language* (E. Hanfmann, Ed., & G. Vakar, Trans.). Cambridge, MA: MIT Press.

Vygotsky, L. S. (1978). *Mind in society: The development of higher psychological processes.* Cambridge, MA: Harvard University Press.

Walmsley, S. A., & Walp, T. P. (1990). Integrating literature and composing into the language arts curriculum: Philosophy and practice. *Elementary School Journal, 90*(3), 251–274.

Webb, M. (1988, Spring). Peer helping relationships in urban schools. *Equity and Choice, 4*(3), 35–48.

Wiggins, G. (1992, May). Creating tests worth taking. *Educational Leadership, 49*(8), 26–33.

Williams, D. I., Jr., & Chavkin, N. F. (1989, October). Essential elements of strong parent involvement programs. *Educational Leadership, 47*(2), 19–20.

Willis, S. (1991, June). Forging new paths to success: Promising programs for teaching disadvantaged students. *ASCD Curriculum Update.*

Worthen, B. R. (1993, February). Critical issues that will determine the future of alternative assessment. *Phi Delta Kappan, 74*(6), 444–454.

2

Diverse Teaching Strategies for Diverse Learners

Marietta Saravia-Shore

That minority and low-income children often perform poorly on tests is well known. But the fact that they do so because we systematically expect less from them is not. Most Americans assume that the low achievement of poor and minority children is bound up in the children themselves or their families. "The children don't try." "They have no place to study." "Their parents don't care." "Their culture does not value education." These and other excuses are regularly offered up to explain the achievement gap that separates poor and minority students from other young Americans.

But these are red herrings. The fact is that we know how to educate poor and minority children of all kinds—racial, ethnic, and language—to high levels. Some teachers and some entire schools do it every day, year in and year out, with outstanding results. But the nation as a whole has not yet acted on that knowledge....

—Commission on Chapter 1 (1992, pp. 3–4)

This chapter describes a multitude of teaching strategies shown by research to be effective in educating diverse student learners. Diverse student learners include students from racially, ethnically, culturally, and linguistically diverse families and communities of lower socioeconomic status. If educators act on the knowledge research offers, we can realize the educational excellence we desire for all children.

Facing the Achievement Gap

According to *Diplomas Count: An Essential Guide to Graduation Policy and Rates* (Olson, 2006), the national graduation rate is 69.6 percent. This report estimates that in 2006 more than 1.2 million students—most of them members of minority groups—will not graduate from high school in four years with a regular diploma. Nationally, while close to 30 percent of students do not graduate, only "51.6 percent of Black students, 47.4 percent of American Indian and Alaskan Native students, and 55.6 percent of Hispanic students graduated from high school on time with a standard diploma," compared with more than three-quarters of non-Hispanic whites and Asians (Olson, 2006, p. 6).

Moreover, *Diplomas Count* tells us that the average graduation rate in urban districts is 60 percent, compared to a 75 percent graduation rate in suburban communities. School systems with high levels of racial segregation have a graduation rate of only 56.2 percent, compared to 75.1 percent in school systems with low levels of racial segregation. Nationally, more than one-third of students (35 percent) fail to make the transition from 9th to 10th grade. In summary, *the patterns in poor school districts mirror those found in racially segregated districts.*

Demographer Harold Hodgkinson, who advocates universal preschool education as a means of providing true equal educational opportunity, reflects on the diversity in U.S. schools (2003):

The most diverse group in the United States is our youngest children, and they will make the nation more diverse as they age. Almost 9 million young people ages 5 to 17 speak a language other than English in their home and 2.6 million of them have difficulty speaking English. For our Children's Class of 2000, we could estimate that almost one-half million are being raised in families that speak no English at home, and that at least 125,000 will need special attention in preschool and kindergarten to learn to speak and read English.

About one-third of our black and Hispanic children are being raised in poverty while 10% of non-Hispanic whites live in poverty. However, the largest number of poor children are white while the highest percentage of poor children are black and Hispanic. Of the 14 million children ages birth to 18 living in poverty in 2000, 9 million were white and 4 million were black. Four million Hispanics were living in poverty, but were included in both white and black totals, as Hispanics are not a "race."

Regardless of race, the children in married couple families are much less likely to be poor (about 8%) while 29% of white children and 52% of black and Hispanic children who live with a single mother are likely to be poor. Almost half of these single mothers are working, usually at very low-wage jobs. (pp. 4–5)

Closing the Achievement Gap

Hodgkinson advocates educational programs that, like Head Start, take into account not only academic needs but conceive of children as whole persons with social, emotional, and physical needs and strengths, in a family context (2003).

Overall, the evidence that high-quality education before the child's fifth birthday can yield lifetime benefits is undebatable. We know how to do it. Why don't we make such programs available to all? There are few federal programs in any agency that can support results like these, yet Head Start enrollment has usually hovered below 50% of those eligible. (p. 11)

However, many schools do not have the opportunity to work with children at such a young age. Thus, they must start work closing the achievement gap in later years. Burris and

Welner (2005) documented changes in schooling practice that closed the achievement gap between black and Latino students and white and Asian students in middle and high school in the diverse Rockville Centre School District in New York. The district instituted detracking (that is, heterogeneous grouping of high- and low-achievers in all classes) and accelerated learning by gradually eliminating remedial classes and offering all students rigorous classes in mathematics, global history, International Baccalaureate English, and history—classes previously offered only to the highest achievers.

Their five-year study found a dramatic rise in the rate of students passing all eight New York State Regents tests to receive a Regents high school diploma. Before detracking, only 32 percent of the African American and Latino students in the graduating class of 2000 earned Regents diplomas, while 88 percent of white and Asian students did so. After detracking and accelerated learning had been instituted for five years, 82 percent of African American and Latino students in the graduating class of 2003 earned Regents diplomas; 97 percent of white or Asian students did so. In fact, "The Regents diploma rate for [detracked] minority students [82 percent] surpassed New York State's rate for white or Asian American students" (Burris & Welner, 2005, p. 598).

Burris and Welner (2005, p. 595) concluded that when "all students—those at the bottom as well as those at the top of the [achievement] gap—have access to first-class learning opportunities, all students' achievement can rise."

Hodgkinson (2003) highlighted another model—the Schools of the 21st Century—that regarded students as whole persons in their family context. This "is one of the most successful models for putting together all of the factors . . . that contribute to the positive academic, emotional, and social development of young children" (p. 14), including (1) school-based programs; (2) strong links between early childhood and schools; (3) strong parental support and involvement; (4) universal access; (5) a focus on children's physical, social, emotional, and intellectual development; (6) strong staff training and development; and (7) a commitment to serving working families. Schools of the 21st Century is now offered in over 1,400 schools in a wide variety of communities across the United States. Although the core components just mentioned are always present, the program is flexible enough to maximize the program's success in the unique "fingerprint" of each community setting.

Hodgkinson concluded: "Although we do not know how to reduce poverty . . . , there is an abundance of research on how to successfully reduce the *effects* of poverty on our youngest children" (p. 16).

Today, as in the past, teachers are being challenged to broaden their repertoire of teaching strategies to meet the needs and strengths of students from a tremendous diversity of backgrounds and cultures. These learners—African Americans, American Indians, Asian Americans, Hispanics, and many others—face societal discrimination, live in conditions of poverty, or both. The ways in which we teach these young people exert a powerful influence on their linguistic, social, cognitive, and general educational development.

Research suggests, for example, that effective instruction acknowledges students' gender differences and reaffirms their cultural, ethnic, and linguistic heritages. Many effective instructional approaches build on students' backgrounds to further the development of their abilities. Critically important is recognizing that the use of effective instructional practices as demonstrated by research will improve achievement for all children, including those who are not minorities or children of poverty. The implementation of sound, research-based strategies that recognize the benefits of diversity can build a better future for all of us.

Embracing Diversity

The broad range of experiences and perspectives brought to school by culturally, linguistically, and ethnically diverse students offer a powerful resource for everyone to learn more—in different ways, in new environments, and with different types of people. Every single person in this enormously diverse and ever-changing system has the power to serve as an invaluable resource for all others—students, teachers, and the community as a whole. Rather than constituting a problem for students and educators, the growing diversity in U.S. classrooms necessitates and encourages the development and use of diverse teaching strategies designed to respond to each student as an individual.

The United States is fortunate, for it includes not only immigrants but also political refugees, indigenous Americans, and descendants of people (sometimes brought against their will) from every continent on the globe. This boundless diversity has resulted in the inventions, discoveries, ideas, literature, art, music, films, labor, languages, political systems, and foods that enrich American culture. These same resources also have the potential for enriching the American classroom. Immigrant students bring us opportunities to be explored and treasures to be appreciated, and they help us challenge the status quo.

Adopting a truly global perspective allows us to view culturally and linguistically diverse students and their parents or guardians as resources who provide unparalleled opportunities for enrichment. However, we need a greater repertoire of approaches to teaching and learning to cope with varied styles of learning. Teachers and students alike must cultivate interpersonal skills and respect for other cultures. The new world economy demands this global view. After all, our markets and economic competition are now global, and the skills of intercultural communication are necessary in politics, diplomacy, economics, environmental management, the arts, and other fields of human endeavor.

Surely a diverse classroom is the ideal laboratory in which to learn the multiple perspectives required by a global society and to put to use information concerning diverse cultural patterns. Students who learn to work and play collaboratively with classmates from various cultures are better prepared for the world they face now—and the world they will face in the future. Teaching and learning strategies that draw on the social history and the everyday lives of students and their cultures can only assist this learning process.

Teachers promote critical thinking when they make the rules of the classroom culture explicit and enable students to compare and contrast them with other cultures. Students can develop cross-cultural skills in culturally and linguistically diverse classrooms. For such learning to take place, however, teachers must have the attitudes, knowledge, and skills to make their classrooms effective learning environments for all students. Given the opportunity, students can participate in learning communities within their schools and neighborhoods and be ready to assume constructive roles as workers, family members, and citizens in a global society.

Zeichner (1992) has summarized the extensive literature that describes successful teaching approaches for diverse populations. From his review, he distilled 12 key elements for effective teaching for ethnic- and language-minority students.

1. Teachers have a clear sense of their own ethnic and cultural identities.

2. Teachers communicate high expectations for the success of all students and a belief that all students can succeed.

3. Teachers are personally committed to achieving equity for all students and believe that they are capable of making a difference in their students' learning.

4. Teachers have developed a bond with their students and cease seeing their students as "the other."

5. Schools provide an academically challenging curriculum that includes attention to the development of higher-level cognitive skills.

6. Instruction focuses on students' creation of meaning about content in an interactive and collaborative learning environment.

7. Teachers help students see learning tasks as meaningful.

8. Curricula include the contributions and perspectives of the different ethnocultural groups that compose the society.

9. Teachers provide a "scaffolding" that links the academically challenging curriculum to the cultural resources that students bring to school.

10. Teachers explicitly teach students the culture of the school and seek to maintain students' sense of ethnocultural pride and identity.

11. Community members and parents or guardians are encouraged to become involved in students' education and are given a significant voice in making important school decisions related to programs (such as resources and staffing).

12. Teachers are involved in political struggles outside the classroom that are aimed at achieving a more just and humane society.

Educating Diverse Students

For the sake of clarity, this chapter breaks the teaching strategies into two main sections. The first section, "Strategies for Culturally and Ethnically Diverse Students," contains strategies appropriate for children whose primary language may or may not be English. The second section, "Strategies for Linguistically Diverse Students,"

contains strategies that specifically address the unique needs of learners of English as a second language. Each strategy includes a brief discussion of the strategy as well as examples of the strategy in use. Resources at the end of each entry allow the reader to explore additional information and resources.

Strategies for Culturally and Ethnically Diverse Students

Generally, U.S. schools provide students of diverse backgrounds with instruction quite different from that provided to students of mainstream backgrounds. For example, poor children and culturally and linguistically diverse students tend to receive inferior instruction because they are usually placed in the bottom reading groups or sent out of the classroom for remedial instruction.

Research also shows that schools tend to discriminate against students of diverse backgrounds through assessments that do not value their home language and through the use of teaching procedures that fail to build on the strengths of their culture or home languages (Garcia & Pearson, 1991; Goldman & Hewitt, 1975; Nieto, 2004; Oakland & Matuszek, 1977). Still other studies demonstrate that many teachers fail to communicate effectively with students from diverse backgrounds; typical (and hard to change) instructional procedures often violate the behavior norms of these students' home cultures (Au, 1980; Cazden, 1988; Delpit, 1988; Heath, 1983; Ogbu, 1982). Also, teachers may have low expectations for students of diverse backgrounds and thus fail to present them with challenging and interesting lessons.

A number of researchers have found many identifiable factors associated with the level of young people's performance in school (First, 1988; Ima & Labovitz, 1991; Ima & Rumbaut, 1989, 1991; National Coalition of Advocates for Students, 1988; Quality Education for Minorities Project, 1990). Schools have control over some factors but not others. If teachers understand these factors and their effects on young people who are newly arrived in the United States, they will be better able to assess their needs and strengths and find innovative ways of helping them adjust to their new schools and to life in a new culture. Some of these critical factors and their effects include the following issues.

• The level of the family's socioeconomic resources is associated with success in school but is conditioned by other factors, such as immigrant status.

• Prior education in the country of origin is associated with success in school.

• The age of entrance into the United States affects success in the English language, as well as other academic areas, but the degree of success is also conditioned by literacy in the home language. Those children who enter the United States before puberty will have an advantage in school.

• The longer the length of the stay in the United States, the greater the success in school. Unfortunately, this effect is offset by a reduction of motivation that comes through acculturation into the American society.

• Intact family and home support systems are associated with success in school. Not surprisingly, unaccompanied minors and students from single-parent families are at greater risk of failure in school.

In this context, it is important to understand how we define various ethnic groups (see "Major U.S. Ethnic Groups," p. 48). For example, Asian Americans are often viewed incorrectly as a single ethnic group. There are, however, many distinct subgroups of Asian Americans, each with its own culture, religion, and unique perspective. Generalization across such subgroups can lead to misperceptions and a failure to recognize and address specific concerns and needs. It is also important to understand that the overall descriptor "Southeast Asian" generally refers to those who report their own ethnic identity as Vietnamese, Laotian, Cambodian, or Hmong. The recent tendency to stereotype Asians as "high achievers" may mask significant and unique educational challenges and needs.

Similarly, Hispanics or Latinos are also composed of many distinct subgroups. Although the U.S. Census Bureau classifies all Spanish-speaking peoples under the general heading "Hispanic origin," this term includes all persons who identify themselves as members of families from Mexico, Central and Spanish-speaking South America, the Spanish-speaking Caribbean islands, or Spain. Furthermore, people of Hispanic origin may be of any race.

Finally, it is important to be aware that agencies dealing with population data refer to Alaskan Natives or American Indians as one group,

Major U.S. Ethnic Groups

The U.S. Census recognizes five primary ethnic groupings in the United States: African Americans or blacks; American Indians and Alaskan Natives; Asian Americans; Hispanic Americans or Latinos; and Native Hawaiians or Pacific Islanders.

African Americans or **blacks** refers to those of African ancestry who may have lived for generations in the United States. Blacks also include Afro-Caribbeans from the West Indies and Haiti and blacks from other islands, such as the Bahamas and Trinidad.

American Indians, also called Native Americans, were the original populations of North America before the arrival of the Spaniards, who were followed by the English, French, and other Europeans. American Indian groups often prefer to be called by their tribal affiliation or the nation to which they belong (i.e., the Navajo nation).

Alaskan Natives refers to indigenous Alaskans including Eskimos, Aleuts, and Inuits.

Asian Americans include all national-origin groups from Asia, some of whom come from technologically advanced countries like Japan. Others come from countries where some of the population have access to advanced technology and others do not, such as Korea, China, Vietnam, and India.

Hispanic Americans or **Latinos** are national-origin groups from the Spanish-speaking Caribbean, Mexico, Central America, and Spanish-speaking South America who reside in the United States. Hispanics also include descendants from Spain, while Latinos are those from the Americas living in the United States. People of Mexican descent are the largest Hispanic group in the United States, and many prefer to be called by their specific national origin (such as Mexican American). Others may prefer terms they call themselves (such as Chicanos).

Native Hawaiians or **Pacific Islanders** refers to groups of indigenous people who have lived for centuries in the Hawaiian Islands or other Pacific Islands such as Fiji, Samoa, Tonga, the Marquesas, and Tahiti.

even though the customs, languages, and cultures of the many tribes and nations of these two groups are vastly different.

Considerable evidence supports this crucial conclusion: the differences in achievement observed between and among students of culturally and ethnically diverse backgrounds and students of mainstream backgrounds are *not* the result of differences in ability to learn. Rather, they are the result of differences in the quality of the instruction these young people have received in school. Moreover, many students who are at risk of failure in U.S. schools have styles of learning that are at odds with traditional instructional practices. A multitude of complex factors contribute to students' at-risk status; many of these factors—crime, drugs, and poverty, among others—are beyond the control of educators. But educators do have the power to replace ineffective instructional practices. The strategies that follow have been demonstrated to be effective in increasing student achievement.

Strategy 2.1:

Maintain high standards and demonstrate high expectations for all ethnically, culturally, and linguistically diverse students.

Discussion

Students learn more when they are challenged by teachers who have high expectations for them, encourage them to identify problems, involve them in collaborative activities, and accelerate their learning (Burris & Welner,

2005). Teachers who express high expectations convey the belief that their students have the ability to succeed in demanding activities. Such teachers avoid repetitive rote learning; instead, they involve young people in novel problem-solving activities. They ask open-ended questions requiring students to use their judgment and form opinions. They choose activities where students must use analytic skills, evaluate, and make connections. They expect students to conduct research, complete their homework, and manage their time effectively.

Now that detracking and accelerated learning with support have been shown to be effective, teachers can confidently advocate for them. Hugh Mehan (2007, p. 11) defines "detracking" as offering "a rigorous academic curriculum to all students accompanied by an extensive system of academic and social supports, or 'scaffolds.'" He notes that "detracking goes beyond just technical or structural changes, but involves a cultural change in teachers' beliefs, attitudes and values, changes in the curriculum, and the organization of instruction" (2007, p. 2).

According to Mehan (2007), research has shown that

the schools' practice of tracking neither provides students with equal educational opportunities nor serves the needs of employers for a well-educated workforce. Students from low-income and ethnic or linguistic minority backgrounds are disproportionately represented in low-track classes and they seldom move up to high-track classes. Students placed in low-track classes seldom receive the educational resources that are equivalent to students who are placed in high-track classes. They often suffer the stigmatizing consequences of negative labeling. They are not prepared well for careers or college. (p. 8)

In an attempt to provide greater educational equity, educators in California schools have been trying an alternative to tracking since the 1980s. In San Diego, one such program—Achievement Via Individual Determination (AVID)—has revamped the curriculum, course structures, and pedagogical strategies into "multiple pathways" to college and career so that students are better prepared and have more options when they complete high school. AVID "untracks" low-achieving ethnic and language-minority students by placing both low- and high-achieving students in the same rigorous academic program. Students are taught explicitly how to study, how to work with teachers, and how to write college applications. These are skills often passed on by parents who have attended college, but they must be taught to students whose parents lack this form of "cultural capital."

The AVID program has successfully prepared underrepresented students for college. From 1988 to 1992, 94 percent of AVID students enrolled in college, compared to 56 percent of all high school graduates. African Americans and Latinos enrolled in college in numbers that exceeded both local and national averages (Mehan, Hubbard, Lintz, & Villanueva, 1994; Mehan, Villanueva, Hubbard, & Lintz, 1996). (Mehan & Hubbard, 1999, p. 1)

Classroom Examples

Jaime Escalante captured media attention with his success in teaching calculus to Hispanic students. His high expectations for his students and their subsequent accomplishments were the subject of the film *Stand and Deliver*. Yet many teachers who will never be the subject of a Hollywood film have inspired and guided pupil achievement. Again and again, research emphasizes the overwhelming importance of the teacher's belief that all students can learn (Gibson & Ogbu, 1991; Knapp, Shields, & Turnbull, 1993; Winfield & Manning, 1992).

When teachers believe that students can learn, they communicate these expectations explicitly, thus encouraging young people, and they also spend more time creating challenging activities. They ask higher-order questions that require not only identification and categorization but also comprehension and analysis, application to other situations, synthesis, and value judgments.

Heath and McLaughlin (1994) have found that one of the reasons for the effectiveness of after-school youth programs organized by community-based organizations is that staff members, often operating on a shoestring budget, depend on students to take some of the responsibility for activities. Young people plan, teach others, and perform a variety of tasks vital to the program. When students are brought into the planning and become coaches for others, they are given "adult" responsibilities and challenges; everyone must be able to depend on everyone else to show up on time and do his or her part.

In addition, involving students in the financial aspects of such operations (whether by fundraising or making requests of foundations) fosters involvement, responsibility, and the learning of math skills. Students acquire social skills along with communication and performance skills. In such collaborative work, diversity of skills is seen as a resource for the entire group; everyone brings something different to the table. When journal writing is a required part of students' group responsibilities, they reflect on what they are learning, practice writing skills, and keep the staff informed of their individual progress and well-being.

Resources

Carter & Chatfield, 1986; Chall, Jacobs, & Baldwin, 1990; Gibson & Bhachu, 1991; Gibson & Ogbu, 1991; Heath & McLaughlin, 1994; Knapp, Shields, & Turnbull, 1993; Levin & Hopfenberg, 1991; McDermott & Goldman, 1998; Mehan, 2005, 2007; Mehan & Hubbard, 1999; Mehan, Hubbard, Lintz, & Villanueva, 1994; Mehan, Villanueva, Hubbard, & Lintz, 1996; Oakes, Wells, Datnow, & Jones, 1997; Quality Education for Minorities Project, 1990; Tharp & Gallimore, 1988; Winfield & Manning, 1992.

Strategy 2.2:

Show students you care by getting to know their individual needs and strengths and sharing their concerns, hopes, and dreams.

Discussion

Students tend to want to participate and do their best when a teacher is nurturing and caring. Nel Noddings (1995) advocates that when society around us concentrates on materialistic messages, "we should care more genuinely for our children and teach them to care" (p. 24). Of course we want academic achievement for our students, she notes, but "we will not achieve even that unless our children believe they themselves are cared for and learn to care for others" (p. 24).

Noddings describes a practice called "looping," where teachers stay with the same group of students for two or more years. Looping was cited in high-performing schools in Oklahoma, Illinois, and New Jersey in the *Just for the Kids Study of Best Practices in 20 States* (National Center for Educational Accountability [NCEA], 2006). By following the same group of students for two or more years, teachers get to know their students' needs and strengths better; trust develops between teacher and students and among classmates. Looping also offers teachers the opportunity to provide more differentiated instruction, even tailoring lessons to individual children.

Classroom Examples

Noddings's definition of caring "implies a continuous search for competence." She observes, "Parents and teachers show caring by cooperating in children's activities, sharing their own dreams and doubts, and providing carefully for the steady growth of the children in their charge" (1995, p. 24). Noddings suggests using integrated curricular themes to teach caring to students.

> In the domain of "caring for self" we might consider life stages, spiritual growth, and what it means to develop an admirable character; in exploring caring for intimate others, we might include units on love, friendship, and parenting; under caring for strangers and global others, we might study war, poverty, and tolerance. (p. 25)

Younger students also get excited when they learn that they can care for the environment through recycling projects, joining others in cleaning and beautifying local parks, starting a community garden, or planting a tree. These themes could be adapted for students from elementary school through high school.

In addition, Noddings suggests alternative methods of staff organization in schools. Elementary students would benefit from having the continuity of the same teacher or a stable group of specialists for two or more years. Even at the high school level, students might benefit if their teacher taught two subjects to the same 30 students rather than one subject to 60 different students.

By learning the strengths and challenges each student faces, teachers can refer children and their families to community-based organizations that provide after-school homework help and programs in sports and the arts. High-performing schools also tend to have systems in place to provide extra help for struggling learners or high-achieving students taking challenging coursework (Viadero, 2006), according to the NCEA's *Just for the Kids Best Practices Studies and Institutes: Findings from 20 States.*

Teachers need support in this work. Developing communities of teachers focused on student work was another practice cited by the NCEA. Successful schools accomplish goals through collaboration. The teachers in one Selma, California, high school hold "focus lesson meetings" in which educators from different disciplines meet and give feedback on one teacher's lesson plan, then try out the revision in one of their classes and give further feedback. Others have "scoring parties" to develop common ideas about what constitutes high-quality student work.

Resources

NCEA, 2006; Noddings, 1995; Viadero, 2006.

Strategy 2.3:

Understand students' home cultures to better comprehend their behavior in and out of the classroom.

Discussion

Educators must understand and respect the many different ways of being a parent and expressing concern about the education of one's children. For example, Gibson (1983, 1988) reports that Punjabi immigrant parents in California believe it is the teacher's task to educate and that parents should not be involved in what goes on at school. Punjabi parents support their children's education by requiring that homework be done and ensuring that their youngsters do not "hang out" with other students but instead apply themselves to schoolwork. Even though the parents themselves may be forced to take more than one job, they do not allow their children to work so that they have time to complete their homework. As a result, Punjabi students as a group have higher rates of graduation and college acceptance than other immigrant groups.

Parental involvement is well established as being correlated with student academic achievement (Epstein, 2005). However, teachers may have concerns about the attitudes of "familism" among Mexican American students, which is defined as the "expressed identification with the interests and welfare of the family" (Valenzuela & Dornbusch, 1994, p. 19). Valenzuela and Dornbusch challenge "the dominant myth that academic achievement is obstructed by collective orientations." In sampling 492 adolescent students of Mexican origin, they found that neither parental education nor familism alone was related to academic achievement, but the two variables working together *were* associated with academic achievement. They suggested that when young people have relatives who have attended a U.S. high school, they have access to more social capital. Also, being part of a dense social network of relatives enhances the opportunity for "multiple alternatives for academic support."

Classroom Examples

Seek information about students' home cultures by asking them to interview their parents about their lives as children, the stories they remember, favorite poems, and family recipes. The results of these interviews can inform the teacher about the rich diversity in his or her classroom. The interviews also can be made into booklets and, subsequently, reading materials for the entire class to share.

Parent-teacher organizations can hold meetings at times convenient for parents to attend, and they can provide translators for those who do not speak English. A room in the school can be set aside for parents to meet and to discuss issues concerning their children's education or the school community. Teachers can visit parents in their homes, or they can use parent-teacher meetings as a time to discuss homework and discipline.

Parents who are welcomed into the school in ways that are culturally appropriate for them become more accessible both as resources and as learners. Immigrant parents can learn both

English as a second language (ESL) and survival skills for their new culture. Parents who are bilingual may be asked to translate for those who have not yet achieved fluency in a new language. Parents who attend workshops can learn family literacy and math activities that enhance their own abilities to support their children's learning of these skills. When students see that their parents are respected by the school, there may be less of the conflict between home and school cultures that can cause a breakdown of discipline within the family.

Resources

Arvizu, 1992; Coballes-Vega, 1992; Gibson, 1983, 1987, 1988; Gibson & Bhachu, 1991; Hamilton, Blumenfeld, Akoh, & Miura, 1989; Heath, 1986; Jordan, Au, & Joseting, 1983; Keefe, 1984; Laosa, 1982; Phillips, 1972; Saravia-Shore & Martinez, 1992; Strickland & Ascher, 1992; Valenzuela & Dornbusch, 1994; Wong-Fillmore & Valadez, 1986.

Strategy 2.4:
Encourage active participation of parents or guardians.

Discussion

Parents and guardians are a child's first teachers, but they are not always aware of the ways in which they mold children's language development and communication skills. Children learn their language at home; the more interaction and communication they have at home, the more children learn. Teachers can support this crucial role by sharing information about the link between home communication and children's learning.

For example, teachers can act as "culture brokers" by talking with parents to emphasize the key role they play in their children's education. Teachers can assist parents in understanding the expectations of the school and their classroom as they elicit from parents their own expectations of teachers and students. Teachers also can suggest ways in which parents might converse more often with their children to prepare them for communication in the classroom.

Parents may not be aware of how they support their children's academic efforts when they discuss the importance of education and take them to informal educational resources in the community. Teachers play an enormously important role in referring parents to community resources such as children's museums, art and science museums, and community-based organizations that offer homework help and arts and sports programs. Teachers also may recommend ESL and GED programs to parents who want to continue their own education.

Classroom Examples

Children learn the importance of language in expressing ideas, feelings, and requests if parents or guardians respond to them and acknowledge their thoughts. Children also need guidance in learning patterns of communication that are necessary in the classroom, including how to make a request, ask a question, and respond to a question.

If parents or guardians are literate in any language, they can read to their children in that language to encourage reading for pleasure and to help children begin to make the connection between oral language and reading. Even if parents or guardians are not literate, they can use wordless books or create prose as they hold their children and "read" with them.

Even the simplest evidence of caring about the importance of literacy pays huge dividends in a young person's schooling. Parents or guardians can take time to talk with their children about any activity they are doing together—eating a meal, for example—thereby encouraging language development. These conversations between parent and child are beneficial whether they are in the home language or in English. Parents or guardians can ask their children questions about whatever activity they are engaged in and how it relates to another activity, as well as ask how they feel about the activity or what they predict may happen next. They are thus modeling the kinds of communication patterns that young people will use in school. At the same time, of course, simply giving children the gift of attention pays huge dividends.

Programs in family literacy can help parents acquire or strengthen their own literacy skills, making them better able to assist their children's development of literacy. The National Center for Family Literacy, with headquarters in Louisville, Kentucky, is a leader in this effort. Other techniques, such as the use of recorded books, allow adults and children to learn reading skills together. Children are encouraged to read when they see their parents reading and have their parents read to them. Quite simply, reading for fun encourages more reading.

A significant resource for teachers and PTAs is the National Network of Partnership Schools (NNPS) at Johns Hopkins University. Their materials assist with parent involvement in schools; their website includes summaries of research on family involvement. For example, NNPS studies (Epstein, 2005) showed that

> through high school, family involvement contributed to positive results for students, including higher achievement, better attendance, more course credits earned, more responsible preparation for class, and other indicators of success in school (Catsambis, 2001; Simon, 2004). Catsambis and Beveridge (2001) analyses indicated that students in neighborhoods with high concentrations of poverty had lower math achievement test scores, but this effect was ameliorated by on-going parental involvement in high school. NNPS studies at the high school level indicated that it is never too late to initiate programs of family and community involvement, as the benefits accrue through grade 12. (p. 2)

Research (Epstein & Van Voorhis, 2001; Van Voorhis, 2003, 2004) on "homework and targeted outcomes reinforce the importance of well-designed, subject-specific or goal-linked activities for family and community involvement for strongest impact on student achievement and success in school" (cited in Epstein, 2005, p. 2). Sheldon and Epstein (2005a) documented that when teachers implement math homework requiring parent/child interactions and offer math materials for families to take home, "the percentage of students attaining math proficiency increased from one year to the next" (cited in Epstein, 2005, p. 2). Similarly, Sheldon and Epstein (2005b) found that when teachers involve families in subject-specific interventions in reading and related language arts, "students' reading skills and scores are positively affected" (cited in Epstein, 2005, p. 2). Moreover, NNPS studies found "significant results of subject-specific family involvement [in homework] for students' science report card grades and homework completion" (cited in Epstein, 2005, p. 2).

Resources

Arvizu, 1992; Carbo, 1978, 1989; Carbo, Dunn, & Dunn, 1986; Catsambis, 2001; Catsambis & Beveridge, 2001; Dornbusch, Ritter, Leiderman, Roberts, & Fraleigh, 1987; Epstein, 2005; Epstein & Sheldon, 2006; Epstein & Van Voorhis, 2001; Lee, 1986; McIntosh, 1983; Sheldon & Epstein, 2005a, 2005b; Simon, 2004; Snow, 1986; Tharp et al., 1984; Valverde, Feinberg, & Marquez, 1980; Van Voorhis, 2003, 2004.

Strategy 2.5:

Tap into students' backgrounds to enhance learning.

Discussion

Students' self-esteem and motivation are enhanced when teachers elicit their experiences in classroom discussions and validate what they have to say. Young people become more engaged in lessons when they are brought into the initial dialogue by being asked what they know about the topic and what they want to know. If their questions are written down and used to form a guide for inquiry into the topic, students are far more likely to be interested in doing further research than if the questions simply come out of a text. The teacher also obtains a better understanding of students' previous knowledge about a subject—a pre-assessment, as it were—that can guide the planning of the subsequent lesson.

Classroom Examples

One way in which teachers can ensure recognition of students' contributions is to use "semantic webbing." At the beginning of learning a new topic, the teacher asks students what they know about that topic; the simplest way to do this is to brainstorm a multitude of associations with the topic. For example, the teacher or one of the students might put the topic "culture" in a center circle on the chalkboard. Then, the recorder notes students' associations in circles around the center circle.

As a next step, the class can discuss (and connect with lines) all the related aspects of "culture," making a web of relationships on the board. This work can be expanded by categorizing the subtopics. The teacher also can ask students what they want to know about the topic at hand. Students' questions, recorded for later use, can serve as guides for research. Students are more likely to be interested in researching a topic when they begin with their own real questions. Those real questions lead them on an ever-widening path of investigation.

Implementing this strategy can be as simple as asking children to voice their questions about a given topic at the beginning of a lesson. After gathering student questions, the teacher can ask whether any student already has information about the topic. Before drawing on books and other resources, the students themselves can be resources by using their own knowledge and prior experiences.

Resources

Au & Jordan, 1981; Boggs, 1985; Coballes-Vega, 1992; Gallimore, Boggs, & Jordan, 1974; Heath, 1983; Jordan, 1981; Lee & Lee, 1980; Protheroe & Barsdate, 1992; Rodriguez, 1989; Taylor, 1983; Tharp, 1989a, 1989b, 1991, 1992; Torres-Guzman, 1992; Trueba, Jacobs, & Kirton, 1990.

Strategy 2.6:

Choose culturally relevant curriculum and instructional materials that recognize, incorporate, and reflect students' heritage and the contributions of various ethnic groups.

Discussion

Students' self-esteem is strengthened when they see and read about the contributions made by their own racial or ethnic groups to the history and culture of the United States. Whenever possible, teachers adapt the curriculum to focus lessons on topics that are meaningful to students. This kind of focus allows students to practice language, thinking, reading, and writing skills in real, meaningful, and interactive situations. Students also come to realize that teachers value and appreciate each child's culture and language.

Classroom Examples

Teachers can select texts or, if necessary, supplementary materials (such as children's literature written by a variety of authors) that incorporate the perspectives, voices, historical events, poetry, artwork, journals, and illustrations of the range of racial and ethnic groups that make up U.S. society (and that may well be represented in the classroom). Teachers can ask students to interview their parents about their history, including their culture, poetry, music, recipes, novels, and heroes. The student can videotape, audiotape, or write the interview and share it with the rest of the class.

In interviews conducted by the Latino Commission (Rodriguez, 1992), high school students observed that they feel left out when the curriculum of the school contains nothing that relates to their own culture. Conversely, they feel that both they and their culture are valued when their culture is included in the curriculum. For younger students, children's books about young people in their own cultural context can provide avenues for discussion and comparison of the similarities and differences between the culture of their parents and that of the school or community in which they now live.

Resources

Banks, 1993; California State Department of Education, 1986; Cummins, 1986; Heath, 1983; Knapp & Turnbull, 1990; Nieto, 2004; Rodriguez, 1992; Saravia-Shore & Arvizu, 1992; Staton-Spicer & Wulff,

1984; Taylor, 1983; Valverde, Feinberg, & Marquez, 1980; Wong-Fillmore & Valadez, 1986.

Strategy 2.7:

Identify and dispel stereotypes.

Discussion

If the teacher allows sexist or racist language and stereotypes to pass unchallenged, students will be harmed in two ways: (1) by the demeaning depiction of their group, which may become part of their self-concept and (2) by the limitations they will feel on their ability to live and work harmoniously with others in their classroom and in their society.

Teachers can select texts or supplementary materials to address the issue of stereotyping. The supplementary materials should be written by a variety of authors who incorporate a wide range of perspectives on historical events, poetry, artwork, journals, music, and illustrations of women and men, as well as varied ethnic and racial groups. Teachers also can point out sexist language and ethnic, racial, or gender stereotypes in everyday instructional materials.

Weis and Fine (2001) have documented the development of a sense of community and the contesting of stereotypes across the usual boundaries of race, class, and gender in two different school situations. In the first, racial and class stereotypes dissolved in a 9th grade literature class guided by two teachers in a racially integrated public school in Montclair, New Jersey. The school has a range of socioeconomic groups, from those living in conditions of extreme wealth to those living in conditions of dire poverty. The school is tracked academically, but the world literature class documented by Michelle Fine was detracked. The teachers asked questions that demanded taking a position and defending it. Students also were asked to develop a new perspective by getting inside the minds and emotions of the literary characters being studied and saying what they might say. Teachers guided the students over the semester as they developed a new consciousness of the range of abilities of their classmates, irrespective of race.

Weis and Fine (2001) also documented an abstinence program among 8th grade girls in the Arts Academy, an urban magnet school in Buffalo, New York. The students differed only in racial identity; all lived in conditions of poverty. However, they developed an identity as a group and distanced themselves from others of their same background who were taking a different path that they saw as unproductive (hanging around men, smoking and drinking, and becoming pregnant at an early age). The group came to see that they shared common problems and could share solutions across racial lines. Through the facilitation of a staff member from the gender-based prevention outreach service Womanfocus, invited by the school guidance counselor, these girls came to share many aspects of their personal lives over the course of the semester. Supporting one another, they planned to graduate from high school, go on to college, and succeed. In doing so, they contested the notions of femininity, victimhood, and race prevailing in their neighborhoods.

Classroom Examples

Identifying and dispelling sterotypes can be as simple as pointing out examples of sexist language in everyday curriculum materials, such as the use of "man" for "human" or the use of the pronoun "he" in referring to both men and women. The teacher can move beyond simple awareness of such stereotypes by asking students how such language makes them feel.

To encourage exploration of how it feels to be in another's shoes, the teacher also can ask students if they would like to be labeled "non-Eastern" because they live in the Western Hemisphere—just as many North Americans refer to those who live in the Eastern Hemisphere as "non-Western." The teacher might also ask white and Asian students whether they would prefer to be called "nonblack," in the same manner that blacks and Asians are often referred to as "nonwhite."

The teacher can compare the dichotomy used in categorizations of racial groups in the United States (i.e., black and white) with the continuum of racial and ethnic groups in South America, where there are more than 20 such categories or distinctions. These striking differences lend themselves to a discussion of the social construction or definition of racial groups; students enjoy the opportunity to research the history and derivation of these definitions.

Resources

Boutte, LaPoint, & Davis, 1993; Demetrulias, 1991; Haw, 1991; Martinez & Dukes, 1991; McIntosh, 1983; Rakow, 1991; Sadker, Sadker, & Long, 1993; Sadker, Sadker, & Steindam, 1989; Valverde, Feinberg, & Marquez, 1980; Weis & Fine, 2001.

Strategy 2.8:
Create culturally compatible learning environments.

Discussion

Research has shown that students learn more when their classrooms are compatible with their own cultural and linguistic experience (Au, 1980; Jordan, 1984, 1985, 1995; National Coalition of Advocates for Students, 1988; Saville-Troike, 1978; Trueba & Delgado-Gaitan, 1985). When the norms of interaction and communication in a classroom are very different from those to which students have been accustomed, they may experience confusion and anxiety, be unable to attend to learning, and not know how to appropriately seek the teacher's attention or participate in discussions. By acknowledging students' cultural norms and expectations concerning communication and social interaction, teachers can appropriately guide student participation in instructional activities.

Research on the effectiveness of culturally compatible classrooms has been conducted with Hawaiian children as well as with Navajo and African American children (Au, 1980; Gilbert & Gay, 1985; Henry & Pepper, 1990; Irvine, 1990; Jordan, 1995; Little Soldier, 1989;

59

Pepper & Henry, 1989). The aspects of culture that influence classroom life most powerfully are those that affect the social organization of learning and the social expectations concerning communication.

The organization of the typical U.S. classroom is one of whole-class teaching in which the teacher as leader instructs, assigns texts, and demonstrates to the whole class. Such whole-class instruction is often followed by individual practice and assessment.

By contrast, Jordan (1995) reported on the results among Hawaiian students in public schools whose reading achievement improved greatly after culturally compatible classrooms were implemented through the Kamehameha Early Education Program (KEEP). In an ethnographic study of the students' home life, Jordan and colleagues in the Hawaiian Community Research Project in the late 1960s and early 1970s found that older siblings were responsible for taking care of younger siblings and doing tasks cooperatively in the home without direct parental supervision. Consequently, these educators structured their 3rd grade classroom into learning centers. After direct instruction from the teacher, small mixed-gender groups of four or five students could assist one another with tasks at the centers, without the direct supervision of teachers—similar to their home situation. Meanwhile, the teachers worked with small groups of students using

comprehension-oriented, direct instruction reading lessons using particular sociolinguistic and cognitive patterns

and a system for managing child behavior which built on standard contingency management to assist the teacher in presenting herself as a person who was both "tough and nice," these being key attributes of adults that Hawaiian children like and respect. (Jordan, 1995, p. 91)

In a collaboration with the Rough Rock Demonstration School in Arizona, Jordan (1995) reported that the same approaches were tried with 3rd grade Navajo students, but the techniques did not work well with them. They learned that in Navajo culture, boys and girls were expected to stay in same-gender groups. Also, because their dwellings were so far apart, they didn't have experiences with many children outside of school in peer companion groups as the Hawaiian children did. Thereafter, changes were made in the classroom organization, and the Navajo children were more comfortable working at learning centers with just one other child of the same gender.

According to Tharp (1992), teaching and learning are more effective when they are contextualized in the experiences, skills, and values of the community and when learning is a joint productive activity involving both peers and teachers. Learning is furthered by "instructional conversations"—dialogues between teachers and learners about their common learning activities.

Classroom Examples

A teacher notices that a Chinese American girl tends not to raise her hand to participate in discussions. The teacher discovers that the child is afraid to respond in front of the whole class because she is still learning English and worries that others will laugh at her. The teacher divides the class into groups of four to do collaborative research so that the girl can practice speaking in English in a smaller group.

Too often, when young people speak a language other than English and are learning English as a second language, teachers of ESL or reading in English may restrict their activities to the lowest level of decoding and phonics, levels that do not challenge students intellectually. Only when students have the opportunity to continue learning in their native language can they operate at their cognitive level and grow intellectually. After reading a book or article in their native language, they can be challenged with comprehension, application, and analysis questions—the higher-order thinking skills. Moll, Diaz, Estrada, and Lopes (1992) found that the level of questioning is much more restricted in ESL reading groups than in native-language reading groups.

Jordan, Tharp, and Baird-Vogt (1992) found that Hawaiian children's academic achievement increased when certain aspects of their home culture were integrated into the elementary classroom. The use of a culturally appropriate form of communication called "talk story" engaged the students more fully. In addition, Hawaiian students were more comfortable in school when they were recognized as being able to take responsibility for maintaining the order and cleanliness of their classroom. In their homes, Hawaiian children have many responsibilities for the care of younger siblings and cooperate in doing household chores. They felt more "at home" when they could come in early, straighten up the room, and set out other students' work for the day. Teachers made the classroom more culturally compatible by learning about the culture of the home.

Resources

Au, 1980; Au & Jordan, 1981; Au & Mason, 1981; Bloome, 1985; Calfee et al., 1981; Dunn, Beaudy, & Klavas, 1989; Dunn & Griggs, 1990; Hirst & Slavik, 1989; Jordan, 1995; Jordan, Tharp, & Baird-Vogt, 1992; Michaels, 1981; Moll, Diaz, Estrada, & Lopes, 1992; Philips, 1983; Saravia-Shore & Arvizu, 1992; Teale, 1986; Tharp, 1992; Wong-Fillmore, 1983.

Strategy 2.9:
Use cooperative learning strategies.

Discussion

One of the most difficult issues faced by teachers in multiethnic classrooms is that students, particularly those from ethnic groups suffering social discrimination, tend to cluster in cliques based on ethnicity. Students may observe that one peer group draws itself apart and, in reaction, may come to feel that they must do so as well.

To break down this defensive withdrawal into ethnic groups, teachers need to give students time to get to know each other and to find that they share common ground, common problems, and common feelings. One way to break down artificial barriers between students is to encourage them to participate in a small group over an extended period of time, collaborating on a shared activity with a shared goal that can only be achieved by working together.

Children who have an opportunity to work in cooperative learning groups with fellow students of other races and ethnicities get to know those students as real people rather than as stereotypes. As students learn together and get to know one another, mutual respect and friendships can develop.

Classroom Examples

The teacher assigns students to groups of five or six and gives each student a specific task in the scientific experiment they are to do collaboratively. One reads and sets up the materials for the experiment; one performs the experiment. Another student records their results, another illustrates their findings, yet another reads the recorded experience to the rest of the class, and so forth.

The social skills that support such cooperative learning must be taught. Students must learn to listen and give feedback, to manage conflict, to lead, to contribute, and to take responsibility for a part of the task. Teachers need to allow groups ample time to "process" their own performance in a task by talking about their interaction and how it could be improved. Tasks that include positive interdependence as part of the activity—that is, tasks requiring each person in the group to be dependent on the whole group's doing well in order to achieve the goal—are more likely to be successful. Especially effective are "jigsaw" tasks, which cannot be completed unless everyone helps or unless each participant

learns one piece of the job and teaches the others. Cooperative learning is more than having students sit next to each other; it involves structuring young people's need to communicate, to get to know one another, and to work together.

Resources

Au, 1980; Carbo, Dunn, & Dunn, 1986; Coballes-Vega, 1992; Dunn, 1989; Garcia, 1992; Hirst & Slavik, 1989; Johnson & Johnson, 1982; Johnson, Johnson, & Holubec, 1994; Philips, 1972; Saravia-Shore, 1993; Slavin, 1980, 1987, 1991.

Strategy 2.10:

Capitalize on students' cultures, languages, and experiences.

Discussion

Learning is more likely to occur when young people's expectations about how to interact with adults and other children match the teachers' and administrators' expectations for such interaction.

Saravia-Shore and Martinez (1992) found that Puerto Rican high school dropouts who had succeeded in an alternative high school credited their increased achievement to the difference in the way adults treated them in each school. They reported that they felt they were treated as children in the regular high school, but the staff members of the alternative school treated them as adults.

Specifically, their new teachers expected that they do their homework because they had enrolled in order to pass the GED examination. Teachers in the alternative high school showed an understanding of the students' cultural norm of having families at an early age and being responsible for other members of their family. Since they knew the students had genuinely pressing responsibilities (including caring for their families and working to support them), they did not criticize students for being late to class, so long as their work was completed. Simply put, the students felt that the teachers in the alternative school understood their life experiences and cared about their success.

Classroom Examples

Jordan, Tharp, and Baird-Vogt (1992) have shown that when teachers incorporate the home culture's expected patterns of interaction and discourse, students feel more comfortable in school and participate more actively in learning situations. When students are used to caring for other children at home, they have a foundation for cooperative learning and peer teaching. They can succeed with cooperative learning and peer teaching if they are given the opportunity to use them and the support of the teacher. If children are accustomed to having responsibilities in caring for their physical environment at home, they often feel comfortable in caring for and managing the school environment as well.

Resources

Au, 1980; Au & Mason, 1981; Calfee et al., 1981; Heath, 1986; Jacob & Jordan, 1987; Jordan, 1995; Jordan, Tharp, & Baird-Vogt, 1992; Knapp & Turnbull, 1990; Philips, 1983; Saravia-Shore & Martinez, 1992; Torres-Guzman, 1992.

Strategy 2.11:
Integrate the arts in the curriculum.

Discussion

Nothing makes learning come alive more than engaging students in arts activities that encourage dialogue on issues that are important to them. Providing opportunities for students to express themselves through the visual and performing arts enables them to learn about and develop their talents and multiple intelligences: not only verbal and mathematical intelligences but also visual, spatial, musical, interpersonal, and intrapersonal intelligences (Gardner, 1983).

Young children benefit from being encouraged to make sense of their world and their relationships through drawing and painting graphic images. Encouraging students to use their imaginations and taking time to elicit their interpretations of visual arts through open-ended questions in a classroom setting is valuable in itself. Yet these conversations also enable students to understand, as they listen to other classmates, the multitude of interpretations that are possible when viewing the same work of art.

Parents can be invited to accompany their children as a group to an art museum and to observe the teacher asking children to describe what they see and what the artwork means to them. Once they've made such a visit, parents may be more comfortable taking their children back to the museum.

Similarly, poetry can be a jumping-off place for discussions. The works of Billy Collins,

Langston Hughes, Maya Angelou, and Bob Dylan often spark students to write their own poetry. Then, students can learn how to perform their own work.

Researchers summarized the results of 145 programs that integrated the arts in curriculum in *Critical Links: Learning in the Arts and Student Academic and Social Development* (Deasy, 2002). They agreed that "well-crafted arts experiences produce positive academic and social effects" (p. iii). One of the *Critical Links* studies reported the effects of the Chicago Arts Partnerships in Education (CAPE) on students' academic performance. In CAPE schools, teams of teachers and teaching artists planned and taught curriculum units that typically integrated a visual art form with an academic subject (such as reading or social studies). The results "demonstrated that the low SES children in arts-integrated schools perform better than those in comparison schools in terms of [standardized tests of mathematics and reading] test scores" (Deasy, 2002, p. 72).

DeMoss and Morris (2002) investigated the question of how the arts support cognitive growth in students. They interviewed 30 students in CAPE schools in 10 classes led by veteran teacher/artist partnerships. They found that "students from all achievement levels displayed significant increases in their ability to analytically assess their own learning following arts-integrated units," while "no such gains were associated with traditional instructional experiences" (2002, p. 1). In addition, DeMoss and Morris documented these benefits of CAPE.

Observations of final performances in the arts-integrated units corroborated students' own assessments. Students who had difficulties controlling their behavior and staying on task performed their parts in final events with seriousness and competency. . . . As students across the board indicated in their interviews, the kinds of activities that the arts provide engage children more deeply in their learning by creating an intrinsic responsibility for the learning activities. This finding held particularly true for those children hardest to reach by traditional approaches. (pp. 20–21)

In this case, the arts contributed to analytically deeper, experientially broader, and psychologically more rewarding learning. These developments could have significant positive effects on students' general cognitive growth over time, particularly if students experience arts-integrated learning in their classrooms on a regular basis. (p. 24)

A more recent study demonstrating the benefits of integrating visual arts in the curriculum on young children's cognitive development was reported in the *New York Times* (Kennedy, 2006). Third grade students in the Learning through Art program sponsored by the Solomon R. Guggenheim Museum were found to have "performed better in six categories of literacy and critical thinking skills—including thorough description, hypothesizing, and reasoning—than did students who were not in the program"

(Kennedy, 2006, p. 1). In this program, the Guggenheim Museum sends teaching artists to the schools where they collaborate with the teacher for 90 minutes per class one day a week over a 10- or 20-week period, helping students and teachers learn about and make art. Groups of students are also taken to the Guggenheim two or three times in that period to see exhibitions.

Classroom Examples

Posters of artwork can enliven a classroom and be a starting point for enriching conversations. If there are restrictions on displaying such work on the walls, use inexpensive foam core panels that fold out and stand up as the background for a classroom gallery. Invite children to describe the artwork on the posters and create a story about what is happening in the pictures—what may have happened before and what may happen next.

Children can learn how to mix primary colors, discovering the secondary colors that are created when any two primary colors are combined. Children enjoy painting, whether it's finger paint for the youngest students or tempera paint for middle and high school students. Students can do collaborative arts projects, putting together individual pieces into quilts or developing murals. Seek out illustrated children's paperback books, such as Jacob Lawrence's *The Great Migration*. Lawrence uses art to interpret the history of African Americans who migrated from the South to the North during the early 20th century. Such visual references to historical events bring social studies to life.

Photography is another art form that children can learn from an adult, be it a teacher, a teacher's colleague, or a parent. Students can use disposable cameras to select locations, people, and objects from their environment to photograph; the photos can be posted in the classroom "gallery" and discussed or used to build a story, play, or poem. Photographic "essays" are another way of sharing one's home culture with others.

Middle and high school students enjoy "poetry slams" in which they compete to be the best performer of their own poems. Learning songs is another way to experience poetry. From the youngest children's songs of Woody Guthrie to favorite world folk songs to the songs of social justice in the Civil Rights Movement, music illuminates the human condition and makes social studies more memorable. Students can even read plays aloud in the classroom, and later the students themselves can write and perform plays for the class.

Resources

Catterall & Waldorf, 1999; Deasy, 2002; DeMoss & Morris, 2002; Fiske, 1999; Gardner, 1983; Kennedy, 2006; Korn and Associates, 2005; Levin, 2003.

Strategy 2.12:
Promote students' health.

Discussion

Caring for students includes positively influencing their decisions related to their physical well-being. Congress passed the Child Nutrition

Act in June 2004, requiring school districts to craft "wellness" policies. Such policies should include goals for nutrition education and ways to increase the physical activity of all students.

Educators who are aware of the growing epidemic of childhood obesity and diabetes are alarmed. According to Kleinfield (2006a, p. A1), "One in three children born in the United States [in 2001] are expected to become diabetic in their lifetimes, according to a projection by the Centers for Disease Control and Prevention. The forecast for Latinos is even bleaker: one in every two."

Nationally, the growing problem of overweight youngsters affects minority students disproportionately. Childhood Type 2 diabetes, the most common form, is often linked to obesity. Being overweight has become a major medical problem among Latino/Hispanic families. In the 2003–04 Child Trends study, 25.3 percent of Mexican American males from ages 6–11 were overweight as defined by the Centers for Disease Control and Prevention—the highest rate in that age group. Compare their rate to the figure for black males (17.5 percent) and for white males (18.5 percent) of the same age group. Among girls ages 6–11, the highest percentage (26.5) of overweight youngsters was black females, followed by 19.4 percent of Mexican American girls and 16.9 percent of white females. In the 12–19 age range, black females were the highest percent of overweight youngsters at 25.4 percent. Moreover, "Asians, especially those from Far Eastern nations like China, Korea, and Japan, are acutely susceptible to Type 2 diabetes, the most common form of the disease" (Santora, 2006, p.

A1). In addition, they develop Type 2 diabetes at far lower weights than people of other races; at any weight they are 60 percent more likely than whites to contract the disease.

Teachers can help to counteract television commercials for fast food, larger portions, sodas, sugary snacks, and sedentary lifestyles that feed childhood obesity and often lead to diabetes, particularly among Asians, Latinos, and African Americans. A *New York Times* study of East Harlem in New York City found a 31 percent rate of diabetes among the 90 percent Latino and African American population there (Kleinfield, 2006b). Unfortunately, "even as health authorities pronounced obesity a national problem, daily participation in gym classes dropped to 28 percent in 2003 from 42 percent in 1991, according to the Centers for Disease Control and Prevention" (Santora, 2006, p. A23).

Classroom Examples

To promote healthier eating habits, teachers can assign research projects comparing the calories in fast foods in various restaurants, soft drinks (including diet sodas), breakfast foods, and snacks (fried versus baked chips, the nutrition facts about various kinds of microwave popcorn). If each child researches one product, the class can create a chart comparing all of them. A similar class project could ask students to act as detectives, uncovering the amount of high-fructose corn syrup in various products by investigating and recording the information on the ingredients label. Teachers of older students can show the film *Super Size Me*, which puts a human face on the effects of fast foods and also contains information about nutritious foods.

Teachers interested in making wellness a part of the curriculum can integrate units on the health benefits of food with complex carbohydrates (beans and multigrain or whole grain bread) compared to highly refined carbohydrates (such as white bread and most pastas). They also might help students investigate why eating apples and other fruits as snacks is healthy as well as delicious; the health benefits of leafy green vegetables; making sandwiches or wraps of roasted vegetables; the higher levels of mercury in larger fish compared to smaller fish; and the benefits of olive oil compared to butter and margarine.

One school district in Texas used the Get FIT (Families in Training) program for a nine-week summer intervention camp for their students who were overweight. For five days each week, students exercised, ate healthy snacks and lunches, and learned about good nutrition; their parents came to the school one night a week to learn about nutrition to support their children. The program, developed by Peggy Visio, a dietitian and adjunct professor, also introduced the 130 5th graders to dancing, kickboxing, yoga, swimming, and volleyball. The benefits of involving parents are clear: they can support a healthier lifestyle in the home and advocate for healthy lunches and snacks in school.

Teachers also can encourage students to take advantage of sports programs offered by community organizations like Girls and Boys Clubs, the YMCA, and the Police Athletic League. Community-based organizations often sponsor summer camps and after-school programs. Taking part in sports; yoga; tai chi; or simple deep, slow breathing also helps reduce stress. Even inviting a well-informed parent or a teacher or a health professional from a local hospital to share information on healthy nutrition, exercise, and stress reduction will positively influence students in this area.

Resources

Harvard Medical School, 2006; Kleinfield, 2006a, 2006b; Santora, 2006; Zehr, 2006.

Strategy 2.13:
Develop community ties and build community schools.

Discussion

Teachers can explore community schools as models for an educational approach that puts children at the center and addresses cognitive, social, emotional, and physical needs and strengths. A recent report from the ASCD Commission on the Whole Child (Blank & Berg, 2006) provides examples of successful community schools. Community schools aim to develop students who are "academically proficient and physically and emotionally healthy and respectful, responsible, and caring; who can contribute to the community and the world" (Blank & Berg, 2006, p. 3). Community schools also offer "structured enrichment activities and acknowledge students' need for choice, control, competence, and belonging" (p. 7).

Community schools open their classrooms to community-based organizations and resources that support children through after-school homework help and enrichment programs as well as supportive programs for parents, such as ESL, GED preparation, parenting courses, and parent and community leadership workshops in the evening. Some community schools have dental clinics on site; others have nurseries so that teenage mothers can complete school. Some schools in high asthma areas have clinics in the school so students can get assistance and miss less school.

Community schools make an array of community resources accessible to support children and families in reaching their potential. When schools, parents, and community organizations pool their resources, they can provide "supportive environments that nurture students' social, emotional, physical, moral, civic and cognitive development" (Blank & Berg, 2006, p. 10).

The ASCD Commission identified several nonschool factors that influence academic achievement such as nutrition, parent participation in their child's school, time watching television, mobility, and mothers' educational level. Important, too, is research by McLaughlin and colleagues (1994) showing that adolescents who participate regularly in community-based youth development programs—including arts, sports, and community service—have better academic and social outcomes as well as higher educational and career aspirations than other teens. The idea is to "build on children's learning styles . . . and support the basic needs of children and their families, including health, nutrition, and economic and social well-being" (Blank & Berg, 2006, p. 6).

Classroom Examples

Chicago, Illinois, has one of the largest community school initiatives in the United States. Of Chicago's 613 schools, 102 now operate as community schools. They serve an average of 15,000 students and their families each year. A study by Blank and Berg (2006, p. 16) showed that "81 percent of community schools are showing improvement in academic achievement compared to 74 percent of regular public schools" (p. 17). In Indianapolis, Indiana, a community high school started in 2000 now has 49 community partners. These organizations offer mental and physical health consultation, day-care and after-school programs, college preparation, and adult education programs. Their students' standardized test scores have risen 10 to 15 points every year since the program began. The sophomores tested in 2003 outscored those in all the traditional high schools in Indianapolis.

Resources

Blank & Berg, 2006; McLaughlin, Irby, & Langman, 1994.

Strategy 2.14:
Incorporate multiple forms of assessment.

Discussion

In recent years, standardized testing has been used to drive school reform, with decidedly mixed results. The Coalition for Authentic Reform in Education (CARE) suggests that rather than relying on a single standardized test for high-stakes decisions such as promotion to the next grade, authentic assessment of student work (such as student exhibitions, portfolios, products, and performance tasks) is preferable (Valenzuela, Valenzuela, Sloan, & Foley, 2001, p. 321). Multiple indicators of academic performance and progress on schoolwork throughout the year should be a part of this approach.

Valenzuela and colleagues suggest an approach that would take into account: "1) input (the adequacy of resources), 2) process (the quality of instruction), and 3) output (what students have learned as measured by tests or other indicators)" (p. 321). The use of standardized testing alone tends to focus on output, neglecting the other two dimensions. Students who live in communities of poverty often do not have the access to resources or highly qualified teachers that students in wealthier districts do. Thus, they are far from experiencing equal educational opportunity.

Among many others, Hodgkinson (2003) has suggested that the focus of the current high-stakes standardized testing system is too narrow:

An additional problem involves the heavy preoccupation with reading and math readiness skills and abilities in the early years of schooling. While these skills are obviously important, factors that are less focused on academics, such as self-confidence, resilience, caring, emotional development, and supportive family members may be just as important. . . . Given the national preoccupation with "high-stakes testing" as the *only* measure of student, school, district, state, and perhaps national educational success, and the constant testing of those areas that are most easily measured, such as reading and math subskills, a preschool program that has also emphasized social/emotional development may be seen as "soft" or "afraid to face facts."

Although it seems overdone, elementary schools right down to kindergarten in a few cases are being assessed by student scores on the NAEP, Iowa Tests of Basic Skills, IQ, or the state achievement tests. (One of the hidden agendas here is that educational success will be defined by the student's ability to take standardized multiple-choice tests.) Half of the elementary schools in Fairfax County, Virginia, are evaluating their kindergartners using an 11-page report card, assessing language, reading, writing, math, science, social studies, health, movement, art, and music as well as social and emotional development. Rather than checkmarks for "sometimes," "usually," and "consistently," parents are encountering terms such as "pre early emergent," "early emergent," "emergent," and "novice." Some parents may have a hard time grasping these assessment results. They will need some help to understand the difference between seeing an "A" on their child's report card and looking at a child's stage of development, regardless of the advantage of getting a better feeling of what students are *really* learning. Unless parents are prepared for this change, the desirable shift to see learning as growth, using a *variety* of clinical and statistical measures, may not catch on. (p. 13)

The *Just for the Kids Study of Best Practices* (NCEA, 2006) also noted that "all of the high-performing schools we visited draw data from multiple assessments and use those data to inform every decision."

Classroom Examples

In addition to the outcome skills of reading and mathematics, most of us want our students to develop such habits of mind as questioning, observing closely, making connections, creating meaning, valuing their experience, identifying patterns, exhibiting empathy, and evaluating their own work. Students become more aware of these capacities when they are identified, discussed, and assessed.

Lincoln Center Institute has developed an assessment tool to assess habits of mind that are not measurable through standardized tests. Looking to the 30-year history of philosophy and practice at the institute, Madeleine Fuchs Holzer developed definitions for nine capacities for imaginative learning. For example, she defined "creating meaning" as creating interpretations on the basis of previous capacities (such as questioning, noticing deeply, identifying patterns, and making connections), seeing these

in light of others in the community, creating a synthesis, and expressing it in your own voice (Holzer, 2007).

Holzer shared the capacities with faculty from at least eight colleges and numerous elementary and high schools during the Lincoln Center Institute Summer Institute. She encouraged and received feedback about them and revised the capacities through several iterations. The institute published the definitions of the capacities (Holzer, 2007) and then asked a consultant, Drew Dunphy, to work with a group of teachers from the High School for Arts, Imagination and Inquiry in New York City to develop rubrics for the capacities.

There are several advantages to working as a team to develop rubrics. Teachers can spot gaps in colleagues' efforts and work to strengthen them. In addition, when teachers develop and own an assessment instrument, students' goals and outcomes become more consistent. By identifying the development of these capacities as their goal, teachers let students know that they value the expression of these innate qualities of thought and emotion.

Another assessment that engages students in the process is the use of portfolios. Teachers and students can develop portfolios containing samples of their classwork and teacher-made tests over the year. Asking students to review their portfolios bimonthly and select the best examples of their work for that time period coaches them in self-assessment and enables them to see their progress. The teacher can share these portfolios on parents' night to show how students are doing. In addition, if students don't perform well on a standardized test used in a high-stakes event, such as promotion to the next grade, their work samples could also be used to show that they are ready for the next grade.

Resources

Hodgkinson, 2003; Holzer, 2007; NCEA, 2006; Scheurich, Skria, & Johnson, 2000; Valenzuela, Valenzuela, Sloan, & Foley, 2001.

Strategies for Linguistically Diverse Students

The term "linguistically and culturally diverse students" encompasses a vast array of young people. As President John F. Kennedy famously suggested, America is a "nation of immigrants." Students who come to school speaking a native language other than English—from homes and communities in which English is not the language of communication—have often been perceived by the English-speaking majority as the most educationally vulnerable. Now that so many dual-language bilingual programs have been in place for the past 20 years, however, we can see that coming to a school that supports becoming bilingual and biliterate can actually be an advantage.

As the world becomes more economically interdependent, the advantages of bilingualism and cross-cultural understanding are better understood. According to the American Council on the Teaching of Foreign Languages, the number of high school students who are enrolled in foreign language programs in public high schools has grown steadily from 1978—when

3.2 million (23 percent of the public high school population) were enrolled in such classes—to the year 2000, when 5,899,400 (43.8 percent of that population) were enrolled in such classes.

Recent research has redefined the nature of how we understand the educational vulnerability of linguistically and culturally diverse students. Stereotypes and myths have begun to give way, laying a foundation on which to reconceptualize existing educational practices.

Current thinking emphasizes the *value* of speaking more than one language. Rather than being considered "disadvantaged" as speakers of a language other than English, such students are now being considered potentially bilingual and biliterate. The first language (L1) is now considered a base on which English language learners (ELLs) can build "additive" bilingualism (learning a second language [L2] while becoming literate in their first language and eventually literate in both).

Teachers wishing to see evidence of the effectiveness of various programs for ELLs should be aware of the work of Thomas and Collier (2002), who conducted the most comprehensive longitudinal research study to date on the long-term academic effectiveness of eight different K–12 programs for language-minority students, as well as English monolingual students who participate in two-way immersion (also called dual-language) programs.

Thomas and Collier researched English as a second language (ESL), transitional bilingual education, developmental bilingual education (DBE), one-way (one group learning bilingually) and two-way (two groups learning each other's language as a second language) bilingual programs, as well as the placement of ELLs in mainstream classes. Their 2002 report of their study (from 1985 to 2001) covers six sites in the United States. In researching more than 200,000 student records each year, they converted standardized test scores into normal curve equivalents and percentages. They found the following highlights.

- Enrichment 90-10 [90 percent instruction in L1 and 10 percent in L2] and 50-50 one-way and two-way developmental bilingual education (DBE) programs (or dual-language, bilingual immersion) are the only programs . . . found . . . that assist [English language learners] to fully reach the 50th percentile in both L1 and L2 in all subjects and to maintain that level of high achievement, or reach even higher levels through the end of schooling. The fewest dropouts come from these programs. (p. 7)
- Parents who refuse bilingual/ESL services for their children should be informed that their children's long-term academic achievement will probably be much lower as a result, and they should be strongly counseled against refusing bilingual/ESL services when their child is eligible. The research findings of this study indicate that ESL or bilingual services, as required by *Lau v. Nichols*, raise students' achievement levels by significant amounts. (p. 7)

Another significant finding: ELL students who attend remedial, segregated programs do not close the achievement gap after being placed in mainstream classes. Instructional gains are best accomplished in an enrichment, not a remedial, program, Thomas and Collier observed. They cautioned against short-term bilingual education (one to three years). They found that it takes a minimum of four years of bilingual schooling or four years of schooling in a student's L1 in the home country and four years in bilingual programs for students to reach grade-level performance in English (the 50th percentile on the subtest of reading in English).

Thus the most efficient schooling is in dual-language programs where both L1 and L2 are learned simultaneously and students have the opportunity to talk with students fluent in that L2. Thomas and Collier found that the strongest predictor of student achievement in English (L2) was formal L1 schooling in either the home country or the host country (United States). "The more L1 grade-level schooling, the higher L2 achievement," they noted (2002, p. 7).

An exciting finding (Thomas & Collier, 2002, p. 7) was that "bilingually schooled students outperform comparable monolingually schooled students in academic achievement in all subjects, after 4–7 years of dual language schooling." The authors also noted

An enrichment bilingual/ESL program must meet students' developmental needs: linguistic (L1–L2), academic, cognitive, emotional, social, physical. Schools need to create a natural learning environment in school, with lots of natural, rich language (L1, L2), both oral and written, used by students and teachers; meaningful, "real world" problem-solving; all students working together; media-rich learning (video, computers, print); challenging thematic units that get and hold students' interest; and using students' bilingual-bicultural knowledge to bridge to new knowledge across the curriculum. (p. 8)

Because one of the goals of bilingual programs in the 21st century is to prepare students to be proficient bilingually in the workplace, Thomas and Collier (2002, p. 5) also researched the achievement of native Spanish speakers in Spanish and native English speakers in a dual-language bilingual program.

Native-English speakers in two-way bilingual immersion programs maintained their English, added a second language to their knowledge base, and achieved well above the 50th percentile in all subject areas on norm-referenced tests in English. These bilingually schooled students equaled or outperformed their comparison groups being schooled monolingually, on all measures. (p. 5)

[For ELLs, the] number of years of primary language schooling, either in home country or in host country, had more influence than socioeconomic status when the number of years of schooling was 4 or more years. In addition, the L2 academic achievement of older immigrant arrivals with strong grade-level schooling completed in L1 in the home country was less influenced by low socioeconomic status and more dependent on number of years completed. Likewise, students of low socioeconomic status who were born in the U.S. or arrived at a very young age achieved at high levels in L2 when grade-level schooling was provided in both L1 and L2 in the U.S. (2002, p. 6)

Today, educators prefer that students develop linguistic facility in both English and their home language, rather than learn English only and lose the home language, only to have to relearn a second language later in their school years. Research shows that students' cognitive development proceeds more readily in their native language and that students learn content more easily in the native language while they are learning English as a second language.

An interdisciplinary approach to curriculum—breaking from many decades of separation among the various disciplines—is a powerful ally in teaching culturally and linguistically diverse children. Instead of teaching reading as a separate subject, for instance, teachers now view reading as a process for learning concepts and exploring subjects and their connections. Cooperative learning groups and peer tutoring work well in conjunction with computer-mediated language learning. And parents are partners in their children's schooling, as well as resources for teachers in understanding young people's cultural patterns of communication and interaction.

The following strategies synthesize the approaches that research emphasizes as most promising in raising the achievement levels of linguistically diverse students.

Resources

Barona & Garcia, 1990; Bredo, Henry, & McDermott, 1990; Cavazos, 1989; Center for Demographic Policy, 1993; Chan, 1983; Cummins, 1981; Cummins & Swain, 1986; DeAvila & Duncan, 1980; Dolly, Blaine, & Power, 1988; First & Willshire-Carrera, 1988; Hakuta, 1986; Hakuta & Garcia, 1989; Hakuta & Gould, 1987; Ima & Rumbaut, 1989; Matute-Bianchi, 1986; Ogbu, 1987; Pang, 1990; Thomas & Collier, 2002; Wong-Fillmore, 1983; Wong-Fillmore & Valadez, 1986.

Strategy 2.15:

Establish truly bilingual classrooms.

Discussion

Students who come to school with a home language other than English learn more from programs in which their native language is one of the languages of instruction. By continuing to learn subject content in their native language, the students do not fall behind in their academic subjects while acquiring English. Potentially bilingual students who are in developmental or late-exit bilingual programs for five years seem to progress at a faster rate in subjects presented in English than do their counterparts in early-exit bilingual programs.

When potentially bilingual students continue to learn in their home language while learning English, they continue to develop cognitively and acquire skills (such as reading) that can later be transferred to English. Once they have learned vocabulary in English, they can comprehend what they decode. The context of learning is more difficult if instruction is entirely in a student's second language. Students taught solely in the second language also risk losing the opportunity to become bilingual and biliterate.

A school that respects the language and culture of its ethnically and linguistically diverse students (and their parents or guardians) develops educational situations that maximize the resources these students bring to school. Instead of being confused and distressed by trying to cope in a language they cannot understand, students continue to learn content and skills and develop a feeling of efficacy as well as belonging to their new school. If the school context does not allow for this linguistic and cultural diversity, students are more likely to feel alienated and confused.

Classroom Examples

When the number of students in a school who speak the same language merits the establishment of a bilingual program, encouraging young people to learn content in their native language while learning English as a second language is likely to increase overall learning. Students can learn subjects such as mathematics, science, and social studies in their native language until they have learned sufficient English to study the academic content in English.

With the help of such programs as Logo-Writer, students can use computers to do programming and word processing in their native language. In one 6th grade classroom, for example, new immigrant students compared dwellings around the world. They saw photographs of different types of dwellings and learned that cultural responses to different ecological systems were one of the reasons for differences among earlier cultures. Igloos were adaptations to their environment just as the adobe "apartments" of Native Americans in the southwestern United States were adaptations to theirs. The builders of both types of dwellings used available resources. Using Spanish, students learned to program geometrical shapes to represent igloos and Anasazi dwellings. They also wrote about the structures in Spanish.

Resources

California State Department of Education, 1986; Carter & Chatfield, 1986; Chamot & O'Malley, 1994; Cummins, 1981, 1986; Cziko, 1992; Hakuta & Garcia, 1989; Hakuta & Gould, 1987; Ramirez, Yuen, Ramey, & Pasta, 1991; Saravia-Shore & Arvizu, 1992; Wong-Fillmore & Valadez, 1986.

Strategy 2.16:

Embrace dual-language strategies.

Discussion

Students proficient in languages other than English learn more effectively in dual-language learning situations. They continue to learn content in their native language while learning English as a second language by interacting with monolingual English-speaking students who are also learning a second language.

This approach is valuable for several reasons. First, young people's native language is affirmed and respected when it becomes a subject being taught to their English-speaking peers. Second, potentially bilingual students can share their native-language expertise as peer tutors to English-speaking students who are learning a second language for enrichment; in the process, they gain experience working in English as well. Third, the long-term gains are greater because, in this additive bilingual strategy, students proficient in languages other than English become bilingual and biliterate. Fourth, students are not segregated into classes for potentially bilingual students or monolingual English-speaking students; all are integrated and become bilingual over a period of five or six years.

In some schools, students spend half the day in an immersion situation, learning content in English, and the other half immersed in learning content in their native language. In other schools, students initially learn specific subjects such as math, art, music, or physical education in English, their second language. Sometimes, monolingual English-speaking students are immersed in a second language, such as Spanish, with native Spanish speakers.

Based on many years of working with scores of two-way immersion programs, Howard and Christian (2002) have specific suggestions for implementing two-way immersion bilingual programs. They follow Thomas and Collier (2002) and others in suggesting a minimum of four to six years of bilingual instruction. They advocate two possible approaches:

- 50 percent of instruction in L1 and 50 percent in L2 from kindergarten through middle school, or
- 90 percent in the native language with 10 percent in L2 for grades K–1, 80 percent in the native language and 20 percent in L2 for grades 2–3, and 50/50 by 4th grade and beyond.

They stress that academic instruction needs to be of high quality and that there be "optimal language input that is comprehensible, interesting, and of sufficient quantity, and opportunity for output . . . including explicit language arts instruction" in both L1 and L2, so that students become bilingual and biliterate (Howard & Christian, 2002, p. 6).

To accomplish these practices, teachers' use of the Sheltered Instruction Observation Protocol (SIOP) is recommended. Howard and Christian (2002) also suggest other teaching practices including constructivist, child-centered, active discovery learning. Along with August and Hakuta (1998), they recommend a teaching method known as "instructional conversation," which "provides students with opportunities for extended dialogue in areas that have educational value as well as relevance for them" (Howard & Christian, 2002, p. 7). Cooperative learning offers students opportunities for conversations in both languages if the groups are structured to include equal numbers of native speakers of both L1 and L2. Cooperative learning is also an opportunity to develop cross-cultural understanding.

Classroom Examples

Teachers can enhance the learning of a second language by structuring informal situations in which students who are proficient in languages other than English act as peer tutors for monolingual English-speaking students learning a second language and vice versa. Second-language learning for both groups is enhanced when they can communicate informally at certain times during the school day in their second language. This alternative social organization of learning a second language does not rely solely on the teacher as the locus of teaching. Students become teachers and resources for one another; second-language learning is reciprocal.

Students learning Spanish as a second language, for example, can be encouraged to use the language in functional situations. Younger students can learn aspects of Latino cultures by using recipes in Spanish to cook Mexican, Dominican, and Puerto Rican dishes. Or they can learn about the music of each culture by learning to sing songs in Spanish. Older students can learn about the rain forests in Central and South America; they might, as one example, graph the number of medicines derived from plants in this ecosystem.

Resources

August & Hakuta, 1998; Deem & Marshall, 1980; Garcia, 1987/1988, 1988, 1991, 1992; Gee, 1982; Herbert, 1987; Howard & Christian, 2002; Krashen & Biber, 1988; Lindholm, 1988; Saravia-Shore & Arvizu, 1992; Short, Crandall, & Christian, 1989.

Strategy 2.17:

Use integrated, holistic approaches to language experiences for second-language learners instead of rote drill and practice.

Discussion

Rote drill and practice are boring and lack meaning for young people; holistic experiences are much more engaging. For example, students can use language-experience approaches to learn science in English. In doing so, they connect doing and observing an experiment to speaking, writing, and reading. Because their oral language is written down for later reading, they can understand what they read, and their reading has meaning.

Research on the learning of second languages shows the value of an increased emphasis on "communicative competence" (Garcia, 1987/1988, 1988; Valdez-Pierce, 1991). To be competent in communicating, students need to go beyond simply mastering the rules of grammar. They also must learn how to apply social and cultural rules. Students learning a second language must learn, for example, that the informal language used with peers and friends may not be appropriate in more formal situations, such as making a request of a teacher or answering questions during a job interview. Students must learn how to take turns in a conversation, when to talk and keep still, how to "demonstrate" listening, and when to be direct or indirect. These culturally appropriate ways of speaking can be learned when students hear stories, see dramas, read books with dialogue, and write and act out plays.

"Teaching through conversation" is among the Five Standards for Effective Pedagogy proposed by Tharp, Estrada, Dalton, and Yamauchi (2000) to improve learning outcomes for all students—but especially those of diverse ethnic, cultural, linguistic, or economic backgrounds. Other researchers also support the approach of engaging students through instructional conversation (Howard & Christian, 2002). As previously discussed, instructional conversation is an extended dialogue that is educational and relevant to students' lives. Tharp and colleagues advocate a holistic approach that employs all five standards, including: teachers and students producing together, developing language and literacy across the curriculum, connecting school to students' lives, teaching complex thinking, and teaching through instructional conversation.

Classroom Examples

The teacher begins reading a children's story by first showing the illustrations and asking the students to describe them. After reading the story, the teacher asks a student to retell it. Subsequently, the teacher may ask the students to write the story as a play with a different ending or to write a continuation of the story. This technique helps young people see the connection between writing and reading.

The teacher asks students to break into groups of five. Each group is responsible for writing and illustrating a story. Group members must first negotiate who will do which tasks in English, then which events to illustrate. They must agree on the sequence of events and number them sequentially. One way of structuring this activity is to provide pages labeled "main characters," "problem to be solved," "first event," "second event," "third event," and "resolution of problem."

High school students can be assigned to watch one scene of a play that takes place in the culture they are learning about. They then form groups and write the scene as they recall it. After the groups respond to one another's efforts and refine the dialogue (perhaps by referring to the video of the play), they act out the scene. A subsequent assignment might call on them to change the role and status of one of the characters and decide how that character would speak: What might he or she say differently? How would the other characters respond? The students can then act out the scene, using the same basic content but saying things in a different way to someone with a different social role.

Students can also imagine real-life situations in which they might find themselves and act out the parts of different speakers, alternating in social roles. They can get feedback from peers who are members of the linguistic group they are studying.

Resources

Garcia, 1987/1988; Heath, 1986; Krashen, 1982; Ovando, 1993; Tharp, Estrada, Dalton, & Yamauchi, 2000; Tharp et al., 2004.

Strategy 2.18:

Teach language through subject matter rather than specific linguistic skill exercises.

Discussion

The learning of language cannot be separated from what is being learned. Too often, students with limited proficiency in English are required to learn the abstract or grammatical aspects of language as opposed to the functional and communicative aspects. These more important functional skills are best developed in conjunction with the learning of content.

When students learn a second language in a functional way (similar to the way they learned their first language), the process has real meaning. Learning makes sense and is more interesting. Students also benefit by learning cross-cultural skills. Learning greetings in a second language, for example, as well as the "polite" behavior associated with that language enables young people to communicate more easily in a new culture. Learning how to request food at a dinner table requires basic grammar and polite behavior. Students can go on to discuss how polite behavior differs in different cultures and what "polite" means in the classroom among friends, in a restaurant, and in the school cafeteria.

Classroom Examples

Instead of removing students from a content lesson in mathematics because they are not yet proficient in English, the teacher can pair bilingual and monolingual students in small groups and provide math-related tasks within those groups. Bilingual students will assist the monolingual students in completing these tasks while providing natural models of language development within the content domain.

Pairs of students may perform a simple experiment in their classroom: They are to find out "what will happen if. . . ?" Labels on the objects they use guide their inquiry. Students write the steps of their experiment in the form of an experience chart and tell what happened when they followed the steps. If they are stuck, they can ask another pair of students for help. The sequence of steps is then written and may be illustrated with pictures. Another day, they can use the experience chart to practice reading aloud in English.

For older students who have learned the processes of mathematics (addition, subtraction, multiplication, division) in their native language, and particularly for those who already know the Arabic number system, a review of the math process in English is an effective way of learning functional English. When young people understand a process in numerical form, they can learn the vocabulary and the rules for asking questions and stating solutions.

Resources

Carter & Chatfield, 1986; Cuevas, 1984; Garcia, 1987/1988; Lucas, Henze, & Donato, 1990; Wong-Fillmore & Valadez, 1986.

Strategy 2.19:
Adopt sheltered English strategies.

Discussion

Often, schools cannot form bilingual classrooms because their students are so linguistically diverse that the number of children speaking any one language is insufficient for a separate class. In these settings, pullout programs should be avoided; they stigmatize children. Yet sheltered English and content-embedded ESL programs benefit students who are proficient in languages other than English. Such programs ensure that students have ample time to use English themselves rather than sitting as a passive audience for the teacher.

The Sheltered Instruction Observation Protocol was developed to assist teachers in using sheltered English strategies. SIOP was constructed by Short and Echevarria (1999) based on the research concerning best practices, as well as on the experiences of middle school teachers and researchers who collaborated in developing the observation tool. The participating teachers used sheltered instruction in traditional ESL classes, content-based ESL classes, and sheltered content classes. SIOP provides concrete examples of sheltered instruction that teachers can use to support ELL students' understanding of instructional content. Several teachers might use SIOP as the basis for supporting each other as a learning community while they try out new strategies and discuss their practice, sharing questions and solutions.

Classroom Examples

The sheltered English strategy makes learning of content more comprehensible to English language learners. The strategy includes

- Speaking at a rate and level of complexity appropriate to the proficiency level of students.
- Using visual aids and graphic organizers as well as math manipulatives.
- Building on prior knowledge.
- Providing frequent opportunities for interaction among L1 and L2 speakers.
- Modeling academic tasks.
- Reviewing key content and vocabulary.

In sheltered English classrooms, teachers provide many examples and hands-on activities so students can comprehend abstract as well as concrete instructional materials. This approach need not be complex. For example, the teacher may demonstrate an activity and describe in simple terms what she is doing. As she draws a face, she tells the children, "I am drawing eyes," and "I am drawing a mouth," and "These are teeth." The visual references make comprehension quicker and easier, and the modeling of language enables children to learn new grammatical structures. Even the use of drawing as a teaching device may model for students the effectiveness of nonverbal means of mastering their new language and new culture; this activity may lead to the use of drawing as a tool for peer tutoring.

Resources

Cummins, 1984; Edward, Wesche, Krashen, Clement, & Krudenier, 1984; Garcia, 1987/1988, 1988, 1991, 1992; Krashen, 1982, 1985; Short & Echevarria, 1999.

Strategy 2.20:
Practice English in flexible, heterogeneous cooperative learning groups.

Discussion

Students proficient in languages other than English learn more by being actively engaged in cooperative learning than by listening passively. Students whose native language is other than English benefit from working in cooperative learning groups with native English speakers because they can hear a native model of English and practice their English in authentic communicative situations.

Teachers who structure cooperative learning situations for ELLs enable their students to become more actively engaged in learning. Potentially bilingual students need to practice generating and rehearsing their second language. Small groups in which each child has a specific role and specific tasks enable youngsters to learn more than if they are merely passive listeners. For this reason, cooperative learning groups are more productive than whole-class instruction because small groups (three or four students) challenge children to use language more frequently. However, the students must be grouped around meaningful tasks so that they use language for work-related communication. Cooperative strategies have been demonstrated to work well with Chicano (Garcia, 1991), Laotian, Cambodian, Hmong (Ima, Galang, Lee, & Dinh Te, 1991), and Japanese students.

Classroom Examples

In a junior high science class, students identify some of the problems in their neighborhood. They then collaboratively develop a questionnaire to use to interview people in the community to find out what they identify as neighborhood problems. If their community has many residents who speak a language other than English, they may need a second version of the questionnaire in that language. After forming teams to interview community members about the neighborhood problems, students return to school, record the responses, and graph them by frequency. They can then discuss whether there is a problem that they can work together to solve, what resources they need to solve it, and the pros and cons of various suggestions for achieving a solution.

In another example, younger students may be assigned to research one of two Native American groups: the Algonquin or the Iroquois. Their goal is to discover the adaptive strategies each group used to take advantage of the environment for their dwellings, clothing, food, and transportation. The students are assigned to different roles, such as researcher, recorder, reporter, illustrator, or graph maker (to graph the results of the research).

The teacher gives each group a coloring book containing line drawings of people from the Algonquin and Iroquois nations pursuing activities of daily life. The students can interpret the drawings to identify means of transportation, materials from which dwellings were made, and so forth. They display their findings on a chart,

and they also write a brief narrative describing the drawing.

Resources

Cummins, 1986; DeAvila & Duncan, 1979; Garcia, 1991, 1992; Howard & Christian, 2002; Ima, Galang, Lee, & Dinh Te, 1991; Saravia-Shore, 1993; Slavin, 1980, 1987, 1991; Tharp et al., 2004; Tharp & Gallimore, 1991.

Strategy 2.21:
Use cross-age and peer tutoring.

Discussion

Teachers have a foundation on which to build cross-age peer tutoring when their students' cultures emphasize the care of younger children by older siblings (Puerto Rican, Hawaiian, and Chicano cultures, for example). Research shows that cross-age tutoring enhances learning for those who are tutored and for the tutors themselves. Heterogeneous cross-ability grouping promotes student tutoring through the sharing of different skills in different contexts. For example, a student who is still learning English may be strong in math and can assist an English-speaking classmate with a mathematics project.

Teachers can provide learning opportunities for students who are proficient in languages other than English by organizing their classroom to include cross-age tutoring and peer tutoring. Students who are proficient in another language, such as Spanish, can provide language models and practice for monolingual English speakers learning Spanish. In some learning situations, Spanish can be used to converse about a shared activity. In another situation in which English is the primary language, the tutoring roles can be reversed.

Classroom Examples

Students are studying number systems. Using the chalkboard, a student who speaks only English demonstrates the use of zero in the Arabic number system to a native Spanish speaker by showing math problems and then working with the other student to solve them. After learning the Mayan number system, the native Spanish speaker then demonstrates, in Spanish, the Mayan number system and its use of place and zero to the English-speaking student, explaining that the Mayans were the first world culture to use a symbol for zero.

Resources

Moll, Diaz, Estrada, & Lopes, 1992.

Strategy 2.22:
Respect community language norms.

Discussion

Establishing communication is the most important consideration in teaching. In many bilingual populations, language alternation (or code switching) is frequently used for more effective communication. In conversations, either teacher or student may change the language in midstream to catch the listener's attention, to emphasize something, to clarify, to elaborate, or to address those in a group who may understand the second language more readily. Therefore,

students and teachers should be able to readily use these naturally occurring alternations to achieve communication in the classroom.

In discussing the whole language approach, in which language is taught naturally as it occurs within any social environment, Goodman (1986) has noted, "Whole language programs respect the learners—who they are, where they come from, how they talk, what they read, and what experiences they [have] already had." Both Edelsky (1986) and Huerta-Macias and Quintero (1992) include code switching as part of this whole language approach.

Classroom Examples

In a reading exercise conducted in English, a student hesitates in answering a comprehension question posed by the teacher. The teacher rephrases the question in the child's native language, and the child proudly responds to the question in her native language. In this scenario, the teacher focuses on the goal of story comprehension and alternates language use to achieve this goal.

In a family literacy program, five families come together for 90 minutes once a week after school. Their teacher conducts the classes in both Spanish and English, alternating according to the linguistic abilities and preferences of parents and children. This strategy enables parents and children to feel comfortable in expressing themselves in either language. Their activities include conversing, reading, writing, and creating art projects. The parents tend to use Spanish to express themselves; the teacher alternates between speaking Spanish with the parents and

English with the children. The children also use both languages freely as they speak to their parents, their brothers and sisters, and the teacher.

In developing literacy, the specific language used is not as important as encouraging communication between parents and their children. The intent here is to use the language skills of the parents as a resource so that they can continue assisting their children with reading and writing skills at home. This communication—and the development of an enjoyment of reading and writing together—are the primary goals. Other outcomes include developing respect for the parents' native language, helping the student to develop biliteracy, and developing the native language as a resource while acquiring literacy in English.

Resources

Bowman, 1989; Carter & Chatfield, 1986; Duran, 1981; Edelsky, 1986; Garcia, 1988, 1991, 1992; Garcia, Maez, & Gonzalez, 1983; Genishi, 1981; Goodman, 1986; Huerta, 1980; Huerta-Macias & Quintero, 1992; Poplack, 1981; Valdez-Fallis, 1977; Zentella, 1992.

Strategy 2.23:

Organize teaching around thematic, interdisciplinary units.

Discussion

Linguistically diverse students have been shown to benefit from interdisciplinary approaches. Students proficient in languages other than English can learn content with greater comprehension if their learning is interdisciplinary.

For students learning English as a second language, thematic approaches enhance learning and comprehension because the new learning is incremental and added to a theme that the students already understand. Having a base vocabulary related to the theme provides students a context in which to fit new learning from the various disciplines. Vocabulary is reinforced by its use in different subject contexts.

Focusing on a theme and relating various disciplines to that theme enables students to better understand each new area, since it is connected to a known core. When there is a theme, the vocabulary and skills can be developed in connection with the content. This approach provides coherence to students who are proficient in languages other than English. Instead of trying to learn about several separate and distinct areas with diverse vocabularies simultaneously, they can work within a broad, unifying theme.

Classroom Examples

The bilingual science program Descubrimiento (DeAvila & Duncan, 1980) is an example of an interdisciplinary program that integrates science content and processes, foreign language learning, and English as a second language. Because students set up, conduct, analyze, report, and write up the experiments as group members, they learn a second language, either English or Spanish, while they are acquiring science skills and content. They also learn to work cooperatively. All the skills of communication in each language are used on different days to learn, question, record, and share what has been learned from the science experiment.

Resources

Carter & Chatfield, 1986; Garcia, 1992; Gardner, 1983; Krashen, 1982, 1985; Lucas, Henze, & Donato, 1990; Pease-Alvarez, Garcia, & Espinosa, 1991.

Strategy 2.24:
Enhance language learning with computers and peer tutors.

Discussion

Teachers can create situations in which two potentially bilingual students use a common computer to more readily learn English as a second language. While sharing a word processing program, two second-language learners have the opportunity to generate language, create dialogues, interview each other, assist each other with corrections, and act as an audience for the other's writing. However, one computer shared by a whole class of students does not allow for as much language practice as does pairing students who have access to a computer laboratory.

The kinds of software used for language learning also make a difference. Some language-learning programs simply translate drill and practice into computer formats. Other programs—desktop publishing software, for example—motivate students to write in their second language, since they know that their writing will be edited collaboratively and then published, to be read by classmates and parents or guardians.

The Internet can also be used to correspond with "sister schools" in the same city, another state, or even another country. Individual correspondence or bilingual newsletters written by students can develop their writing and literacy skills in both their native and second languages.

Classroom Examples

By using computers, teachers can challenge students to provide more of their own interpretation and to generate their own text, rather than simply perform rote drill-and-practice activities. For example, a teacher can show a photograph of two people interacting to a pair of students at the computer. Their task is to imagine the identity of each person and to develop a dialogue in which each of them assumes the voice of one of the people in the photograph. Each responds to the other and gives feedback if he or she is "out of character" or needs assistance.

The teacher also can structure situations in which students use computers to strengthen writing skills in their second language by providing assignments that have an immediate communicative purpose. For example, teachers assign two students to a computer and ask each to provide peer tutoring to the other. Students can interview each other via the computer— one asking questions via the computer and the other writing the answers.

Writing a play or a news story together can be enjoyable and rewarding. When writing a news story, one student can act as the correspondent and interview the "newsmaker" or "informant." Students can also interview one another about their various countries of origin and write a book for the whole class by combining their individual accounts.

At the high school level, as an ongoing classroom project, bilingual students can learn to use desktop publishing software to collaboratively produce a bilingual monthly newsletter that they can exchange with a bilingual class in a sister school in another district. The newsletter may include poems; jokes; community surveys; methods of dealing with problems at school; or interviews with conflict mediators, faculty members, or parents, all telling about their jobs. By exchanging newsletters with a sister school (and possibly including a column that allows students from the other school to tell how they deal with concerns and problems), students are using language to learn about real-life concerns.

Cummins, Brown, and Sayers (2007) suggest further bilingual strategies with students using both L1 and L2 and computer programs to create movies, audio CDs, and Web pages. Students can share the outcomes of their projects aimed at generating new knowledge, creating literature, doing action research, and addressing the social realities of their community in both languages. When they exchange their work with other classes, students can use computers and other technology to create and share literature and art and explore issues of social relevance to them and their communities (projects like "Voices of Our Elders" or "The Social History of Our Community").

Cummins also suggests that bilingual students from kindergarten on can bring in words in either L1 or L2 and explore their meanings in each language with peers and teacher,

incorporating their words into a technology-supported bilingual dictionary developed by the entire class.

For older students in bilingual or L2 immersion classes, Cummins suggests developing critical literacy by comparing the way that the same news events and issues are reported in L1 and L2 on the Web.

Resources

Andelin, Naismith, Roberts, Feuer, Fulton, St. Lawrence, & Zuckerkandel, 1987; Cummins, 2005; Cummins, Brown, & Sayers, 2007; Mehan, 1989; Mehan, Moll, & Riel, 1985; Moll, Diaz, Estrada, & Lopes, 1992; Philips, 1972; Roberts et al., 1987; Sayers, 1989; Sayers & Brown, 1987.

Strategy 2.25:
Help students build "social capital."

Discussion

While students with college-educated parents usually have a network of social relationships to facilitate academic success (a form of social capital), students whose parents did not attend college often lack these kinds of networks.

Gibson and Bejinez's (2002) ethnography documented how adult caring and building social capital influenced the persistence of Mexican migrant students in school. They studied the federally funded Migrant Education Program (MEP) at Hillside, California, an integrated high school with approximately equal proportions of white (45 percent) and Mexican (42 percent) students. Gibson and Bejinez examined how the MEP staff "facilitated student engagement by creating caring relationships with students, providing them with access to institutional support, and implementing activities that build from and serve to validate students' home cultures" (Gibson & Bejinez, 2002, p. 155). MEP teachers who came from migrant backgrounds and were college educated provided role models for the migrant students and explicitly assisted them with tutoring and the college application process. They established an office where students could socialize as well as find information and support.

Gibson and Bejinez also drew on the literature on caring as "a precondition for students to feel trust and belonging within the school environment in order to establish beneficial school-based relationships" (p. 157). They "found caring relationships between migrant teachers and students to be at the very heart of the [MEP] program's success in engaging students academically and keeping them in school" (p. 159).

Finally, Gibson and Bejinez built on the research on the school structures and personnel facilitating "the minority students' ability to withstand the assimilationist pressures of school." Minority students who felt there was a safe place for them to speak Spanish as well as English and to build upon their culture—bringing their multiple identities to school rather than concealing them—had a sense of belonging instead of marginalization and alienation. This sense of belonging in school has been correlated with engagement with schoolwork and perseverance in the face of obstacles (Gandara, 1995; Gibson & Bhachu, 1991).

Classroom Examples

In the Gibson and Bejinez (2002) study, one MEP teacher noted, "We have good communication, and we keep on pushing them. That's why our office is always packed. They know we have high expectations, and I think that they're really trying to meet them" (p. 168).

The dual-language programs discussed here enable all students to build on their native language while learning a second. Students also know that in a reciprocal relationship they are both teaching and learning. As did Weis and Fine (2001), Gibson and Bejinez found that anti-Mexican, anti-immigrant, anti-Spanish stereotypes were contested both in the MEP office and by the school's Mexican Students Association, where students could take leadership in organizing, fund-raising, and celebrating their native culture. They did so by holding a graduation banquet dinner at which they honored their parents. Gibson has called this "additive acculturation," that is, acculturation without assimilation.

Teachers can encourage students to share aspects of their native cultures through assignments in social studies in which a particular country's history and culture is researched by a small group of students and then presented to the entire class to support student pride in their culture and learning about others. Other activities include building a classroom library of autobiographies and children's books in various languages, assigning Web sites where students can research their culture, or hosting international days that celebrate students' cultures.

Resources

Bourdieu & Passeron, 1977; Gandara, 1995; Gibson, 2000; Gibson & Bejinez, 2002; Gibson & Bhachu, 1991; Weis & Fine, 2001.

Bibliography

Andelin, J., Naismith, N. C., Roberts, L. G., Feuer, M., Fulton, K., St. Lawrence, J., & Zuckerkandel, M. (1987). *Trends and status of computers in schools: Use in Chapter 1 programs and use with limited English proficient students.* Washington, DC: U.S. Congress Office of Technology Assessment.

Arvizu, S. F. (1992). Home-school linkages: A cross-cultural approach to parent participation. In M. Saravia-Shore and S. F. Arvizu (Eds.), *Cross-cultural literacy: Ethnographies of communication in multiethnic classrooms* (pp. 37–56). New York: Garland.

Au, K. H. (1980, Summer). Participation structures in a reading lesson with Hawaiian children: Analysis of a culturally appropriate instructional event. *Anthropology and Education Quarterly, 11*(2), 91–115.

Au, K. H., & Jordan, C. (1981). Teaching reading to Hawaiian children: Finding a culturally appropriate solution. In H. Trueba, G. P. Guthrie, & K. H. Au (Eds.), *Culture and the bilingual classroom* (pp. 139–152). Rowley, MA: Newbury House.

Au, K. H., & Mason, J. M. (1981). Social organizational factors in learning to read: The balance of rights hypothesis. *Reading Research Quarterly, 17*(1), 115–152.

August, D., & Hakuta, K. (Eds.). (1998). *Educating language-minority children.* Washington, DC: National Academy Press.

Banks, J. A. (1993). Approaches to multicultural curriculum reform. In J. A. Banks & C. A. M. Banks (Eds.), *Multicultural education: Issues and perspectives* (pp. 192–219). Boston: Allyn and Bacon.

Barona, A., & Garcia, E. (1990). *Children at risk: Poverty, minority status, and other issues in educational equity.* Washington, DC: National Association of School Psychologists.

Blank, M., & Berg, A. (2006). *All together now: Sharing responsibility for the whole child.* Alexandria, VA: Association for Supervision and Curriculum Development.

Bloome, D. (1985). Reading as a social process. *Language Arts, 62*(2), 134–142.

Boggs, S. T. (1985). *Speaking, relating, and learning: A study of Hawaiian children at home and at school.* Norwood, NJ: Ablex.

Bourdieu, P., & Passeron, J. C. (1977). *Reproduction in education, society, and culture.* London: Sage.

Boutte, G. S., LaPoint, S., & Davis, B. (1993, November). Racial issues in education: Real or imagined? *Young Children, 49*(1), 19–23.

Bowman, B. T. (1989, October). Educating language-minority children: Challenges and opportunities. *Phi Delta Kappan, 71*(2), 118–120.

Bredo, E., Henry, M., & McDermott, R. P. (1990). The cultural organization of teaching and learning. *Harvard Education Review, 60*(2), 247–258.

Burris, C. C., & Welner, K. G. (2005, November). Closing the achievement gap by detracking. *Phi Delta Kappan, 86*(8), 594–598.

Calfee, R., Cazden, C., Duran, R., Griffin, M., Martus, M., & Willis, H. (1981). *Designing reading instruction for cultural minorities: The case of Kamehameha Early Education Program.* Cambridge, MA: Harvard University, Graduate School of Education. (ERIC Document Reproduction Service No. ED 215039).

California State Department of Education. (1981). *School and language minority students: A theoretical framework.* Los Angeles: Evaluation, Dissemination, and Assessment Center, California State University.

California State Department of Education. (1986). *Beyond language: Social and cultural factors in schooling language minority students.* Los Angeles: Evaluation, Dissemination, and Assessment Center, California State University.

Carbo, M. (1978, December). Teaching reading with talking books. *The Reading Teacher, 32*(3), 267–273.

Carbo, M. (1989). *How to record books for maximum reading gains*. Roslyn Heights, NY: National Reading Styles Institute.

Carbo, M., Dunn, R., & Dunn, K. (1986). *Teaching students to read through their individual learning styles*. Englewood, NJ: Prentice-Hall.

Carter, T. P., & Chatfield, M. L. (1986). Effective bilingual schools: Implications for policy and practice. *American Journal of Education, 95*(1), 200–234.

Catsambis, S. (2001). Expanding knowledge of parental involvement in children's secondary education: Connections with high school seniors' academic success. *Social Psychology of Education, 5,* 149–177.

Catsambis, S., & Beveridge, A. A. (2001). Does neighborhood matter? Family, neighborhood, and school influences on eighth grade mathematics achievement. *Sociological Focus, 34*(4), 435–457.

Catterall, J., & Waldorf, L. (1999). The Chicago arts partnerships in education evaluation. In E. B. Fiske (Ed.), *Champions of change: The impact of the arts on learning* (pp. 47–62). Washington, DC: Chief Council of State School Officers.

Cavazos, L. (1989). Building bridges for at-risk children. *Education Digest, 55*(3), 16–19.

Cazden, C. B. (1988). *Classroom discourse: The language of teaching and learning*. Portsmouth, NH: Heinemann.

Center for Demographic Policy. (1993, Summer). *CDP Newsletter 1,* 4.

Chall, J. S., Jacobs, V. A., & Baldwin, L. E. (1990). *The reading crisis: Why poor children fall behind*. Cambridge, MA: Harvard University Press.

Chamot, A. U., & O'Malley, J. M. (1994). Instructional approaches and teaching procedures. In K. Spangenberg-Urbschat & R. Pritchard (Eds.), *Kids come in all languages: Reading instruction for ESL students* (pp. 82–107). Newark, DE: International Reading Association.

Chan, K. S. (1983). Limited English speaking, handicapped, and poor: Triple threat in childhood. In Mae Chu-Chang with V. Rodriguez (Eds.), *Asian- and Pacific-American perspectives in bilingual education: Comparative research* (pp. 153–171). New York: Teachers College Press.

Coballes-Vega, C. (1992, January). *Consideration in teaching culturally diverse children*. Washington, DC: ERIC Clearinghouse on Teacher Education. (ERIC Document Reproduction Service No. EDO-SP 90/2)

Commission on Chapter 1. (1992). *Making schools work for children in poverty*. Washington, DC: American Association for Higher Education. (ERIC Document Reproduction Service No. ED362618).

Cuevas, G. J. (1984). Mathematics learning in English as a second language. *Journal for Research in Mathematics Education, 13*(7), 134–144.

Cummins, J. (1981). The role of primary language development in promoting educational success for language minority students. In California State Department of Education (Ed.), *Schooling and language minority students: A theoretical framework* (pp. 3–49). Los Angeles: National Dissemination and Assessment Center.

Cummins, J. (1984). *Bilingualism and special education: Issues in assessment and pedagogy*. Clevedon, England: Multilingual Matters.

Cummins, J. (1986). Empowering minority students: A framework for intervention. *Harvard Education Review, 56*(1), 18–36.

Cummins, J. (2005). *Challenging monolingual instructional assumptions in second language immersion and bilingual programs*. Presentation at AERA Annual Meeting, Montreal.

Cummins, J., Brown, K., & Sayers, D. (2007). *Literacy, technology, and diversity: Teaching for success in changing times*. Boston: Pearson/Allyn and Bacon.

Cummins, J., & Swain, M. (1986). *Bilingualism in education: Aspects of theory, research, and practice*. London: Longman.

Cziko, G. A. (1992, March). The evaluation of bilingual education. *Educational Researcher, 21*(2), 10–15.

Deasy, R. (Ed.). (2002). *Critical links: Learning in the arts and student academic and social development*. Washington, DC: Arts Education Partnership.

DeAvila, E. A., & Duncan, S. E. (1979). Bilingualism and cognition: Some recent findings. *NABE Journal, 4*(1), 15–50.

DeAvila, E. A., & Duncan, S. E. (1980). Definition and measurement of bilingual students. In *Bilingual program, policy and assessment issues* (pp. 47–62). Sacramento: California State Department of Education.

Deem, J. M., & Marshall, W. J. (1980). Teaching a second language to Indochinese refugees when no program exists. *Journal of Reading, 23*(7), 601–605.

Delpit, L. D. (1988). The silenced dialogue: Power and pedagogy in educating other people's children. *Harvard Education Review, 58*(3), 280–298.

Demetrulias, D. M. (1991, Spring). Teacher expectations and ethnic surnames. *Teacher Education Quarterly, 18*(2), 37–43.

DeMoss, K., & Morris, T. (2002). *How arts integration supports student learning: Students shed light on the connections.* Available: www.capeweb.org/rcape.html

Diplomas Count: An essential guide to graduation policy and rates. (2006, June 22). *Education Week, 25*(41S).

Dolly, J. M., Blaine, D. D., & Power, K. M. (1988). *Performance of educationally at-risk Pacific and Asian students in a traditional academic program.* Paper presented at the AERA annual meeting, New Orleans.

Dornbusch, S. M., Ritter, P. L., Leiderman, P. H., Roberts, D. F., & Fraleigh, M. J. (1987). The relation of parenting style to adolescent school performance. *Child Development, 58*(5), 1233–1257.

Dunn, R. (1989, Summer). Do students from different cultures have different learning styles? *International Education, 16*(50), 40–42. (Available from the Association for the Advancement of International Education, New Wilmington, PA).

Dunn, R., Beaudy, J. A., & Klavas, A. (1989). Survey of research on learning styles. *Educational Leadership, 46*(6), 50–58.

Dunn, R., & Griggs, S. (1990). Research on the learning styles characteristics of selected racial and ethnic groups. *Reading, Writing, and Learning Disabilities, 6*(3), 261–280.

Duran, R. (Ed.). (1981). *Latino language and communicative behavior.* Norwood, NJ: Ablex.

Edelsky, C. (1986). *Writing in a bilingual program.* Norwood, NJ: Ablex.

Edward, H., Wesche, M., Krashen, S., Clement, R., & Krudenier, B. (1984). Second language acquisition through subject-matter learning: A study of sheltered psychology classes at the University of Ottawa. *Canadian Modern Language Review, 41*(2), 268–282.

Epstein, J. L. (2005, September). Developing and sustaining research-based programs of school, family and community partnerships: Summary of five years of NNPS research. Available: www.partnership-schools.org

Epstein, J. L., & Sheldon, S. B. (2006). Moving forward: Ideas for research on school, family, and community partnerships. In C. F. Conrad & R. Serlin (Eds.), *SAGE handbook for research in education: Engaging ideas and enriching inquiry* (pp. 117–138). Thousand Oaks, CA: Sage.

Epstein, J. L., & Van Voorhis, F. L. (2001). More than minutes: Teachers' roles in designing homework. *Educational Psychologist, 36*(3), 181–194.

First, J. M. (1988, November). Immigrant students in U.S. public schools: Challenges and solutions. *Phi Delta Kappan, 70*(3), 205–210.

First, J. M., & Willshire-Carrera, J. W. (1988). *New voices: Immigrant students in U.S. public schools.* Boston: National Coalition of Advocates for Students.

Fiske, E. B. (Ed.). (1999). *Champions of change: The impact of the arts on learning.* Washington, DC: Council of Chief State School Officers.

Gallimore, R., Boggs, J., & Jordan, C. (1974). *Culture, behavior, and environment.* Beverly Hills, CA: Sage.

Gallimore, R., & Tharp, R. G. (1990). Teaching mind in society: Teaching, schooling, and literate discourse. In L. Moll (Ed.), *Vygotsky and education: Instructional implications and applications of sociohistorical psychology* (pp. 175–205). Cambridge, UK: Cambridge University Press.

Gandara, P. (1995). *Over the ivy walls: The educational mobility of low-income Chicanos.* Albany, NY: State University of New York Press.

Garcia, E. (1987–1988, Winter). *Effective schooling for language minority students* [NCBE Occasional Papers in Bilingual Education, No. 1]. Wheaton, MD: National Clearinghouse for Bilingual Education.

Garcia, E. E. (1988). Attributes of effective schools for language minority students. *Education and Urban Society, 20*(4), 387–398.

Garcia, E. E. (1991). *The education of linguistically and culturally diverse students: Effective instructional practices.* NCRCDSLL Educational Practice Reports. Paper EPR01. Santa Cruz, CA: Center for Research on Education, Diversity & Excellence. Available: http://repositories.cdlib.org/crede/ncrcdslleducational/EPR01

Garcia, E. E. (1992). Linguistically and culturally diverse children: Effective instructional practices and related policy issues. In H. Waxman, J. Walker de Felix, J. E. Anderson, & H. P. Baptiste (Eds.), *Students at risk in at risk schools: Improving environments for learning* (pp. 65–86). Newbury Park, CA: Corwin Press.

Garcia, E. E., Maez, L., & Gonzalez, G. (1983). *The incidence of language switching in Spanish/English bilingual children of the United States.* Tempe, AZ: Bilingual/Bicultural Education Center, Arizona State University. (ERIC Document Reproduction Service No. ED BE015018)

Garcia, G. E., & Pearson, P. D. (1991, April). *Literacy assessment in a diverse society* (Technical Report No. 525). Champaign, IL: Center for the Study of Reading, University of Illinois.

Gardner, H. (1983). *Frames of mind: The theory of multiple intelligences.* New York: BasicBooks.

Gee, P. L. (1982). *Reading and mathematics achievement of eighth-grade Chinese-American students enrolled in bilingual or monolingual program.* Unpublished doctoral dissertation, University of San Francisco.

Genishi, C. (1981). Code-switching in Chicano six-year-olds. In R. Duran (Ed.), *Latino language and communicative behavior* (pp. 133–152). Norwood, NJ: Ablex.

Gibson, M. A. (1983). *Home-school-community linkages: A study of educational opportunity for Punjabi youth.* [Final Report]. Stockton, CA: South Asian American Education Association.

Gibson, M. A. (1987, December). The school performance of immigrant minorities: A comparative view. *Anthropology and Education Quarterly, 18*(4), 262–275.

Gibson, M. A. (1988, Spring). Punjabi orchard farmers: An immigrant enclave in rural California. *International Migration Review, 22*(1), 28–50.

Gibson, M. A. (2000). Situational and structural rationales for the school performance of immigrant youth: Three cases. In H. Vermeulen and J. Perlmann (Eds.), *Immigrants, schooling, and social mobility: Does culture make a difference?* (pp. 72–102). London: Macmillan.

Gibson, M. A., & Bejinez, L. F. (2002). Dropout prevention: How migrant education supports migrant youth. *Journal of Latinos and Education, 1*(3), 155–175.

Gibson, M. A., & Bhachu, P. K. (1991). Ethnicity and school performance: A comparative study of South Asian pupils in Britain and America. *Ethnic and Racial Studies, 11*(3), 239–262.

Gibson, M. A., & Ogbu, J. U. (Eds.). (1991). *Minority status and schooling: A comparative study of immigrant and involuntary minorities.* New York: Garland Publishing.

Gilbert, S. E., & Gay, G. (1985, October). Improving the success in school of poor black children. *Phi Delta Kappan, 67*(2), 133–137.

Goldman, R. E., & Hewitt, B. (1975). An investigation of test bias for Mexican American college students. *Journal of Educational Measurement, 12,* 187–196.

Gonzalez, R. D. (1990, January). When minority becomes majority: The changing face of English classrooms. *English Journal, 79*(1), 16–23.

Goodman, K. (1986). *What's whole in whole language?* Exeter, NH: Heinemann.

Hakuta, K. (1986). *The mirror of language: The debate on bilingualism*. New York: BasicBooks.

Hakuta, K., & Garcia, E. (1989). Bilingualism and education. *American Psychologist, 44*(2), 286–299.

Hakuta, K., & Gould, L. (1987, March). Synthesis of research on bilingual education. *Educational Leadership, 44*(6), 38–45.

Hamilton, V. L., Blumenfeld, P. C., Akoh, H., & Miura, K. (1989, Winter). Japanese and American children's reasons for things they do in school. *American Educational Research Journal, 26*(4), 545–571.

Harvard Medical School. (2006). *Stress management: Techniques for preventing and easing stress*. The Special Health Report from Harvard Medical School. Big Sandy, TX: Harvard Health Publications.

Haw, K. F. (1991, Spring). Interactions of gender and race—a problem for teachers? A review of the emerging literature. *Educational Researcher, 33*(1), 12–21.

Heath, S. B. (1983). *Ways with words: Language, life and work in communities and classrooms*. New York: Cambridge University Press.

Heath, S. B. (1986). Sociocultural Contexts of Language Development. In California State Department of Education (Ed.), *Beyond language: Social and cultural factors in schooling language minority students* (pp. 143–186). Los Angeles: Evaluation, Dissemination, and Assessment Center, California State University.

Heath, S. B., & McLaughlin, M. W. (1994, September/October). Learning for anything everyday. *Journal of Curriculum Studies, 26*(5), 471–489.

Henry, S. L., & Pepper, F. C. (1990). Cognitive, social, and cultural effects on Indian learning style: Classroom implications. *Journal of Educational Issues of Language Minority Students, 7*, 85–95.

Herbert, C. (1987). *San Diego Title VII two-way bilingual program*. San Diego, CA: San Diego Unified School District.

Hirst, L., & Slavik, C. (1989). Cooperative approaches to language learning. In J. Reyhner (Ed.), *Effective language education practices and Native American language survival* (pp. 133–142). Billings, MT: Eastern Montana College Press.

Hodgkinson, H. L. (2003). *Leaving too many children behind: A demographer's view on the neglect of America's youngest children*. Washington, DC: Institute for Educational Leadership.

Holzer, M. F. (2007). *Teaching and learning at Lincoln Center Institute*. New York: Lincoln Center Institute for the Visual and Performing Arts.

Howard, E. R., & Christian, D. (2002). *Two-way immersion 101: Designing and implementing a two-way immersion education program at the elementary level*. Santa Cruz, CA: Center for Research, Diversity, and Excellence, University of California, Santa Cruz. Available: http://repositories.edlib.org/crede/edupractrpts/ep09

Huerta, A. G. (1980). The acquisition of bilingualism: A code-switching approach. In R. Bauman & J. Sherzer (Eds.), *Language and speech in American society: A compilation of research papers in sociolinguistics* (pp. 1–28). Austin, TX: Southwest Education Development Lab.

Huerta-Macias, A., & Quintero, E. (1992, Summer/Fall). Code-switching, bilingualism, and biliteracy: A case study. *Bilingual Research Journal, 16*(3–4), 69–90.

Ima, K., Galang, R., Lee, E., & Dinh Te, H. (1991, Summer). *What do we know about Asian and Pacific Islander language minority students?* Report to the Bilingual Education Office, California Department of Education. San Diego, CA: San Diego State University.

Ima, K., & Labovitz, E. M. (1991). *Language proficiency, ethnicity, and standardized test performance of elementary school students*. (ERIC Document Reproduction Service No. ED 341700)

Ima, K., & Rumbaut, R. G. (1989, June). Southeast Asian refugees in American schools: A comparison between fluent-English-proficient and limited-English-proficient students. *Topics in Language Disorders, 9*(3), 54–75.

Irvine, J. J. (1990). *Black students and school failure: Policies, practices, and prescriptions.* Westport, CT: Greenwood Press.

Jacob, E., & Jordan, C. (Eds). (1987). Explaining the school performance of minority students. *Anthropology and Education Quarterly, 18*(4).

Johnson, D. W., & Johnson, R. T. (1982). *Joining together: Group theory and group skills* (2nd ed.). Englewood Cliffs, NJ: Prentice-Hall.

Johnson, D. W., Johnson, R. T., & Holubec, E. J. (1994). *The new circles of learning.* Alexandria, VA: Association for Supervision and Curriculum Development.

Jordan, C. (1981). *Educationally effective ethnology: A study of the contributions of cultural knowledge to effective education of minority children.* Unpublished doctoral dissertation, University of California at Los Angeles.

Jordan, C. (1984). Cultural compatibility and the education of Hawaiian children: Implications for mainland educators. *Educational Research Quarterly, 8*(4), 59–71.

Jordan, C. (1985, Summer). Translating culture: From ethnographic information to educational program. *Anthropology and Education Quarterly, 16*(2), 104–123.

Jordan, C. (1995). Creating cultures of schooling: Historical and conceptual background of the KEEP/Rough Rock collaboration. *Bilingual Research Journal, 19*(1), 83–100.

Jordan, C., Au, K. H., & Joseting, A. K. (1983). Patterns of classroom interaction with Pacific Islands children: The importance of cultural differences. In Mao Chu-Chang & V. Rodriguez (Eds.), *Asian- and Pacific-American perspectives in bilingual education: Comparative research.* New York: Teachers College Press.

Jordan, C., Tharp, R., & Baird-Vogt, L. (1992). Just open the door: Cultural compatibility and classroom rapport. In M. Saravia-Shore & S. F. Arvizu (Eds.), *Cross-cultural literacy: Ethnographies of communication in multiethnic classrooms* (pp. 3–18). New York: Garland.

Keefe, S. E. (1984). Real and extended families among Mexican Americans and Anglo Americans: On the meaning of close family ties. *Human Organization, 43*(1), 65–69.

Kennedy, R. (2006, July 27). Guggenheim study suggests arts education benefits literacy skills. *New York Times,* pp. 1–2.

Kleinfield, N. R. (2006a, January 9). Diabetes and its awful toll quietly emerge as a crisis. *New York Times,* pp. A1, A18–A19.

Kleinfield, N. R. (2006b, January 10). Living at an epicenter of diabetes, defiance, and despair. *New York Times,* pp. A1, A20–A21.

Knapp, M. S., Shields, B. J., & Turnbull, B. (1993). *Study of academic instruction for disadvantaged students: Academic challenge for the children of poverty: Findings and conclusions.* Washington, DC: Office of Policy and Planning, U.S. Department of Education.

Knapp, M. S., & Turnbull, B. (1990). *Better schooling for the children of poverty: Alternatives to conventional wisdom.* Study of Academic Instruction for Disadvantaged Students. Vol. 1: Summary. Washington, DC: Policy Studies Associates; Menlo Park, CA: SRI International.

Korn, R., & Associates. (2005). *Solomon R. Guggenheim Museum Teaching Literacy Through Art Year One: 2004–05 Study.* Available: www.learningthroughart.org/research_findings.php

Krashen, S. (1982). *Principles and practices in second language acquisition.* Hayward, CA: Alemany Press.

Krashen, S. (1985). *The input hypothesis: Issues and implications.* New York: Longman.

Krashen, S., & Biber, D. (1988). *On course: Bilingual education's success in California.* Sacramento: California Association for Bilingual Education.

Laosa, L. (1982). School, occupation, culture, and family: The impact of parental schooling on the parent-child relationship. *Journal of Educational Psychology, 74*(6), 791–827.

Lee, E. (1986). *Chinese parents' support for the bilingual education program.* Unpublished doctoral dissertation, University of the Pacific.

Lee, E. S., & Lee, M. R. (1980). *A study of classroom behaviors of Chinese American children and immigrant Chinese children in contrast to those of black American children and white American children in an urban Head Start program.* Unpublished doctoral dissertation, University of San Francisco.

Levin, H. (2003, July 3). Interview on PBS from WGBH. Boston: WGBH Educational Foundation.

Levin, H., & Hopfenberg, W. (1991, January). Don't remediate: Accelerate! *Principal, 70*(3), 11–13.

Lindholm, K. J. (1988). *Edison elementary school bilingual immersion program: Student programs after one year of implementation.* Los Angeles: Center for Language Education and Research.

Little Soldier, L. (1989, October). Cooperative learning and the native American student. *Phi Delta Kappan, 71*(2), 161–163.

Lucas, T., Henze, R., & Donato, R. (1990). Promoting the success of Latino language minority students: An exploratory study of six high schools. *Harvard Educational Review, 60*(3), 315–334.

Martinez, R., & Dukes, R. L. (1991, March). Ethnic and gender difference in self-esteem. *Youth and Society, 22*(3), 218–338.

Matute-Bianchi, M. E. (1986). Ethnic identities and patterns of school success and failure among Mexican-descent and Japanese-American students in a California high school: An ethnographic analysis. *American Journal of Education, 95*(1), 233–255.

McDermott, R., & Goldman, S. (1998). Review of constructing school success: The consequences of untracking low-achieving students. *Anthropology and Education Quarterly, 29*(1), 125–126.

McIntosh, P. (1983). *Interactive phases of curricular re-vision: A feminist perspective.* Wellesley, MA: Wellesley College Center for Research on Women.

McLaughlin, M., Irby, M. A., & Langman, J. (1994). *Urban sanctuaries: Neighborhood organizations in the lives and futures of inner-city youth.* San Francisco: Jossey-Bass.

Mehan, H. (1989). Microcomputers in classrooms: Educational technology or social practice? *Anthropology and Education Quarterly, 20*(1), 4–22.

Mehan, H. (2005). *Assessment, equity, and opportunity to learn.* Paper presented at the AERA Annual Conference, Montreal.

Mehan, H. (2007). *Restructuring and reculturing schools to provide students with multiple pathways to college and career.* Los Angeles: University of California Institute for Democracy, Education and Access.

Mehan, H., & Hubbard, L. (1999). *Tracking "untracking": Evaluating the effectiveness of an educational innovation.* Santa Cruz, CA: Center for Research on Education, Diversity and Excellence.

Mehan, H., Hubbard, L., Lintz, A., & Villanueva, I. (1994). *Tracking untracking: The consequences of placing low track students in high track classes.* (Research Report No. 10). Washington, DC: National Center for Research on Cultural Diversity and Second Language Learning.

Mehan, H., Moll, L. C., & Riel, M. (1985). *Computers in classrooms: A quasi-experiment in guided change* (NIE Report 6-83-0027). Washington, DC: National Institute of Education.

Mehan, H., Villanueva, I., Hubbard, L., & Lintz, A. (1996). *Constructing school success: The consequences of untracking low-achieving students.* Cambridge, UK: Cambridge University Press.

Michaels, S. (1981). Sharing time: Children's narrative styles and differential access to literacy. *Language in Society, 10*(3), 423–442.

Moll, L. C., Diaz, S., Estrada, E., & Lopes, L. M. (1992). Making contexts: The social construction of lessons in two languages. In M. Saravia-Shore and S. F. Arvizu (Eds.), *Cross-cultural literacy: Ethnographies of communication in multiethnic classrooms* (pp. 339–366). New York: Garland.

National Center for Educational Accountability. (2006, July 14). *Just for the Kids study of best practice studies and institutes: Findings from 20 states.* Available: http://www.just4kids.org/jftk/twenty_states.cfm

National Coalition of Advocates for Students. (1988). *New voices: Immigrant Students in U. S. public schools.* Boston: Author.

Nieto, S. (2004). *Affirming diversity: The sociopolitical context of multicultural education* (4th ed.). Boston/ New York: Pearson/Allyn and Bacon.

Noddings, N. (1995, November). Teaching themes of caring. *Education Digest, 61*(3), 24–28.

Oakes, J., Wells, A., Datnow, A., & Jones, M. (1997). Detracking: The social construction of ability, cultural politics, and resistance to reform. *Teachers College Record, 98*(3), 482–510.

Oakland, T., & Matuszek, P. (1977). Using tests in non-discriminatory assessment. In T. Oakland (Ed.), *Psychological and educational assessment of minority children* (pp. 52–69). New York: Brunner/Mazel.

O'Donnell, C. R., & Tharp, R. G. (1990). Community intervention guided by theoretical development. In A. S. Bellack, M. Hersen, & A. E. Kazdin (Eds.), *International handbook of behavior modification and therapy* (2nd ed.) (pp. 251–266). New York: Plenum Press.

Ogbu, J. (1982). Cultural discontinuities and schooling. *Anthropology and Education Quarterly, 13*(4), 291–307.

Ogbu, J. U. (1987). Variability in minority school performance: A problem in search of an explanation. *Anthropology and Education Quarterly, 18*(4), 312–334.

Olson, L. (2006, June 22). The down staircase. *Diplomas count: Education Week, 25*(41S), 5–6, 10–11.

Ovando, C. J. (1993). Language diversity and education. In J. A. Banks & C. A. M. Banks (Eds.), *Multicultural education: Issues and perspectives* (2nd ed., pp. 215–235). Needham Heights, MA: Allyn and Bacon.

Pang, V. O. (1990, Fall). Asian-American children: A diverse population. *Educational Forum, 55*(1), 49–66.

Pease-Alvarez, C., Garcia, E., & Espinosa, P. (1991). Effective instruction for language minority students: An early childhood case study. *Early Childhood Research Quarterly, 6*(3), 347–362.

Pepper, F., & Henry, S. (1989). Social and cultural effects on Indian learning style: Classroom implications.

In B. J. Shade (Ed.), *Culture, style, and the educative process*. Springfield, IL: Charles C. Thomas.

Philips, S. (1972). Participant structures and communicative competence. In C. Cazden, V. P. John, & D. Hymes (Eds.), *Functions of language in the classroom* (pp. 370–392). New York: Teachers College Press.

Philips, S. (1983). *The invisible culture: Communication in classroom and community on the Warm Springs Indian Reservation*. New York: Longman.

Poplack, S. (1981). Syntactic structure and social function of code-switching. In R. Duran (Ed.), *Latino language and communication behavior*. Norwood, NJ: Ablex.

Protheroe, N. J., & Barsdate, K. (1992, March). Culturally sensitive instruction. *Streamlined Seminar, 10*(4), 1–4.

Quality Education for Minorities Project. (1990, January). *Education that works: An action plan for the education of minorities: Report summary*. Cambridge: Massachusetts Institute of Technology.

Rakow, L. F. (1991, Summer). Gender and race in the classroom: Teaching way out of line. *Feminist Teacher, 5*(1), 10–13.

Ramirez, J. D., Yuen, S., Ramey, D. R., & Pasta, D. J. (1991, February). *Final report: Longitudinal study of structured English immersion strategy early-exit and late-exit transitional bilingual education programs for language minority children* (Vols. 1 & 2). Washington, DC: U.S. Department of Education.

Rodriguez, C. E. (1989). *Puerto Ricans born in the U.S.A.* Winchester, MA: Unwin Hyman.

Rodriguez, C. E. (1992). *Student voices: High school students' perspectives on the Latino dropout problem*. Report of the Fordham University, College at Lincoln Center Student Research Project. New York: Latino Commission on Educational Reform.

Sadker, M., Sadker, D., & Long, L. (1993). Gender and educational equity. In J. A. Banks & C. A. M. Banks (Eds.), *Multicultural education* (2nd ed.) (pp. 106–123). Needham Heights, MA: Allyn and Bacon.

Sadker, M., Sadker, D., & Steindam, S. (1989). Gender equity and educational reform. *Educational Leadership, 46*(6), 44–47.

Santora, M. (2006, January 12). East meets west, adding pounds and peril. *New York Times*, pp. A1, A22–A23.

Saravia-Shore, M. (1993). Professional development for an education that is multicultural: The cross-cultural interdisciplinary cooperative (CICL) model. In F. Rivera-Batiz (Ed.), *Reinventing urban education: Multiculturalism and the social context of schooling* (pp. 277–302). New York: IUME Press, Teachers College, Columbia University.

Saravia-Shore, M., & Arvizu, S. F. (Eds.). (1992). *Cross-cultural literacy: Ethnographies of communication in multiethnic classrooms.* New York: Garland.

Saravia-Shore, M., & Martinez, H. (1992). An ethnographic study of home/school role conflicts of second generation Puerto Rican adolescents. In M. Saravia-Shore & S. F. Arvizu (Eds.), *Cross-cultural literacy: Ethnographies of communication in multiethnic classrooms* (pp. 227–252). New York: Garland.

Saville-Troike, M. (1978). *A guide to culture in the classroom.* Arlington, VA: National Clearinghouse for Bilingual Education.

Sayers, D. (1989). Bilingual sister classes in computer writing networks. In D. Johnson & D. Roen (Eds.), *Richness in writing: Empowering ESL students.* New York: Longman.

Sayers, D., & Brown, K. (1987, April). Bilingual education and telecommunications: A perfect fit. *The Computing Teacher, 14*(7), 23–24.

Scheurich, J. J., Skria, L., & Johnson, J. F. (2000, December). Thinking carefully about equity and accountability. *Phi Delta Kappan, 82*(4), 293–299.

Sheldon, S. B., & Epstein, J. L. (2005a). Involvement counts: Family and community partnerships and math achievement. *Journal of Educational Research, 98*(4), 196–206.

Sheldon, S. B., & Epstein, J. L. (2005b). School programs of family and community involvement to support children's reading and literacy development across the grades. In J. Flood & P. Anders (Eds.), *Literacy development of students in urban schools: Research and policy.* Newark, DE: International Reading Association.

Short, D. J., Crandall, J., & Christian, D. (1989). *How to integrate language and content instruction: A training manual.* Los Angeles: Center for Language Education and Research. (ERIC Document Reproduction Service No. ED 292304)

Short, D. J., & Echevarria, J. (1999). *The sheltered instruction observation protocol: A tool for teacher-researcher collaboration and professional development.* Santa Cruz, CA: Center for Research on Education, Diversity, and Excellence. Educational Practice Reports. Available: http://repositories.cdlib.org/crede/edupractrpts/epr03

Simon, B. S. (2004). High school outreach and family involvement. *Social Psychology of Education, 7*(2), 185–209.

Slavin, R. (1980). *Using student team learning* (3rd ed.). Baltimore: Johns Hopkins University Press.

Slavin, R. (1987). Cooperative learning: Can students help students learn? *Instructor, 96*(7), 74–78.

Slavin, R. (1991, February). Synthesis of research on cooperative learning. *Educational Leadership, 48*(5), 71–82.

Snow, M. (1986). *Innovative second language education: Bilingual immersion programs.* Los Angeles: University of California, Center for Language Education and Research.

Staton-Spicer, A. O., & Wulff, D. H. (1984, October). Research in communication and instruction: Categorization and synthesis. *Communication Education, 33*(4), 377–391.

Strickland, D., & Ascher, C. (1992). Low income African-American children and public schooling. In P. W. Jackson (Ed.), *Handbook of research on curriculum* (pp. 609–625). New York: Macmillan.

Taylor, D. (1983). *Family literacy: Young children learning to read and write.* Portsmouth, NH: Heinemann.

Teale, W. H. (1986). Home background and young children's literacy development. In W. H. Teale & E. Sulzby (Eds.), *Emergent literacy: Writing and reading* (pp. 173–206). Norwood, NJ: Ablex.

Tharp, R. G. (1989a). Psycho-cultural variables and constants: Effects on teaching and learning in schools. *American Psychologist, 44*(2), 349–359.

Tharp, R. G. (1989b). Culturally compatible education: A formula for designing effective classrooms. In H. T. Trueba, G. Spindler, & L. Spindler (Eds.), *What do anthropologists have to say about dropouts?* New York: Falmer Press.

Tharp, R. G. (1991). Cultural diversity and treatment of children. *Journal of Cultural and Clinical Psychology, 59*(6), 799–812.

Tharp, R. G. (1992). Cultural compatibility and diversity: Implications for the urban classroom. *Teaching Thinking and Problem Solving, 14*(6), 1–4. (Available from Research for Better Schools, Philadelphia)

Tharp, R. G., Doherty, R. W., Echevarria, J., Estrada, P., Goldenberg, C., Hilberg, R. S., & Saunders, W. M. (2004). *Research evidence: Five standards for effective pedagogy and student outcomes* (Technical Report No. G1). Santa Cruz, CA: University of California, Santa Cruz Center for Research on Education, Diversity and Excellence.

Tharp, R. G., Estrada, P., Dalton, S. S., & Yamauchi, L. (2000). *Teaching transformed: Achieving excellence, fairness, inclusion, and harmony.* Boulder, CO: Westview Press.

Tharp, R. G., Jordan, C., Speidel, G. E., Au, K. H., Klein, T. W., Calkins, et al. (1984). Product and process in applied developmental research: Education and the children of a minority. In M. E. Lamb, A. L. Brown, & B. Rogoff (Eds.), *Advances in developmental psychology* (Vol. III, pp. 91–141). Hillsdale, NJ: Lawrence Erlbaum.

Tharp, R., & Gallimore, R. (1991). *The instructional conversation: Teaching and learning in social activity.* Santa Cruz: National Center for Research on Cultural Diversity and Second Language Learning, University of California.

Thomas, W. P., & Collier, V. (2002). *A national study of school effectiveness for language minority students' long-term academic achievement.* Santa Cruz: University of California, Santa Cruz, Center for Research on Education, Diversity, and Excellence.

Torres-Guzman, M. E. (1992). Stories of hope in the midst of despair: Culturally responsive education for Latino students in an alternative high school in New York City. In M. Saravia-Shore & S. F. Arvizu (Eds.), *Cross-cultural literacy: Ethnographies of communication in multiethnic classrooms* (pp. 477–490). New York: Garland.

Trueba, H., & Delgado-Gaitan, C. (1985). Socialization of Mexican children for cooperation and competition: Sharing and copying. *Journal of Educational Equity and Leadership, 5*(3),189–204.

Trueba, H. T., Jacobs, L., & Kirton, E. (1990). *Cultural conflict and adaptation: The case of Hmong children in American society.* New York: Falmer.

U.S. Census Bureau. (2006, August 9). *Facts for features.* Available: http://www.census.gov/Press-Release/www/releases/archives/facts_for_features_special_editions/007276.html

Valdez-Fallis, G. (1977). *Code-switching and the classroom teacher.* Arlington, VA: Center for Applied Linguistics.

Valdez-Pierce, L. (1991). *Effective schools for language minority students.* Chevy Chase, MD: Mid-Atlantic Equity Center. (Available from the publisher at 5454 Wisconsin Ave., Suite 1500, Chevy Chase, MD 20815)

Valenzuela, A., & Dornbusch, S. M. (1994, March). Familism and social capital in the academic achievement of Mexican origin and Anglo adolescents. *Social Science Quarterly, 75*(1), 18–36.

Valenzuela, R., Valenzuela, A., Sloan, K., & Foley, D. (2001, December). Let's treat the cause, not the symptoms: Equity and accountability in Texas revisited. *Phi Delta Kappan, 83*(4), 318–321.

Valverde, L., Feinberg, R. C., & Marquez, E. M. (1980). *Educating English-speaking Hispanics.* Alexandria, VA: Association for Supervision and Curriculum Development.

Van Voorhis, F. L. (2003). Interactive homework in middle school: Effects on family involvement and students' science achievement. *Journal of Educational Research, 96*(9), 323–339.

Van Voorhis, F. L. (2004). Reflecting on the homework ritual: Assignments and designs. *Theory Into Practice, 43*(3), 205–212.

Viadero, D. (2006, July 14). "Best practices" distilled from studies of more than 250 schools. *Education Week, 25*(44), p. 20.

Weis, L., & Fine, M. (2001). Extraordinary conversations in public school. *Qualitative Studies in Education, 14*(1), 497–523.

Winfield, L. F., & Manning, J. (1992). Changing school culture to accommodate student diversity. In M. E. Dilworth (Ed.), *Diversity in teacher education: New expectations* (pp. 181–214). San Francisco: Jossey-Bass.

Wong-Fillmore, L. (1983). The language learner as an individual: Implications of research on individual differences for the ESL teacher. In M. A. Clarke & J. Handscombe (Eds.), *On TESOL '82: Pacific perspectives on language learning and teaching* (pp. 157–171). Washington, DC: Teachers of English to Speakers of Other Languages (TESOL).

Wong-Fillmore, L. (1991). When learning a second language means losing a first. *Early Childhood Research Quarterly, 6*(3), 323–346.

Wong-Fillmore, L., & Valadez, C. (1986). Teaching bilingual learners. In M. C. Wittrock (Ed.), *Handbook of research on teaching* (pp. 630–647). New York: Macmillan.

Zehr, M. A. (2006, July 12). Recipes for life. *Education Week*, pp. 38–41.

Zeichner, K. M. (1992). *Educating teachers for cultural diversity*. East Lansing, MI: National Center for Research on Teacher Learning.

Zentella, A. C. (1992). Individual differences in growing up bilingual. In M. Saravia-Shore & S. F. Arvizu (Eds.), *Cross-cultural literacy: Ethnographies of communication in multiethnic classrooms* (pp. 211–226). New York: Garland.

3

Strategies for Increasing Achievement in Reading

Marie Carbo

Our schools are called on to shoulder the responsibility for bringing about world-class levels of literacy in the United States. Today, we are still far from that momentous goal. Fewer than *one-third* of U.S. students in grades 4, 8, and 12 currently read at or above grade level, according to the results on the most recent National Assessment of Educational Progress (NAEP) in 2005 (Romano, 2005). Low reading ability holds back many students, making it virtually impossible for them to understand their subjects and causing them to fall even further behind in their schoolwork. The current levels of reading achievement still fall far short of what is needed in the workplace, in colleges, and in the international arena.

Although international competition is growing, U.S. students graduating from high school or college and entering the workforce are increasingly *less* literate. The serious implications of these alarming statistics for America's future are described by retired global-marketing officer Robert L. Wehling:

I've been watching very, very closely the educational progress in Asia—China, India, Vietnam, Singapore, and several others. . . . They're making rapid progress, whereas we're making minuscule progress. And I don't think the average American understands the impact of this for our future, because they're going to have the bulk of the intellectual and creative talent in the world, and that has devastating consequences for us. (Olson, 2005, p. 24)

If our young people are to participate successfully on the world stage, sweeping changes are necessary in the way our students are taught to read, and then tested on what they are able to read. We need clear guidelines for accelerating the development of the most important, fundamental, and vital ability addressed in the schools: the ability to read.

The State of the Art of Reading Instruction

According to Grover J. Whitehurst of the Department of Education, there are "substantial declines in reading for pleasure, and it's showing up in our literacy levels" (Dillon, 2005a). Declines in reading for pleasure are extremely serious because students who enjoy reading and read a great deal improve their reading skills at much faster rates than do students who read very little for pleasure (Allington, 2001; Anderson, 1996; Cipielewski & Stanovich, 1992; Krashen, 1993). When reading for pleasure declines substantially, as it has, so does reading ability.

A particularly disturbing trend in the 2007 NAEP data indicates a continuing decline in the reading abilities of boys (National Center for Education Statistics, 2007). Specifically,

between grades 4 and 8, the literacy gap between boys and girls doubles, with girls ending up a year and a half ahead of boys, on average. In fact, the gender gap is so serious that at the elementary level, boys are twice as likely as girls to be diagnosed with learning disabilities and placed in special education classes (Carbo, 2007; Tyre, 2006). Based on these data, it's not surprising that between 1980 and 2001, there was a 71 percent rise in boys who said they didn't like school (Newkirk, 2003).

The gender gap has caused a shift at the college level as well; men are now a minority in our colleges. In 1972, men represented 58 percent of undergraduates; today that figure is 44 percent. The widening achievement gap between boys and girls "has profound implications for the economy, society, families, and democracy" according to Margaret Spellings, U. S. Secretary of Education (Tyre, 2006).

Even more foreboding, the literacy levels of college graduates are falling. Only 31 percent of *college graduates* demonstrated reading proficiency on the National Assessment of Adult Literacy given in 2003 by the U.S. Department of Education, compared with 40 percent in 1992. And 14 percent of college graduates scored at the basic proficiency level, which demonstrates an ability to read and understand only short, commonplace texts (Dillon, 2005b). These results are seriously inadequate. Our students *can* and *must* make much higher reading gains rapidly. Low reading ability correlates strongly with the high dropout rate in our high schools; moreover, those who have low reading ability and are living at the poverty level find it more difficult to secure good jobs and move into the middle class (Carbo, 2007).

Finally, a high percentage of U.S. students appear to be performing at the proficient reading level on their state exams, but a very low percentage perform at that same level on the more valid and accurate NAEP. For example, 87 percent of Georgia 4th graders scored at the proficient level on their state exam, but only 26 percent of them scored at the proficient level on the NAEP (Ravitch, 2005). Other states with similarly striking discrepancies include Alabama, Idaho, New York, North Carolina, Tennessee, and Texas. Easy state tests are extremely dangerous; they make it appear that students are doing well when they're not, lulling educators and the public into keeping the reading instruction that exists, rather than looking into why their students are not doing well.

These kinds of data strongly suggest that the education community has not provided reading programs for U.S. students that accomplish two critically important reading goals: significant increases in students' reading comprehension and reading for pleasure. Unfortunately, instead of counteracting students' lack of interest in reading by making learning to read easy and fun, schools are teaching and reteaching a multitude of reading skills that are often unnecessary for many students, focusing on preparing students for tests, and ignoring what students say they want to read. In other words, much of what is being done today to improve literacy disregards important research in reading, learning styles, and how the brain learns and is likely to worsen the reading problem and increase the number of bored, stressed students who dislike reading—exactly what we don't want.

The Effect of No Child Left Behind

The overriding objective of the No Child Left Behind (NCLB) Act is to close the achievement gap in grades K–3, especially for children who are poor or underachieving, or for whom English is a second language. NCLB defines "good" schools as those that are effective with every group of children they serve. Few would argue the merits of that vitally important goal; however, many educators are gravely concerned about a lack of funds to implement NCLB, impossibly high standards, an overemphasis on reading and math to the detriment of other subjects, and an overly narrow definition of success that seems to equate to passing annual tests (Franklin, 2006).

Has reading achievement actually improved during the period of time since NCLB has been implemented? Whether we can claim improvement depends, it seems, on how the data are analyzed. Secretary Spellings (2006) stated that "over the last five years, our 9-year-olds have made more progress in reading than in the previous 28 combined." Spellings was referring to the reading gains made on the NAEP by 9-year-olds between 1999 and 2004.

Gerald Bracey (2006) analyzed the regular NAEP 2005 assessments, not the trend data, and found that "fourth-grade reading reached the same level as it had at the onset of NCLB in 2002 . . . the proportion of students at or above the proficient level was static for fourth-graders at 31% and fell for eighth-graders from 33% to 31%" (p. 152). According to a multitude of recent reports, the reading gap between Hispanic or African American students and whites is apparent in kindergarten, worsens through 12 years of public education, and shows "very few signs of closing" (Dillon, 2006b).

The focus of NCLB on closing the achievement gap is important. Since the law was enacted, the reading scores of African American and Hispanic students have increased somewhat, but overall the reading achievement of U.S. students has remained static. Currently, only one-third of students read at or above grade level. U.S. students—all of them, at every grade level and in every socioeconomic group—deserve much, much more.

Reading Strategies That Promote Achievement

The 1990s were one of the most turbulent periods in the history of reading research and instruction. It was a time many referred to as the "Reading Wars" because reading experts with strong opposing positions seemed to have no common ground of agreement. Fortunately, there is now broad agreement among reading experts about which reading strategies facilitate learning to read and which reading strategies make learning to read difficult (Flippo, 1998, 2001; Reutzel & Smith, 2004). These "expert opinion" studies, as well as research in reading, brain behavior, learning styles, and reading styles, inform this chapter.

Strategy 3.1:
Stop doing what doesn't work.

Discussion

One of the major concerns of educators is how to add on reading strategies and materials to an already crowded reading program. If your students read well, perform well on various reading tests, and read a great deal for their own pleasure, you probably need only fine-tune your reading program. But if your students are not performing well in reading, read very little (or not at all) for their own enjoyment, or both, it's highly likely that major changes are needed. The first step toward implementing those changes is to stop or reduce what doesn't work so you have adequate instructional time to do what does work.

Reading experts agree that the following reading practices make learning to read difficult. This list draws heavily from Reutzel and Smith's (2004) excellent synthesis of the important findings of Flippo (1998, 2001).

• *Isolated instruction*—teaching reading separately from writing, listening, or speaking; teaching letters and sounds in isolation with flash cards and other devices; teaching only phonics as a way of deciphering words.

• *Drill and mastery*—following the script in the teacher's edition faithfully during instruction instead of responding to students' needs; using worksheets and workbooks to practice every skill and lesson; using even more worksheets with struggling readers; teaching letters

101

and words until mastery is achieved before advancing to new letters and words; focusing instruction on skills instead of comprehension.

• *Control*—selecting and discussing reading materials decided by the teacher; using short, choppy reading selections with controlled vocabularies; using texts with no new, previously taught words.

• *Competition*—making learning to read a contest with points, prizes, winners, and losers.

• *Implicit instruction and avoidance of modeling*—avoiding reading aloud, especially after primer books are completed; too little modeling of reading for specific teaching purposes or for enjoyment.

• *Negative expectations and ability grouping*—communicating negative reading attitudes to students; discussing and emphasizing high-stakes testing, keeping students in static reading groups.

• *Rote accountability*—requiring book reports for every text or story read; using skill practice sheets for each chapter or story.

• *Mode of reading practice*—using "round robin reading"; too little use of silent reading.

Classroom Examples

Reading materials and strategies that are not producing high reading gains and increased reading for pleasure need to be examined closely. Because high-interest reading materials and student choice are extremely important, an effective first step for principals and their teachers is to meet by grade level to evaluate their reading materials. At these meetings, stories that are confusing or boring for students can be greatly reduced or even eliminated, as can worksheets that are unnecessary, boring, or overly repetitive.

With the additional time created, teachers can: read aloud daily to their students; discover and discuss students' reading interests; add and use supplemental, high-interest reading materials; discuss and model important reading strategies with the stories that remain; provide group and individual writing experiences that relate to stories read; have students pantomime or act out stories; and take the time to enjoy texts and stories with their students.

Resources

Allington, 2001; Barber, Carbo, & Thomasson, 1998; Caine, Caine, McClintic, & Klimek, 2005; Eldredge, Reutzel, & Hollingsworth, 1996; Flippo, 1998, 2001; International Reading Association, 1999; Jensen, 1998; Kozol, 2005; Reutzel & Smith, 2004; Sprenger, 1999, 2003.

Strategy 3.2:

Read aloud to students to model accuracy, fluency, vocabulary, and comprehension.

Discussion

Reading aloud is important at all grade levels, especially for students in the primary grades, struggling readers at any level, young people with a limited knowledge of English, and those who have had little or no experience listening to written English (Carbo, 2007). Students need to listen to good reading models in order to become familiar with both the patterns and rhythms of well-written language and the wide range of exciting, informative reading materials that are available to them. The enthusiasm, interest, and delight that the person reading exhibits while reading aloud to students is contagious and motivating.

Hoffman, Roser, and Battle (1993) suggest this possible model read-aloud program with seven features: (1) designating a daily legitimate time and place for reading aloud; (2) carefully selecting quality texts that include stories with "enduring themes and meaty plots, [and] poems that touch and enlighten"; (3) allowing readers and listeners to explore interrelationships among books; (4) encouraging personal responses to the readings; (5) establishing small conversation groups; (6) offering a variety of opportunities to respond to the readings and to extend them; and (7) rereading selected pieces.

Classroom Examples

If students have had limited experiences being read to, 10 to 15 minutes at least three times daily should be set aside for reading aloud. A wide variety of literature and expository texts can be read to students, with illustrations shown and discussed as appropriate. Many different people can be scheduled to read aloud to students, such as teachers, the principal, authors, parents, or older students. Students of all ages, including older struggling readers, need to see and hear people enjoying reading as they read aloud, and then experience that enjoyment themselves.

In addition to listening to stories, sometimes emerging readers can follow along in the text while they listen, so that they connect the spoken and printed word. To help young people better understand the content, teachers should relate the reading materials to the students' background and experiences, and encourage students to read a text selection silently to themselves before reading it aloud for discussion.

Resources

Adams, 1990; Anderson, Heibert, Scott, & Wilkinson, 1985; Carbo, 1978a, 1978b; Chomsky, 1978; Dickinson & Smith, 1994; Durkin, 1966; Hoffman, Roser, & Battle, 1993; Holdaway, 1979, 1982; Kapinus, Gambrell, & Koskinen, 1987; McCauley & McCauley, 1992; Morrow, 1989; Samuels, Schermer, & Reinking, 1992; Strickland & Morrow, 1989; Teale & Sulzby, 1986; Trelease, 2006; Wasik & Slavin, 1990; Yopp, 1995.

Strategy 3.3:

Create a literacy-rich environment with reading materials that are developmentally appropriate, well organized, varied in subject matter and level of difficulty, and complementary to students' interests, abilities, backgrounds, and reading styles.

Discussion

Students tend to become more motivated to read and will read for longer periods of time when they are given opportunities to choose reading materials that accommodate their interests, abilities, and reading styles. Older struggling readers benefit greatly when they can choose reading materials that interest them (see "Grade 6 Reading Interests," p. 104). Emerging readers, particularly those from diverse linguistic, cultural, or socioeconomic backgrounds, often benefit from exposure to a wide variety of reading materials that honor different cultures. Challenging reading materials—neither too easy nor too hard—that are at or slightly above students' reading levels are usually most effective. The common practice of providing struggling readers with easy reading materials for long periods of time generally hinders reading achievement.

Initially, teachers provide emerging readers with easy reading materials that allow them to experience success, such as journals, children's stories, books with repetitive phrases and predictable language, big books, recorded books, correspondence, picture books, and environmental print (words that youngsters encounter every day). Both the environmental print in classrooms and the books in class libraries should reflect students' first languages, as well as English.

Grade 6 Reading Interests

- Scary books and stories
- Comics, cartoons, magazines about popular culture
- Books and magazines about sports, cars, and trucks
- Series books
- Funny books
- Books about animals

(Worthy, Moorman, & Turner, 1999)

The most effective teachers of reading expose students to a wide range of graded reading materials that become increasingly complex. They use well-organized textbooks that skillfully integrate relevant, subject-specific information. Articles from periodicals and newspapers help students connect reading to the topics and issues of the real world and introduce real-world materials into the classroom. Basal readers, texts, and workbooks represent only a small sampling of the many available resources that encourage reading. Young people should be able to make extensive use of a variety of reading resources, especially high-quality literature for children and adolescents.

Classroom Examples

Teachers can determine students' interests, abilities, and learning- or reading-style preferences through observations, interviews, checklists, and inventories. An inventory of reading interests, for example, might ask students to identify their favorite authors, topics, and the kinds of reading materials they like to read. This information can guide the selection of materials and can also be shared with students.

In classrooms designed to encourage reading, teachers label many objects, post written charts and directions, and stock well-organized libraries with a variety of reading materials, including poetry, storybooks, newspapers, magazines, book recordings, reading games, and software. Physical features of libraries that increase children's voluntary use of books include a central area, partitioned and private places to read, comfortable seating, a display of some attractive book covers, literature-oriented displays and props, and books organized into categories (Fractor, Woodruff, Martinez, & Teale, 1993).

A large repertoire of written materials that reflect students' interests and backgrounds should be available in classrooms and school libraries. These materials should reflect the diverse cultures and experiences of the youngsters. Teachers can encourage students to write about their experiences, publish their writing in school, and share their writing with classmates. Students may choose to write about topics such as their families, their interests, the country in which they were born, and holiday celebrations.

Teachers should provide time for students to browse through reading materials in the library and to choose, discuss, and share their reading interests and favorite reading materials with their peers. A student-devised card catalog can list favorite books and why and for whom they are recommended. Teachers should help students keep records of what they read and the purposes for which they read in order to help youngsters become aware of the important role reading plays in their lives.

Resources

Allington, 1984; Anderson, Heibert, Scott, & Wilkinson, 1985; Carbo, 2007; Chall, 1993; Durkin, 1966; Fractor, Woodruff, Martinez, & Teale, 1993; Heald-Taylor, 1987; Holdaway, 1979, 1982; Neuman, 1999; Salinger, 1988; Strickland & Morrow, 1989; Sulzby, 1985; Teale, 1984, 1987.

Strategy 3.4:
Encourage reading for pleasure.

Discussion

Students who like to read and who read often for their own pleasure are likely to improve in reading fluency, vocabulary, and comprehension at a much faster rate than students who don't. Such students are called "engaged readers." These are youngsters who take books out of the library and read for substantial amounts of time, simply because they want to do so. Engaged reading is *not* assigned reading, nor is it affected by extrinsic rewards, such as distributing points or gifts. Engaged reading is reading that students do *because they want to read*. The amount of engaged reading is an excellent predictor of reading achievement. The cognitive abilities required to perform well in reading comprehension are developed and strengthened through large amounts of engaged reading (Guthrie, Schafer, & Huang, 2001).

Classroom Examples

To stimulate interest in reading and to provide practice, teachers provide literacy-rich environments and time for students to read for pleasure. They build in uninterrupted periods of time (from 10 to 45 minutes, depending on students' developmental ages, interests, and abilities). During these periods, teachers permit students to choose from a variety of interesting, high-quality, developmentally appropriate reading materials, ranging from the readily understandable to the challenging. For struggling readers, teachers make available recorded readings. Emerging readers may work with recordings of challenging reading materials to help increase their confidence, comprehension, and fluency.

Teachers provide a variety of environments and activities to help students associate reading with pleasure (e.g., snacks, pillows, rugs, lamps). Students are given time to interact with peers in discussions about stories and books. Teachers permit students to choose classroom materials, or they provide guidelines for students. For example, at times students might be required to select books from a list of biographies, books about history, or award-winning books.

After introducing students to a variety of reading materials, a teacher might help youngsters to form and join various book clubs, based on their reading interests (for instance, the Mystery Club, the Adventure Club, or the History Club). The class can work together to design a poster for each book club, and students can sign their names on the poster if they are interested in reading a certain type of book with a group, or after they have read a specific number of books of that type. Teachers can provide class time for students to meet and discuss their mutual interests and readings. Students can be encouraged to devise discussion questions for group meetings and to lead discussion groups.

Resources

Allington, 2001; Alvermann, 2002; Anderson, Heibert, Scott, & Wilkinson, 1985; Cipielewski & Stanovich, 1992; Clarke, 2006; Goodman, 1984; Guthrie, Schafer, & Huang, 2001; Guthrie & Wigfield,

2000; Hiebert & Raphael, 1998; Holdaway, 1979; Karweit, 1989; Moorman & Turner, 1999; Pressley, 1998, 2001; Smith & Wilhelm, 2002; Strickland & Morrow, 1989; Taylor, Frye, & Maruyama, 1990; Trelease, 2006; Vacca & Vacca, 1999; Wigfield, 1997.

Strategy 3.5:

Use assisted reading methods to enable students to read challenging materials with good fluency and comprehension.

Discussion

Many youngsters in the early grades do not receive the necessary amount and kind of modeling they need to become fluent readers. Children who are barely able to read may spend a good deal of time practicing reading with a partner, who also can barely read. Or they may sit quietly during sustained silent reading pretending to read a book, trying to do what they are not yet able to do: independently read books that interest them. At a time in their school career when they desperately need to hear and see good reading being modeled, they may not receive it.

When these students reach middle or high school, they are often years behind in reading and still do not receive the modeling they require to move ahead (Carbo, 2007). Through the use of certain assisted reading methods, effective support is provided to students, especially older struggling readers. For example, Heckelman (1969) reported that older students reading at least three years below level gained 1.9 years in reading comprehension in just six weeks with the neurological impress method, and Queiruga (1992) reported that 33 10th grade special education students who were reading from six to nine years below grade level gained 2.2 years in reading comprehension using the recording method described in Figure 3.2 (p. 108).

The appropriate use of assisted reading methods provides the modeling that young readers and struggling readers need. The idea behind this group of reading methods is simple and powerful. Students who are not yet independent readers, especially those reading below their potential, need frequent modeling of high-interest reading materials. During this modeling, a competent reader reads aloud a portion of a high-interest, somewhat challenging story or text, while the less able reader listens to and looks at the words being read. If done correctly, after several repetitions of this process, the less-able reader is usually able to read back the passage with good fluency and comprehension.

Assisted reading methods help students to read with good fluency and accuracy. When that happens, the brain is freed to attend to the *meaning* of what is being read. If students spend a great deal of attention trying to decode words, they are unable to give necessary attention to understanding what they are reading (Carbo, 2007; LaBerge & Samuels, 1974; Perfetti, 1985; Stanovich, 1980). The correct use of assisted reading methods provides the scaffolding that emerging and at-risk readers need to *bypass* the decoding process, read fluently, and concentrate on meaning.

Classroom Examples

There are many kinds of assisted reading methods. To understand their relationship and purpose, refer to the Continuum of Assisted Reading Methods (see Figure 3.2, p. 108). Those methods that provide the most assistance to the reader are at the base of the model. Moving from the bottom to the top of the continuum, each method provides increasingly less assistance or modeling. The strategies at the bottom of the continuum should be used for sufficient periods of time during reading instruction so that beginning readers and at-risk readers become fluent in their reading.

For example, the recording method on the continuum has enabled students to make unusually high gains in reading fluency and comprehension, especially older struggling readers (Barber, Carbo, & Thomasson, 1998; Carbo, 1978a, 1978b; Molbeck, 1994; Queiruga, 1992). This method of recording differs from others in that very small amounts of text are recorded on one tape side or CD track, at a slower than usual pace, in chunked phrases with good expression. The student listens to the brief recorded passage two or three times while following along in the text, and then soon afterward reads that passage, or a portion of it, aloud to a teacher, a peer, or a volunteer. This recording method has enabled most at-risk readers to master and fluently read back passages that are above their grade level. To hear stories and books recorded with this method visit the National Reading Styles Institute Web site at www.nrsi.com.

When a student is struggling to read using an assisted reading method, a method that is lower

FIGURE 3.2

Continuum of Assisted Reading Methods

By Marie Carbo

Low Teacher Involvement, High Student Independence

Sustained Silent Reading	Each person in the classroom, including the teacher, reads alone. Emphasis is placed on self-selection of reading materials and reading for pleasure.
Paired Reading	Two students take turns reading a passage or story.
Choral Reading	Two or more read a passage in unison.
Echo Reading	The teacher reads aloud a small portion of a reading selection (e.g., a sentence or paragraph), and the student reads it back.
Recorded Books	Less able readers listen one to three times to short amounts of text recorded at a slower-than-usual pace, and then read the passage aloud (Carbo, 1978a).
Neurological Impress	The teacher sits behind the youngster and reads into the child's ear. The student holds the book and reads in unison with the teacher, while the teacher tracks the words (Heckelman, 1969).
Shared Reading	The teacher reads a story while pointing to the words. After a few readings, youngsters are encouraged to read along with the teacher.

High Teacher Involvement, Low Student Independence

©1993 by Marie Carbo. *Release your students' learning power.* Syosset, NY: National Reading Styles Institute.

on the continuum should be used. For instance, when a competent reader and a struggling reader are pair reading, the competent reader often is instructed to correct the struggling reader. The echo method would be a better choice than pair reading for these two youngsters. Instead of directing the two children to take turns reading, the competent reader would be instructed to read a portion of the story first (possibly a paragraph). Then the struggling reader would read that same paragraph back to the competent reader. The students would continue in this way until the designated selection was finished. In this way, the struggling reader hears the passage modeled before reading it.

Resources

Bradsby, Wise, Mundell, & Haas, 1992; Brooks, 1991; Carbo, 1978a, 1978b, 2007; Chomsky, 1978; Dowhower, 1991; Heckelman, 1969; Hoffman, 1987; Koskinea et al., 1999; Krashen, 2002; Kuhn & Stahl,

2000; LaBerge & Samuels, 1974; Molbeck, 1994; Morris & Nelson, 1992; Perfetti, 1985; Queiruga, 1992; Reutzel, Hollingsworth, & Eldredge, 1994; Stanovich, 1980.

Strategy 3.6:

Accommodate students' interests, abilities, and reading styles.

Discussion

According to William Glasser, students need to feel important in school; they need to be able to say, "Someone listens to me; someone thinks that what I have to say is important; someone is willing to do what I say." When their basic needs for recognition and power are ignored, many children "pay little attention to academic subjects" and, instead, engage "in a desperate search for . . . acceptance" that can lead to behavioral problems (Gough, 1987). This observation is particularly true for adolescent readers.

On the other hand, students whose teachers accommodate their interests, abilities, and styles tend to experience a sense of power, which can lead, in turn, to more effective learning and improved behavior. Instructional approaches that virtually force students to learn to read, ignoring what they have already learned and using materials that fail to engage them, tend to ensure failure and loss of self-esteem. Approaches that capitalize on students' strengths and interests tend to increase their self-confidence and their reading achievement.

Struggling readers, in particular, need to learn how to capitalize on their learning strengths while compensating for their weaknesses.

Teachers can identify young people's interests, abilities, and reading styles through observations, artwork, checklists, interviews, and inventories. They can then use this information to plan instruction; they can also share it with students and their parents, along with suggestions for work that can be accomplished at home.

Classroom Examples

Teachers can learn to observe students' reading styles and plan instruction based on their observations. They might, for example, ask students to draw pictures related to reading. Students could draw pictures of where they like to read, such as a favorite reading chair or couch, and their preferred type of lighting. Or teachers might ask students to describe their favorite reading partners and their favorite time of day for reading. Teachers could share their observations with other teachers, students, and students' parents or guardians. Inventories such as the Reading Style Inventory (Carbo, 1992a) provide computerized profiles that describe students' reading styles and compatible reading strategies.

To identify students' reading interests, teachers can design a simple Reading Interests Inventory; youngsters could even help design this inventory as a class or schoolwide project. The Reading Interests Inventory can be used as a guide for selecting and accumulating books for a class or school library. The inventory should, of course, include questions about students' interests, such as

- Their general interests (e.g., sports, food, software, baseball, cars, chess, dancing, kites, music, machinery).

- The types of reading materials they enjoy (e.g., storybooks, books with facts, textbooks, readers, comic books, magazines, newspapers, plays, poems, picture books).

- The types of books they enjoy (e.g., adventure, science fiction, humor, science, history, romance, mystery, mythology, fiction, nonfiction).

Resources

Allington, 1984; Anderson, Heibert, Scott, & Wilkinson, 1985; Barber, Carbo, & Thomasson, 1998; Carbo, 1987, 1989, 1992a, 1992b; Carlisle & Beeman, 2000; Clay, 1979; Dunn, Griggs, Olson, Gorman, & Beasley, 1995; Garcia & Pearson, 1990; Gough, 1987; Grant, 1985; International Reading Association, 1999; Kapinus, Gambrell, & Koskinen, 1987; Love, 1988; Mohrmann, 1990; Morrow, Sharkey, & Firestone, 1993; Oglesby & Suter, 1995; Palincsar & Brown, 1984; Pearson, Roehler, Dole, & Duffy, 1992; Skipper, 1997; Slavin & Cheung, 2004; Snyder, 1994, 1997; Thies, 1999/2000.

Strategy 3.7:

Activate students' prior knowledge to help students understand and respond to reading selections.

Discussion

Students bring their own unique prior knowledge to the reading of any text. They often profit from guidance and support as they access their background experiences related to the information in a reading selection. To activate students' prior knowledge, teachers may ask students to draw on their personal experiences, perhaps by remembering a similar story, a place they visited, or something that happened to them. Teachers can assist this process by showing pictures, encouraging the sharing of anecdotes, and using graphic aids related to the story and vocabulary.

Teachers can help youngsters link their own language to unfamiliar vocabulary or to a "bookish" syntactical sequence. To do this, teachers might use language features contained in the story during the discussion of the story, carefully and deliberately enunciate unusual words, use particular sentence patterns two or three times, or ask students to repeat several times difficult language or pronunciation after hearing the teacher's model. These techniques help ready the mind and ear of the students and enable them to process novel words, phrases, and concepts more easily (Clay, 1991).

Teachers can ask questions to help students consider their relevant prior knowledge. Specific strategies—for example, K-W-L (what I *know*, what I *want* to learn, and what I *learned*)—help to structure the activation, application, and integration of students' prior knowledge. Reciprocal teaching allows students to consistently activate and apply prior knowledge as they make predictions about a reading selection.

Classroom Examples

The teacher using K-W-L draws three columns on the board with the following headings: "Know," "Want to Learn," and "Learned." Students offer information that they already know about the topic to be written in the first column. Then, to guide their reading, students generate questions about what they want to find out from their reading. After completing the reading, students fill in the third column with descriptions of what they have learned.

In addition to the K-W-L strategy, previewing techniques such as probable passages and story frames, graphic organizers, and guided reading may be used in the classroom. To create a probable passage and story frame, the teacher chooses vocabulary words from a reading selection and helps students categorize the words according to the elements of a story frame (e.g., setting, characters, problem, solution, ending). The students use the story frame to predict a story line, writing the categorized terms into a "probable passage"—that is, the probable direction of the story. Students then read the selection. Finally, they modify the story frame and probable passage to reflect the actual reading selection.

To develop a graphic organizer, the teacher identifies and lists all of the vocabulary that students need in order to understand a story (or other type of text). The teacher chooses an appropriate diagram as a visual framework for the selection. This diagram, or graphic organizer, will help students grasp the text's organization and the relationships between the concepts. The teacher presents the graphic organizer by explaining the terms and their relationship to one another. Students may then elaborate on their experiences with the topic.

Resources

Anderson, Heibert, Scott, & Wilkinson, 1985; Anderson & Pearson, 1984; Clay, 1979, 1991; Kapinus, Gambrell, & Koskinen, 1987; Ogle, 1986; Pearson, Roehler, Dole, & Duffy, 1992; Stahl & Vancil, 1986; Strickland & Morrow, 1989; Wang & Palincsar, 1989.

Strategy 3.8:

Use systematic, varied strategies for recognizing words in meaningful contexts to promote fluency and to give students control over their reading.

Discussion

Teachers need to use methods that help students master the complexity of reading rather than simply focus on isolated skills. Reading instruction should always support the notion of reading as a tool for building meaning and understanding. Students should be provided with a repertoire of strategies for recognizing words, including the use of phonics, context, word family patterns, and structural analysis. Young people who experience difficulty using one method should be given the opportunity to try an alternative approach that better accommodates their reading style. Instruction should be fun and thought-provoking; it should complement the interests and strengths of each student.

Classroom Examples

Teachers need to teach students different strategies for decoding words, such as reading ahead a bit and using context clues, sounding out words, or comparing new words to patterns within words they already know. Direct

111

instruction and application in meaningful reading situations supports the development of reading fluency and independence as students find that they can apply strategies in an even wider range of contexts. Inquiry is often useful for helping students discover for themselves patterns and relationships among words.

For students who find inquiry methods frustrating, direct instruction should be used. For example, those who have difficulty with context clues may find phonics or structural analysis particularly helpful. On the other hand, when students have great difficulty sounding out words because they cannot hear or remember letter sounds, the teacher should emphasize context clues and other approaches that students can use. Ultimately, students should have a repertoire of strategies that they can apply flexibly in a variety of contexts.

Resources

Adams, 1990; Anderson, Heibert, Scott, & Wilkinson, 1985; Brophy, 1987; Brophy & Good, 1986; Clay, 1979; Fisher, Frey, & Williams, 2002; Garcia & Pearson, 1990; Gough, 1987; Grant, 1985; Holdaway, 1979; Love, 1988; Moore, Bean, Birdyshaw, & Rycik, 1999; Passow, 1990; Samuels, Schermer, & Reinking, 1992; Stahl, Duffy-Hester, & Stahl, 1998.

Strategy 3.9:
Model skills and strategies for successful reading.

Discussion

Explicit modeling of reading processes and the application of strategies increase reading achievement. For example, assisted reading methods (discussed in Strategy 3.5 and described in Figure 3.2) model fluent, expressive reading for students. These reading methods enable students to simultaneously see and hear the words in stories. They build students' sight vocabulary, fluency, listening, vocabulary, and comprehension.

Other modeling and scaffolding strategies enable students to understand how, what, and why a person reads. These include inquiry strategies that promote divergent thinking, different levels of thinking, and personal responses. Additional modeling and scaffolding strategies include reciprocal teaching and Question-Answer Relationships, or QAR (Raphael, 1982).

Classroom Examples

Reciprocal teaching is a structured approach that allows students to gradually and independently apply reading strategies within a meaningful context. The teacher reads a section of the text, models a summary of what was read, asks a question about the text, clarifies potential areas of confusion, and predicts what will come next. After several instances of such modeling, the teacher turns over the leadership of the group to a student, and that student provides the modeling. This teaching strategy can be varied to allow for the gradual introduction of reading strategies, one at a time, or the use of collaborative approaches, such as students working in pairs to develop their summaries, questions, clarifications, and predictions.

The use of Question-Answer Relationships involves teaching students how to analyze a question in order to find the correct answer or answers. Students learn how to place questions in one of three categories: *Right There, Think and Search,* and *On My Own.* The *Right There* category is for questions that have an answer explicit in the reading—that is, the words in the question and the words in the answer are *Right There* in the same sentence. *Think and Search* also involves a question that has an answer in the reading, but this answer requires information from more than one sentence or paragraph. *On My Own* involves a question for which the answer must be found in the reader's own knowledge; in other words, the information is relevant to the story but does not appear in it. Students receive feedback concerning their ability to identify a QAR as *Right There, Think and Search,* or *On My Own;* their ability to use the QAR to locate the answer; and their ability to provide an adequate answer.

Resources

Adams, 1990; Anderson, Heibert, Scott, & Wilkinson, 1985; Bloome, 1985; Cazden, 1983; Morrow, 1989; Paris, 1986; Pearson & Fielding, 1991; Pearson, Roehler, Dole, & Duffy, 1992; Pressley, Woloshyn, Lysynchuk, & Martin, 1990; Raphael, 1982; Slavin, 1980, 1986; Strickland & Morrow, 1989; Sturtevant, 2003; Wang & Palincsar, 1989; Wasik & Slavin, 1990.

Strategy 3.10:

Integrate reading, writing, listening, and speaking activities to enable students to make natural connections among the disciplines.

Discussion

When students have the opportunity to engage in a range of language activities, they can observe and use the patterns of language in different ways. By listening to stories, for instance, they learn that stories have structure and similar components, such as characters and plot. This knowledge helps to guide their own reading. Story writing enables students to learn firsthand about the types of decisions that authors need to make. When writing a story, students can apply the knowledge of writing style, story structure, and language that they have gained from listening to, speaking about, and reading stories.

Talking with adults and peers about what they have read or written gives students insights into the meaning of texts and how that meaning is conveyed through language. Students develop these insights not only through listening to peers but also through the process of articulating their own perceptions and interpretations. When teachers are sensitive to and accepting of the differences in the expressive language abilities of diverse youngsters, they show that they are ready to assist students in their language development.

Besides allowing students to make connections among the varied uses of language, integrated activities provide opportunities for students to perceive the differences in the uses of language for different purposes and in different contexts. For example, students learn that writing a story often requires language different from that used in retelling a story.

Classroom Examples

To assist emerging readers and writers, teachers model and describe the purposes and writing styles of authors, and encourage students to draw parallels between these models and their own writings. They also encourage students to listen to the ideas and interpretations of their peers through student-directed discussions of reading selections (possibly in small reading groups). As students develop their reading and writing abilities, teachers introduce them to more difficult and varied writing styles, which they may discuss, review, critique, and imitate.

Asking students to imitate the writing style of an author is an activity that helps students integrate reading, writing, listening, and speaking. This is especially appropriate for students who have listened to many stories by the same author. The teacher begins the activity by calling attention to the author's style, such as how the author usually begins a story, develops the plot, or describes the characters. Students then write stories in the same style. They might then send their stories to the author along with an invitation to visit their classroom to talk about writing.

Resources

Anderson, Heibert, Scott, & Wilkinson, 1985; Calkins, 1983; Clay, 1979, 1986; Cunningham & Hall, 1998; Goodman, Goodman, & Hood, 1989; Harste, Short, & Burke, 1988; Heald-Taylor, 1987; Hiebert & Raphael, 1998; Holdaway, 1979; Langer & Applebee, 1983; Larrick, 1987; Pressley, 1998, 2001; Strickland & Morrow, 1989; Teale, 1987; Tierney, Soter, O'Flahavan, & McGinley, 1989.

Strategy 3.11:
Promote home/school partnerships.

Discussion

Many school-age children in the United States today watch too much television and read too little. Voluntary reading and library use decline sharply throughout the grades, making it difficult for many students, especially those at risk of academic failure, to learn to read well enough to function effectively in school.

Schools need to emphasize the importance of reading at home through a variety of activities with parents, guardians, and families. Workshops can be offered at convenient times to

• Help parents understand the importance of reading at home.

• Demonstrate techniques for reading with youngsters.

• Provide hands-on practice with shared reading activities.

• Show parents or guardians how to secure a library card for their child.

• Demonstrate how to use recordings of books in the home.

• Help parents or guardians understand their child's particular interests and style of learning.

Parents or guardians should be given specific activities that will enable them to play an active role in monitoring and assisting with assigned homework or school tasks. They need to be encouraged to regularly read aloud to children while limiting television viewing to less than 10 hours weekly.

Classroom Examples

Teachers might offer an intergenerational reading workshop in which parents and guardians are shown procedures for effectively reading a book to a child; for example, positioning the book during reading, involving the child in the story through questions and comments, and taking turns with the child to read the story using some of the assisted reading methods described in Strategy 3.5 and Figure 3.2.

To teach parents these assisted reading methods, teachers need to model the method first and then ask parents to practice the method. An effective procedure is to videotape a method being used correctly in the classroom, play the videotape for parents, model the method with a student, and then discuss the method and list the procedures with parents. Parents can be asked to practice the method with their own child. At an intergenerational workshop, parents can actually practice an assisted reading method with their child.

To help parents or guardians provide books for their children at home, teachers might establish a classroom library of books that students can check out. During the workshop for parents or guardians, the procedures for securing and using a library card can be role played and

discussed. Parents can learn how to create games that help children practice sight words and build their vocabulary. Parents usually enjoy learning how to read to their child and appreciate lists of possible books to borrow or purchase.

Resources

Anderson & Pearson, 1984; Benjamin & Lord, 1996; Chall, 1993; Gilliam, Gerla, & Wright, 2004; Jordan, Snow, & Porche, 2000; Morrow, 1990; Morrow & Young, 1997; Neuman, Caperelli, & Kee, 1998; Ollila & Mayfield, 1992; Slavin & Cheung, 2004; Strickland & Morrow, 1989; Taylor & Strickland, 1986; Teale, 1984, 1987; Trelease, 2006.

Strategy 3.12:

Provide authentic purposes, materials, and audiences for reading, writing, listening, and speaking.

Discussion

In the real world, people do things for real purposes. For example, adults may write to entertain and inform others, to persuade, to bring about action, to manage activities, to gain personal insights, or to keep records.

In school, students need audiences and purposes for reading, writing, and speaking that relate to the world outside of school. Teachers need to provide young people not only with well-written books and stories whose primary purpose is to entertain and inform, but also with materials related to the world outside the classroom, such as newspapers, maps, directions, brochures, advertisements, and directories.

Classroom Examples

Teachers can provide authentic purposes, materials, and audiences for students with activities such as planning and conducting a school fair, writing and performing in a play, or raising money for a trip. During a project, youngsters might take notes, devise schedules, share work, make posters and costumes, discuss problems that arise, and report their findings.

Interdisciplinary teaching and learning occur quite naturally when youngsters work on large-scale projects. If, for example, students first identify a local environmental or community problem, they might then read newspaper items about the problem, science and social studies articles and texts, and relevant laws. After discussion, and possibly debates, they could write their own editorials, articles, and letters, and they might find it necessary to begin corresponding with people who are knowledgeable about the issue. Students might place key pieces of the information they accumulate in a large book or portfolio; they might also design bulletin boards to display their work. And they might share with other classes the knowledge they've gained. These are but a few of the multitude of activities and learning situations that could be classified as "authentic."

Resources

Anderson, Heibert, Scott, & Wilkinson, 1985; Brophy, 1987; Bussis, Chittenden, Amarel, & Klausner, 1985; Clay, 1979; Goodman, Goodman, & Hood, 1989; Hansen, 1987; Harste, Woodward, & Burke, 1984; Jongsma, 1989; Knapp & Turnbull, 1990; Langer & Applebee, 1983; Pearson & Fielding, 1991; Pressley, 2001; Wolf, 1989.

Bibliography

Adams, M. J. (1990). *Beginning to read: Thinking and learning about print.* Cambridge, MA: Bradford Books/MIT Press.

Allington, R. L. (2001). *What really matters for struggling readers: Designing research-based programs.* New York: Addison Wesley Longman.

Alvermann, D. E. (2002, Summer). Effective literacy instruction for adolescents. *Journal of Literacy Research, 34*(2), 189–208. (ERIC Document Reproduction Service No. EJ672862)

Anderson, R. C. (1996). Research foundations to support wide reading. In V. Greaney (Ed.), *Promoting reading in developing countries.* Newark, DE: International Reading Association.

Anderson, R. C., Heibert, E. H., Scott, J. A., & Wilkinson, I. A. (1985). *Becoming a nation of readers: The report of the commission on reading.* Urbana, IL: Illinois University, Center for the Study of Reading and Washington, DC: National Academy of Education.

Anderson, R. C., & Pearson, P. D. (1984). *A schema–theoretic view of basic processes in reading comprehension* (Technical Report No. 306). Cambridge, MA: Bolt, Beranek, and Newman; and Urbana, IL: Illinois University, Center for the Study of Reading.

Barber, L., Carbo, M., & Thomasson, R. (1998). *A comparative study of the reading styles program to extant programs of teaching reading.* Bloomington, IN: Phi Delta Kappa.

Benjamin, L. A., & Lord, J. (1996). *Family literacy.* Washington, DC: Office of Education Research and Improvement.

Bloome, D. (1985). Reading as a social process. *Language Arts, 62*(2), 134–142.

Bracey, G. W. (2006). The 16th Bracey report on the condition of public education. *Phi Delta Kappan, 78*(2), 151–166.

Bradsby, S., Wise, J., Mundell, S., & Haas, S. (1992). Making a difference for L.D. students: Matching reading instruction to reading styles through recorded books. *Research in the Classroom.* (ERIC Document Reproduction Service No. ED 347765)

Brooks, J. D. (1991). *Teaching to identified learning styles: The effects upon oral and silent reading and listening comprehension.* Unpublished doctoral dissertation, University of Toledo.

Brophy, J. (1987, October). Synthesis of research on strategies for motivating students to learn. *Educational Leadership, 45*(2), 40–48.

Brophy, J., & Good, T. L. (1986). Teacher behavior and student achievement. In M. C. Wittrock (Ed.), *Handbook of research on teaching* (3rd ed.). New York: Macmillan and London: Collier Macmillan.

Bussis, A., Chittenden, E., Amarel, M., & Klausner, E. (1985). *Inquiry into meaning: An investigation of learning to read.* Hillsdale, NJ: Erlbaum.

Caine, R. N., Caine, G., McClintic, C., & Klimek, K. (2005). *12 brain mind learning principles in action.* Thousand Oaks, CA: Corwin Press.

Calkins, L. M. (1983). *Lessons from a child: On the teaching and learning of writing.* Exeter, NH: Heinemann.

Carbo, M. (1978a). How to make books talk to children. *The Reading Teacher, 32*(3), 267–273.

Carbo, M. (1978b). A word imprinting technique for children with severe memory disorders. *Teaching Exceptional Children, 11*(1), 3–5.

Carbo, M. (1987). Deprogramming reading failure: Giving unequal learners an equal chance. *Phi Delta Kappan, 69*(3), 97–202.

Carbo, M. (1992a). *Reading style inventory.* Syosset, NY: National Reading Styles Institute.

Carbo, M. (1992b). Eliminating the need for dumbed-down textbooks. *Educational Horizons, 70*(4), 189–193.

Carbo, M. (2007). *Becoming a great teacher of reading: Achieving high rapid reading gains with powerful, differentiated strategies.* Thousand Oaks, CA: Corwin Press.

Carlisle, J. F., & Beeman, M. M. (2000). The effects of language of instruction on the reading and writ-ing achievement of first-grade Hispanic children. *Scientific Studies of Reading, 4*(4), 331–353.

Cazden, C. B. (1983). Adult assistance to language development scaffolds, models, and direct instruction. In R. P. Parker & F. A. Davis (Eds.), *Developing literacy: Young children's understanding of language.* Newark, DE: International Reading Association.

Chall, J. S. (1993). Why poor children fall behind in reading: What schools can do about it. *Effective School Practices, 12*(2), 29–36.

Chomsky, C. (1978). When you still can't read in third grade after decoding, what? *Language Arts, 53*(3), 288–296.

Cipielewski, J., & Stanovich, K. (1992). Predicting growth in reading ability from children's exposure to print. *Journal of Experimental Child Psychology, 54*(1), 74–89.

Clarke, B. (2006). Breaking through to reluctant readers. *Educational Leadership, 63*(5), 66–69.

Clay, M. M. (1979). *The early detection of reading difficulties.* Portsmouth, NH: Heinemann.

Clay, M. M. (1986). Constructive processes: Talking, reading, writing, art, and craft. *The Reading Teacher, 39*(8), 764–770.

Clay, M. M. (1991). Introducing a new storybook to young readers. *The Reading Teacher, 45*(4), 264–279.

Cunningham, P., & Hall, D. (1998). The four blocks: A balanced framework for literacy in primary classrooms. In K. R. Harris, S. Graham, & D. Deshler. *Teaching every child every day: Learning in diverse schools and classrooms.* Cambridge, MA: Brookline Books.

Dickinson, D. K., & Smith, M. W. (1994). Long-term effects of preschool teachers' book readings on low–income children's vocabulary and story comprehension. *Reading Research Quarterly, 29*(2), 104–122.

Dillon, S. (2005a, October 20). Education law gets first test in U.S. schools [Online article]. *New York Times.* Available: http://www.nytimes.com/2005/10/20/national/20exam.html

Dillon, S. (2005b, December 16). Literacy falls for graduates from college, testing finds [Online article]. *New York Times*. Available: http://www.nytimes.com/2005/12/16/education/16literacy.html

Dillon, S. (2006a, September 23). Report says education officials violated rules [Online article]. *New York Times*. Available: http://www.nytimes.com/2006/09/23/education/23education.html?_r=1&oref=slogin

Dillon, S. (2006b, November 20). Schools slow in closing gaps between the races [Online article]. *New York Times*. Available: http://www.nytimes.com/2006/11/20/education/20gap.html?ei=5094&en=50afd2f22c6d9

Dowhower, S. L. (1991). Speaking of prosody: Fluency's unattended bedfellow. *Theory in Practice, 30*(3), 158–164.

Dunn, R., Griggs, S. A., Olson, J., Gorman, B., & Beasley, M. (1995). A meta-analytic validation of the Dunn and Dunn model of learning style preference. *Journal of Educational Research, 88*(6), 353–361.

Durkin, D. (1966). *Children who read early: Two longitudinal studies.* New York: Teachers College Press.

Eldredge, J. L., Reutzel, D. R., & Hollingsworth, P. M. (1996). Comparing the effectiveness of two oral reading practices: Round-robin reading and the shared book experience. *Journal of Literacy Research, 28*(2), 201–225.

Fisher, D., Frey, N., & Williams, D. (2002). Seven literacy strategies that work. *Educational Leadership, 60*(3), 70–73.

Flippo, R. F. (1998). Points of agreement: A display of professional unity in our field. *The Reading Teacher, 52*(1), 30–40.

Flippo, R. F. (2001). *Reading researchers in search of common ground.* Newark, DE: International Reading Association.

Foertsch, M. A. (1992). *Reading in and out of school: Factors influencing the literacy achievement of American students in Grades 4, 8, and 12, in 1988 and 1990.* Washington, DC: Office of Educational Research and Improvement.

Fractor, G. S., Woodruff, M. C., Martinez, M. G., & Teale, W. H. (1993). Let's not miss opportunities to promote voluntary reading: Classroom libraries in the elementary school. *The Reading Teacher, 46*(6), 476–484.

Franklin, J. (2006). NCLB a year before reauthorization. *Education Update, 48*(7), 1, 7–8.

Garcia, G. E., & Pearson, P. D. (1990). Modifying reading instruction to maximize its effectiveness for all students. Cambridge, MA: Bolt, Beranek, and Newman.

Gilliam, B., Gerla, J. P., & Wright, G. (2004). Providing minority parents with relevant literacy activities for their children. *Reading Improvement, 41*(4), 226–234.

Goodman, H. S., Goodman, Y. M., & Hood, W. J. (1989). *The whole language evaluation book.* Portsmouth, NH: Heinemann.

Gough, P. B. (1987, May). The key to improving schools: An interview with William Glasser. *Phi Delta Kappan, 68*(9), 656–662.

Grant, S. M. (1985, October). The kinesthetic approach to teaching: Building a foundation for learning. *Journal of Learning Disabilities, 18*(8), 455–462.

Guthrie, J. T., Schafer, W. D., & Huang, C. (2001). Benefits of opportunity to read and balanced instruction on the NAEP. *Journal of Educational Research, 94*(3), 145–162.

Harste, J., Woodward, V., & Burke, C. (1984). *Language stories and literacy lessons.* Portsmouth, NH: Heinemann.

Heald-Taylor, G. (1987). Predictable literature selections and activities for language arts instruction. *The Reading Teacher, 41*(1), 6–12.

Heckelman, R. G. (1969). A neurological-impress method of remedial reading instruction. *Academic Therapy Quarterly, 4*(4), 277–282.

Hiebert, E. H., & Raphael, T. E. (1998). *Early reading instruction.* New York: Harcourt Brace.

Hoffman, J., Roser, N. L., & Battle, J. (1993). Reading aloud in classrooms: From the modal to a 'model'. *The Reading Teacher, 46*(6), 496–503.

Holdaway, D. (1979). *The foundations of literacy.* Exeter, NH: Heinemann.

Holdaway, D. (1982). Shared book experience: Teaching reading using favorite books. *Theory Into Practice, 21*(4), 293–300.

International Reading Association. (1999). *Summary of adolescent literacy: A position statement for the commission on adolescent literacy of the International Reading Association.* Washington, DC: Author.

IRA responds to report on Reading First. (2006, October/November). *Reading Today, 24*(2), 1.

Jensen, E. (1998). *Introduction to brain compatible learning.* San Diego: The Brain Store.

Jongsma, K. S. (1989). Portfolio assessment. *The Reading Teacher, 43*(3), 264–265.

Jordan, G. E., Snow, C. E., & Porche, M. V. (2000). Project EASE: The effect of a family literacy project on kindergarten students' early literacy skills. *Reading Research Quarterly, 35*(4), 524–546.

Kapinus, B. A., Gambrell, L. B., & Koskinen, P. S. (1987). Effects of practice in re-telling upon the reading comprehension of proficient and less proficient readers. In J. E. Readence & R. S. Baldwin (Eds.), *Research in literacy: Merging perspectives.* 36th Yearbook of the National Reading Conference. Rochester, NY: National Reading Conference.

Karweit, N. (1989). Effective kindergarten programs and practices for students at risk. In R. E. Slavin, N. L. Karweit, & N. A. Madden (Eds.), *Effective programs for students at risk.* Boston: Allyn and Bacon.

Koskinea, P. S., Blum, I. H., Bisson, S. A., Phillips, S. M., Creamer, T. S., & Baker, T. K. (1999). Shared reading, books, and audio tapes: Supporting diverse students in school and at home. *The Reading Teacher, 52*(8), 430–444.

Kozol, J. (2005). Confections of apartheid: A stick-and-carrot pedagogy for the children of our inner-city poor. *Phi Delta Kappan, 87*(4), 264–275.

Krashen, S. (1993). *The power of reading: Insights from the research.* Englewood, CO: Libraries Unlimited.

Krashen, S. (2002). More smoke and mirrors: A critique of the national reading panel report on fluency. In R. L. Allington (Ed.), *Big brother and the national reading curriculum.* Portsmouth, NH: Heinemann.

Kuhn, M. R., & Stahl, S. A. (2000). *Fluency: A review of development and remedial practices.* Ann Arbor, MI: Center for the Improvement of Early Reading Achievement.

LaBerge, D., & Samuels, S. J. (1974). Toward a theory of automatic information processing in reading. *Cognitive Psychology, 6,* 293–323.

Langer, J. A., & Applebee, A. N. (1983). Instructional scaffolding: Reading and writing as natural language activities. *Language Arts, 60*(2), 168–175.

Larrick, N. (1987). Illiteracy starts too soon. *Phi Delta Kappan, 69*(3), 184–189.

Love, L. (1988, May). *The effect of reading games on the improvement of fourth grade reading skills scores.* Unpublished master's thesis, Kean College, New Jersey.

McCauley, J. K., & McCauley, D. S. (1992). Using choral reading to promote language learning for ESL students. *The Reading Teacher, 45*(7), 526–533.

Molbeck, C. H. (1994). Using recorded books with reluctant readers. *WSRA Journal, 38*(2), 39–42.

Moore, D. W., Bean, T. W., Birdyshaw, D., & Rycik, J. A. (1999). *Adolescent literacy: A position statement for the Commission on Adolescent Literacy of the International Reading Association.* Newark, DE: International Reading Association. (ERIC Document Reproduction Service No. ED437640)

Morris, D., & Nelson, L. (1992). Supported oral reading and low achieving second graders. *Reading Research and Instruction, 32*(1), 49–63.

Morrow, L. M. (1982). Relationships between literature programs, library corner designs, and children's use of literature. *Journal of Educational Research, 75*(6), 339–344.

Morrow, L. M. (1990). Preparing the classroom environment to promote literacy during play. *Early Childhood Research Quarterly, 5*(4), 537–554.

Morrow, L. M., Sharkey, E., & Firestone, W. A. (1993, Spring). *Promoting independent reading and writing through self-directed literary activities in a collab-*

orative setting (Reading Research Report No. 2). Athens, GA: National Reading Research Center.

Morrow, L. M., & Young, J. (1997). Parent, teacher, and child participation in a collaborative family literacy program: The effects of attitude, motivation, and literacy achievement. *Journal of Educational Psychology, 89,* 736–742.

National Association of Secondary School Principals. (2005). *Creating a culture of literacy: A guide for middle and high school principals.* Reston, VA: Author.

National Center for Education Statistics. (2007). *The nation's report card: Reading.* Washington, DC: U.S. Department of Education. Available: http://nces.ed.gov/nationsreportcard/reading

Neuman, S. B. (1999). Books make a difference: A study of access to literacy. *Reading Research Quarterly, 34*(3), 286–311.

Neuman, S. B., Caperelli, B. J., & Kee, C. (1998). Literacy learning, a family matter. *The Reading Teacher, 52*(3), 244–252.

Newkirk, T. (2003, September 10). The quiet crisis in boys' literacy [Online article]. *Education Week.* Available: http://www.edweek.org/ew/articles/2003/09/10/02newkirk.h23.html?querystring=comic%20books&print=1

Ogle, D. (1986). K–W–L: A teaching model that develops active comprehension of expository text. *The Reading Teacher, 39*(6), 564–570.

Oglesby, F., & Suter, W. N. (1995). Matching reading styles and reading instruction. *Research in the Schools, 2*(1), 11–15.

Ollila, L. O., & Mayfield, M. I. (1992). Home and school together: Helping beginning readers succeed. In S. J. Samuels & A. E. Farstrup (Eds.), *What research has to say about reading instruction.* Newark, DE: International Reading Association.

Olson, L. (2005, December 7). Nationwide standards eyed anew. *Education Week, 25*(14), 24.

Palincsar, A. S., & Brown, A. L. (1984). Reciprocal teaching of comprehension-fostering and comprehension-monitoring activities. *Cognition and Instruction, 1*(12), 117–175.

Palincsar, A. S., Englert, C. S., Raphael, T. E., & Gavelek, J. R. (1991, May/June). Examining the context of strategy instruction. *Remedial and Special Education, 12*(3), 43–53.

Paris, S. G. (1986). Teaching children to guide their reading and learning. In T. E. Raphael (Ed.), *The contexts of school–based literacy.* New York: Random House.

Pearson, P. D., & Fielding, L. (1991). Comprehension instruction. In R. Barr, M. L. Kamil, P. B. Mosenthal, & P. D. Pearson (Eds.), *Handbook of reading research* (Vol. 2). New York: Longman.

Pearson, P. D., Roehler, L. R., Dole, L. A., & Duffy, G. G. (1992). Developing expertise in reading comprehension. In S. J. Samuels & A. E. Farstrup (Eds.), *What research has to say about reading instruction.* Newark, DE: International Reading Association.

Perfetti, C. A. (1985). *Reading ability.* New York: Oxford University Press.

Pressley, M. (1998). *Reading instruction that works: The case for balanced teaching.* New York: Guilford.

Pressley, M. (2001). *Effective beginning reading instruction* (Executive summary and paper commissioned by the National Reading Conference). Chicago: National Reading Conference.

Pressley, M., Woloshyn, V., Lysynchuk, L., & Martin, V. (1990). A primer of research on cognitive strategy instruction: The important issues and how to address them. *Educational Psychology Review, 2*(1), 1–58.

Queiruga, L. (1992). *A reading styles experiment with learning–disabled high school students.* Syosset, NY: National Reading Styles Institute.

Raphael, T. E. (1982, November). Question-answering strategies for children. *The Reading Teacher, 36*(2), 186–190.

Ravitch, D. (2005, November 7). Every state left behind [Online article]. *New York Times.* Available: http://www.nytimes.com/2005/11/07/opinion/07ravitch.html

Reutzel, D. R., Hollingsworth, P. M., & Eldredge, L. (1994). Oral reading instruction: The impact on student reading development. *Reading Research Quarterly, 29*(1), 40–62.

Reutzel, D. R., & Smith, J. A. (2004). Accelerating struggling readers' progress: A comparative analysis of expert opinion and current research recommendations. *Reading & Writing Quarterly, 20*(1), 63–89.

Romano, L. (2005, October 20). Test scores move little in math, reading. *Washington Post*, pp. 20, A1–3.

Salinger, T. (1988). *Language arts and literacy for young children*. Columbus, OH: Merrill.

Samuels, S. J., Schermer, N., & Reinking, D. (1992). Reading fluency techniques for making decoding automatic. In S. J. Samuels & A. E. Farstrup (Eds.), *What research has to say about reading instruction* (2nd ed.). Newark, DE: International Reading Association.

Skipper, B. (1997). Reading with style. *American School Board Journal, 184*(2), 36–37.

Slavin, R. (1980, March). Cooperative learning: Can students help students learn? *Instructor, 96*(7), 74–78.

Slavin, R. (1986). *Using student team learning* (3rd ed.). Baltimore: Johns Hopkins University Press.

Slavin, R. E., & Cheung, A. (2004). *A synthesis of research on language of reading instruction for English language learners*. Institute of Education Sciences, U.S. Department of Education (Grant No. OERI–R–117–40005).

Smith, M. W., & Wilhelm, J. D. (2002). *Reading don't fix no Chevy's: Literacy in the lives of young men*. Portsmouth, NH: Heinemann.

Snyder, A. E. (1994). On the road to reading recovery. *The School Administrator, 51*(1), 23–24.

Snyder, A. E. (1997). *Utilization of a systemic design and learning styles model as a paradigm for restructuring education*. Unpublished doctoral dissertation, Tennessee State University.

Spellings, M. (2006, April 27). Remarks presented at U.S. Department of Education No Child Left Behind Summit, Philadelphia. Available: www.ed.gov

Sprenger, M. (1999). *Learning and memory: The brain in action*. Alexandria, VA: Association for Supervision and Curriculum Development.

Sprenger, M. (2003). *Differentiation through learning styles and memory*. Thousand Oaks, CA: Corwin Press.

Stahl, S. A., Duffy-Hester, A. M., & Stahl, K. A. D. (1998). Everything you wanted to know about phonics (but were afraid to ask). *Reading Research Quarterly, 33*(3), 338–355.

Stahl, S. A., & Vancil, S. J. (1986, October). Discussion is what makes semantic maps work in vocabulary instruction. *The Reading Teacher, 40*(1), 62–67.

Stanovich, K. E. (1980). Toward an interactive-compensatory model of individual differences in the development of reading fluency. *Reading Research Quarterly, 16*(1), 32–71.

Strickland, D. S., & Morrow, L. M. (1989). *Emerging literacy: Young children learn to read and write*. Newark, DE: International Reading Association.

Sturtevant, E. (2003). *The literacy coach: A key to improving teaching and learning in secondary schools*. Washington, DC: Alliance for Excellent Education.

Sulzby, E. (1985). Children's emergent reading of favorite storybooks: A developmental study. *Reading Research Quarterly, 20*(4), 458–481.

Taylor, B. M., Frye, B. J., & Maruyama, G. M. (1990). Time spent reading and reading growths. *American Educational Research Journal, 27*(2), 351–362.

Taylor, D., & Strickland, D. S. (1986). *Family storybook reading*. Portsmouth, NH: Heinemann.

Teale, W. H. (1984). Reading to young children: Its significance for literacy development. In H. Goelman, A. Oberg, & F. Smith (Eds.), *Awakening to literacy*. Portsmouth, NH: Heinemann.

Teale, W. H. (1987). Emergent literacy: Reading and writing development in early childhood. In J. E. Readence & R. S. Baldwin (Eds.), *Research in literacy: Merging perspectives*. Needham Heights, MA: Allyn and Bacon.

Thies, A. P. (1999/2000). The neuropsychology of learning styles. *National Forum of Applied Educational Research Journal, 13*(1), 50–62.

Tierney, R. J., Soter, A., O'Flahavan, J. F., & McGinley, W. (1989). The effects of reading and writing upon thinking critically. *Reading Research Quarterly, 24*(2), 134–173.

Trelease, J. (2006). *The read-aloud handbook* (6th ed.). New York: Penguin.

Tyre, P. (2006, January 30). The trouble with boys [Online article]. *Newsweek*. Available: http://www.msnbc.msn.com/id/10965522/site/newsweek/print/1/displaymode/1098/

Vacca, R. T., & Vacca, J. L. (1999). *Content area reading* (6th ed.). New York: Longman.

Wang, M. C., & Palincsar, A. S. (1989). Teaching students to assume an active role in their learning. In M. C. Reynolds (Ed.), *Knowledge base for the beginning teacher*. New York: Pergamon.

Wasik, B. A., & Slavin, R. E. (1990). Preventing early reading failure with one-to-one tutoring: A best evidence synthesis (Report No. 6). Baltimore: The Johns Hopkins University Center for Research on Effective Schooling for Disadvantaged Students.

Wigfield, A. (1997). Children's motivations for reading and reading engagement. In J. T. Guthrie & A. Wigfield (Eds.), *Reading engagement: Motivating readers through integrated instruction*. Newark, DE: International Reading Association.

Wolf, D. P. (April 1989). Portfolio assessment: Sampling student work. *Educational Leadership, 46*(7), 35–39.

Worthy, J., Moorman, M., & Turner, M. (1999). What Johnny likes to read is hard to find in school. *Reading Research Quarterly, 34*(1), 12–27.

Yopp, H. K. (1995). Read-aloud books for developing phonemic awareness: An annotated bibliography. *The Reading Teacher, 48*(6), 538–543.

4

Strategies to Promote Equity in Mathematics Education

Beatriz S. D'Ambrosio and Signe E. Kastberg

In 1995, D'Ambrosio, Johnson, and Hobbs wrote a chapter for *Educating Everybody's Children* (1995) titled "Strategies for Increasing Achievement in Mathematics." The focus then was to convey to readers the importance of teaching all children to understand mathematics in order to empower learners as young mathematicians. In reviewing that chapter for this revision, we realized that most of what had been described as effective teaching strategies in 1995 has not changed. We updated the references and made some minor changes in the text to more closely align this revised chapter with a focus on promoting equity by teaching all children to understand mathematics.

What *has* changed significantly in the past decade, however, is the context for conversations about teaching all children. Two major events have drastically shaped the opportunities for all children to learn mathematics. First, the release in 2000 of the *Principles and Standards for School Mathematics* (PSSM) by the National Council of Teachers of Mathematics (NCTM) set important directions for curriculum, instruction, and assessment in schools. Second, the passage of the No Child Left Behind (NCLB) Act in 2001 focused much public attention on testing, accountability, and the quality of teachers. The introduction of these two major documents into the national conversation about teaching and learning has unearthed many tensions—shifting between issues raised by teachers and educators to those raised by politicians and vocal members of the community.

Unfortunately, NCLB has demanded such intense focus on increasing test scores that many teachers and educators who are advocates for children have been silenced. The education and well-being of children in the United States may no longer be attended to as some school districts search for strategies to raise test scores rather than strategies to enhance student learning. According to several authors (Gutierrez, 2002; Howard, 2006), the main ingredient for promoting success for children in schools is believing in their ability and disposition to learn and to succeed. Too many teachers, educators, parents, and politicians do not believe in all children's ability to learn. Until all teachers, educators, parents, and especially politicians come to see all children as wanting and able to learn, we will continue to oppress some of them in our schools and, as a result, continue to witness their struggle to succeed in an environment of domination and coercion.

In the sections that follow, we supplement the chapter written in 1995 with commentary on the impact of the forces that have affected U.S. education in the past decade. First, we discuss the impact of the NCTM standards document (PSSM) and the resulting reform curriculum intended to help teachers implement the standards. Second, we discuss the NCLB Act; though a deep discussion of NCLB is beyond the scope of this chapter, we hope to plant the seeds for readers to further investigate the relationship among NCLB, the rhetoric that accompanies it, and its impact on the success of children who are underachieving in school.

NCTM Standards

The authors of the new version of the NCTM *Principles and Standards for School Mathematics* (2000) placed special emphasis on issues of equity by making the "equity principle" the first principle to be considered in teaching mathematics. The view of equity in school mathematics is grounded in the vision of "a classroom, school, or district where all students have access to high-quality, engaging mathematics instruction. There are ambitious expectations for all, with accommodations for those who need it" (p. 3). The equity principle makes three main points. First, for equity to be achieved, "high expectations and worthwhile opportunities for all" (p. 12) are required. Second, with the goal of supporting all students in their learning of important mathematics, accommodations must be provided. Third, achieving equity will require "resources and support for all classrooms and all students" (p. 14).

Combined with the other principles, the equity principle sets the vision for a school experience that empowers *all* students as learners of mathematics. In doing so, the PSSM document also empowers teachers to view themselves as mathematicians (to explore this point, see Schifter, 1998), to view every child as able to do mathematics, and to value the experience of the classroom community in exploring mathematics, with all members contributing to the collective knowledge that emerges from that experience. The PSSM document contains the underlying assumption that teachers have the best interest of children at heart. A deep respect for the work of teachers pervades the document.

Numerous empirical studies suggest that teachers have children's interest at heart when they make instructional decisions. For example, Sztajn (2003) explored the motivations and instructional practices of two elementary school teachers in light of their knowledge of reform as it was articulated in *Curriculum and Evaluation Standards for School Mathematics* (National Council of Teachers of Mathematics, 1989). Sztajn found that teachers' instructional decisions regarding "what is best, however, are value-laden; they are mediated by the distinct social contexts in which teachers operate and the different children they teach" (2003, p. 71). Thus students from different socioeconomic backgrounds were given the opportunity to learn different mathematics. The focus of instruction for children from lower socioeconomic backgrounds was basic skills and procedures. These results were echoed in reports of larger-scale studies undertaken by Spillane (2001) and by Kannapel, Aagaard, Coe, and Reeves (2001). Beliefs about who can learn, and under what conditions, are refuted by other studies that illustrate success among children labeled by schools. Schools label students in a wide variety of ways including by socioeconomic status, race, ethnicity, and elegibility for special education

services. The work of Gutstein (2003) and Gutierrez (1999, 2001) are among the examples that illustrate the success of such children under conditions of high expectations, challenging curriculum, and collegial collaboration.

Unfortunately, the PSSM document does not comment on the structures of the school system and society that hinder the success of children with diverse backgrounds (Berry, 2005; Weissglass, 2000). Recent studies of high-achieving, high-poverty schools have revealed that the changes required for achieving significant gains in student performance are systemic in nature. For instance, a systemic change that characterizes schools whose students achieve significant performance gains is the creation of cultures of high expectations and caring. According to a review conducted by the Center for Public Education (2005), "Much of the research points to the presence of such a culture as 'necessary' or even the 'dominant theme' in making it possible for a school to succeed in a high-poverty community" (p. 3).

Although the success of schools in the United States is typically measured by students' performance and achievement on state standardized tests, the current national political agenda has placed undue emphasis on the use of standardized tests as the only means of measuring success. As a result, teachers are coerced into teaching skills as opposed to good mathematics. Kannapel and Clements (2005), in their study of high-performing, high-poverty schools, found that these schools place a heavy emphasis on ongoing assessments that serve as diagnostic tools to determine individual student needs. In successful schools, teachers use the results of assessment to plan instruction that meets the academic needs of their students. Assessment results are studied carefully and used to drive the instruction in these schools. Although the teaching of skills is part of the instruction, these schools work to support children in developing higher-order thinking skills. (We say more about this in the section addressing the NCLB Act.)

In considering high expectations and worthwhile opportunities for all, Hiebert and his colleagues (1997) describe the importance of the tasks chosen for instruction in supporting all students. They describe tasks with multiple access points as those that allow students to engage in meaningful inquiry by drawing on whatever mathematical knowledge and experiences they know are useful in solving the task at hand. Tasks with multiple access points create opportunities for all students to engage in the construction of mathematical understanding. Tasks that limit students' accessibility can result in a meaningless experience for many. Still, tasks must be problematic and deal with important mathematical ideas in order for the student to garner something meaningful from the assignment.

Hiebert and his colleagues (1997) further develop strategies for achieving equity by emphasizing the importance of classroom communication and reflection. They suggest that classroom communication should create opportunities for all children to share their thinking and their unique strategies for solving problems. This practice allows all children's ideas and thoughts to be valued by the teacher and by their peers. As a result, children feel like members of a classroom community in which *everyone's* ideas, right or wrong, contribute to everyone's growth in understanding the mathematics involved in a problem.

Despite these recommendations, we are still concerned about the question of how to motivate all learners to engage and to be involved in the activities posed to a class. Recent work with students typically considered at risk of failure sheds light on what may help many students who are "falling through the cracks" and achieving far below their abilities in mathematics. Underachieving students are very often students of color, students of low socioeconomic status, or students who have been identified by the school system as children with special needs. This trend may suggest that educators should examine the talents of children and explore learning experiences that build on and develop these talents. Using this approach, the understandings all children bring to the learning of mathematics are valued and used to change what society knows about mathematics and how it views the discipline.

Standards-Based (or Reform) Curricula

Teachers who want to teach mathematics by using high-quality problems and tasks have often had to create their own materials. In the past 10 to 15 years, several curricula have been published that support a vision of mathematics instruction well aligned with the teaching strategies suggested throughout this chapter and throughout the PSSM. These materials—often referred to as standards-based curricula or reform curricula—are based on extensive field testing and research and were designed with much input from practicing teachers.

Several studies of the impact of standards-based curriculum materials on the achievement of all children have been conducted in recent years. Findings have been controversial. Some authors have suggested that children from disadvantaged backgrounds struggle with these materials (Lubienski, 2000, 2002), but others have found that the benefits of exposure to high-quality mathematical tasks organized through these materials greatly outweigh the difficulties of using such materials (Boaler, 2002a; Gutstein, 2003; Gutstein, Lipman, Hernandez, & de Los Reyes, 1997; Walker, 2006). Walker found evidence that children who had been failing in school mathematics, when exposed to reform curricula, became heavily committed to the work of the classroom community and active participants in the work of their groups. She found that many of these children took on leadership roles in their groups and took creative approaches to problem solving that shifted the work of their group from simply solving problems to doing mathematics as young mathematicians. These findings support the work of Gloria Ladson-Billings (1994, 1995, 1998), in which she eloquently defines culturally relevant pedagogy as the practices of teachers who succeed in teaching children of color.

Other studies have found that the performance of children labeled by schools can improve with the use of reform curricula (see,

for example, Riordan & Noyce, 2001; Schoenfeld, 2002). These studies go further, analyzing the curricula themselves and attributing success to different features of the curricula. One important finding for the purpose of this chapter is the comparison of the performance of children who use reform curricula with that of all other students. Assessment of procedural skills revealed no significant differences, although children using reform curricula were found to outperform their counterparts on problem-solving and reasoning tasks. These findings suggest that teaching for understanding supports children's learning of tools (often referred to as procedures) as well as their learning of problem solving and reasoning (Senk & Thompson, 2003).

These reform curricula have provided teachers with materials that support teaching for understanding. Unfortunately, teachers find themselves torn between the rhetoric of teaching for understanding (for instance, the big overarching ideas of most state standard documents) and testing for procedural skills. Initial emphasis by states and districts on standards-based practice seemed to stimulate some teachers to initiate reform practices (Wilson & Floden, 2001); however, as mandates increased, "the room the staff has enjoyed for making their own professional decisions shrinks ... as does their sense of ownership and autonomy" (Wilson & Floden, 2001, p. 198). Although the use of open-ended items on state assessments initially provoked a flurry of activity, as teachers provided more opportunity for students to solve such problems (Wilson & Floden, 2001), the narrow focus of the scoring rubrics used to evaluate student responses illustrates that the expectation is still the demonstration of procedures expected by the item developers (Norton, 2007).

Much of the testing of children emphasizes the evaluation of their procedural efficiency as opposed to their understanding of mathematics. Teachers often find themselves having to make difficult choices about what is best for the learners while under pressure from district administrators (and often parents) to teach to the tests—a form of teaching that is driven by a focus on the teaching of procedures and basic skills.

The No Child Left Behind Act

The NCLB Act of 2001 has created a different set of problems for teachers and schools. Although, as we noted earlier, it is beyond the scope of this chapter to delve into great detail about NCLB, we feel it is important to point out that NCLB has had an enormous impact on the lives of teachers and children since its passage. With the advent of NCLB, almost every state in the nation has articulated a set of standards (Reys, Dingman, Sutter, & Teuscher, 2005). In several states, teams of teachers have participated in the design of standards documents, in the creation of standards-based materials, in the choice of curriculum that supports the state standards, and in the design and delivery of professional development for colleagues. One might venture to say that the participation of teachers should have led to the creation of materials that have the best interest of learners in mind. Unfortunately,

the needs of children are far from the focus of much of this activity at the state or district level. The pressure to succumb to a federal mandate has silenced the voices of most well-intentioned teachers and administrators.

With the passage of NCLB, schools and teachers are under pressure to prove that teachers are highly qualified, and yet there is little agreement as to what "highly qualified" means. Schools are under pressure to increase scores on achievement tests, and yet there is little agreement as to what constitutes a passing score, or what should be included on a test in order to measure performance.

Current analysis of results on the National Assessment of Educational Progress (NAEP) sheds light on the difficulties of determining test items that are capable of revealing what children know and can do (D'Ambrosio, Kastberg, & Lambdin, 2007; Pellegrino, 2002). Consequently, teachers find themselves trying to teach to a moving target (Schoenfeld, 2002). Although the rhetoric of state standards is about teaching for understanding, the details describing each standard are usually laid out as a bulleted set of skills and procedures to be mastered at each grade level. Hence the testing becomes focused on evaluating children's proficiency with skills.

Not only are teachers struggling with the tensions of multiple (and sometimes conflicting) goals for instruction, but so are the children. Many children find themselves in classrooms with multiple authority figures, each with clearly different goals for them. The collaboration between the classroom teacher and the special education professional, for example, is often tense and counterproductive. The goals of each of these professionals for teaching mathematics are often at odds. This is a simple reflection of two fields—both engaged in teaching children mathematics, with distinct purposes and strategies—that approach teaching and learning from very different paradigms regarding how children learn. Whereas classroom teachers often work to provide opportunities for children to acquire identity and agency in their mathematical experiences (Boaler & Greeno, 2000), modifications proposed by the special education professionals tend to reject the view of children as autonomous mathematical thinkers (for a review of special education literature regarding mathematics teaching and learning, see Koontz, 2005). Hence the children, particularly those who carry labels, find themselves torn between the mathematics constructed through their classroom activity and the "support" provided by their special education teachers.

Another serious result of NCLB has been the emphasis placed on the success of multiple subgroups within a school. The determination of adequate yearly progress (AYP) requires that "all schools meet an absolute level of performance in reading and mathematics that is uniformly applied to all subgroups of students within a school . . . and defines subgroups as economically disadvantaged students, students from major racial and ethnic groups, students with disabilities, and students with limited English proficiency" (Kim & Sunderman, 2005, p. 3). Kim and Sunderman show that these requirements have resulted in greater inequities among schools. These authors found that schools failing

to make AYP are typically those with multiple subgroups, whereas schools with few subgroups are more likely to make AYP. Furthermore, Kim and Sunderman report that many schools that fail to make AYP have often achieved higher gains in student performance than some other schools in the district that make AYP. These results are alarming; they require the attention of schools, administrators, and particularly policymakers. If, in fact, our goal is to close the achievement gap between children in poor communities and those from economically advantaged communities, then we must consider a very different perspective on assessment, progress, accountability, and sanctions.

Connecting to the Previous Version of This Chapter

The pages that follow reflect a vision of instruction that deeply respects teachers and children. This vision requires that teachers believe in themselves and in their students as mathematicians. This vision is one of a classroom that fosters a community of practice in which investigations are mathematical in nature and members of the community are empowered to pose and investigate their own problems. This vision values and respects the input of all members of the classroom community.

Unfortunately, this vision exists in stark contrast to the current reality of most schools, especially those serving children who strive to succeed despite social and economic hardship—schools in which success is measured exclusively by scores on standardized tests. For a vision of success for all students to be realized, it will be necessary for a great many members of our society to relinquish their belief that some children cannot succeed, and to replace that false belief with a deeply held understanding that success is accessible to all children. Only in light of this revised belief will teachers become empowered to "enact an equitable classroom" (Gutierrez, 2002). According to Gutierrez, "from Freire's point of view, our goal as researchers is to try to help teachers develop the ability to create spaces of uncoerced interactions" (p. 168). This will be possible only if we critically reexamine the culture of schools and explore how the structure of schools tends to serve as an instrument of coercion for both teachers and children. Teachers are coerced to teach without attending to the needs of the children, and children are coerced to behave and perform in "prescribed" ways. Our greater understanding of power relations in schools will be the first step toward liberating teachers and students in order to create a space in which the vision described in the PSSM can be enacted and in which all children can have equal opportunities to engage in learning meaningful and worthwhile mathematics.

The preceding paragraphs set a lofty and demanding vision for all mathematics teachers and all advocates for children. While teachers, administrators, parents, politicians, and policymakers invest intellectually and creatively in the systemic restructuring of schools in order to better meet the needs of all children, there are several instructional strategies that can promote equity in mathematics learning. In the rest of this chapter, we describe strategies that focus instruction on facilitating understanding of mathematics by all children, thus promoting a more equitable approach to the mathematics classroom experiences of all children. These paragraphs represent slight modifications from the 1995 chapter.

Mathematics Strategies That Promote Equity and Achievement

The following strategies, intended to enhance students' understanding of mathematics, are supported by research about how students learn most effectively. The strategies fall into three broad categories dealing with student learning, content applications and integration, and instructional approaches.

Strategy 4.1:
Encourage exploration and investigation.

Discussion

Students who engage in mathematical explorations and investigations reshape their understanding of mathematics as an area in which they can be creative. This type of activity develops flexibility in their reasoning skills and allows students to use their existing knowledge to explore new situations, hence extending their knowledge base.

As young people engage in mathematical activities, they raise questions that reflect their curiosity about mathematics. They ask "what if" questions that explore the implications of those questions for the mathematical concept being explored. Students' success in mathematics is related to their ability to ask good questions and to raise interesting conjectures based on them.

Classroom Examples

As students walk into the room, they see a problem on the board, which they are to work on in small groups. They immediately begin exploring the problem, which is rich enough to allow many different strategies for its solution. Throughout the working session, the teacher circulates around to the different groups, observing the work and asking questions to help students verbalize the strategies they are using. After sufficient time for exploration, all groups share their solutions and compare the different approaches used to reach them.

Giving students an opportunity to explore concepts before being "taught the rules" is appropriate at all levels. At the high school level, students can use graphing calculators to explore the role of the coefficients in the graphical representation of linear functions. Measuring a table with paper clips, pencils, and notebooks helps younger children build number sense while coming to understand the need for standard units of measure.

Resources

Blais, 1988; Borasi, 1992; Brown & Walter, 1990; Campione, Brown, & Connell, 1988; Davis, Maher, & Noddings, 1990; Fosnot & Dolk, 2001; Kroll, 1989; Romberg & Kaput, 1999; Wearne & Hiebert, 1989.

Strategy 4.2:
Use students' prior knowledge.

Discussion

The knowledge that students bring to a new experience will greatly shape their understanding of new concepts. If we understand the learning of mathematics as a constructive process, we can plan activities that will allow students to construct knowledge based on concepts they already understand. Given a problem-solving task, for example, students must bring to that task what they already know in order to develop solutions that are personally meaningful to them. Their differing strategies and approaches to a problem will indicate the different mathematical constructions they rely on to solve a given problem.

To build instruction based on students' meanings and understandings, teachers must ask many questions throughout a teaching session. Students who reach the same answer for a problem may have solved it in very different ways. The process of sharing their solutions not only helps them see other possible solutions, but also helps the teacher understand their thinking. Several successful programs of mathematics instruction use the instructional strategy of encouraging students to use what they know in order to invent procedures to solve problems whose answers they do not know.

Classroom Examples

As 2nd graders think about subtraction problems, they are encouraged to use what they know to solve problems with new difficulties, such as 27 − 8. One child might think to herself that 28 − 8 = 20, so 27 − 8 must then be 19. Another child might think that 27 − 7 = 20, so one less would be 19. Yet another child might think of 27 − 8 as 10 − 8 = 2 and 2 + 17 = 19. Multiple strategies are possible for this problem, and children's understanding of subtraction without regrouping can lead to their successful solution of subtraction with regrouping, even if that algorithm has not yet been introduced.

Somewhat older students who know how to find the area of a rectangle can be challenged to discover a method for finding the area of a triangle or a parallelogram. Providing paper shapes and scissors or other tools and encouraging students to experiment will enable them to start with what they already know and construct new knowledge that they will be able to use more flexibly and retain longer.

Resources

Carpenter & Fennema, 1992; Cocking & Mestre, 1988; D'Ambrosio, 2004; Fosnot & Dolk, 2001; Garofalo, 1989; Kilpatrick, Swaford, & Findell, 2001; Lehrer, Jacobson, Kemeny, & Strom, 1999; NCTM, 1995; Peterson, Fennema, & Carpenter, 1991.

Strategy 4.3:

Use multiple representations to illustrate mathematical ideas.

Discussion

Individuals who have made strong connections among different mathematical concepts demonstrate a greater conceptual understanding of those ideas. Teachers need to emphasize several different representations of mathematical ideas to help children make the many conceptual connections. These include concrete, oral, and graphic representations, as well as the traditional symbolic representations.

Students need to learn to "translate" from one of these "languages of mathematics" to another. For example, given an equation or a number sentence, students should be able to draw a diagram or make a model with manipulatives and also write a problem that is represented by the equation. Similarly, given a verbal problem, students should be able to write an equation as well as represent it graphically or with manipulatives.

The use of manipulatives (concrete or virtual) in classroom activities greatly enhances students' visualization of mathematical ideas. Manipulatives allow students to explore and investigate mathematical relationships that will later be translated into symbolic form. They serve as an alternative representation of concepts and should be used whenever ideas are introduced. The key to the successful use of manipulatives lies in the bridge (which must be supported by the teacher) between that artifact and the formalized statement of the underlying mathematical concepts. A weak link can defeat the purpose of the use of manipulatives.

The effective use of manipulatives requires three stages: (1) the use of the manipulatives alone, followed by (2) the use of the manipulatives side by side with symbolic paper-and-pencil representations, and then (3) the use of the symbolic representation alone. Not allowing sufficient time for students to transition between their understandings of manipulatives as representations of their mathematics to written representations meant to signify their thinking could result in overreliance on manipulatives. The use of manipulatives should lead to the construction of representations that are more easily shared with peers, teachers, and the larger world. This shift in representation, when motivated by students' desire to share their thinking or findings, can be used as the basis for investigating the world with mathematics.

Contrary to popular belief, the use of manipulatives should not be restricted to younger students or to students having difficulties. At any grade level, manipulatives can facilitate students' exploration of new mathematical ideas at a concrete level, before the formalization of those ideas.

Classroom Examples

Manipulatives range from commercial products (such as Unifix cubes, base 10 blocks, or Cuisenaire rods) to everyday objects (bottle tops, dice, dominoes, or paper squares). They can also be teacher-made (game boards or geoboards) or student-made (pentominoes or three-dimensional shapes). A more recent option, virtual manipulatives, is available electronically, often in the form of interactive applets. The benefits of supporting children's learning as they use real or virtual manipulatives are reported in the literature.

Games using dice and dominoes can help children construct meaning for the idea of units of 10. These experiences will support children's

understanding of place value as they transition into the use of base 10 blocks to understand the idea of regrouping. Geometric representations of tenths, hundredths, and thousandths make the understanding and ordering of decimals meaningful for most children. Algebra can be introduced using counters in two colors for positive and negative numbers and squares for variables.

The study of probability is enlivened by activities involving the collection of data from rolling dice, spinning spinners, grabbing objects from bags, or playing different games. Using such manipulatives spurs students' curiosity and motivates them to further explore simulations and other applications of actual and theoretical probability.

Resources

Clements & Del Campo, 1989; Gilfeather, 1989; Hiebert & Lefevre, 1986; Joyner, 1990; Kilpatrick, Swaford, & Findell, 2001; Laborde, 2002; Reimer & Moyer, 2005; Ross & Kurtz, 1993; Sarama & Clements, 2002; Skemp, 1987; Smith, 2003.

Strategy 4.4:
Use real-world problem-solving activities.

Discussion

The use of real-world problems in the classroom helps students come to value mathematics as a useful tool that can be applied to out-of-school activities. Real-world problems provide opportunities to relate mathematics to students' own interests and concerns; they draw on students' previous experiences; they link mathematics to other subjects; and they allow students to use their accumulated knowledge in mathematics as well as in other subjects. And, possibly best of all, applying mathematical knowledge to personally relevant situations is highly motivating for students.

Classroom Examples

Real-world problem solving in mathematics takes many forms. Projects requiring the collection and analysis of data relevant to a genuine problem can lead to changes in the students' school or community. Younger children can do surveys of food preferences and share them with the cafeteria manager; older students might analyze the results of community recycling efforts. Situations arising from student interest or community need are open-ended and encourage young people to generate their own creative directions for exploration and investigation. Students can visit appropriate sites and involve community members who have expertise in their area of inquiry. Problems of this type also empower students to use mathematics to explore inequities in their world; this can be a precursor to engagement in society (Gutstein, 2006).

Writing their own mathematics problems based on their personal experiences or those of family members is an important and effective way for students to see the relevance of mathematics to their daily lives. The teacher can ask students to write problems involving their classmates or community members that are based on current topics of study such as multiplication, measurement, or square roots. These problems

can then be used on a quiz, in a game of math Jeopardy, or in reviewing for a test. Students enjoy having their peers solve problems they have written.

Resources

Austin, 1991; Cobb, Yackel, Wood, Wheatley, & Merkel, 1988; Fosnot & Dolk, 2001; Kastberg, D'Ambrosio, McDermott, & Saada, 2005; Kilpatrick, 1987; Lesh & Doerr, 2003; Lesh, Landau, & Hamilton, 1983; Lester, 1989; Nelissen, 1999; Russell & Friel, 1989; Swetz & Hartzler, 1991.

Strategy 4.5:

Integrate mathematics with other content areas.

Discussion

Students who have experiences that link mathematics to other subject areas are able to apply previously acquired knowledge to new situations. Teachers have many opportunities to integrate mathematics with other areas of the curriculum and thus enhance learning. Experiences of this type help students understand the power of mathematics to interpret problems in the social and physical sciences; such experiences also help them link the curricular subjects in ways that are real to them. Focusing on real-life, significant issues makes mathematics more relevant to students.

Classroom Examples

Learning to communicate mathematical understandings is a critical element of instruction. As students keep journals, write math autobiographies, describe mathematical processes, make conjectures, and justify solutions to problems, they enhance their oral and written language skills. Students discover that using what they learned in language arts can strengthen their knowledge of mathematics.

Similarly, young people must come to use their mathematics skills as they study other subjects. Interdisciplinary activities organized around a common theme require students to connect mathematics to science, history, economics, art, physical education, and other subjects. Students may be asked to analyze measurements collected during a science experiment or to accumulate data on a presidential candidate's success in various regions of the country as indicated by the polls during an election campaign. Fractions are integral to reading music; geometry is an essential component of art; and measurement is vital in physical education. Challenging students to go through their school day without using mathematics (not just arithmetic) anywhere except in math class can support the development of an understanding of the vital connections among mathematics and the learning of science, social studies, and other subjects.

The local newspaper is a wonderful tool for discovering the connections between math and other subjects. Every page uses numbers and shapes in news articles, advertisements, sports reports, and weather forecasts. Using the newspaper in mathematics is yet another vehicle for helping students see the importance of math for their future.

Resources

Beyth-Maron & Dekel, 1983; Borasi & Siegel, 2000; Czerniak, Weber, Sandmann, & Ahern, 1999; D'Ambrosio, Kastberg, McDermott, & Saada, 2004; Jacobs, 1993; Kurtzke, 1990.

Strategy 4.6:

Use culturally relevant materials as a springboard for mathematics instruction.

Discussion

The process of legitimizing the mathematics practiced in different cultural settings is a way of increasing students' respect for their social and cultural heritage and, consequently, increasing their self-respect and self-confidence. Mathematics is practiced in different ways in different cultures. These practices can be valued and legitimized through their use in classroom instruction. Many of these mathematical activities are highly relevant to the students in a classroom, as they can be made to reflect students' own life experiences.

Integrating the history of mathematics with the study of new mathematical topics can show students how mathematics is linked to real-world problems and how mathematical knowledge evolved from the needs of different social or cultural groups. A study of the history of mathematics can also reveal, for example, how notions of rigor in mathematical proofs have evolved over time. What was considered a proof in the early history of mathematics would not meet today's standards of rigor. Students come to realize that these standards are socially agreed upon, and the classroom community can establish its own internal criteria for what will count as proof.

Culturally relevant materials can be used in multicultural experiences to motivate the development of mathematical topics, simultaneously stimulating young people's appreciation and understanding of other cultures and other realities. This type of experience reinforces the importance of valuing and respecting everyone's cultural heritage.

Classroom Examples

Students can explore the different ways in which the numeration system evolved in various cultural settings, such as in the Mayan, Chinese, Babylonian, or Arabic cultures. Comparison of these different systems of numeration and the needs from which they evolved can lead to a better understanding of the underlying structures of our own society's current system of numeration.

Games from other cultures that use reasoning or other mathematics skills help students realize the importance of mathematics in every time and place: Senet and Wari originated in Africa; origami and the tangram puzzle came from Asia; Patolli and a walnut shell game are part of the Native American heritage. Having a collection of these activities in the classroom and using them for a change of pace is an effective way to apply this strategy.

Another way of using culturally relevant materials is to teach concepts by relating them to students' current experiences. The local newspaper is a prime source of ideas for problem solving

and applications of mathematics in the community. Teachers in Boston may relate instruction to the Boston subway system, and Florida teachers may create a unit on the tourism industry. Connecting mathematics to the local job market is culturally relevant and appropriate in any part of the United States.

Resources

Arcavi, 1991; D'Ambrosio, 1985, 2007; Gutstein, 2006; Moses & Cobb, 2001; Moses, Kamii, Swap, & Howard, 1989; Powell & Frankenstein, 1997; Secada, 1991; Zaslavsky, 1973, 1989.

Strategy 4.7:
Provide students with opportunities to use technology.

Discussion

Students benefit greatly from the use of technology as an alternative way of representing mathematical ideas. Several dimensions of the ever-growing power of technology may be used to explore mathematics instruction.

First, technology can be used as a tool for problem solving. Calculators, spreadsheets, graphing utilities, and structured mathematical environments (such as Mathematica and Fathom) are used to engage students in solving problems that involve real data, problems that can be approached using many different strategies, and problems that would be cumbersome to solve without the use of such tools.

Second, technology can be used to generate exploratory mathematical environments called microworlds. Computer software such as

Geometer's Sketchpad, Shape Makers, TIMA: Bars, and SimCalc, to name a few, create a mathematical environment in which students can explore mathematical ideas.

Classroom Examples

Using geometry-based computer software to explore the effect of maximizing the area of a quadrilateral gives students insights that are difficult to acquire using only paper and pencil. The trial-and-error strategy for problem solving is easily applied when a student can quickly consider various options. Software programs exist that allow students to use such manipulatives as base 10 blocks to connect concrete materials with the appropriate picture representations and symbols. Computers can make the drill and practice of skills more interesting and can motivate students to continue practice—and eventually reach higher levels of achievement.

Scientific calculators facilitate solving statistics problems; they relieve students of tedious calculations and allow them to spend their time on the more critical skills of data analysis. Simple four-function calculators can help elementary students explore patterns in multiplication, such as the results of multiplying numbers by 9, 99, or 999. After considering a few examples, students can analyze the pattern that emerges, predict other products, and verify their predictions by further exploring the products. Graphing calculators greatly expand the options for teaching algebra. Students can easily explore the effect on a curve of modifying its equation, or they can enter data and determine if it can be represented by an algebraic function. The graphing calculator

can help students make important connections between algebra and geometry.

Teachers should spend time helping students understand appropriate uses of technology. Through experience, young people can determine what computations can be done more efficiently by mental math, by paper and pencil, or by calculator. High school students can see computer-generated fractals and realize that technology is opening the way to new discoveries and new frontiers of mathematics. Unless young people are taught mathematics with the use of technology, they are learning skills that may be obsolete by the time they finish high school.

Resources

Fey, 1992; Kaput, 1992; Kaput, Noss, & Hoyles, 2002; Kastberg & Leatham, 2005; Kendal & Stacey, 1999; Olive, 1991, 2000; Schwartz & Yerushalmy, 1985; Steffe & Olive, 2002; Steffe & Wiegel, 1994; Thompson, 1989.

Strategy 4.8:

Encourage oral and written discourse in the classroom.

Discussion

The sharing of mathematical thinking is an essential aspect of the classroom environment. Much of the current research on students' construction of knowledge points to social interaction as an important aspect of the construction process. Students should be encouraged to explain their thinking, to express their thinking to their peers, and to share their ideas. This process of sharing helps young people organize their thoughts and their solution strategies. It also helps them build a rationale for justifying the strategies they have chosen. Debates that arise as a result of sharing multiple solutions can be used to help students understand that the consideration of diverse perspectives is critical to the creation of powerful mathematical ideas.

Mathematical communication is considered to be an essential part of the learning process, particularly in a classroom environment that encourages group work, student involvement, and student-generated solution strategies, as well as student-generated problems. Communication provides a forum for students to negotiate meaning and to reflect on their solution strategies. Oral as well as written communication of mathematical thinking should be encouraged and sustained in classrooms.

Classroom Examples

Students can keep journals in their mathematics classes. They write in their journals daily and report the results of their mathematics investigations and problem-solving episodes each day. Journal entries can be on a topic of the student's choice, or they can be prompted with open-ended statements such as these: "Division is called repeated subtraction because. . . ." "What would you most like more help with in math?" "Based on the graphs, I conclude. . . ." The students' written work provides the teacher with evidence of each student's contributions to the group work, as well as each student's growth resulting from group activities.

Asking students to write a short paragraph summarizing new insights and areas of difficulty at the end of a homework assignment can help focus homework review sessions. Students can be given one minute at the beginning of class to write a summary of the previous day's lesson, instead of the teacher providing such a review, as is usually the case.

Resources

Ball & Bass, 2003; Borasi & Rose, 1989; Borasi & Siegel, 2000; Cobb, Yackel, & McClain, 2000; Collins, Hawkins, & Carver, 1991; Countryman, 1992; Forman, 2003; Gutstein, 2006; Johnson, 1983; Keith, 1988; Lampert, 1998; Powell & Ramnauth, 1992; Sherin, 2002a; Waywood, 1992; White, 2003.

Strategy 4.9:
Encourage collaborative problem solving.

Discussion

Research indicates that student achievement rises in classroom environments in which students engage in collaborative problem-solving activities. Successful collaborative problem solving should be a crucial goal of mathematics instruction, because collaboration is the most prevalent problem-solving mode in the world of work for which students are preparing. Learners who are engaged cooperatively in problem-solving activities are all involved in sharing and negotiating meanings, in verbalizing their understandings, in trying to understand one another's strategies, in providing constructive criticism, and in being actively involved in learning.

Cooperatively, students tackle challenging problems that are often beyond their individual abilities, and they are generally more highly motivated to persevere in finding solutions.

It is critical that the classroom environment be structured in a way that permits all students to make significant contributions to problem-solving experiences. Students must learn how to work in groups in order to get the most out of the collaborative experience. Elementary school teachers may need to organize the cooperative activity by assigning students specific roles or tasks. Generally, a group is given only one set of materials so that they must work together on the solution. There are a variety of collaborative problem-solving structures that ensure participation by each student in the group.

Classroom Examples

Collaborative problem solving can take the form of long-term projects or shorter activities that can be completed in a single class period or less. Students enjoy puzzles in which each person in a group of four is given a different clue and they must combine the clues to reach the solution. Students develop both number sense and mental math skills when they are challenged, for example, to find a number that is even, is a multiple of three, has an integral square root, and has two digits.

Homework assignments can be efficiently reviewed in small groups. The teacher hopes, of course, that each problem will have been correctly solved by at least one person in each group. If not, by working together and sharing strategies, the group members can reach an answer that all understand. The teacher is called on only when everyone in the group is stumped. Students can also help one another prepare for tests by working collaboratively to determine what content will be covered and creating and reviewing sample questions together.

Resources

Davidson, 1985; Good, Reys, Grouws, & Mulryan, 1990; Lindquist, 1989; Noddings, 1989; Siegler, 2003; Slavin, 1990; Webb & Mastergeorge, 2003; Yackel & Cobb, 1996.

Strategy 4.10:
Use student thinking to enhance learning.

Discussion

Children must realize that their way of thinking is important and will be heard and carefully reflected on by their peers. An environment that encourages the sharing of ideas will also encourage the development of students' self-confidence and willingness to contribute to group activities.

In a constructivist teaching environment, all students' ways of thinking are shared, explored, and extended. Instead of examining errors, teachers should question the processes used to obtain solutions. Often, as they share their thinking, young people refine their thoughts and point out inconsistencies in their previous expressions of ideas. The learning environment must encourage this level of reflection.

Too often in mathematics instruction, students' answers are simply assessed as correct or incorrect, and the discussion moves on to another problem. Simply telling a child that an answer is correct or incorrect discourages the reflection necessary to turn problem solving into a learning experience.

Classroom Examples

Traditionally, classroom discussion has been a two-way dialogue between the teacher and one student at a time. Changing the teacher's role to that of a facilitator who expects students to respond to each other's questions communicates that the views of individual students are respected and that students are responsible for their own learning. Teachers and students must allow one another enough "think time," because not all students can respond immediately to questions.

Taking time regularly to talk with young people individually about their progress in mathematics communicates that the teacher values their ideas and cares whether they succeed. This kind of discussion can be a formal interview in which the teacher asks specific questions, or it can be less structured, focusing on journal entries or a review of student work. The suggestions dealing with communication and cooperative learning (see Strategies 4.8 and 4.9) are applicable here; the activities provide opportunities for students' ideas to be expressed and valued.

Resources

Borasi, 1987, 1996; D'Ambrosio, 2004; Irwin, 2001; Koehler, 1990; Lappan & Schram, 1989; Resnick, 1987; Schoenfeld, 1989; Sherin, 2002b; Steffe &

D'Ambrosio, 1995; Sullivan & Clarke, 1991; Wilson, 1990.

Strategy 4.11:
Offer an enriched curriculum and challenging activities.

Discussion

Mathematics instruction—indeed, instruction in every subject—has been greatly hindered by the mistaken notion that mathematics should be "dumbed down" for underachieving students. This misconception is directly related to tracking and ability grouping, which increase both academic and social inequalities among children. These practices, in turn, increase students' feelings of inadequacy and helplessness regarding mathematics. Teachers' expectations of students' abilities to learn mathematics affect the type of instruction they deliver to students in different ability groups.

All students should engage in challenging mathematical activities. They should experience mathematics as an inquiry-based discipline in which they ask many questions and allow their curiosity and creativity to guide their exploration and investigation of mathematical concepts. All students should investigate open-ended problem-solving experiences.

Unfortunately, underachieving students generally experience a much less interesting, less challenging, and, consequently, less motivating curriculum. To many such students, mathematics means merely rote memorization, and the work required of them is repetitive and mathematically trivial.

Mathematics instruction, if it is to be meaningful to all young people, must ensure that students will develop higher-order thinking skills and engage in mathematical activity beyond the mere mastery of skills and procedures.

Classroom Examples

Measurement, geometry, statistics, probability, and functions are a few of the topics identified by the NCTM as part of a complete mathematics curriculum. Unfortunately, these topics may get little attention when the major portion of classroom time is devoted to computation skills. A richer curriculum attends to topics involving hands-on activities and demonstrating the applications of arithmetic. These activities are generally more motivating to students and require higher-level thinking. In using calculators for computation, for instance, even students who have not mastered traditional algorithms can participate and benefit. Resource materials with enrichment activities, projects, and challenging problems must be readily available.

Interdisciplinary activities that connect mathematics with science and other subjects are also part of an enriched curriculum. Students enjoy opportunities to apply the mathematics they are learning by undertaking projects that benefit the school and community. They may choose to delve deeper into a mathematics topic such as the Fibonacci sequence, the golden rectangle, tesselations, or the history of mathematics or architecture.

Resources

Boaler, 2002a, 2002b; Carnegie Corporation of New York, 1990; Haberman, 1991; Knapp & Shields, 1990; Levin & Hopfenberg, 1991; Means, Chelemer, & Knapp, 1991; Oakes, 1986; Senk & Thompson, 2003; Silver, Smith, & Nelson, 1995; Stein, Grover, & Henningsen, 1996.

Strategy 4.12:

Use a variety of problem-solving experiences.

Discussion

Success in solving mathematical problems is related to students' experiences with problem solving. A lack of flexibility in students' thinking strategies reflects their lack of experience with nonroutine and open-ended problems. When confronting problem-solving situations, students often rely on such ineffective strategies as key words.

Many types of problems should be incorporated into the curriculum, including problems that can be solved in many different ways, problems that may have several correct answers, problems that may involve decision making and allow for various interpretations, and problems that may require students to determine what might be the interesting questions that merit exploration.

Experience with nonroutine problems and open-ended problems helps students shed the false perception that success in mathematics is linked to one's ability to recognize the correct procedure to use. When students recognize that they have many alternatives to use when they are faced with a problem, we see an increase in their level of perseverance and willingness to try new strategies.

Classroom Examples

Textbooks illustrate a wide variety of problem-solving strategies, including drawing a diagram, making an organized list, working backward, and solving a simpler problem. Students need many opportunities to learn and apply such strategies, which can be used to solve nonroutine problems. Too often, however, instructional time is devoted primarily to the most common strategy for solving an equation, while alternative strategies receive little attention.

Problems with multiple solutions can be presented as weeklong challenges. Each Monday, the teacher can put one on a bulletin board. Here are some examples:

- Find hexominoes (grids of six adjacent squares) that can be folded into a cube.
- Find combinations of coins that total $1.00.
- Describe an illustration of the Fibonacci sequence.
- Write a rational number between 1/2 and 1.

Nonroutine problems are rich sources of collaborative work for small groups of students. Students find it exciting when several small groups reach a common solution by following different strategies. Such explorations prepare young people to apply mathematics in their out-of-school world and in their future jobs.

Resources

Barron et al., 1998; Boaler, 1997; Hiebert et al., 1996; Lester, 1989; Peterson, 1988; Schoenfeld, 1989; Shavelson, Webb, Stasz, & McArthur, 1989.

Bibliography

Arcavi, A. (1991). The benefits of using history. *For the Learning of Mathematics, 11*(2), 11.

Austin, J. D. (Ed.). (1991). *Applications of secondary school mathematics*. Reston, VA: National Council of Teachers of Mathematics.

Ball, D. L., & Bass, H. (2003). Making mathematics reasonable in school. In J. Kilpatrick, W. G. Martin, & D. Schifter (Eds.), *A research companion to Principles and Standards for School Mathematics* (pp. 27–44). Reston, VA: National Council of Teachers of Mathematics.

Barron, B. J. S., Schwartz, D. L., Vye, N. J., Moore, A., Petrosino, A., Zech, L., & Bransford, J. D. (The Cognition and Technology Group at Vanderbilt). (1998). Doing with understanding: Lessons from research on problem- and project-based learning. *Journal of the Learning Sciences, 7*(3–4), 271–311.

Berry, R. Q. (2005). Introduction: Building an infrastructure for equity in mathematics education. *High School Journal, 88*(4), 1–5.

Beyth-Maron, R., & Dekel, S. (1983). A curriculum to improve thinking under uncertainty. *Instructional Science, 12*(1), 67–82.

Blais, D. M. (1988). Constructivism: A theoretical revolution for algebra. *Mathematics Teacher, 81*(8), 624–631.

Boaler, J. (1997). *Experiencing school mathematics: Teaching styles, sex, and setting.* Buckingham, UK: Open University Press.

Boaler, J. (2002a). Learning from teaching: Exploring the relationship between reform curriculum and equity. *Journal for Research in Mathematics Education, 33*(4), 239–258.

Boaler, J. (2002b). Paying the price for "sugar and spice": Shifting the analytical lens in equity research.

Mathematical Thinking and Learning, 4(2–3), 127–144.

Boaler, J., & Greeno, J. (2000). Identity, agency, and knowing in mathematical worlds. In J. Boaler (Ed.), *Multiple perspectives on mathematics teaching and learning* (pp. 171–200). Westport, CT: Ablex.

Borasi, R. (1987, November). Exploring mathematics through the analysis of errors. *For the Learning of Mathematics, 7*(3), 2–8.

Borasi, R. (1992). *Learning mathematics through inquiry.* Portsmouth, NH: Heinemann.

Borasi, R. (1996). *Reconceiving mathematics instruction: A focus on errors.* Norwood, NJ: Ablex.

Borasi, R., & Rose, B. (1989). Journal writing and mathematics instruction. *Educational Studies in Mathematics, 20*(4), 347–365.

Borasi, R., & Siegel, M. (2000). *Reading counts: Expanding the role of reading in mathematics classrooms.* New York: Teachers College Press.

Brown, S. I., & Walter, M. I. (1990). *The art of problem posing* (2nd ed.). Hillsdale, NJ: Erlbaum.

Campione, J. C., Brown, A. L., & Connell, M. L. (1988). Metacognition: On the importance of understanding what you are doing. In R. I. Charles & E. A. Silver (Eds.), *The teaching and assessing of mathematical problem solving* (pp. 93–114). Reston, VA: National Council of Teachers of Mathematics.

Carnegie Corporation of New York. (1990, Summer/Fall). Ensuring minorities' success in mathematics, engineering, and science: The MESA program. *Carnegie, 35*(3–4), 7.

Carpenter, T., & Fennema, E. (1992). Cognitively guided instruction: Building on the knowledge of students and teachers. *International Journal of Educational Research, 17,* 457–470.

Center for Public Education. (2005, August 22). *Research review: High-performing, high-poverty schools.* Alexandria, VA: National School Boards Association.

Clements, M. A., & Del Campo, G. (1989). Linking verbal knowledge, visual images, and episodes for mathematical learning. *Focus on Learning Problems in Mathematics 11*(1–2), 25–33.

Cobb, P., Yackel, E., & McClain, K. (2000). *Symbolizing and communicating in mathematics classrooms: Perspectives on discourse, tools, and instructional design.* Mahwah, NJ: Erlbaum.

Cobb, P., Yackel, E., Wood, T., Wheatley, G., & Merkel, G. (1988, September). Creating a problem-solving atmosphere. *Arithmetic Teacher, 36*(1), 46–47.

Cocking, R. R., & Mestre, J. (Eds.). (1988). *Linguistic and cultural influences on learning mathematics.* Hillsdale, NJ: Erlbaum.

Collins, A., Hawkins, J., & Carver, S. M. (1991). A cognitive apprenticeship for disadvantaged students. In B. Means, C. Chelemer, & M. S. Knapp (Eds.), *Teaching advanced skills to at-risk students: Views from theory and practice* (pp. 216–243). San Francisco: Jossey-Bass.

Countryman, J. (1992). *Writing to learn mathematics: Strategies that work, K–12.* Portsmouth, NH: Heinemann.

Czerniak, C. M., Weber, W. B., Jr., Sandmann, A., & Ahern, J. (1999). A literature review of science and mathematics integration. *School Science and Mathematics, 99*(8), 421–431.

D'Ambrosio, B. S. (2004). Preparing teachers to teach mathematics within a constructivist framework: The importance of listening to children. In D. Thompson & T. Watanabe (Eds.), *The work of mathematics teacher educators: Exchanging ideas for effective practice* (AMTE Monograph Series Vol. 1, pp. 135–150). San Diego: Association of Mathematics Teacher Educators.

D'Ambrosio, B. S., Kastberg, S. E., & Lambdin, D. (2007). Designed to differentiate: What is NAEP measuring? In P. Kloosterman & F. K. Lester (Eds.), *Results and interpretations of the 2003 mathematics assessment of the National Assessment of Educational Progress* (pp. 289–309). Reston, VA: National Council of Teachers of Mathematics.

D'Ambrosio, B. S., Kastberg, S. E., McDermott, G., & Saada, N. (2004). Beyond reading graphs: Student reasoning with data. In P. Kloosterman & F. K. Lester (Eds.), *Results and interpretations of the 1990 through 2000 mathematics assessments of the National Assessment of Educational Progress* (pp. 363–381). Reston, VA: National Council of Teachers of Mathematics.

D'Ambrosio, U. (1985). Ethnomathematics and its place in the history and pedagogy of mathematics. *For the Learning of Mathematics, 5*(1), 44–48.

D'Ambrosio, U. (2007). Peace, social justice, and ethnomathematics. In B. Sriraman (Ed.), *International perspectives on social justice in mathematics education: Monograph 1 of the Montana mathematics enthusiast* (pp. 25–34). Missoula, MT: University of Montana Press.

Davidson, N. (1985). Small-group learning and teaching in mathematics: A selective review of the literature. In R. Slavin, S. Sharan, S. Kagan, R. Lazarowitz, C. Webb, & R. Schmuck (Eds.), *Learning to cooperate, cooperating to learn* (pp. 211–230). New York: Plenum.

Davis, R. B., Maher, C. A., & Noddings, N. (1990). Constructivist views on the teaching and learning of mathematics. *Journal of Research in Mathematics Education* (Monograph No. 4). Reston, VA: National Council of Teachers of Mathematics.

Fey, J. T. (Ed.). (1992). *Calculators in mathematics education.* Reston, VA: National Council of Teachers of Mathematics.

Forman, E. A. (2003). A sociocultural approach to mathematics reform: Speaking, inscribing, and doing mathematics within communities of practice. In J. Kilpatrick, W. G. Martin, & D. Schifter (Eds.), *A research companion to Principles and Standards for School Mathematics* (pp. 333–352). Reston, VA: National Council of Teachers of Mathematics.

Fosnot, C., & Dolk, M. (2001). *Young mathematicians at work.* Portsmouth, NH: Heinemann.

Garofalo, J. (1989). Beliefs, responses, and mathematics education: Observations from the back of the classroom. *School Science and Mathematics, 89*(6), 451–455.

Gilfeather, M. (1989). *Conceptually based mathematics instruction: An investigation with a classroom of fourth and fifth grade students.* Unpublished doctoral dissertation, Indiana University, Bloomington.

Goldin, G. A. (2003). Representations in school mathematics: A unifying research perspective. In J. Kilpatrick, W. G. Martin, & D. Schifter (Eds.), *A research companion to Principles and Standards for School Mathematics* (pp. 275–285). Reston, VA: National Council of Teachers of Mathematics.

Goldin, G. A., & Shteingold, N. (2001). Systems of representations and the development of mathematical concepts. In A. A. Couco (Ed.), *The roles of representation in school mathematics* (pp. 1–23). Reston, VA: National Council of Teachers of Mathematics.

Good, T., Reys, B., Grouws, D., & Mulryan, C. (1990, December/January). Using work groups in mathematics instruction. *Educational Leadership, 47*(4), 56–62.

Gutierrez, R. (1999). Advancing urban Latina/o youth in mathematics: Lessons from an effective high school mathematics department. *The Urban Review, 31*(3), 263–281.

Gutierrez, R. (2001). Advancing African-American, urban youth in mathematics: Unpacking the success of one math department. *American Journal of Education, 109*(1), 63–111.

Gutierrez, R. (2002). Enabling the practice of mathematics teachers in context: Toward a new equity research agenda. *Mathematical Thinking and Learning, 4*(2–3), 145–187.

Gutstein, E. (2003). Teaching and learning mathematics for social justice in an urban, Latino school. *Journal for Research in Mathematics Education, 34*(1), 37–73.

Gutstein, E. (2006). *Reading and writing the world with mathematics: Toward a pedagogy for social justice.* London: Routledge Falmer Press.

Gutstein, E., Lipman, P., Hernandez, P., & de los Reyes, R. (1997). Culturally relevant mathematics teaching in a Mexican-American context. *Journal for Research in Mathematics Education, 28*(6), 709–737.

Haberman, M. (1991, December). The pedagogy of poverty versus good teaching. *Phi Delta Kappan, 73*(4), 290–294.

Hiebert, J., Carpenter, T. P., Fennema, E., Fuson, K., Human, P., Murray, H., et al. (1996). Problem solving as a basis for reform in curriculum and instruction: The case of mathematics. *Educational Researcher, 25*(4), 12–21.

Hiebert, J., Human, P., Carpenter, T. P., Fennema, E., Fuson, K. C., Wearne, D., et al. (1997). *Making sense: Teaching and learning mathematics with understanding.* Portsmouth, NH: Heinemann.

Hiebert, J., & Lefevre, P. (Eds.). (1986). *Conceptual and procedural knowledge: The case of mathematics.* Hillsdale, NJ: Erlbaum.

Hodges, H. (1989). *ASCD's 3-High Achievement Model.* Unpublished manuscript for the ASCD Urban Middle Grades Network, Alexandria, Virginia.

Howard, S. (2006). No Child Left Behind: The scene behind the act. In T. S. Poetter, J. C. Wegwert, & C. Haerr (Eds.), *No Child Left Behind and the illusion of reform: Critical essays by educators* (pp. 41–48). Lanham, MD: University Press of America.

Irwin, K. (2001). Using everyday knowledge of decimals to enhance understanding. *Journal for Research in Mathematics Education, 32*(4), 199–220.

Jacobs, H. H. (1993, February). Mathematics integration: A common-sense approach to curriculum development. *Arithmetic Teacher, 40*(6), 301–302.

Johnson, M. L. (1983). Writing in mathematics classes: A valuable tool for learning. *Mathematics Teacher, 76*(2), 117–119.

Joyner, J. M. (1990). Using manipulatives successfully. *Arithmetic Teacher, 38*(2), 6–7.

Kannapel, P., Aagaard, L., Coe, P., & Reeves, C. (2001). The impact of standards and accountability on teaching and learning in Kentucky. In S. Fuhrman (Ed.), *From the capitol to the classroom: Standards-based reform in the states* (100th Yearbook of the National Society for the Study of Education, pp. 242–262). Chicago: University of Chicago Press.

Kannapel, P., & Clements, S. K. (2005). *Inside the black box of high-performing, high-poverty schools.* Lexington, KY: Prichard Committee for Academic Excellence.

Kaput, J. (1992). Technology and mathematics education. In D. A. Grouws (Ed.), *Handbook of research on mathematics teaching and learning* (pp. 515–556). New York: Macmillan.

Kaput, J., Noss, R., & Hoyles, C. (2002). Developing new notations for a learnable mathematics in the computational era. In L. English (Ed.), *The handbook of international research in mathematics education* (pp. 51–73). Mahwah, NJ: Erlbaum.

Kastberg, S. E., D'Ambrosio, B., McDermott, G., & Saada, N. (2005). Context matters in assessing students' mathematical power. *For the Learning of Mathematics, 25*(2), 10–15.

Kastberg, S., & Leatham, K. (2005). Research on graphing calculators at the secondary level: Implications for mathematics teacher education. *Contemporary issues in technology and teacher education, 5*(1), 25–37.

Keith, S. Z. (1988, December). Explorative writing and learning mathematics. *Mathematics Teacher, 81*(9), 714–719.

Kendal, M., & Stacey, K. (1999). Varieties of teacher privileging for teaching calculus with computer algebra systems. *International Journal of Computer Algebra in Mathematics Education, 6*(4), 233–247.

Kilpatrick, J. (1987). Problem formulating: Where do good problems come from? In A. H. Schoenfeld (Ed.), *Cognitive science and mathematics education* (pp. 123–148). Hillsdale, NJ: Erlbaum.

Kilpatrick, J., Swaford, J., & Findell, B. (Eds.). (2001). *Adding it up: Helping children learn mathematics.* Washington DC: National Research Council.

Kim, J. S., & Sunderman, G. L. (2005). Measuring academic proficiency under the No Child Left Behind Act: Implications for educational equity. *Educational Researcher, 34*(8), 3–13.

Knapp, M., & Shields, P. M. (1990, June). Reconceiving academic instruction for the children of poverty. *Phi Delta Kappan, 71*(10), 753–758.

Koehler, M. S. (1990). Classrooms, teachers, and gender differences in mathematics. In E. Fennema & G. C. Leder (Eds.), *Mathematics and gender* (pp. 128–148). New York: Teachers College Press.

Koontz, T. Y. (2005). Instructional strategies for improving student achievement: Prevention and intervention. In S. Wagner (Ed.), *PRIME: Prompt intervention in mathematics education* (pp. 99–130). Columbus, OH: Ohio Resource Center for Mathematics, Science, and Reading/Ohio Department of Education.

Kroll, D. L. (1989). Connections between psychological learning theories and the elementary mathematics curriculum. In P. R. Trafton (Ed.), *New directions for elementary school mathematics* (1989 Yearbook, pp. 199–211). Reston, VA: National Council of Teachers of Mathematics.

Kurtzke, J. F. (1990). The baseball schedule: A modest proposal. *Mathematics, 83*(5), 346–350.

Laborde, C. (2002). Integration of technology in the design of geometry tasks with Cabri-Geometry. *International Journal of Computers for Mathematical Learning, 6*(3), 287–317.

Ladson-Billings, G. (1994). *The dreamkeepers: Successful teachers of African American children.* San Francisco: Jossey-Bass.

Ladson-Billings, G. (1995). Making mathematics meaningful in multicultural contexts. In W. G. Secada, E. Fennema, & L. B. Adajian (Eds.), *New directions for equity in mathematics education* (pp. 126–145). New York: Cambridge University Press.

Ladson-Billings, G. (1998). Just what is critical race theory and what's it doing in a nice field like education? *International Journal of Qualitative Studies in Education, 11*(1), 7–24.

Lampert, M. (1998). *Talking mathematics in school.* Cambridge, UK: Cambridge University Press.

Lappan, G., & Schram, P. (1989). Communication and reasoning: Critical dimensions of sense making in mathematics. In P. Trafton & A. P. Schulte (Eds.), *New directions for elementary school mathematics* (1989 Yearbook, pp. 13–30). Reston, VA: National Council of Teachers of Mathematics.

Lehrer, R., Jacobson, C., Kemeny, V., & Strom, D. (1999). Building on children's intuitions to develop mathematical understanding of space. In E. Fennema & T. R. Romberg (Eds.), *Mathematics classrooms that promote understanding* (pp. 63–87). Mahwah, NJ: Erlbaum.

Lesh, R., & Doerr, H. (2003). *Beyond constructivism: Models and modeling perspectives on mathematics problem solving, learning, and teaching.* Mahwah, NJ: Erlbaum.

Lesh, R., Landau, M., & Hamilton, E. (1983). Conceptual models in applied mathematical problem solving. In R. Lesh & M. Landau (Eds.), *Acquisition of mathematics concepts and processes* (pp. 263–343). New York: Academic Press.

Lester, F. K. (1989, November). Mathematical problem solving in and out of school. *Arithmetic Teacher, 37*(3), 33–35.

Levin, H., & Hopfenberg, W. (1991, January). Don't remediate: Accelerate! *Principal, 70*(3), 11–13.

Lindquist, M. (1989). Mathematics content and small-group instruction in grades 4–6. *Elementary School Journal, 89*(5), 625–632.

Lubienski, S. T. (2000). Problem solving as a means toward "mathematics for all": An exploratory look through a class lens. *Journal for Research in Mathematics Education, 31*(4), 454–482.

Lubienski, S. T. (2002). Research, reform, and equity in U.S. mathematics education. *Mathematical Thinking and Learning, 4*(2–3), 103–125.

Means, B., Chelemer, C., & Knapp, M. (Eds.). (1991). *Teaching advanced skills to at-risk students: Views from theory and practice.* San Francisco: Jossey-Bass.

Moses, R., & Cobb, C., Jr. (2001). *Radical equations: Civil rights from Mississippi to the Algebra Project.* Boston: Beacon Press.

Moses, R. P., Kamii, M., Swap, S. M., & Howard, J. (1989). The Algebra Project: Organizing in the spirit of Ella. *Harvard Educational Review, 59*(4), 423–443.

Mullis, I. V. S., Dossey, J. A., Owen, E. H., & Phillips, G. W. (1991, June). *The state of mathematics achievement: NAEP's 1990 assessment of the nation and the trial assessment of the states.* Princeton, NJ: Educational Testing Service/National Assessment of Educational Progress.

National Council of Teachers of Mathematics. (1989). *Curriculum and evaluation standards for school mathematics.* Reston, VA: Author.

National Council of Teachers of Mathematics. (1995). *Assessment standards for school mathematics.* Reston, VA: Author.

National Council of Teachers of Mathematics. (2000). *Principles and standards for school mathematics.* Reston, VA: Author.

Nelissen, J. M. C. (1999). Thinking skills in realistic mathematics. In J. H. M. Hamers, J. E. H. van Luit, & B. Csapo (Eds.), *Teaching and learning thinking skills* (pp. 189–214). Lisse, the Netherlands: Swets and Zeitlinger. Available: http://www.fi.uu.nl/publicaties/literatuur/6259.pdf

Noddings, N. (1989). Theoretical and practical concerns about small groups in mathematics. *Elementary School Journal, 89*(5), 607–623.

Norton, A. (2007). What's on your report card? *Teaching Children Mathematics, 13*(6), 315.

Oakes, J. (1986). Tracking, inequality, and the rhetoric of school reform: Why schools don't change. *Journal of Education, 168*(1), 61–80.

Olive, J. (1991). Logo programming and geometric understanding: An in-depth study. *Journal for Research in Mathematics Education, 22*(2), 90–111.

Olive, J. (2000). Computer tools for interactive mathematical activity in the elementary school. *International Journal of Computers for Mathematical Learning, 5*(3), 241–262.

Pellegrino, J. (2002). Knowing what students know. *Issues in Science and Technology, 19*(2), 48–52.

Peterson, P. L. (1988). Teaching for higher-order thinking in mathematics: The challenge for the next decade. In D. A. Grouws & T. J. Cooney (Eds.), *Perspectives on research for effective mathematics teaching* (pp. 2–26). Hillsdale, NJ: Erlbaum; and Reston, VA: National Council of Teachers of Mathematics.

Peterson, P., Fennema, E., & Carpenter, T. (1991). Using children's mathematical knowledge. In B. Means, C. Chelemer, & M. Knapp (Eds.), *Teaching advanced skills to at-risk students: Views from theory and practice* (pp. 68–101). San Francisco: Jossey-Bass.

Powell, A., & Frankenstein, M. (1997). *Ethnomathematics: Challenging eurocentrism in mathematics education.* New York: State University of New York Press.

Powell, A. B., & Ramnauth, M. (1992, June). Beyond questions and answers: Prompting reflections and deepening understandings of mathematics using multiple-entry logs. *For the Learning of Mathematics, 12*(2), 12–18.

Reimer, K., & Moyer, P. (2005). Third-graders learn about fractions using virtual manipulatives: A classroom study. *Journal of Computers in Mathematics and Science Teaching, 24*(1), 5–25.

Resnick, L. (1987). Constructing knowledge in school. In L. S. Liben (Ed.), *Development and learning: Conflict or congruence?* (pp. 19–25). Hillsdale, NJ: Erlbaum.

Reys, B., Dingman, S., Sutter, A., & Teuscher, D. (2005, March). *Development of state-level mathematics curriculum documents: Report of a survey.* Available: http://www.mathcurriculumcenter.org/ASSM_report.pdf

Riordan, J., & Noyce, P. (2001). The impact of two standards-based mathematics curricula on student achievement in Massachusetts. *Journal for Research in Mathematics Education, 32*(4), 368–398.

Romberg, T. A., & Kaput, J. J. (1999). Mathematics worth teaching, mathematics worth understanding. In E. Fennema & T. A. Romberg (Eds.), *Mathematics classrooms that promote understanding* (pp. 3–18). Mahwah, NJ: Erlbaum.

Ross, R., & Kurtz, R. (1993). Making manipulatives work: A strategy for success. *Arithmetic Teacher, 40*(5), 254–257.

Russell, S. J., & Friel, S. N. (1989). Collecting and analyzing real data in the elementary school classroom. In P. Trafton & A. Schulte (Eds.), *New directions for elementary school mathematics* (pp. 134–148). Reston, VA: National Council of Teachers of Mathematics.

Sarama, J., & Clements, D. H. (2002). Building blocks for young children's mathematical development. *Journal of Educational Computing Research, 27*(1), 93–110.

Schifter, D. (1998). Learning mathematics for teaching: From a teachers' seminar to the classroom. *Journal of Mathematics Teacher Education, 1*(1), 55–87.

Schoenfeld, A. (1989). Problem solving in context(s). In R. I. Charles & E. A. Silver (Eds.), *The teaching and assessing of mathematical problem solving* (pp. 82–92). Reston, VA: National Council of Teachers of Mathematics.

Schoenfeld, A. (2002). Making mathematics work for all children: Issues of standards, testing, and equity. *Educational Researcher, 31*(1), 13–25.

Schwartz, J., & Yerushalmy, M. (1985). *The geometric supposer.* Pleasantville, NY: Sunburst Communications.

Secada, W. G. (1991). Selected conceptual and methodological issues for studying the mathematics education of the disadvantaged. In M. S. Knapp & P. M. Shields (Eds.), *Better schooling for the children of poverty: Alternatives to conventional wisdom* (pp. 149–168). Berkeley, CA: McCutchan.

Senk, S., & Thompson, D. (2003). *Standards-based mathematics curricula: What are they? What do students learn?* Mahwah, NJ: Erlbaum.

Shavelson, R. J., Webb, N. M., Stasz, C., & McArthur, D. (1989). Teaching mathematical problem-solving: Insights from teachers and tutors. In R. I. Charles and E. A. Silver (Eds.), *The teaching and assessing of mathematical problem solving* (pp. 203–231). Reston, VA: National Council of Teachers of Mathematics.

Sherin, M. G. (2002a). A balancing act: Developing a discourse community in a mathematics classroom. *Journal of Mathematics Teacher Education, 5*(3), 205–233.

Sherin, M. G. (2002b). When teaching becomes learning. *Cognition and Instruction, 20*(2), 119–150.

Siegler, R. S. (2003). Implications of cognitive science research for mathematics education. In J. Kilpatrick, W. G. Martin, & D. Schifter (Eds.), *A research companion to Principles and Standards for School Mathematics* (pp. 289–303). Reston, VA: National Council of Teachers of Mathematics.

Silver, E. A., Smith, M. S., & Nelson, B. S. (1995). The QUASAR project: Equity concerns meet mathematics education reform in the middle school. In W. G. Secada, E. Fennema, & L. B. Adajian (Eds.), *New directions for equity in mathematics education* (pp. 9–56). New York: Cambridge University Press.

Skemp, R. R. (1987). *The psychology of learning mathematics.* Hillsdale, NJ: Erlbaum.

Slavin, R. (1990, December/January). Research on cooperative learning: Consensus and controversy. *Educational Leadership, 47*(4), 52–54.

Smith, S. P. (2003). Representation in school mathematics: Children's representations of problems. In J. Kilpatrick, W. G. Martin, & D. Schifter (Eds.), *A research companion to Principles and Standards for School Mathematics* (pp. 263–274). Reston, VA: National Council of Teachers of Mathematics.

Spillane, J. (2001). Challenging instruction for "all students": Policy, practitioners, and practice. In S. Fuhrman (Ed.), *From the capitol to the classroom: Standards-based reform in the states* (100th Yearbook of the National Society for the Study of Education, pp. 217–242). Chicago: University of Chicago Press.

Steffe, L. P., & D'Ambrosio, B. S. (1995). Toward a working model of constructivist teaching: A reaction to Simon. *Journal for Research in Mathematics Education, 26*(2), 146–159.

Steffe, L. P., & Olive, J. (2002). Design and use of computer tools for interactive mathematical activity (TIMA). *Journal of Educational Computing Research, 27*(1), 55–76.

Steffe, L. P., & Wiegel, H. G. (1994). Cognitive play and mathematical learning in computer microworlds.

Educational Studies in Mathematics, 26(2–3), 111–134.

Stein, M. K., Grover, B., & Henningsen, M. (1996). Building student capacity for mathematical thinking and reasoning: An analysis of mathematics tasks used in reform classrooms. *American Educational Research Journal, 33,* 455–488.

Sullivan, P., & Clarke, D. (1991). Catering to all abilities through good questions. *Arithmetic Teacher, 39*(2), 14–18.

Swetz, F., & Hartzler, J. S. (Eds.). (1991). *Mathematical modeling in the secondary school curriculum.* Reston, VA: National Council of Teachers of Mathematics.

Sztajn, P. (2003). Adapting reform ideas in different mathematics classrooms: Beliefs beyond mathematics. *Journal of Mathematics Teacher Education, 6*(1), 53–75.

Thompson, P. (1989). Artificial intelligence, advanced technology, and learning and teaching algebra. In S. Wagner & C. Kieren (Eds.), *Research issues in the learning and teaching of algebra* (pp. 135–161). Reston, VA: National Council of Teachers of Mathematics.

Walker, V., with D'Ambrosio, B. S., & Kastberg, S. E. (2006). A developing mathematical community. In J. O. Masingila (Ed.), *Teachers engaged in research: Inquiry into mathematics practice, grades 6–8* (pp. 81–97). Reston, VA: National Council of Teachers of Mathematics.

Waywood, A. (1992). Journal writing and learning mathematics. *For the Learning of Mathematics, 12*(2), 34–43.

Wearne, D., & Hiebert, J. (1989). Constructing and using meaning for mathematical symbols: The case of decimal fractions. In J. Hiebert & M. Behr (Eds.), *Number concepts and operations in the middle grades* (pp. 220–235). Hillsdale, NJ: Erlbaum; and Reston, VA: National Council of Teachers of Mathematics.

Webb, N. M., & Mastergeorge, A. M. (2003). The development of students' helping behavior and learning in peer-directed small groups. *Cognition and Instruction, 21*(4), 361–428.

Weissglass, J. (2000). No compromise on equity in mathematics education: Developing an infrastructure. In W. Secada (Ed.), *Changing the faces of mathematics: Perspectives on multiculturalism and gender equity* (pp. 5–24). Reston, VA: National Council of Teachers of Mathematics.

White, D. Y. (2003). Promoting productive mathematical classroom discourse with diverse students. *Journal of Mathematical Behavior, 22*(1), 37–53.

Wilson, L. D., & Kenney, P. A. (2003). Classroom and large-scale assessment. In J. Kilpatrick, W. G. Martin, & D. Schifter (Eds.), *A research companion to Principles and Standards for School Mathematics* (pp. 53–67). Reston, VA: National Council of Teachers of Mathematics.

Wilson, P. S. (1990, Summer/Fall). Inconsistent ideas related to definitions and examples. *Focus on Learning Problems in Mathematics, 12*(3–4), 111–129.

Wilson, S., & Floden, R. (2001). Hedging bets: Standards-based reform in classrooms. In S. Fuhrman (Ed.), *From the capitol to the classroom: Standards-based reform in the states* (100th Yearbook of the National Society for the Study of Education, pp. 193–216). Chicago: University of Chicago Press.

Yackel, E., & Cobb, P. (1996). Sociomathematical norms, argumentation, and autonomy in mathematics. *Journal for Research in Mathematics Education, 27*(4), 458–477.

Zaslavsky, C. (1973, November). Mathematics in the study of African culture. *Arithmetic Teacher, 20,* 532–535.

Zaslavsky, C. (1989, September). People who live in round houses. *Arithmetic Teacher, 37*(1), 18–21.

5

Strategies for Increasing Achievement in Writing

Sally Hampton

The current emphasis on reading has absorbed much of the American school day. Students' reading proficiency is measured annually, and often teacher evaluations are either explicitly or implicitly tied to state testing scores. As a result of this trend, in many classrooms the "language arts" have become simply "reading."

Teaching has changed, too. The emphasis on standards and assessments has caused—no, *forced*—multitudes of teachers to focus almost solely on what is tested and how to prepare students to do well on the test at hand. Many varieties of tests— practice tests, tests with "predictive validity," district assessments, tests to monitor ongoing growth/proficiency—all take up classroom time and drive teaching. Increased emphasis on student accountability has resulted in fewer opportunities for students' inquiry, less time for student-centered instruction, and an overall compression of the curriculum in order to provide more time for testing.

Although writing is one of the subjects assessed in the National Assessment of Educational Progress (NAEP), the assessment is not done every year, and it is not a state-level assessment (see "The State of Writing Today"). Although NAEP may influence practice, it is the state standards that drive accountability.

150

The State of Writing Today: NAEP 2002 Results

Scores on the writing assessment of the National Assessment of Educational Progress (NAEP) increased significantly between 1998 and 2002 for students in grades 4 and 8. The writing proficiency of 12th graders, however, did not improve. Yet even with the rise in scores at grades 4 and 8, there is reason for serious concern.

To understand why we should be concerned, first consider the NAEP achievement levels. The NAEP has identified three general levels of achievement:

- **Basic,** which denotes partial mastery of the prerequisite knowledge and skills essential for proficiency at each grade;
- **Proficient,** which denotes solid academic performance for each grade assessed, requiring students to demonstrate competence in challenging subject-matter knowledge, application of such knowledge to real-world situations, and analytical skills appropriate to the subject matter; and
- **Advanced,** which signifies superior performance.

It is a matter of grave concern when the NAEP reports that at each level—grades 4, 8, and 12—only 2 percent of students reach the advanced level. Moreover, at grade 4, only 26 percent are proficient; at grade 8, 29 percent are proficient; and at grade 12, 22 percent are proficient. To understand the scope of the problem in the area of writing, consider the percentage of students who score at the *below-basic* and *basic* levels: 72 percent at grade 4, 69 percent at grade 8, and 77 percent at grade 12 (National Center for Education Statistics, 2002).

Each student tested must respond to two 25-minute tasks. The kinds of writing tested are narrative, informative, and persuasive. Most important is that writers be able to organize their writing effectively, include detail to illustrate and elaborate their ideas, and demonstrate appropriate control of conventions. That only 2 percent at each of the three grade levels perform at an advanced level is troubling, and even more so is the fact that so many of our students perform at the basic and below-basic levels.

Unless writing is a state priority, teachers may hesitate to focus more instructional time on it. Yet *not* to teach writing is to overlook a powerful resource—one that can increase students' content knowledge and develop the kinds of literacy required in contemporary society, as well as improve reading comprehension.

Research reflects that reading and writing are related language-based processes. The link between these two processes can be made explicit and improve both through knowledge of genre and midlevel structures, such as cause and effect, comparison and contrast, and claim and evidence (Chomsky, 2006; Gee, 2001). Teaching reading and writing together enhances student engagement, learning, and reasoning.

How Reading and Writing Are Alike—and Also Different

At some level, the processes of reading and writing are strikingly similar. Both are acts of composing. A reader composes meaning from text, and a writer composes meaning into text. In both cases, background knowledge and experience are essential. And both processes require some specialized and linguistic knowledge in order to build meaning. Students who are writers have an advantage as readers. They understand what and why an author does things—either to cue a reader that something is essential or to employ a strategy that will lift the level of language in the text. Donald Murray (1993) once said that reading with a writer's eye was like a player of a sport watching that sport being played by others. The player—or, by comparison, the student who writes—has an edge. A student who writes understands the strategies being executed in a piece of writing and can follow what is going on with knowing eyes—seldom confused or surprised.

Despite their similarities, the cognitive and linguistic patterns of thinking for reading and writing are distinctive—even when students are reading and writing about the same topic.

If there were not such distinctions, students would automatically know how to write when they learn how to read.

Why Genre Knowledge Is Essential—and How It Can Be an Overarching Construct for Readers and Writers

As writers, students draw on their knowledge of genre to organize their writing. In like manner, as readers, students draw on their knowledge of genre to anticipate and follow where a text is going. Judith Langer (1986) tells us that a genre sets up certain expectations, shared understandings between the reader and writer. For example, when a reader encounters a memoir, he knows that he will be reading about some specific event or series of events that shaped a person's character, as opposed to a biography, which chronicles a person's entire life. When a reader encounters procedural writing, she expects to see how a process is carried out. She expects that the text will take her through a process step-by-step, guided by transition words such as *first*, *next*, and *then*. When a reader encounters an argument—frequently an editorial piece in a newspaper—the reader expects a claim to be made and then evidence offered in support of that claim. These expectations are rule-governed, not idiosyncratic, and their intent is to cue the reader. A writer employs them intentionally so the reader can use them as signposts to meaning. That same writer, when reading, understands how a text is ordered and is guided by these same signposts.

Not to make students aware of genre knowledge is to deny them academic success. The student who is required to produce a report but who does not know the expectations for how a writer of reports is expected to present information to a reader is immediately disadvantaged. That writer must draw at best on a "felt sense" of how information might be ordered, what kind of stance or persona could be effective, how much information should be provided, and what level of specificity is required. By comparison, the student who is genre-savvy and is aware of the various expectations attached to informational writing can simply elect which genre expectations to guide his or her writing, which to disregard, and if or where to vary the form. This second student obviously enjoys a tremendous advantage over the first student.

When genres drive instruction, students gain a deepening understanding of a relatively small number of forms and have the opportunity to "get better" at these forms through the grades. Genres provide a coherent view about what constitutes good writing and a meta-language for feedback, while they afford teachers a framework into which strategies can be plugged. When instruction builds around genre, teachers have language to talk about such things as flashback and naming, and back-story and forecasting.

How To Teach Reading and Writing Together

Reading and writing taught together enrich students' language and thinking capacities, and together they are hallmarks of a literate person. It only makes good sense, then, that they be integrated so students get the most out of each. What is also essential is *how* these processes are taught. For instruction to be effective, students need to have some choice—about what to read and the topic of their writing. When students have some control over what they choose to read, they are likely to invest themselves in developing a full understanding of the text, and so work hard to comprehend what they are reading. Similarly, when writers have some choice over what to write about, they will probably work harder to communicate simply because the topic is meaningful to them.

In order to make the connections between reading and writing obvious to students, the two processes should be taught together. There needs to be a sense of process; both reading and writing are, after all, processes. There is likely, for readers, to be an initial understanding of the text that may hold up or may need to be revised as the text unfolds. Writers, too, revise. They produce early drafts that may need only a little tinkering with or—more typically—may need substantial revision to communicate adequately and well. There also needs to be an effort from the teacher to make the reading/writing relationship explicit, through genre knowledge and understanding of midlevel structure and strategies, and to establish expected behaviors—habits of good readers and good writers—that guide what students do.

Primary writers. For primary students, the relationship between reading and writing is obvious. The two processes are almost two sides of the same coin, and knowledge of one supports the learning of the other. Drawing on their understanding of sound/letter correspondence, readers decode. Drawing on the same skills to form the words that tell their stories, writers encode. Also, sounding out a word helps students to read and to spell it; knowledge of signal words and phrases allows a writer to join ideas in an appropriate way and allows readers to connect ideas and understand the relationship between those ideas.

Moreover, as they write, primary children read and reread, especially as their texts get longer and more complicated. Lucy Calkins (1983) has observed that young writers read to savor what they've written, to regain momentum, and to edit. In fact, almost 30 percent of the time primary students spend on writing is actually spent reading.

Upper-elementary writers. A strong writing program supports content learning for students in grades 4 and above. Various kinds of writing—stories or reports, for example—include particular types of information. This information is organized or linked in common ways. Good readers seek the types of information that fit into these structures, and they use such information as an aid to understanding and remembering content. Writers, of course, learn these categorical structures (i.e., genre and midlevel structures, such as comparison/

contrast) in order to organize what they are communicating. So their writing supports their learning of the structures that will aid them as readers in retaining content.

Another way in which writing supports content learning has to do with a writer's need to understand the expectations and constraints imposed by different subject areas. Science generally requires students to record observations and write up experiments. As children do such writing, they internalize the vocabulary of science; they learn to think as a scientist does. There are two obvious benefits: first, these students are grounded in science; second, they are acquiring the language and expectations of the discipline. As a result, they can handle a relatively complex reading load.

Secondary writers. When Ernest Boyer (Tagg, 1986), then president of the Carnegie Foundation for the Advancement of Teaching, was asked how to know if a given high school was doing a good job, he answered that simply asking all the seniors to write an essay on a subject of their choice and then reading those essays would reveal more about the quality of the school than would any other measure. Writing reveals what we know; more than anything else, it is a measure of our learning.

Academically, of course, at the secondary level being able to write means survival. The high school term paper, subject-matter portfolios, college application letters, the SAT, ACT, and AP tests all measure student writing proficiency. If, as the 2002 NAEP scores reveal, only 2 percent of 12th graders tested were at an advanced level, success at the college level would seem to be a challenge for almost all graduates. Writing—and writing of several kinds—must be addressed in the high school curriculum.

Typically, high school students write to display knowledge in various content-area courses—a task that continues through the college years. Learning how to address a topic directly and to recast primary- and secondary-source materials effectively are skills that develop over time with ongoing feedback and practice. At the secondary level, writing reveals not only what the writer knows about writing strategies and organizational patterns, it also reveals the writer's understanding of the subject and the clarity of the writer's thinking. As writers work to shape content, they must cluster ideas appropriately, employ vocabulary specific to the topic, and provide sufficient detail to communicate ideas effectively. Working and reworking the writing deepens writers' understanding of a specific subject as it increases facility with language and thinking.

Writing Strategies That Promote Achievement at All Grade Levels

The following set of strategies, which are grounded in both research and experience in the field, should be the foundation for a comprehensive and coherent writing program. They are strongly recommended for accelerating writing ability and creating more good writers, especially among the lower third of students in schools:

- Establish a workshop environment in the classroom.
- Establish productive writing habits.
- Establish a genre-based curriculum.
- Use writing in all subject areas.
- Encourage reading.
- Embed studies in the curriculum.
- Use rubrics as a tool for formative assessment.
- Involve students in the evaluation process.
- Include contextual instruction in grammar.
- Model the writing process.

Strategy 5.1:
Establish a workshop environment in the classroom.

Discussion

A writer's workshop is a classroom management structure that offers teachers maximum opportunity to work both one-on-one and with small groups of students while the remainder of the class is engaged in productive learning. During a writer's workshop, those students not working directly with the teacher work on refining their own writing. Some students draft pieces while others plan, revise, or edit their writing.

Properly established, the writer's workshop provides a tightly structured learning environment that puts in place daily procedures and practices for students to follow. The workshop also creates a community that enables students to learn, to move about

155

the classroom purposefully, to use all the resources of the classroom efficiently, and to be independent and responsible. Students are taught what to do (practices) and when to do these things. They learn problem-solving procedures so that they can work independently while the teacher is conferring with individual students or providing instruction to a small group of students who share a common need.

Unlike classrooms that rely on centers in order for teachers to differentiate instruction, the writer's workshop does not require planning time for the teacher to stock and grade activities. The workshop, instead, requires that students use the writing process to individually develop pieces of work, and then the teacher and each student meet to discuss that work. Hence, both the teacher's planning time and the students' work time focus on important learning.

Classroom Examples

The writer's workshop usually begins with a relatively short, focused whole-group lesson after which students practice the concept taught during the lesson and then either work on their own writing or receive instruction one-on-one or in a small group with the teacher.

If, for example, the teacher has noticed that students need help with their introductions, she might give a lesson on how to write introductions using rhetorical questions. She can provide examples of this kind of opener and talk about why it is effective. She can then ask students to try this strategy by going back to one of their previous pieces and revising their introduction

so that it includes a rhetorical question, or else beginning the piece they plan to work on next by using this particular strategy.

There are usually rules posted on the wall that the students and teachers have agreed upon. These rules address problems that students need to solve (what to do when you can't spell a word) or procedures that need to be followed (how to find a response partner or how to schedule a conference with the teacher).

There are also rubrics on the wall that students use to assess their own writing. The rubrics reflect the classroom curriculum and have been constructed jointly by the teacher and students. The rubrics also help guide the writing response groups and the student/teacher conferences. Students are free to move about the room in order to use the classroom walls as a resource.

Resources

Atwell, 1998; Bomer, 1995; Calkins, 1983; Fiderer, 1993; Graves, 1991; Peterson, 1992; Ray & Laminack, 2001.

Strategy 5.2:
Establish productive writing habits.

Discussion

The writer's workshop introduces the idea that during the school year, students will work to become writers. In order for this transformation to take place, students learn about and practice the habits, and the habits of mind, that writers cultivate. They read a series of mentor texts— books or articles—worth studying in order to analyze how these texts communicate so well. Students visit Web sites to learn what writers themselves say about how to become a successful writer. In short, they apprentice themselves to writers and study the techniques these writers practice.

Apprenticeship learning has a long history in the research literature as being an effective mode of instruction. Students should have the opportunity to learn about writing from real writers. To ensure this opportunity, the teacher introduces students to the writing habits of a select number of writers whose works (mentor texts) the students study to understand organization and style. Students maintain "sourcebooks" in which they keep track of the strategies and the organizing structures that they learn about, and then employ these skills in pieces they are working to produce.

So what do recognized writers say about their practice? Stephen King says, "If you want to be a writer, you must do two things above all others: read a lot and write a lot. There's no way around these two things that I'm aware of, no short cut." William Goldman said, "Writing is essentially about going into a room by yourself and doing it." Graham Greene: "It's just the question of working, of being willing to put in the time." Robert Southley: "By writing much, one learns to write well." And James Thurber: "Don't get it right, get it written."

Therefore, one habit student writers should develop is to write regularly and—if King is to be believed—read regularly. The more, the better. Another habit professional writers promote is revision. Writing about something of interest or something that is meaningful is a good habit for any writer. Another valuable habit is finding a good reader—an editor or response partner or group—to help refine your writing. Still another is learning from the style of other writers. Careful writers are deliberate; they care not just about what is said but take care to say things well.

Including in the workshop library a few of the many collections of "writerly advice" offered by professional writers can help inspire novice student writers to improve. Such collections offer insights into writerly habits that can serve to mentor writing development.

Classroom Examples

Students are encouraged to adopt, as a fundamental goal, improving themselves as writers. In order to understand what would help to bring about this transformation, a teacher may suggest that the class adopt as mentors the authors of several books that the students especially like. Next, the class studies information about the authors, including how they live their lives as writers. Then the class compiles a list of writerly habits. Drawn from their study of favorite authors and from the list of these authors' writerly habits, students set goals for themselves.

For example, a teacher working with students could translate professional writers' habits into such meaningful classroom behaviors as

- Write every day.
- Read a lot.
- Work hard at writing.
- Share my writing with others to get suggestions for improvement.
- Reread my writing.

- Revise my writing to make it better.
- Borrow ideas and words from other writers.

Resources

Farnham-Diggory, 1990; Goldberg, 1986; Kovacs & Preller, 1993; Murray, 1993; Ray, 1999.

Strategy 5.3:
Establish a genre-based curriculum.

Discussion

At its most basic level, a genre is a type of text, a rough template for organizing information. Written genres have distinguishing features, such as organizational structures, subject matter, vocabulary, and style features. Because genres follow general, predictable patterns in their structure, organization, and language, genre-savvy readers and writers know what to expect when they read a particular genre and how to structure their ideas as they write in a given genre.

State tests, for example, frequently expect students to produce writing samples that conform to genre patterns. Most frequently tested at the elementary level are narratives, the story structure that organizes a series of events chronologically; argument, the genre that builds on a structure of claim, evidence, and reasoning; and informational genres, such as reports, instructions, etc., which are factual in nature and often include such midlevel structures as comparison/contrast or problem/solution.

For students to understand genres, they need examples, or model texts, that illustrate the genre's distinctive features. In teaching informational reports, for example, the teacher might use several science trade books as illustrations of the genre and then point out such features as specialized language; an organizational structure built around topics and subtopics; the inclusion of graphics, charts, and illustrations; and specific, accurate facts and information. In teaching narrative, the teacher might illustrate the genre with a high-quality story and point out such features as the initiating event, the chronology of further events, conflict, resolution, the closing, character development, and description.

Classroom Examples

Genre studies are a popular method for teaching genre structures and their attendant strategies. Although there are several formats for these studies—and many examples available on the Web—what generally happens in a genre study is that the teacher leads students through a study of several books that conform to the same genre pattern, making explicit to students the organizational structures and style features.

For example, if the class undertakes a study of the mystery story, a narrative subgenre, the teacher could choose one book as the starting point and then read through it with the class, calling students' attention to the book's setting, the initiating event, the problem (crime), the protagonist, the antagonist, the use of pacing to build suspense, the layering of clues, and the final resolution.

The students could then divide into small groups, with a different mystery story assigned to each group. The task of the groups would be to tease out what similarities and differences the book that the group has been assigned to study shares with the book read by the teacher. The class could then create a chart of mystery-story features, drawn from the initial book and all the information from all the groups, and use this chart either to produce a class-constructed mystery story or to measure a new book against the criteria chart to determine whether or not that book qualifies as a mystery story.

Resources

Bishop & Ostrom, 1997; Cope & Kalantzis, 1993; Derewianka, 2002; Duke & Bennett-Armistead, 2003; Lattimer, 2003.

Strategy 5.4:
Use writing in all subject areas.

Discussion

Writing is thinking in print. A writer draws from a variety of sources—personal knowledge, observations, and primary-source data, among others—to construct text that allows connections to emerge. This meaning-making crosses disciplines and encourages students to explore relationships between the subjects they are studying and the real-world knowledge they bring to those subjects. What emerges from these connections represents new knowledge for the writer.

Writing—simply putting words on paper—seems to unlock the mind, to organize and synthesize thinking, to shape intelligence. Writing enables the writer to weave together bits of information that may or may not have been previously joined—and in this joining, to discover new meaning. How this meaning is conveyed to a reader causes a writer to make a variety of choices: how to structure the writing as a whole; what pitch or word choice should be used to ensure precise meaning; what ideas to make subordinate; what to assert rather than imply; which combination of sentence forms might best produce the desired cadences.

Teachers in all content areas should encourage writing as a mode of learning. In evaluating writing, teachers should emphasize the degree to which students are able to demonstrate content-specific understandings. Once teachers focus on a student's ability to demonstrate an understanding of content or on the quality of thinking demonstrated in the writing, writing becomes less the province of the English teacher and more a means of examining what a student knows and how well a student thinks.

Classroom Examples

Young science students, for instance, might undertake topic studies in which they research a topic related to what they are learning in science, gathering information from multiple sources (see Strategy 5.6). Mathematics students might be encouraged to explain why a math answer is incorrect or where an answer might have gone wrong. History students might be asked to write about perspective, illustrating how writers' perspectives on an event differ and why this is important to an understanding of history.

Teachers who are working to help students develop various thinking strategies—regardless of the subject being considered—might use writing as a way of gauging improvement. Students might move through a series of assignments: for instance, moving from writing focused on developing the ability to see relationships in a very rudimentary context, to analyzing a relationship within an increasingly complex situation, perhaps even to analyzing a whole series of complex relationships.

Resources

Applebee, 1981; Duke, 2002; Farr & Daniels, 1986; Fulwiler & Young, 1982; Langer, 1986; Langer & Applebee, 1987.

Strategy 5.5:
Encourage reading.

Discussion

Many adults who read extensively admit to favoring a particular genre or topic, such as mystery stories or books about World War II. They also admit to reading the complete works of authors whose style they like. Although teachers can—and, to some degree, should—encourage readers to sample a variety of genres by a range of authors, teachers should also encourage readers to emulate these habits of successful readers and to read deeply within a genre they especially like or to read multiple texts by one author.

Encouraging this kind of reading will benefit students. First, if they read deeply in a genre, students will become increasing familiar with that genre's conventions, and so will be able to anticipate the structure of other books in the same genre. Likewise, if students read multiple texts by a single author, they develop a familiarity with the style of that writer. Consider the 3rd and 4th graders who read the Harry Potter books. In most cases, the first book in this series was a real challenge for the readers. Having met that challenge, however, readers find the rest of the series much easier to read because of the background knowledge they have garnered from the first book.

Those who read regularly internalize the patterns of organization of various types of writing and develop an understanding of and appreciation for the structures of language. Moreover, attentive readers become more sensitive to writers' strategies and can make distinctions between strategies they find effective and those they do not. And it is through reading widely that students expand their vocabularies.

Always, students should be reminded of the relationship between reading and writing. To the extent that we encourage young people to read as writers—looking for what works and what doesn't work—we will encourage discriminating writers, capable of accessing a range of options and strategies. To the extent that we require students to examine closely what makes writing effective, we will help them develop a repertoire of effective writing options.

Students should be encouraged to draw on their experience as writers to solve reading problems and on their experience as readers to solve writing problems. At the very least, reading teachers should make specific references to features of writing when teaching students to read, and writing teachers should talk about accommodating the needs of readers when teaching students to draft text. Teachers of reading should also make explicit to readers the various stylistic strategies employed by particular writers so that students will make connections between these strategies and their own strategies.

Classroom Examples

The most direct way to encourage wide reading is to make engaging materials accessible and to give students time during class to read these materials. Classroom libraries should contain high-interest, age-appropriate texts on a variety of levels so that all students can find something to read. The library should contain a mix of fiction and nonfiction texts as well as blended genres. A mix of 30 percent of each of these text types is desirable. When possible, the library should also contain manuals, magazines, and newspapers.

Book clubs and discussion groups foster discussion and develop comprehension. Establishing a procedure such as Lauren Resnick's Accountable Talk (1999) ensures that students carry on meaningful and productive conversation about what they are reading. Therefore, teachers should encourage talking about the books, and should put a procedure in place to make the conversations thoughtful and civil.

Resources

Bereiter & Scardamalia, 1984; Daniels & Zemelman, 1998; Goldman & Rohestraw, 2000; Kamberelis, 1999; Pappas, Kiefer, & Levstick, 1999; Resnick, 1999; Shanahan, 1988.

Strategy 5.6:
Embed studies in the curriculum.

Discussion

Studies are exercises in learning that require students to spend long blocks of time—at least three weeks—delving deeply into a topic. There are *author* studies, in which students read a collection of texts by the same author in order to compare and contrast their works (using criteria such as subject matter, plot line, use of language, and types of characters), and then write up their findings. There are *genre* studies (see Strategy 5.3), which require that students read a collection of works all conforming to the same set of genre expectations. Students are required to sort out the characteristics of the genre and then write a report about how well the books did or did not conform to the characteristics. And there are *topic* studies, which require students to read widely and deeply on a topic of their choice. Each of these studies engages students deeply as readers and writers, sharpens their ability to analyze, and requires that they order and communicate large chunks of informational material.

Classroom Examples

Topic studies are a productive means of both fostering student interest and providing extensive reading and writing time. To set up a topic study, the teacher should (1) help the students in choosing and narrowing the subject to be researched; (2) supply the necessary resources; and (3) set a schedule for completing the work. Topic studies are most effective when the final product requires a write-up of what the student has learned. The benefits can be compelling; teachers know that a student's strong interest can be a powerful motivator and can enable that student to read and understand very challenging texts.

The student, for example, who chooses to do a topic study on an endangered species will be willing to work through text that she might normally abandon because of its difficulty. And the more deeply the student reads about the endangered species, the easier the reading will become, even though the challenge level of the texts may increase. This growth in reading ability occurs because the student's knowledge about the topic supports her learning. Everything about the topic becomes background knowledge that facilitates the understanding of increasingly difficult texts.

Moreover, when the student writes up what she has learned, not only will the act of writing crystallize what she knows, her commitment to accurately communicating what she knows will cause her to address seriously such issues as paragraphing, the use of headers, maintaining a focus, providing sufficient and relevant detail, and sorting and categorizing information in a transparent way.

Resources

Calkins, 1983; Duke, 2000; Hampton, 2006; McMackin & Siegel, 2002.

Strategy 5.7:
Use rubrics as a tool for formative assessment.

Discussion

Rubrics are familiar features in many writing classrooms, and it is widely accepted that feedback via classroom rubrics can have a significant impact on improving student writing.

Paul Black has studied the value of formative assessment (such as rubrics) on learning gains, and found that formative assessment experiments produce substantial student improvement, considerably more improvement than most educational interventions. Black contends that (Black & Wiliam, 1998) "innovations which include strengthening the practice of formative assessment produce significant, and often substantial, learning gains . . . larger than most of those found for educational interventions."

The problem is that in most classrooms grading is typically overemphasized at the expense of formative assessments, so that the giving of useful advice and learning are underemphasized. Typical feedback to students, when it does exist, is primarily of a social or managerial function.

Black (Black & Wiliam , 1998) continues:

Formative assessment can be a powerful weapon . . . if it is communicated in the right way. Whilst it can help all pupils, it gives particularly good results with low achievers where it concentrates on specific problems with their work, and gives them both a clear understanding of which is wrong and achievable targets for putting it right. . . . Feedback to any pupil should be about the particular qualities of his or her work, with advice on what he or she can do to improve, and should avoid comparisons with other pupils.

In addition, Black warns that "pupils should be trained in self-assessment so that they can understand the main purposes of their learning and thereby grasp what they need to do to achieve."

What Black is telling us is that, under "certain circumstances," feedback (say, classroom rubrics) can contribute significantly to student learning (student writing improvement, for instance). Those "certain circumstances," however, are critical. The rubric must provide feedback about particular, as opposed to general, qualities of the work. It must provide advice about how to improve the work. This advice must set an achievable target. And the feedback must be so intelligible that students can grasp its significance and use it both as a self-assessment tool and as a guide for improvement. Consider each of these "certain circumstances." Certain conditions must be met for the rubrics to be effective.

First of all, the rubrics must be intelligible to students. Ideally, the rubric criteria have all been taught and used by students. Thus they are familiar and well understood, growing out of the writing curriculum. The goal is for students to be able to use the rubric criteria for self-assessment and in peer-response groups and for guidance in revising their work.

Next, the rubrics should provide feedback about particular qualities of the student writing. This means that the rubrics must be highly specific. Criteria such as "well organized" or "well developed" are not helpful. The former would be helpful if it read: "contains a series of events ordered chronologically"; the latter, "provides sufficient detail so the reader can envision the character and setting." Feedback is particularly effective when it is developed around genres, because the genres provide a framework that remains fairly constant through the grades.

Next, to be effective, rubrics must set targets and offer advice. At each score level, a good rubric provides a list of specific criteria that defines performance at that level. Students advance to the next level (the target) by refining the paper to match the criteria in the next score level. So, for example, if a student's paper is at score point 3 and that student wants a score point 4, the student must revise the paper to include all the elements for the higher score currently missing from the paper or must refine the way in which the elements and strategies are developed. Rubrics are not good tools for revision if the distinctions between score levels are set only by qualifiers: "scant" detail, "some" detail, "adequate" detail, and "effective" detail. Better rubrics provide more definitive distinctions: "no sense of introduction," "an introduction that names the topic and provides at least

FIGURE 5.1				
Rubric for Formative Assessment in Writing				
	4	3	2	1
Orientation/ Introduction				
Organization				
Use of detail				
Closure				

minimal context," and "an introduction that names the topic, provides context, and generates reader interest."

Classroom Examples

Because the criteria for the rubrics come from classroom instruction, students are aware that these elements are characteristics of good writing: organization, orientation/introduction, development or use of detail, and closure.

In creating a rubric, the teacher creates a chart that lists these elements down the side of the chart (see Figure 5.1); across the top are the numbers 4, 3, 2, and 1, as follows:

Working with the class, the teacher fills in each cell with a very explicit description—for example, organization might be described as follows:

4. Creates a logical sequence of events that a reader can easily follow.

3. Creates a sequence of events that may have some gaps.

2. Creates a series of events not clearly ordered.

1. Inappropriate event sequence that is not possible to follow.

A score sequence for beginners providing greater detail might look similar to Figure 5.2.

Resources

Black & Wiliam, 1998; Hampton, Murphy, & Lowry, 2004.

Strategy 5.8:

Involve students in the evaluation process.

Discussion

The development of students' writing abilities requires both a coherent writing program and continuing opportunities for students to engage in the writing process. Ideally, such growth in writing ability would be measured against grade-level standards, with students understanding that they are responsible for moving toward these standards. This view of writing development places less emphasis on the evaluation of any single piece of student work and more emphasis on the student's collection (or portfolio) of work, which should show substantive improvement over time and should contain evidence of having reached a certain level of proficiency.

If students are to be held accountable for their growth as writers, then they must be made aware of the inventories, checklists, or rubrics used to judge writing as being successful. And they must be given regular feedback relative to these same criteria. The criteria for evaluation should always grow out of the curriculum and be completely transparent (see Strategy 5.7). These evaluation criteria should guide conversations in response groups and in teacher/student conferences. It is important that all standards, models, and criteria represent age-appropriate proficiency.

When students become aware of what is valued in writing and are shown strategies for developing effective writing, they will work to develop those strategies. For example, once students who produce unelaborated texts recognize that elaboration is a necessary component of effective writing, they can begin to judge the quality of their own work relative to the degree and kind of elaboration they provide. They can be encouraged to revisit earlier pieces and revise these pieces by successfully employing elaboration strategies. These same students may recognize that perhaps they do not elaborate as effectively as professional writers or mentor authors, but they will also realize that they have the ability to elaborate more effectively than they once did. Teachers, too, see writing ability as evolving over time and recognize and celebrate the growth of their students' abilities.

FIGURE 5.2

Rubric of Specific Criteria for Writing Improvement

4	3	2	1
Has effective leads that make the reader want to read more and might: • Introduce the main characters • Include the setting • Lead right into the action of the story • Include feelings, details, and events that are returned to in the ending	Has leads that are simple or rote and that might: • Include setting • Introduce the main character • Lead right into the action of the story	Has a sense that a story is beginning and/or uses only a rote beginning such as "One day" or "Once upon a time."	Has no sense that a story is beginning.

Classroom Examples

A teacher may encourage students to focus on developing proficiency in using a particular strategy or element associated with various forms of discourse—the use of dialogue, for example. The teacher may hold a conference with each student on effective ways to craft dialogue and how often or where to use that particular device. The teacher might ask students to bracket sections of texts where they have used dialogue and to assess its effectiveness relative to earlier efforts or to a model piece of writing. This process allows students to appreciate their progress and encourages further effort and a willingness to revise.

The one-on-one teacher/student conference is always the best way to bring a student into the evaluation process. By establishing a sign-up procedure that requires each student to confer with the teacher on a regular basis, the teacher can prepare by reviewing the student's work before the conference, and the student can be ready to ask for help or to discuss progress being made toward the established goals.

Another effective strategy involves asking students to review all work done prior to producing a final draft. After the review, students produce a reflective piece in which they describe the evolution of their writing, noting specifically what they did to make their work better and what might yet be done were they to consider a further revision. This reflective piece, a form of self-evaluation, might actually be the primary basis for discussion during a teacher/student conference.

Resources

Anderson, 2000; Daniels & Zemelman, 1985; Farr & Daniels, 1986; Hillocks, 1986; Newkirk & Atwell, 1988; Parry & Hornsby, 1988; Robb, 1998; Romano, 1987; Routman, 2000; Sowers, 1988.

Strategy 5.9:

Include contextual instruction in grammar.

Discussion

Research has shown that the study of grammar in isolation does not improve students' writing ability (Andrews et al., 2006; Graham & Perin, 2007). Students should be taught strategies for learning such an important skill in context rather than discretely, so that they can more readily apply their learning in the future.

Traditionally, teachers decided what skills young people needed and taught those skills directly, often in a predetermined sequence; students then practiced the skills in isolation. Teachers emphasized practice and corrected responses, controlling how much practice or how many exercises students required. Only rarely was the skill applied in new, meaningful contexts.

Language use and conventions—punctuation, paragraphing, spelling, capitalization—all exist to accommodate reader understanding. They are, of course, governed by rules; facility in using them requires deep understanding of written language. When students write, they gain this deep understanding. As writers, students actively engage in making decisions about which language and conventions will best present their ideas: long sentences or short sentences, dialogue or indirect quotation, bullets or short paragraphs. Each decision made will have an effect on a reader. But only an informed writer understands the variety of effects and can access a range of options. The more students write, the more understanding they will have about how language and conventions work.

The control of conventions should be taught when and because the learners need to use them to make writing intelligible. So, for example, as primary students move from drawing and labeling pictures to drafting sentences, they need to learn about end punctuation. As their text becomes longer, they should begin to learn about paragraphing. When they write stories, they will likely need to be able to handle quotation marks for dialogue, and so forth.

Teachers should routinely review student writing to determine the most common errors in the use of conventions. The next step is to plan lessons that address these errors. During the lesson, the teacher could discuss the skill or concept and then use the skill or concept in editing a piece of student writing on a transparency. At the end of the lesson, the teacher can direct students to review the text on which they are working or a sample from their writing folders, and have them edit the work using the skill featured in the minilesson.

Classroom Examples

Let us assume that several students are having problems with end punctuation. The teacher could make transparencies of student papers that contain numerous errors of this nature (obscuring the students' names, of course). The teacher could then edit these papers for end punctuation, referencing the appropriate rules and instructing students to edit their own work-in-progress for problems with end punctuation. The teacher's task thus becomes the identification of error patterns, rather than the correction of random errors.

If students maintain their writing in folders, teachers can use these caches of writing as rich resources for revision exercises. One way to use folders to focus on revision is to periodically review one piece of writing from a folder, affixing a sticky note to the piece that details control of conventions, any features that distinguish the piece of writing, and any patterns of errors that mar it. The note will direct subsequent revision efforts, with students attending primarily to the pattern of errors noted to revise the selected piece and perhaps as many as two subsequent pieces. Students themselves may even choose to begin using this system of sticky notes to document certain features of their own work.

Resources

Anderson, 2005; Andrews et al., 2006; Graham & Perin, 2007; Weaver, 1979; Williams, 2003.

Strategy 5.10:
Model the writing process.

Discussion

The writing process movement changed how we think about the way in which real writers produce writing. Before the mid-1980s, many teachers assigned writing; they did not teach writing. Moreover, the first draft was commonly the final draft; there was no knowledge of the writing process.

Today, many teachers afford students time to plan and draft, revise and edit. Students have access to feedback on their writing from response groups made up of other students and to teacher feedback during a writing conference. It is not unusual for even primary students to produce multiple drafts of text before producing a final product. The teaching of writing has come a long way.

On-demand writing and writing in other content areas are frequently overlooked, however, because teachers often focus on the need to get students invested in both what they say and how they express their thoughts using literary strategies. And yet students often face the need to produce these kinds of writing, especially at the secondary level, where the emphasis is less on how eloquently something is expressed than the degree to which a student is able to express a correct understanding of a topic.

The writing process, of course, is still the writing process: good writing requires a plan, an execution, and most frequently some revision. What it means to plan, draft, revise, and edit, however, can vary depending on circumstance.

For example, if a student is taking a timed test, the planning time will be relatively short and the drafting less carefully polished than otherwise, especially if time is short or if no allowance is made for multiple drafts. The writer of an on-demand piece should focus on

organization, clarity, thoroughness, and correctness rather than turns of phrase or artful strategies. Revision for an on-demand piece of writing will possibly allow for crossing through and rewriting words, clauses, even sentences, but will certainly not allow for largely revising and reorganizing the writing. In these circumstances, editing will be crucial, so the writer will need to allow adequate time to examine the piece for any errors. There will be no access to feedback from others or to resources such as a dictionary, so the final rereading will be labor intensive.

By contrast, if a student is preparing a paper as a history assignment, there will be (we hope) adequate time to plan and draft as well as access to feedback and the opportunity to revise. What might matter most, however, is the use of careful and coherent organization structures, footnotes or endnotes, a bibliography, and the inclusion of maps, timelines, and other graphics. Accurate and sufficient detail will also be a focus. All of these elements will be more specific to the writing process than will such elements as the use of metaphor or pacing. Revisions will focus on sufficiency and correctness of information and on the transparency of claims and adequacy of evidence to support the claims.

Classroom Examples

Teachers should model for students the various forms that the writing process can take. Depending on the grade level of the students, the modeling—at least, the planning and drafting stages—can be done on an overhead transparency. The class can offer comment as a form of response, so revision and editing can take place on the transparency. This process, though it may take more than one class period, is most valuable when the teacher thinks aloud while composing. Though all writers' processes are somewhat idiosyncratic, the modeling will illustrate that writing takes work, that it is a process, and that the process is not sequential, but recursive—that is, sometimes we edit as we draft, and sometimes we plan as we revise.

Resources

Avery, 1993; Bomer, 1995; Calkins, 1983; Fletcher & Portalupi, 1998; Graves, 1983; Ray, 1999; Routman, 1991; Zemelman & Daniels, 1988.

Conclusion

All of the strategies in this chapter require that writing be a regular part of the student's day, and that students and teachers understand that *learning to write takes time*. Writing well takes practice and instruction and feedback, but given these strategies all students can learn to express themselves thoughtfully and well. This goal is well within our reach.

Moreover, being able to express oneself in print is the hallmark of a literate person. It is also a skill that is fundamentally important for academic success and for advancement in the workplace. Being nimble with words, approaching a computer screen with confidence and purpose rather than with uncertainty and dread, are things that do not come easily. They grow out of years of practice. They are habits. As such, they should be practiced and respected and held in esteem by educators everywhere.

Bibliography

Anderson, C. (2000). *How's it going?: A practical guide to conferring with student writers*. Portsmouth, NH: Heinemann.

Anderson, J. (2005). *Mechanically inclined*. Portland, ME: Stenhouse.

Andrews, R., Torgerson, C., Beverton, S., Freeman, A., Locke, R., Low, G., et al. (2006). The effect of grammar teaching on writing development. *British Educational Research Journal, 32*(1), 39–55.

Applebee, A. N. (1981). *Writing in the secondary school: English and the content areas*. Urbana, IL: National Council of Teachers of English.

Atwell, N. (1998). *In the middle: New understandings about writing, reading, and learning*. Portsmouth, NH: Boynton/Cook.

Bereiter, C., & Scardamalia, M. (1984). Learning about writing from reading. *Written Communication, 1*(2), 163–188.

Bishop, W., & Ostrom, H. (1997). *Genre and writing: Issues, arguments, alternatives*. Portsmouth, NH: Boynton/Cook.

Black, P., & Wiliam, D. (1998). Inside the black box: Raising standards through classroom assessment. *Phi Delta Kappan, 80*(2), 139–148.

Bomer, R. (1995). *Time for meaning: Crafting literate lives in middle and high school*. Portsmouth, NH: Heinemann.

Butler, A., & Turbill, J. (1984). *Towards a reading-writing classroom*. Rozelle, New South Wales, Australia: Primary English Teaching Association.

Calkins, L. (1983). *Lessons from a child: On the teaching and learning of writing*. Exeter, NH: Heinemann.

Chomsky, N. (2006). *Language and mind* (3rd ed.). Cambridge, UK: Cambridge University Press.

Cope, B., & Kalantzis, M. (1993). *The powers of literacy: A genre approach to teaching writing*. Pittsburgh, PA: University of Pittsburgh Press.

Daniels, H. A., & Zemelman, S. (1998). *Methods that matter: Six structures for best practice classrooms*. Portland, ME: Stenhouse.

Derewianka, B. (2002). *Exploring how texts work*. Newtown, New South Wales, Australia: Primary English Teaching Association.

Duke, N., & Bennett-Armistead, U. S. (2003). *Reading and writing informational text in the primary grades: Research-based practices*. New York: Scholastic.

Farnham-Diggory, S. (1990). *Schooling*. Cambridge, MA: Harvard University Press.

Farr, M., & Daniels, H. (1986). *Language diversity and writing instruction*. New York: Columbia University, Institute for Urban and Minority Education and Urbana, IL: ERIC Clearinghouse on Reading and Communication Skills.

Fiderer, A. (1993). *Teaching writing: A workshop approach*. New York: Scholastic.

Fletcher, R., & Portalupi, J. (1998). *Craft lessons: Teaching writing K–8*. Portland, ME: Stenhouse.

Foorman, B., et al. (1983). The role of instruction in learning to read: Preventing reading failure in at-risk children. *Journal of Educational Psychology, 90*(1), 37–55.

Fulwiler, T., & Young, A. (1982). *Language connections: Writing and reading across the curriculum*. Urbana, IL: National Council of Teachers of English.

Gee, J. (2001). Discourse and sociocultural studies in reading. In R. Barr, P. D. Pearson, M. L. Kamil, & P. Mosenthal (Eds.), *Handbook of reading research* (Vol. 2, pp. 195–208). Hillsdale, NJ: Erlbaum.

Goldberg, N. (1986). *Writing down the bones: Freeing the writer within*. Boston: Shambhala.

Graham, S., & Perin, D. (2007). *Writing next: Effective strategies to improve writing of adolescents in middle and high schools* (Carnegie Corporation Report). Washington, DC: Alliance for Excellent Education.

Graves, D. (1983). *Writing: Teachers and children at work*. Portsmouth, NH: Heinemann.

Graves, D. (1991). *The reading/writing teacher's companion: Build a literate classroom*. Portsmouth, NH: Heinemann.

Hampton, S. (2007). *Connecting reading and writing for literacy learning*. Washington, DC: National Education Association.

Hampton, S., Murphy, S., & Lowry, M. (2004). *Assessment for learning: Using rubrics to improve student writing*. Washington, DC: New Standards.

Kamberelis, G. (1999). Genre development and learning: Children writing stories, science reports, and poems. *Research in the Teaching of English, 33*(4), 403–459.

Kovacs, D., & Preller, J. (1993). *Meet the authors and illustrators: 60 creators of favorite children's books talk about their work* (Vol. 2). New York: Scholastic Professional.

Langer, J. (1986). *Children reading and writing: Structures and strategies*. Norwood, NJ: Ablex.

Langer, J. A., & Applebee, A. N. (1987). *How writing shapes thinking: A study of teaching and learning*. Urbana, IL: National Council of Teachers of English.

Lattimer, H. (2003). *Thinking through genre: Units of study in reading and writing workshop 4–12*. Portland, MA: Stenhouse.

McMackin, M. C., & Siegel, B. S. (2002). *Knowing how: Researching and writing non-fiction 3–8*. Portland, ME: Stenhouse.

Meyer, B., & Rice, E. (1984). The structure of text. In P. D. Pearson (Ed.), *Handbook of reading research*. New York: Longman.

Murray, D. (1993). *Read to write* (3rd ed.). Fort Worth, TX: Harcourt Brace.

National Center for Education Statistics. (2002). *The nation's report card: Writing*. Washington, DC: U.S. Department of Education. Available: http://nces.ed.gov/nationsreportcard/writing

Pappas, C. C., Kiefer, B. S., & Levstick, L. S. (1999). In *An integrated language perspective in the elementary school: An action approach* (3rd ed.). New York: Longman.

Parry, J., & Hornsby, D. (1988). *Write on: A conference approach to writing*. Portsmouth, NH: Heinemann.

Peterson, R. (1992). *Life in a crowded place: Making a learning community*. Portsmouth, NH: Heinemann.

Ray, K. W. (1999). *Wondrous words: Writers and writing in the elementary classroom*. Urbana, IL: National Council of Teachers of English.

Ray, K. W., & Laminack, L. (2001). *The writing workshop: Working through the hard parts (and they're all hard parts)*. Urbana, IL: National Council of Teachers of English.

Resnick, L. B. (1999). Making America smarter. *Education Week Century Series, 18*(40), 38–40.

Robb, L. (1998). *Easy to manage reading and writing conferences: Practical ideas for making conferences work*. New York: Scholastic.

Romano, T. (1987). *Clearing the way: Working with teenage writers*. Portsmouth, NH: Heinemann.

Routman, R. (2000). *Conversations: Strategies for teaching, learning, and evaluating*. Portsmouth, NH: Heinemann.

Sowers, S. (1988). Reflect, expand, select: Three responses in the writing conference. In T. Newkirk & N. Atwell (Eds.), *Understanding writing: Ways of observing, learning, and teaching*. Portsmouth, NH: Heinemann.

Squire, J. (1983). Composing and comprehending: Two sides of the same basic process. *Language Arts, 60*(5), 581–589.

Tagg, J. (1986, March 16). Learning to think—the write way. *Los Angeles Times*, p. 27.

Weaver, C. (1979). *Grammar for teachers: Perspectives and definitions*. Urbana, IL: National Council of Teachers of English.

Williams, J. (2003). *Style: Ten lessons in clarity and grace* (7th ed.). New York: Longman.

6

Strategies for Increasing Achievement in Social Studies

Beverly J. Armento

The primary purpose of social studies is to help young people develop the ability to make informed and reasoned decisions for the public good as citizens of a culturally diverse, democratic society in an interdependent world.

—National Council for the Social Studies (1994, p. 3)

S ocial studies—potentially the most exciting, relevant, important, and empowering component of any student's education—has long been a battleground for educators, politicians, and families. The same questions that have bedeviled the field for decades are still begging for clarity: What should be taught, and when? In what ways? Toward what goals? Local curriculum decision makers and classroom teachers are faced with a bewildering array of choices and receive little direction on how to achieve the subject's "primary purpose" as stipulated by the National Council for the Social Studies.

Complicating matters is the fact that separate curriculum standards exist for a variety of closely related fields, including social studies (National Council for the

Social Studies, 1994); history (National Center for History in the Schools, 1996); geography (National Council for Geographic Education, 1994); civics and government (Center for Civic Education, 1994); and economics (National Council on Economic Education, 1997). Leaders disagree on how these standards should be used to develop a coherent curriculum, disputing, for example, the proper balance of history and the social sciences in the curriculum and whether these subject areas should be taught separately or presented in an integrated fashion.

Despite these serious issues, state policymakers continue to create curriculum frameworks for social studies, textbooks continue to be written to these frameworks, and the National Assessment of Educational Progress (NAEP) continues to administer tests in U.S. history, geography, and civics. In addition, NAEP administered its first test in 12th grade economics in 2006 and has scheduled its first test in world history for 2012.

The most recent NAEP results (civics, 2006; geography, 2001; U.S. history, 2006; and economics, 2006) indicate serious equity concerns, although there have been slight increases in content knowledge at some grade levels. All four tests show significant achievement gaps for low-income students, students from ethnic minority groups, and, to a lesser extent, female students. In addition, the NAEP tests reveal that teachers' pedagogical methods have not kept pace with our current knowledge of effective teaching practices. Many students are learning social studies in very traditional (and likely non-empowering) ways.

It is time for social studies educators to confront these serious ethical issues. Is it our goal to help *all* young people develop the necessary abilities to make decisions for the public good as citizens of a culturally diverse, democratic society in an interdependent world? If the answer is yes, then we must make crucial, systemic changes to the ways we organize and teach social studies.

In this chapter, I discuss strategies that classroom teachers and curriculum leaders can use to actively improve social studies teaching and learning. These strategies are supported by research in social studies and related fields as well as by my many years of experience teaching social studies and preparing effective social studies educators. This chapter does not address issues of curriculum content, but it should be helpful to educators who wish to make learning of *any* content in the social studies more conceptual, more meaningful, and more empowering for all learners.

The State of the Art of Social Studies Instruction

Let's examine the results of the most recent NAEP tests in civics, geography, and U.S. history for grades 4, 8, and 12, and in economics for grade 12. These results are the main sources for national data on students' social studies content knowledge and cognitive processes, although it is important to keep in mind that making generalizations on the basis of these data has its limitations. Because of the breadth of material, each student takes a particular portion of the test, answering two 25-minute sections of multiple-choice and constructed-response questions. The results are then combined to produce an average score for the United States as a whole and for various subgroups divided by gender, ethnicity, income level, and so on. Thus, although these composite scores are based on a nationally representative sample of schools and students, they represent only part of the performance picture. Still, the NAEP results do give us important insight into what is being taught in social studies and how students are performing.

Civics. The conceptual framework for the civics test draws heavily from the 1994 National Standards for Civics and Government. The test has three components: civics knowledge (for example, the foundations of the U.S. political system and the roles of citizens in a democracy); intellectual and participatory skills (for example, identifying, explaining, evaluating, and taking and defending positions); and civic dispositions (for example, assuming the personal, political, and economic responsibilities of a citizen or participating in civic affairs in an informed, thoughtful, effective manner).

• Approximately two out of three students at all three grade levels scored at or above the Basic level in civics knowledge on the 2006 test.

• Only 4th graders' scores improved from 1998 to 2006. Eighth and 12th graders' performance on the 2006 test showed no significant changes from the 1998 test.

• Female students scored higher than male students at the 8th and 12th grade levels.

• At all three grade levels, there were significant disparities in student performance falling along the lines of ethnicity, income level, and parents' level of education. White students tended to score higher than black and Hispanic students, and students from higher-income families and students whose parents had higher levels of education outperformed students from lower-income families with lower levels of education. (Lutkus & Weiss, 2007)

Geography. On the 2001 NAEP geography test, students answered multiple-choice and open-ended questions on content (space and place, 40 percent; environment and society, 30 percent; and spatial dynamics and connections, 30 percent) and on cognitive processes of knowing, understanding, and applying.

• Average scores for 4th and 8th graders were higher in 2001 than in 1994; the performance of 12th graders did not change significantly.

• At all three grade levels in 1994 and 2001, male students earned significantly higher geography scores than female students.

• At all three grade levels, white, Asian/Pacific Islander, and American Indian students earned higher scores than African American and Hispanic students.

• On the 2001 test, the higher the parents' education level, the higher the score of 8th and 12th graders.

• At all three grade levels, the average score for students enrolled in free/reduced-price meal programs was lower than the average score for students not eligible for such programs.

• On the 2001 test, greater percentages of students reported studying maps and globes and learning about countries and cultures in their geography classes than on the 1994 tests. Teachers also reported that they were generally more prepared to teach geography in 2001. (Weiss, Lutkus, Hildebrant, & Johnson, 2002)

U.S. History. The conceptual framework for the 2006 NAEP history test included three dimensions: historical themes (change and continuity in American democracy; the gathering and interactions of people, cultures, and ideas; economic and technological changes; and the changing role of the United States in the world); eight chronological periods (beginnings, colonization, the Revolution, expansion and reform, the Civil War and Reconstruction, the development of modern America, the World Wars, and contemporary America); and two ways of knowing (historical knowledge and perspective and historical analysis and interpretation).

• At all three grade levels, students performed better on the 2006 test than they had on the 1994 and 2001 tests.

• Fourth graders showed the greatest increase at the Basic level of achievement, from 64 percent in 1994 to 70 percent in 2006.

• White, black, and Hispanic students earned higher scores in 2006 than in 1994, but between 2001 and 2006 there were no significant changes in scores for black students at any of the three grade levels or for Hispanic students in grade 12.

• Gains made between 1994 and 2006 by black and Hispanic 4th graders helped narrow the gap with white peers. However, at grades 8 and 12, the gaps between whites and blacks

and Hispanics have not significantly changed, although all groups have improved. (Lee & Weiss, 2007)

Economics. The first NAEP economics test was administered in 2006 to a sample of 11,500 12th graders in 590 public and nonpublic high schools. The conceptual framework revolved around three cognitive categories: knowing (identifying and recalling information and recognizing economic terms and concepts); applying (describing or explaining the relationship between information and economic concepts); and reasoning (using information and economic concepts accurately to solve problems, evaluate issues, and interpret situations). Questions represented a wide range of content from three areas: market economy (microeconomics, or how individuals and businesses make decisions about allocating resources in the marketplace); national economy (macroeconomics, or the sum of decisions made by individuals, businesses, and governments); and international economy (how individuals and businesses interact in foreign markets).

• Seventy-nine percent of students performed at the Basic level or above, with 42 percent performing at the Proficient level and 3 percent at the Advanced level.

• Males tended to score higher than females.

• White and Asian/Pacific Islander students earned higher scores, on average, than other racial/ethnic groups.

- Students from large city schools earned lower scores, on average, than students in other locations.
- Students from higher-income families and students whose parents had higher levels of education scored higher, on average, than did students from lower-income families and those whose parents had lower levels of education. (Mead & Sandene, 2007)

The NAEP data give us only a partial picture of what students are learning and not learning, who is learning and who is not learning, and what teachers are doing and not doing. Still, the patterns that emerge from these data should give all educators cause to pause and question our commitment to equity and excellence in social studies classrooms. Why do these gaps connected to gender, socioeconomic status, and race persist? What are we as social studies educators doing to ensure equitable student access to a high-quality education? How do our pedagogical choices, expectations for students, and allocation of resources contribute to empowering or discouraging each student?

The causes of the achievement gap in social studies and in other areas of the curriculum are multiple and complex. Although some of the underlying social, economic, and political issues must be addressed at policy levels, it is clear from the research that classroom teachers can do much to make a difference in the quality, quantity, and depth of learning for each student.

Assessing Student Achievement in Social Studies

Three basic principles should govern authentic assessment of student learning in social studies. Assessment should

1. Be ongoing, occur in a range of contexts, have real-world applications, and be conducted using a range of materials and techniques.

2. Provide feedback to students and inform instruction.

3. Offer students alternative ways of displaying their competence, and pay attention to students' learning needs, making accommodations as necessary.

Students learn best when new ideas and skills are built onto the knowledge they already possess. This prior knowledge forms a foundation of known facts and concepts on which students can actively generate new ideas. The teacher's first task is to uncover what students already know about a topic as well as the skills and cognitive processes they can use with facility, and then to build on this base. This form of assessment is crucial for all grade levels because the size and nature of the learning gap, once discovered, can inform instructional decisions about content and pedagogy. Successful educators continually tap into prior knowledge by using examples that are easily recognizable to students, asking students to offer examples from their own experiences, and matching instruction to what students already know and can do.

Making prior knowledge and learned knowledge explicit to students can provide important feedback to both students and teachers. For example, before a unit of instruction, the teacher can have students brainstorm about what they know about the topics of the unit. After the unit, students can participate in the same activity. Having students organize their brainstorming into categories and then describe the categories and how they relate to one another yields a sophisticated picture of student learning. The end product of such brainstorming and categorizing should be more accurate, more complete, and more organized than the product of the pre-instruction brainstorming. This informal assessment provides students with a vivid picture of how their knowledge has changed during the unit and provides the teacher with valuable information on how students have processed concepts, how they relate the information to other information, and what new questions they have.

Just as learning must make sense to students, so must assessment procedures. Meaningful assessments stimulate students to become more actively engaged in both learning and assessment; they will come to feel that their responses and efforts will make a difference. Multiple-choice tests can go only so far in assessing the depth of student learning. (It should be noted, however, that all students need to learn how to successfully take formal tests, such as the NAEP and state tests, because these are an inescapable reality of school life. It is also important from an equity point of view to govern student preparation for such tests. All students should learn test-taking skills and have opportunities for prior practice.)

As an alternative to the usual multiple-choice or short-answer quiz, consider conducting an inquiry project culminating in a Social Studies Fair that requires students to orally describe their work, answer questions, and reflect on their learning. Such an event would be a multidimensional measure of what students have learned and how they have learned to use their knowledge and skills. Preparing essays, analyzing primary-source documents, conducting group projects, developing role-plays, preparing research projects, engaging in debate, investigating a current issue in depth and taking social action, or creating a portfolio of work are all ways to supplement the more traditional forms of classroom assessment.

Enhancing Students' Achievement in Social Studies

Pedagogy is a powerful ethical tool. Educators can use it to empower or to thwart; to encourage or to ignore; to honor students' voices or to suppress them; to uncover hidden truths or to gloss over issues; to acknowledge students' cultures and heritages or to overlook the rich and wide range of human variation; to act on their responsibility to educate each child or to seek reasons for inaction. To improve student performance in social studies, educators must make pedagogical choices that promote meaningful learning, critical thinking, and empowered decision making.

Classroom educators should be actively involved in school district and state decisions about the content framework, the texts and resource lists, and staff development. For the sake of this chapter, let us assume that these decisions have been made and that the classroom educator wishes to create an environment where students will

• Develop a deep conceptual understanding of the content, seeing connections between and among ideas and developing skills of insight and reflection.

• Develop critical thinking skills, learning to be thoughtful in their analysis of important issues and being willing and able to take an informed stand on issues.

• Develop the ability to look at issues from different perspectives, analyzing data to inform their views and developing perspective-taking abilities that extend beyond the classroom.

• Develop a commitment to active engagement in society and an expectation that such engagement and action will have consequences.

Unfortunately, students often view social studies as boring, difficult, and irrelevant. Too often, they engage solely in the ritual, sterile tasks of reading from the text and answering questions at the ends of chapters or filling in blanks on worksheets. The dynamic nature of meaningful learning is something that many students in social studies classes never experience. In fact, for many K–3 students, the social studies curriculum does not even exist, having been pushed out by the current emphasis on reading and mathematics. As a result, some students

may not be ready for the challenging textbook reading and large conceptual load in their 4th grade social studies classes. These factors certainly contribute to the NAEP achievement gaps. Thus, the first step toward an improved learning experience for students in social studies is teaching an enriched social studies curriculum, K–12.

Strategies That Promote Achievement in Social Studies

It is important that educators have a clear vision of their own goals for social studies instruction that includes both content-related and pedagogical components. In the area of content, teachers need to address the following questions:

• Will the content be balanced and inclusive?

• Will the content be presented in depth, or will the focus be on breadth of coverage?

• Will the content be enriched by drawing on related areas such as literature, art, music, and drama?

• Will history and the social sciences be integrated or approached separately?

• How will reading, writing, and the language arts be employed to enhance students' literacy skills as well as to facilitate learning of social studies content?

• Will the content be supplemented, as needed, to achieve the desired goals?

Pedagogically, it is important for educators to realize that the actions they take daily have a cumulative effect on what and how students learn, as well as on how that learning is processed, retained, and used. Pedagogical actions (or lack thereof) also influence how students feel about the subject, how interesting or important they think the subject is, how they think the subject relates to their lives, and how deeply engaged they become with the material.

There are many ways of thinking about pedagogical strategies, just as there are many ways of categorizing effective teaching practices. I propose one major overall goal for effective teaching, with four subcategories that take the form of specific pedagogical strategies. A truly effective social studies program intended to help all students attain mastery of the curriculum needs to take place in a learner-centered classroom that acknowledges students' voices and the cultural capital they bring to school, promotes meaningful learning, encourages thoughtfulness and critical thinking, allows for varied points of view, and stimulates social critique and social action. The four specific pedagogical strategies intended to help teachers and their students attain this goal are the following:

1. Create a classroom climate that promotes meaningful learning by emphasizing conceptual understanding, developing visual and verbal tools, using graphic organizers, framing material in time and space, and seeking connections between and among ideas.

2. Create a classroom climate that recognizes students' voices and their cultural capital; acknowledges the voices of "ordinary people" in the social studies material studied; and uses literature, primary-source documents, and other resources as a means of hearing the voices from the past and present and making social studies come alive for students.

3. Create a classroom climate that promotes critical thinking, analysis, inquiry, and thoughtfulness and supports an issues-oriented atmosphere in which multiple viewpoints are expressed, explored, understood, and appreciated.

4. Create a classroom climate that promotes social critique, having students "look underneath" data and issues to find what is typically hidden from view; supports students' voices and social actions on issues; and promotes the notion that active citizen involvement is essential in a democratic society.

Strategy 6.1:
Create a classroom climate that promotes meaningful learning.

Discussion and Classroom Examples

Enabling students to make sense of the social, economic, political, historical, geographic, cultural, psychological, and ethical worlds of the past and present, to see the relevance of this knowledge, and to be able to use it in their everyday lives is one of the major challenges facing the social studies curriculum. Teachers and students are often overwhelmed by the sheer amount of knowledge there is to be learned, recalled, and tested. Educators are sometimes forced to make choices that they think will result in the most efficient way to handle the knowledge overload and end up teaching what they think students will be tested on: political, geographic, and historical facts. Their instruction emphasizes content coverage; students memorize facts that they soon forget; and little meaningful learning about the social world takes place.

This does not have to happen. Teachers have choices. A good first step is to examine the knowledge component of the curriculum and figure out what is important and powerful knowledge, and what is not. Teachers should differentiate between facts, concepts, and generalizations and think about the best ways to teach these different types of knowledge. They can then apply basic learning principles to their teaching of the content, promoting meaningful, enduring understanding, and active engagement with the material.

Factual knowledge, for example, is best learned through association, matching, and practice. Take the learning of continents and oceans, a common objective in the early grades. The teacher can introduce the concepts through the use of globes, world maps, yarn, and name cards that can be affixed to the maps. Students can practice naming and locating the continents and oceans using concentration games, bingo games, or flash cards. This kind of practice can be a fun and easy way for students to learn facts. However, it's important that the teacher introduce these facts conceptually and in context. Students studying a certain region of the United States, for example, might learn the states and capitals of that region; memorizing all 50 states

and capitals at once, on the other hand, would not make good pedagogical sense. In the elementary grades, students can play fact games at learning and practice centers while the teacher uses the social studies portion of class to focus on conceptual and more cognitively challenging learning.

Educators need to place the most emphasis on conceptual learning because it provides the foundation for higher-level thinking and has a generative effect, enabling students to comprehend the many examples of concepts that they will encounter over time. A concept is more than a vocabulary word; it is a term or phrase whose meaning has been derived from observations of patterns from real-life examples.

Concepts (such as *power, scarcity, regions, interdependence, colonization, slavery, migration, continuity, change, resources,* and *poverty*) should be at the center of instruction, with factual examples used to illustrate the broader themes. To learn a concept, students need to be able to recognize examples, generate a concept definition, distinguish examples from nonexamples, and generate new examples of the concept. Abstract concepts (such as *democracy, totalitarianism,* and *progressivism*) are more difficult to grasp, but they also tend to be more powerful cognitive tools because they can be used to explain more examples in sophisticated terms. Conceptual understanding is essential to higher-order thinking, to informed decision making, and to self-generated learning.

Visual tools are an excellent way to stimulate conceptual understanding and fluency, to maintain focus on the most important ideas, to show how these ideas relate to one another, and to enable students to explain what they know and understand. Graphic organizers are powerful visual tools that can be used at all stages of instruction. They enable students to organize information in multiple ways: *hierarchically* (as in an outline, supporting big ideas with secondary ideas); *causally* (showing the factors that caused a particular event or phenomenon); *chronologically* (as in a timeline, showing events that followed or preceded an event); and *relationally* (comparing two or more things). Such methods of organization are powerful because they use patterns, which help learners see how one idea relates to another and are more easily stored in memory than separate bits of information. For example, a relational chart is useful when comparing several different cultures, with the cultures displayed across the top of the chart and comparison questions placed along the vertical axis. Venn diagrams and webs are also useful visual organizational tools.

Before a unit of study, the teacher can ask students to brainstorm what they know about the unit's topic; they can then use a simple graphic to organize this information so that it shows a picture of what they know. Students can engage in the same brainstorming exercise at the end of the unit. The resulting post-instruction diagram should be more accurate, more complete, and more organized and should use a more sophisticated grouping technique.

As students learn to organize their knowledge visually, they begin to recognize that there are multiple ways to organize or explain the same knowledge. Ideas go together in many ways, depending on the purpose of the grouping. The teacher can have students fill in an empty graphic organizer with key information as a lesson progresses, or the class can use a graphic to identify the main ideas of a lesson or unit. Developing their own graphic to illustrate new knowledge learned is an excellent way for students to portray their understanding of the information.

When students study a particular historical event or topic, the teacher should also frame the content in time and space, using timelines and maps or globes. The teacher should not assume that students know where Iraq is or that they can imagine how long ago 1565 was. Students need to see concretely how events lead up to or cause other events, that historical outcomes are not pre-ordained. They need to see places on maps and reflect on those places' locations in relation to where they live. Timelines promote sequential and chronological thinking and are useful for all grade levels as concrete reminders of causal and resulting factors of events being studied. Even young children can begin by making timelines of their school days and their own lives and then apply such timelines to more formal studies in their social studies classes.

At any grade level, some students will come to social studies topics with conceptual gaps in their knowledge. Educators must be able to ascertain those gaps in prior knowledge before starting a new unit of instruction and scaffold instruction accordingly. Scaffolding serves as a conceptual bridge between what students already know and what they need to succeed in the unit. It may mean introducing essential vocabulary, developing some of the central concepts, or highlighting some of the key issues or historical figures studied in the unit. It may also mean applying strategies that facilitate reading comprehension. The larger the reading gap within a class, the more difficulty students will have using grade-level reading materials in social studies. The combination of effective scaffolding and appropriate reading materials will enhance student learning.

Meaningful learning is at the heart of an effective social studies program. It's important to keep in mind that conceptual level often outpaces reading level and that students may understand much more than they are able to read. Do not underestimate students' capability for conceptual thinking. Encourage students to discuss, discuss, discuss—to find new examples, to elaborate on ideas, to build on important concepts, to investigate topics, to graphically present new ideas, to creatively reorganize ideas into new visual representations, to find new avenues for inquiry, to feel free to bring up old and new topics in the classroom, and to feel comfortable expressing their ideas and views.

Resources

Abel, Hauwiller, & Vandeventer, 1989; Adler, 1993; Alleman & Brophy, 1994; Armbruster & Anderson, 1985; Armento, 1993; Au, 1993; Banks & Joyce, 1971; Beck & McKeown, 1988; Brooks & Brooks, 1993; Causey & Armento, 2001; Field, Labbo, Wilhelm, & Garrett, 1996; Franklin & Roach, 1992; Gabella, 1994; Gay, 1991; Groth & Albert, 1997; Harmin, 1994; Hyerle, 1996; Irvin, Lundstrum, Lynch-Brown, & Shepard, 1995; Irvine, 1990; Irvine & Armento, 2001; Kobrin, 1996; Levstik & Barton, 1997; Newmann, 1992; Nieto, 2002; Perfetti, Britt, & Georgi, 1995; Risinger, 1996; Schmidt & Mosenthal, 2001; Sousa, 2001; Strickland & Alvermann, 2004; Teachers' Curriculum Institute, 1994; Thornton, 2005; Werner, 2002; Yell, Scheurman, & Reynolds, 2004.

Strategy 6.2:

Create a classroom climate that recognizes students' voices and their cultural capital and acknowledges the voices of "ordinary people" in the material studied.

Discussion and Classroom Examples

It is vitally important for teachers to realize that students have had a wide variety of experiences before entering the classroom that are valuable and significant to them and their families. Students bring with them their ethnicity, their socioeconomic class, their religion, their nationality, their gender, their language, their abilities and disabilities, their culture, and their heritage. Students should be respected for these assets and for the individual and collective contributions they make to the classroom and school culture. Drawing on students' cultural capital—the valuable knowledge, skills, and tools that they have learned from their cultural backgrounds—is crucial to student engagement and self-respect and demonstrates to students that the content they are studying is relevant to their lives. What better place than in the social studies classroom to explore culture, life experiences, and heritage? Where, if not in social studies, should students expect to see themselves reflected in the curriculum and to feel free and comfortable talking and learning about their lives, their culture, their history, and their issues?

Students should also learn that history is the story not only of political leaders and the elite classes but also of ordinary people, who also make critical decisions, lead movements, make important discoveries, influence ideas and people, and alter the course of events. Students should meet Sybil Ludington as well as Paul Revere in their study of the American Revolution, and see that Rosa Parks's actions set in motion a series of events that helped lead to the civil rights movement (Nash, 1989).

Teachers can use literature, primary-source documents, photographs, music, art, artifacts, poetry, and drama to make voices of the past and present actively heard in the social studies classroom. Such resources, many of which can be found on the Internet, connect students with real people and their actions, enable students to locate and interpret documents, and inject reality and vitality into the social studies classroom. Such investigations can begin with even the youngest students and should extend through the high school years, when students can conduct extensive individual research on topics and issues.

When students investigate topics using primary-source documents, they see the complexity of any given topic and recognize that multiple viewpoints continually compete for attention. They learn that people must inevitably make difficult choices, often with complex consequences. Being able to identify with people of the past and present is crucial for students to see

themselves as active and mutual participants in society.

Social studies must shift from being something students study *about* to being an exploration of every student's world and his or her place in it. For every single student, the same generative question applies: How can I actively participate to make a difference in my world?

Resources

Adler, 1993; Appleby, Hunt, & Jacob, 1994; Armento, 1991a; Banks, 1991, 1994; Banks & Joyce, 1971; Braun, 1992; Crocco, 1997; Danker, 2005; Davis, Yeager, & Foster, 2001; Engle & Ochoa, 1988; Epstein, 1997; Gabella, 1994; Gay, 1991; Groth & Albert, 1997; Harmin, 1994; Irvine & Armento, 2001; Kobrin, 1996; Levstik, 1997; Levstik & Barton, 1997; Nash, 1989; Newmann, 1992; Nieto, 2002; Ramirez & Ramirez, 1994; Risinger, 1996; Schmidt & Mosenthal, 2001; Seixas, 1994; Thornton, 2005; Werner, 2002; Yell, Scheurman, & Reynolds, 2004.

Strategy 6.3:

Create a classroom climate that promotes critical thinking, analysis, inquiry, and thoughtfulness.

Discussion and Classroom Examples

Young children are naturally curious. They want to know the hows and whys of just about everything. Yet once they enter school, the tendency is to shut them down and keep them quiet so that they can "learn," in effect extinguishing their inquisitive natures. But this urge to know is the very attribute students need for optimal learning and for active participation in society. Social studies educators need to nurture students' intrinsic motivation to inquire and probe deeply into subjects, especially in the lower grades. Trying to reinstill such habits in older students is difficult.

Teachers should encourage students to ask questions and to find productive ways of seeking answers to those questions. A wealth of issues are available for consideration, whether they arise from the local community, the formal curriculum, or students' own lives. Teachers should model thoughtfulness and a sense of curiosity about the world and encourage active and informed investigation. Students must discover early the importance of having informed opinions and being able to articulate why they think a certain way and to provide evidence to support their point of view. Even the youngest students can learn how to do this, applying such strategies as the decision tree analysis to problems that arise in the classroom. For example, suppose a kindergarten class has to decide what to do with $25 given to it by the PTA. The teacher can lead the students in a formal analysis, asking them to discuss the following questions:

- What is our problem?
- What are our choices?
- What are the pros and cons of each of our choices?
- For each choice, what will we gain and what will we give up?
- How, then, shall we decide what choice to make?

After the class has made its decision, students can reflect on the consequences of their choice. This same pattern of analysis can be applied to dilemmas that arise in the curriculum, such as the choices faced by a community as it decides how to use certain natural resources, or by a nation as it decides whether or not to go to war.

Skills in reflection and analysis must be overtly taught, reinforced, and applied throughout the school curriculum, from kindergarten through high school. Students should learn to identify an issue that is worthy of investigation and be able to ask and address main and supporting questions that lead to a thorough understanding of the issue. They need to ask themselves, Where can I find the data I need to adequately address these questions? How can I locate resources and data using the Internet, the media center, experts, and other sources? What skills do I need to analyze the data that I've gathered? How can I assess the reliability and validity of the data? How can I reconcile discrepancies? What shall I do with conflicting information? With differing points of view? How can I formulate my own point of view, using the data to justify my view in a thoughtful and articulate manner? How can I respond to alternative conclusions while remaining respectful and open to any new data that might cause me to reconsider my conclusion?

If this kind of thoughtful analysis is what we expect of citizens in a democratic society, then we must first help students develop these attitudes and skills in a variety of settings, with a wide range of content, and in multiple contexts.

The focus on inquiry must begin early and remain a coherent, ongoing component of the social studies curriculum. The first step is to establish a classroom atmosphere that encourages students to ask reasonable questions and seek viable solutions and that provides a safe place for open discourse and informed debate.

Skeel (1996) suggests encouraging students to frame a topic or unit of study as a question. For example, for a unit on the American Revolution, students may ask, Was the American Revolution necessary? The students can then investigate the Revolution from a range of perspectives, study the events leading up to the war, and decide whether it should have happened or could have been avoided. They can look at how decisions were made and examine the consequences of the participants' actions on both sides. This process actively engages students in the inquiry and signals an attitude of questioning that differs considerably from the traditional approach of studying such topics.

An enormous array of politico-economic issues—some intensely personal and some in the larger arena of public policy—faces our students, our nation, and our world. Here are just a few:

- What are the economic benefits and costs of dropping out of school?
- Is there a trade deficit? If so, what difference does it make?
- Are there salary differences between men and women? Between blacks and whites? If so, why? Should there be differences?

- What is the current unemployment rate? If we disaggregated the data, what would we find?
- Why do the patterns (in unemployment rates, salaries, and regional job growth rates, for example) revealed in the data exist, and what are the consequences? What would the data look like in an ideal world that we might design? (Armento, Rushing, & Cook, 1996; Feiner, 1994)

Posing questions such as these in a high school economics class and fostering informed, thoughtful investigations and discourse would transform the course from being boring and irrelevant to being engaging and pertinent to students' lives. Most economics classes deal primarily with the conceptual tools of analysis, teaching students such concepts as supply and demand, markets, trade, and interdependence and anticipating that students will be able to apply those tools later in life to real economic dilemmas. But why wait? Shouldn't we try to inject more authentic learning into classes that many students find difficult and unrelated to their lives?

Every social studies educator should keep in mind the following question: How might we harness young people's inquiring minds to help them see the relevance of social studies to their personal lives; to their roles in the social, economic, and political spheres; and to their roles as citizens of a culturally diverse, democratic society in an interdependent world?

Resources

Agosto, 1991; Armento, Rushing, & Cook, 1996; Berson, 1996; Brooks & Brooks, 1993; Carretero & Voss, 1994; Crocco, 2005; Davis, Yeager, & Foster, 2001; Engle & Ochoa, 1988; Evans, 2004; Evans & Saxe, 1996; Feiner, 1994; Gabella, 1994; Giroux, 1988; Giroux & Simon, 1989; Hahn, 1994; Harmin, 1994; Irvine & Armento, 2001; Kobrin, 1996; Levstik, 1997; Nash, 1989; Newmann, 1991, 1992; Newmann, Secada, & Wehlage, 1995; Oliver & Shaver, 1966; Perfetti, Britt, & Georgi, 1995; Risinger, 1996; Romanowski, 1996; Saul, 1994; Segall, Heilman, & Cherryholmes, 2006; Seixas, 1994; Skeel, 1996; Tunnel & Ammon, 1996; Werner, 2002; Yell, Scheurman, & Reynolds, 2004.

Strategy 6.4:

Create a classroom climate that supports students' voices and promotes the notion that active citizen involvement is essential in a democratic society.

Discussion and Classroom Examples

This final strategy extends the previous one by emphasizing the normative or ethical dimension. Teachers applying this strategy help students to focus on what ought to be and to understand how one's values influence one's choices and actions. This approach is more critical and more difficult and aims to empower students to take social actions based on their informed analysis of issues. When teachers use this strategy, they help students comprehend how a particular society works, where they are located within it, and what its inequitable

characteristics are (Giroux, 1988). Students examine controversial topics, expose and analyze basic issues of inequality, and weigh, discuss, and act on alternative proposals. Such controversial issues often involve race, gender, class, power, privilege, discrimination, and ideology, in contexts ranging from local to global arenas. To successfully examine these issues, students must be able to

• Articulate the problem and related sub-problems.

• Identify and acknowledge their prior knowledge and beliefs about the issue.

• Determine what information and opinions are needed to analyze the issue.

• Locate and analyze these data.

• Account for missing data, conflicting data, and conflicting points of view.

• Uncover patterns in the data.

• Develop a position with supporting data.

• Articulate and justify the position, respond to competing arguments, and make adjustments as necessary.

• Determine and take appropriate social action.

• Reflect on the process and action and determine next steps.

Certain controversial issues may be hard to investigate because of the difficulty in locating necessary information. For example, it is often difficult to locate data on women, ethnic minorities, and people living in poverty, so trying to disaggregate data on these dimensions is not an easy task. Teachers should encourage students to continually ask critical questions of the data they do obtain: What is the source of the data? What biases might the source have? Who is included in (or excluded from) the data? How do I assess the data's accuracy?

Although certain controversial issues have long been included in the curriculum (e.g., slavery in the United States, poverty patterns in the United States and worldwide, and the dropping of the atomic bomb on Hiroshima and Nagasaki), today's curriculum is apt to include many more controversial topics—Japanese internment camps during World War II, immigration patterns, and women in the workplace, for example. Teachers and students are expected to be able to deal analytically and thoughtfully with such topics.

Both teachers and students, however, have their own sets of beliefs and stereotypes on such topics and often hold dogmatic opinions. It takes an effective teacher to move beyond uninformed discourse to thoughtful, reflective, and informed class discussions and to lead students to take an analytical approach to the relevant data. Teachers and students alike must realize that there are many interpretations of life's major issues and that these interpretations are shaped by one's political and social ideology, life experiences, gender, ethnicity, economic class, religion, and position of power.

Resources

Agosto, 1991; Armento, Rushing, & Cook, 1996; Crocco, 2005; Engle & Ochoa, 1988; Evans, 2004; Evans & Saxe, 1996; Feiner, 1994; Giroux, 1988; Giroux & Simon, 1989; Hahn, 1994; Nash, 1989; Newmann, 1991, 1992; Newmann, Secada, & Wehlage, 1995; Oliver & Shaver, 1966; Segall, Heilman, &

Cherryholmes, 2006; Thornton, 2005; Tunnel & Ammon, 1996.

Continuing the Discussion

The four strategies in this chapter, if used effectively, should yield an enriched social studies experience that will demonstrate to students that they are important not only in their classroom but also in their society. Students will be actively engaged in learning how they can make the world a better place. You have the power to continue this discussion by turning to the resources cited for each strategy and beginning to incorporate these approaches into your own practice. We all have it within our power to make social studies the most exciting, relevant, important, and empowering aspect of students' lives and of the school curriculum.

Bibliography

Abel, F. J., Hauwiller, J. G., & Vandeventer, N. (1989). Using writing to teach social studies. *The Social Studies, 80*(1), 17–20.

Adler, S. (1993). *Multicultural communication skills in the classroom.* Boston: Allyn & Bacon.

Agosto, D. (1991). Presenting social issues with videotape. *Media and Methods, 12*(1), 19–20.

Alleman, J., & Brophy, J. (1994). Taking advantage of out-of-school opportunities for meaningful social studies learning. *The Social Studies, 85*(6), 262–267.

American Historical Association. (1998). Criteria for standards in history/social studies/social sciences. *Perspectives, 36*(1), 29.

Appleby, J., Hunt, L., & Jacob, M. (1994). *Telling the truth about history.* New York: Norton.

Armbruster, B. B., & Anderson, T. H. (1985). Producing "considerate" expository text: Or easy reading is damned hard writing. *Journal of Curriculum Studies, 17*(3), 247–263.

Armento, B. J. (1986). Research on teaching social studies. In M. C. Wittrock (Ed.), *Handbook of research on teaching* (3rd ed.) (pp. 942–951). Washington, DC: American Educational Research Association and Macmillan.

Armento, B. J. (1991a). Implications of cultural diversity for the social studies classroom. In G. Nash (Ed.), *A teacher's guide to multicultural perspectives in social studies* (pp. 51–60). Boston: Houghton Mifflin.

Armento, B. J. (1991b). Changing conceptions of research on teaching social studies. In J. P. Shaver (Ed.), *Handbook of research on teaching and learning social studies* (pp. 185–196). New York: Macmillan.

Armento, B. J. (1993, June 11–14). Research on children's learning of history: Issues and implications. *National Council for History Education Annual Conference Proceedings*, Westlake, Ohio.

Armento, B. J., Rushing, F., & Cook, W. (1996). Issues-centered economics instruction. In R. Evans & D. Saxe (Eds.), *Handbook on teaching social issues* (Bulletin 93, pp. 211–219). Washington, DC: National Council for the Social Studies.

Au, K. H. (1993). *Literacy instruction in multicultural settings*. New York: Harcourt, Brace, Jovanovich.

Baker, E. L. (1994). Learning-based assessments of history understanding. *Educational Psychologist, 29*(2), 97–106.

Banks, J. A. (1991). Multicultural education: Its effects on students' racial and gender role attitudes. In J. P. Shaver (Ed.), *Handbook of research on social studies teaching and learning* (pp. 459–469). New York: Macmillan.

Banks, J. A. (1994). *Multiethnic education: Theory and practice* (3rd ed.). Boston: Allyn and Bacon.

Banks, J. A., & Joyce, W. W. (Eds.). (1971). *Teaching social studies to culturally different children*. Reading, MA: Addison-Wesley.

Barton, K. C. (1997a). History—it can be elementary: An overview of elementary students' understanding of history. *Social Education, 61*(4), 13–16.

Barton, K. C. (1997b). 'I just kinda know': Elementary students' ideas about historical evidence. *Theory and Research in Social Education, 24*(4), 407–430.

Beck, I. L., & McKeown, M. G. (1988). Toward meaningful accounts in history texts for young learners. *Educational Researcher, 17*(1), 31–39.

Berson, M. (1996). Effectiveness of computer technology in the social studies: A review of the literature. *Journal of Research on Computing in Education, 28*(4), 486–499.

Bradley Commission on History in the Schools. (1988). *Building a history curriculum: Guidelines for teaching history in schools*. Westlake, OH: National Council for History Education.

Braun, J. A., Jr. (1992). Social technology in the elementary social studies curriculum. *Social Education, 56*(7), 389–392.

Brooks, J., & Brooks, M. (1993). *In search of understanding: The case for constructivist classrooms*. Alexandria, VA: Association for Supervision and Curriculum Development.

Buckles, S., & Watts, M. (1998). National standards in economics, history, social studies, civics, and geography: Complementarities, competition, or peaceful coexistence? *Journal of Economic Education, 29*(2), 157–166.

Carretero, M., & Voss, J. F. (Eds.). (1994). *Cognitive and instructional processes in history and the social sciences*. Hillsdale, NJ: Lawrence Erlbaum.

Causey, V. E., & Armento, B. J. (2001). Strategies for increasing achievement in history. In R. W. Cole (Ed.), *More strategies for educating everybody's children* (pp. 101–118). Alexandria, VA: Association for Supervision and Curriculum Development.

Center for Civic Education. (1994). *National standards for civics and government*. Washington, DC: Author.

Cohen, E., & Lotan, R. A. (Eds.). (1997). *Working for equity in heterogeneous classrooms: Sociological theory in action*. New York: Teachers College Press.

Crocco, M. S. (1997). Making time for women's history . . . when your survey course is already filled to overflowing. *Social Education, 61*(1), 32–37.

Crocco, M. S. (Ed.). (2005). *Social studies and the press: Keeping the beast at bay?* Greenwich, CT: Information Age.

Danker, A. C. (2005). *Multicultural social studies: Using local history in the classroom.* New York: Teachers College Press.

Darling-Hammond, L., Ancess, J., & Falk, B. (1995). *Authentic assessment in action: Studies of schools and students at work.* New York: Teachers College Press.

Davis, O. L., Yeager, E. A., & Foster, S. J. (2001). *Historical empathy and perspective taking in the social studies.* Lanham, MD: Rowman & Littlefield.

Dewey, J. (1933). *How we think.* New York: Heath.

Downey, M. T., & Levstik, L. S. (1991). Teaching and learning history. In J. P. Shaver (Ed.), *Handbook of research on teaching and learning in social studies* (pp. 400–410). New York: Macmillan.

Duis, M. (1996). Using schema theory to teach American history. *Social Education, 60*(3), 144–146.

Engle, S. H., & Ochoa, A. S. (1988). *Education for democratic citizenship: Decision making in the social studies.* New York: Teachers College Press.

Epstein, T. L. (1994). Sometimes a shining moment: High school students' representations of history through the arts. *Social Education, 58*(3), 136–141.

Epstein, T. L. (1997). Sociocultural approaches to young people's historical understanding. *Social Education, 61*(1), 28–31.

Evans, R. W. (2004). *The social studies wars: What should we teach the children?* New York: Teachers College Press.

Evans, R. W., & Saxe, D. (Eds.). (1996). *Handbook on teaching social issues.* New York: Macmillan.

Feiner, S. F. (1994). *Race and gender in the American economy: Views from across the spectrum.* Englewood Cliffs, NJ: Prentice-Hall.

Field, S. L., Labbo, L. D., Wilhelm, R. W., & Garrett, A. W. (1996). To touch, to see, to feel: Artifact inquiry in the social studies classroom. *Social Education, 60*(3), 141–143.

Franklin, M. R., & Roach, P. B. (1992). Teaching reading strategies in social studies contexts. *Social Education, 56*(4), 385–388.

Gabella, M. S. (1994). Beyond the looking glass: Bringing students into the conversation of historical inquiry. *Theory and Research in Social Education, 22*(3), 340–363.

Gagnon, P. (Ed.). (1989). *Historical literacy: The case for history in American education.* Boston: Houghton-Mifflin.

Gardner, H. (1991). *The unschooled mind: How children think and how schools should teach.* New York: BasicBooks.

Gay, G. (1991). Culturally diverse students and social studies. In J. P. Shaver (Ed.), *Handbook of research on teaching and learning in social studies* (pp. 144–156). New York: Macmillan.

Giroux, H. A. (1988). *Teachers as intellectuals: Toward a critical pedagogy of learning.* South Hadley, MA: Bergin and Garvey.

Giroux, H. A., & Simon, R. (1989). *Critical pedagogy and popular culture.* South Hadley, MA: Bergin and Garvey.

Groth, J. L., & Albert, M. (1997). Arts alive in the development of historical thinking. *Social Education, 61*(1), 42–44.

Hahn, C. (1994). Controversial issues in history instruction. In M. Carretero & J. F. Voss (Eds.), *Cognitive and instructional processes in history and the social sciences* (pp. 201–219). Hillsdale, NJ: Lawrence Erlbaum.

Harmin, M. (1994). *Inspiring active learning: A handbook for teachers.* Alexandria, VA: Association for Supervision and Curriculum Development.

Hertzberg, H. W. (1981). *Social studies reform, 1880–1980.* Boulder, CO: Social Science Education Consortium.

Hunt, M. P., & Metcalf, L. (1968). *Teaching high school social studies.* New York: Harper & Row.

Hyerle, D. (1996). *Visual tools for constructing knowledge.* Alexandria, VA: Association for Supervision and Curriculum Development.

Irvine, J. J. (1990). *Black students and school failure*. New York: Greenwood Press.

Irvine, J. J., & Armento, B. J. (2001). *Culturally responsive teaching: Lesson planning for elementary and middle grades*. Boston: McGraw-Hill.

Irvin, J. L., Lundstrum, J. P., Lynch-Brown, C., & Shepard, M. F. (1995). *Enhancing social studies through literacy strategies*. Washington, DC: National Council for the Social Studies.

Kobrin, D. (1996). *Beyond the textbook: Teaching history using documents and primary sources*. Portsmouth, NH: Heinemann.

Lee, J., & Weiss, A. (2007). *The nation's report card: U.S. history 2006* (NCES 2007-474). Washington, DC: National Center for Education Statistics.

Levstik, L. S. (1997). "Any history is someone's history": Listening to multiple voices from the past. *Social Education, 61*(1), 48–51.

Levstik, L. S., & Barton, K. C. (1997). *Doing history: Investigating with children in elementary and middle schools*. Mahwah, NJ: Lawrence Erlbaum.

Lutkus, A., & Weiss, A. (2007). *The nation's report card: Civics 2006* (NCES 2007-476). Washington, DC: National Center for Education Statistics.

Mead, N., & Sandene, B. (2007). *The nation's report card: Economics 2006* (NCES 2007-475). Washington, DC: National Center for Education Statistics.

Nash, G. (1989). History for a democratic society: The work of all the people. In P. Gagnon (Ed.), *Historical literacy: The case for history in American education*. Boston: Houghton-Mifflin.

Nash, G., Crabtree, C., & Dunn, R. E. (1997). *History on trial: Culture wars and the teaching of the past*. New York: Knopf.

National Center for History in the Schools. (1996). *National standards for history, basic edition*. Los Angeles: Author.

National Commission on Social Studies in the Schools. (1989). *Charting a course: Social studies for the 21st century*. Washington, DC: Author.

National Council for Geographic Education. (1994). *National geography standards*. Jacksonville, AL: Author.

National Council for the Social Studies. (1994). *Expectations of excellence: Curriculum standards for social studies*. Washington, DC: Author.

National Council on Economic Education. (1997). *The national voluntary content standards in economics*. New York: Author.

Newmann, F. M. (1991). Promoting higher order thinking in social studies: Overview of a study of sixteen high school departments. *Theory and Research in Social Education, 19*(4), 324–340.

Newmann, F. M. (1992). *Student engagement and achievement in American secondary schools*. New York: Teachers College Press.

Newmann, F. M., Secada, W. G., & Wehlage, G. G. (1995). *A guide to authentic instruction and assessment: Vision, standards, and scoring*. Madison, WI: Wisconsin Center for Education Research.

Nieto, S. (2002). *Language, culture, and teaching: Critical perspectives for a new century*. Mahwah, NJ: Lawrence Erlbaum.

Oliver, D. W., & Shaver, J. P. (1966). *Teaching public issues in the high school*. Boston: Houghton Mifflin.

Perfetti, C. A., Britt, M. A., & Georgi, M. C. (Eds.). (1995). *Text-based learning and reasoning: Studies in history*. Hillsdale, NJ: Lawrence Erlbaum.

Ramirez, G., & Ramirez, J. L. (1994). *Multiethnic children's literature*. Albany, NY: Delmar.

Risinger, C. F. (1996). Webbing the social studies: Using Internet and World Wide Web resources in social studies instruction. *Social Education, 60*(2), 111–112.

Romanowski, M. (1996). Problems of bias in history textbooks. *Social Education, 60*(3), 170–173.

Saul, E. W. (Ed.). (1994). *Milton Meltzer on writing, history, and social responsibility: Non-fiction for the classroom*. New York: Teachers College Press.

Schmidt, P. R., & Mosenthal, P. B. (Eds.). (2001). *Reconceptualizing literacy in the new age of multicultural-*

ism and pluralism. Greenwich, CT: Information Age.

Segall, A., Heilman, E. E., & Cherryholmes, C. H. (Eds.). (2006). *Social studies: The next generation*. New York: Peter Lang.

Seixas, P. (1994). Students' understanding of historical significance. *Theory and Research in Social Education, 22*(3), 281–304.

Skeel, D. (1996). An issues-centered elementary curriculum. In R. Evans & D. W. Saxe (Eds.), *Handbook on teaching social issues* (Bulletin 93, pp. 230–236). Washington, DC: National Council for the Social Studies.

Sousa, D. A. (2001). *How the brain learns* (2nd ed.). Thousand Oaks, CA: Corwin Press.

Strickland, D. S., & Alvermann, D. E. (Eds.). (2004). *Bridging the literacy achievement gap, grades 4–12*. New York: Teachers College Press.

Teachers' Curriculum Institute. (1994). *History alive! Engaging all learners in the diverse classroom*. Menlo Park, CA: Addison-Wesley.

Thornton, S. J. (2005). *Teaching social studies that matters*. New York: Teachers College Press.

Tunnel, M. O., & Ammon, R. (1996). The story of ourselves: Fostering multiple historical perspectives. *Social Education, 60*(4), 212–215.

VanSledright, B. A. (1997). Can more be less? The depth-breadth dilemma in teaching American history. *Social Education, 61*(1), 38–41.

Weiss, A. R., Lutkus, A. D., Hildebrant, B. S., & Johnson, M. S. (2002). *The nation's report card: Geography 2001* (NCES 2002-484). Washington, DC: National Center for Education Statistics.

Werner, W. (2002). Reading visual texts. *Theory and Research in Social Education, 30*(3), 401–429.

Yell, M. M., Scheurman, G., & Reynolds, K. (2004). *A link to the past: Engaging students in the study of history* (Bulletin 102). Silver Spring, MD: National Council for the Social Studies.

7

Strategies for Increasing Achievement in Science

Charles Watson

Because it takes fifteen years to create a scientist or advanced engineer, starting when that young man or woman first gets hooked on science and math in elementary school, we should be embarking on an all-hands-on-deck, no-holds-barred, no-budget-too-large crash program for science and engineering education immediately. The fact that we are not doing this is our quiet crisis. Scientists and engineers don't grow on trees.

—Thomas L. Friedman (2005, p. 275)

Calls for improvements in U.S. science achievement continue unabated. During the last few years, these calls have asserted urgently that without improved science and mathematics achievement, the United States will lag behind in the global economy (U.S. Department of Education, 2000) and efforts to improve national security may be affected. Other countries, such as China and India, are emerging as powerful economic and technological innovators and are producing scientists and engineers at unprecedented rates, surpassing U.S. efforts—another indicator of our inability to improve either achievement in or motivation for the study of science and mathematics. In his book *The World Is Flat*, Thomas Friedman (2005) suggests that the United States is losing the "numbers game" with respect to producing badly needed scientists and engineers. He suggests, too, that students nationwide appear to have little motivation to study mathematics or science and that this "quiet crisis" is largely being ignored.

For a variety of reasons, a great many students consider the study of science to be beyond their grasp. On the 1996 National Assessment of Educational Progress (NAEP), only about 60 percent of high school seniors and about 70 percent of 8th graders met the Basic level of performance in science. When the tests were administered again in 2000, scores of 4th and 8th graders remained at or near the 1996 levels, and 12th graders' scores had declined significantly (National Center for Education Statistics, 2002). In recent years, U.S. students' math and science knowledge has been compared with that of students from many other nations, with unflattering results. In 2000, the Programme for International Student Assessment (PISA) examined mathematics and science literacy among 15-year-old students from countries aligned with the Organisation for Economic Co-operation and Development (OECD). PISA found that the average scores of U.S. students did not differ significantly from the average scores of students in 15 other nations; however, in some countries, including Korea, Japan, and the United Kingdom, 75 percent of students scored higher than U.S. students (Lemke et al., 2001).

Both the NAEP and the PISA assessments required students to plan investigations, interpret data and charts, solve problems, and form conclusions—activities that are often absent in U.S. science classrooms. U.S. students' relatively poor scores may stem from how we interpret science standards, how we teach science in schools, and how students demonstrate understanding (Windschitl, 2006). Teachers and programs tend to place too much emphasis on memorizing facts rather than on applying and understanding concepts through inquiry and active involvement (Lawton, 1997). The current U.S. focus on accountability in the form of high-stakes test scores often tempts principals and teachers to teach to the test and forgo inquiry- and discovery-based instructional strategies, instead having students merely recite facts and regurgitate definitions.

Cultural and traditional factors may also be involved. Fort (1993) suggests that both students and adults in the United States are "science shy": most students fear involvement in science and do not receive the support they need to engage in scientific activities. If U.S. students are to become "science savvy," they need to have more positive experiences with science and gain confidence in their abilities. To achieve this, teachers must rid themselves of their own science shyness. If we want students to experience the joy of being engaged in science, we need to make science and science education less mysterious, less abstract, more clear, and more accessible.

The challenge for teachers is to create engaging classroom activities that align with standards while fostering critical thinking and inquiry (Cavaness, 2004). Providing professional development that links standards with inquiry models is a solid first step in that direction (Harcombe, 2005). Further, aligning science curriculum standards with classroom texts, activities, experiments, and instructional strategies is crucial. The process of aligning the curriculum of a school or even a grade level can lead to valuable reflection on just what is important for students to learn (Martin-Hansen, 2004).

The No Child Left Behind Act of 2001 includes a number of strategies to help schools and teachers meet this challenge. For example, funds from the National Science Foundation and the U.S. Department of Education are being directed toward partnerships between school districts and universities. Businesses, science centers, museums, and other community organizations are being invited to partner with schools to help students become more engaged in science. States are being urged to reward school districts that increase student enrollment in advanced science and mathematics courses. Finally, as of 2007, states are required to measure students' progress in science at least once in each of three grade spans (3–5, 6–9, and 10–12) annually and to report results.

During the last 15 years, many highly regarded organizations—including the National Research Council (NRC), the National Science Teachers Association (NSTA), and the American Association for the Advancement of Science (AAAS)—have published standards and guidelines "calling for improvement in teacher qualifications and the learning environment, and setting levels of expectation for student achievement. The standards reinforce the notion that the pursuit of excellence must be open to all students, regardless of their sex, race, or the community in which they live" (Suter, 1996, p. 3).

In general, the standards call for the following:

- Expect all students to attain a high level of scientific competence.
- Expose all students to the full range of educational opportunities and the demands of an appropriate science curriculum.
- Expect young people to learn science as an active process while focusing on a limited number of concepts.
- Ensure instruction and assessment that stress understanding, reasoning, and problem solving rather than memorization of facts and terminology.
- Create learning environments that involve students actively through discussion, problem solving, hands-on activities, and small-group work.
- Require teachers to act as facilitators of learning through proper management of the learning environment. (Suter, 1996, pp. 4–5)

In addition, the AAAS (1990) states that science teaching should

- Be consistent with the nature of scientific inquiry.
- Reflect scientific values.
- Aim to counteract learning anxieties.
- Extend beyond the school.
- Involve students in activities to produce learning of lasting benefit. (pp. 200–207)

The challenge ahead is clear, for both policy leaders and science teachers. Before students can become science savvy and actively engaged in learning science, both the instructional processes and the ways we view science must change. The summary in Figure 7.1 (pp. 196–197) compares the traditional with the new forms of curriculum, instruction, and assessment.

The State of the Art of Science Education

Science education in the United States has changed significantly during the last several decades. The most visible change is the coordinated effort of science, education, and government sectors to increase scientific literacy for all.

In a world filled with the products of scientific inquiry, scientific literacy is a necessity. Everyone needs to use scientific information to make choices that arise every day. Everyone needs to be able to engage intelligently in public discourse and debate on vital issues involving science and technology. And everyone deserves to share the excitement and personal fulfillment that come from understanding and learning about the natural world (National Research Council, 1996).

The publication of *Benchmarks for Scientific Literacy* (American Association for the Advancement of Science, 1993) and *National Science Education Standards* (National Research Council, 1996) provided road maps of a sort to coordinate this enormously important effort. The associations, agencies, and institutions participating in the effort received guidelines directed toward their respective areas of concern (e.g., assessment, teacher education, or professional development) that also meshed together in pursuit of the overarching goal of scientific literacy for all. In addition, nearly every U.S. state has revised state-level science content standards so that they align with these overarching standards.

So what exactly does *scientific literacy* mean? According to the American Association for the Advancement of Science (1990), a science-literate person is aware that science, mathematics, and technology are interdependent human enterprises; understands key concepts and principles of science; is familiar with the natural world; and uses scientific knowledge and scientific ways of thinking for individual and social purposes. The National Research Council's (1996) definition of scientific literacy includes the following abilities:

- A person can ask, find, or determine answers to questions derived from curiosity about everyday experiences.
- A person can read and understand articles about science in the popular press and converse about the validity of the conclusions therein.
- A person can identify scientific issues underlying national and local decisions and express positions that are scientifically and technologically informed.
- A person can evaluate the quality of scientific information on the basis of its source and the method used to generate it.
- A person can pose and evaluate arguments based on evidence and apply conclusions from such arguments appropriately. (p. 22)

FIGURE 7.1

Comparison of Traditional and New Forms of Science Curriculum, Instruction, and Assessment

Curriculum

Traditional Emphasis	New Emphasis
• Scope and sequence usually aligned with published textbooks	• Science curriculum mapped and aligned with state and national standards
• Science as a body of information and memorization of facts	• Science as a deep understanding of concepts, principles, and applications
• Science disciplines as separate entities	• Interrelationships among life science, physical sciences, technology, and mathematics
• Science as values-free and objective	• Effects of science on ethical, moral, and humanistic principles
• Science for high-ability students and those with aptitudes for math and science	• Science for all students, regardless of ability, background, culture, or other social condition
• Science teachers as technicians and transmitters of science knowledge and skills	• Science teachers as knowledgeable, reflective, and effective members of learning communities

Instruction

Traditional Emphasis	New Emphasis
• Textbook-driven	• Textbooks as one resource among many; teachers with extensive and deep understanding of discipline
• Passive accumulation and memorization of factual information	• Inquiry-based, with students learning principles and concepts through in-depth examination, exploration, and problem solving
• Lecture and demonstration	• Experimentation, use of learning cycle, hands-on activities
• Individual student achievement and competition	• Cooperation, collaboration, collective efforts toward understanding
• Uniform, one-size-fits-all instruction	• Variety of approaches, differentiation, modification of activities and tasks

Assessment	
Traditional Emphasis	*New Emphasis*
• Assessment of easily measured products	• Assessment of a wide range of products related to important concepts
• Assessment of memorized factual information	• Assessment of performances and science-related products and activities
• Summative assessments administered at conclusion of unit	• Formative assessments administered throughout unit
• Teacher assesses all students	• Students involved with assessment and measures of understanding
• Grading based on students' ability to recite or remember factual information; grades usually determined by percentage of correct recalled answers	• Grading based on students' conceptual understanding, solutions to problems, and contextual performance; grades determined through use of extensive rubrics
• Teacher-made tests or standardized tests used exclusively	• Variety of assessments used, including performance ratings, products, and simulations

Adapted from J. B. Kahle (1996), Highlights of the National Research Council's National Science Education Standards. *School Science and Mathematics, 96*(5), 274–275.

Recent research also points to specific teaching strategies that have had remarkable effects on student achievement in all subjects and that should be included as an integral part of science instruction (Marzano, Norford, Paynter, Pickering, & Gaddy, 2001; Marzano, Pickering, & Pollock, 2001). These practices will help students attain a deeper understanding of scientific principles and enhance their performance on mandated tests. These instructional strategies include

• Having students practice identifying similarities and differences.

• Emphasizing summarization and note taking.

• Providing positive recognition of student effort.

• Emphasizing homework and practice.

• Using nonlinguistic representations.

• Promoting cooperative learning.

• Setting objectives and providing feedback.

• Having students generate and test hypotheses.

• Using questions, cues, and advance organizers.

Teachers should avoid responding to pressure for higher test scores by teaching to the test. Instead, they should keep in mind that when students are engaged in science and scientific inquiry, they are much more likely to understand scientific concepts and to retain that content for a longer period of time. This is not to suggest that teachers should ignore state and national standards; it simply means that using sound instructional strategies like those listed above in conjunction with the strategies described later in this chapter will result in both greater depth of knowledge and higher test scores (National Research Council, 2000, 2001).

We can attain the goal of scientific literacy for everyone. We now have a clear statement of what it means to be scientifically literate. If teachers, parents, citizens, and policymakers work together, we can improve the science education of today's children for tomorrow's world.

Assessing Student Achievement in Science

Student assessment in science, as in other subjects, typically involves administering teacher-made or standardized achievement tests composed primarily of multiple-choice, true/false, short-answer, and fill-in-the-blank questions. However, according to the recent reports of the American Association for the Advancement of Science, the National Research Council, and the National Science Teachers Association, educators should start integrating other assessment strategies and formats.

These strategies should, of course, be consistent with the learning objectives of the material being studied. Teachers should be able to answer the question, What do I want students to know or be able to do at the end of this lesson that they

didn't know or couldn't do before? Once they have identified the desired outcomes, teachers should be able to answer the question, How will I know my students learned _____?

For example, if skills in problem solving and critical thinking are desired outcomes (as they should be, if students are expected to achieve scientific literacy), then assessments should provide tasks that require students to demonstrate their skills in these areas. The host of guidelines and standards advocated by national organizations, professional societies, and individual states demand strategies that go far beyond the multiple-choice, paper-and-pencil testing used almost exclusively until now. Today's teachers must be skilled in designing and implementing

• Performance-based assessments that require students to demonstrate skills and apply knowledge and that evaluate a variety of student products.

• Portfolio assessments that measure progress in student performance, attainment of specific goals and objectives, and the quality and value of science experiences.

• Test-based assessments that require students to construct responses indicating their ability to apply learning to new contexts.

Specific science assessment tasks may have students

• Perform various operations to display the proper use of equipment or technology.

• Perform experiments and investigations that require application of learned skills and information.

• Present oral and written reports of their observations and findings from experiments and investigations.

• Keep collections of work and products over time to depict accomplishments and progress.

• Reflect on failures, successes, experiences, and progress.

• Perform self-assessments of accomplishments and products.

• Complete projects and prescribe tasks.

• Design plans for solving practical problems.

• Respond to essay and other constructed-response test items using application, synthesis, and other higher-order mental processes.

• Perform library, Internet, or other research.

• Give oral responses to questions and make oral presentations of ideas, work, and discoveries.

• React to the work of classmates and students from other schools or grade levels.

• Create devices and tools applying science knowledge and understanding.

• Describe observed phenomena, events, and sequences of events.

Teachers can best assess student performance on these tasks by observing students while they are actually completing the tasks. In performance assessments, the process and the behaviors that students demonstrate are a major part of what is being evaluated, whereas some assessments primarily judge the products that result from students' performance. Whether the emphasis is on the process, the product, or both, performance assessments need to be based on specific criteria established before the administration of the assessments.

Unlike conventional paper-and-pencil tests, performance assessment tasks usually do not have single correct answers and therefore are not usually scored by a machine or by someone unfamiliar with the content. Educators can get the most valid results by developing rubrics—scoring guides containing specific criteria—prior to the performance. Rubrics provide clear performance targets and standards toward which students can strive, and they should be shared with students early in the instructional and evaluative process. Teachers should make sure that the rubrics are appropriate for students' backgrounds and developmental levels (Perrone, 1991).

Again, the design, content, and requirements of performance tasks should be aligned with the teacher's own objectives, and the rubrics should be consistent with the identified tasks. Rubrics can be designed to enable the scorer to simply check whether or not each performance criterion has been met or to rate performances or products along a numeric continuum. Teachers can easily design ratings that are similar to the scales used in more traditional grading.

As a final note, it is important to distinguish between instructional activities and assessment activities. These two types of activities may resemble each other, but assessment activities should take place both during and after the instruction and should determine the effectiveness of the instruction. In addition, teachers should use examples and conditions for the assessment activities that are different from those used in the instructional activities. Providing different examples ensures assessment of abilities beyond mere rote memorization (see Figure 7.2).

Enhancing Students' Achievement in Science

Students learn best when they construct their own knowledge through interaction with the objects and people in their environment. This approach to learning—known as *constructivism* (Piaget, 1951), *sense-making* (McIntyre, 1984), or *project learning* (Katz & Chard, 1989)—is driven by student questions rather than by textbooks or curricula. To enhance their natural understanding of science, students need to explore the physical properties of a wide variety of objects; have time to think about their investigations; and share their experiences with others (Gega, 1994). Science instruction extends beyond the school: teachers, families, and the community must work together to increase student achievement. However, as states and organizations review and revise science standards, the best science teachers are also revising their strategies to incorporate the standards into the constructivist approach.

The following powerful, sensible recommendations, which grew out of the American Association for the Advancement of Science's *Benchmarks for Scientific Literacy*, suggest ways of increasing students' proficiency in science:

- Begin investigations with questions that students ask themselves, possibly questions about nature.
- Engage students actively, giving them real items to observe, weigh, measure, compare, count, and categorize.
- Concentrate on collecting and using evidence; integrate science and technology with other forms of expression.
- Use a team approach to learning.
- Deemphasize memorizing technical vocabulary; focus on contextual understanding, adding vocabulary for communication purposes.
- Welcome curiosity, creativity, and a healthy spirit of questioning.

Let us also consider the relationship between academic success and motivation and self-confidence. For many students, science provokes feelings of anxiety and fear of failure. Find strategies that enhance students' self-esteem. Build on their successes, maintain equal expectations for boys and girls, and support the roles of women and minorities in science.

Strategies That Promote Achievement in Science

The instructional strategies in the remainder of this chapter are based on sound research and instructional principles that have yielded positive results in students' science achievement and understanding of scientific principles. Briefly, the strategies point toward

FIGURE 7.2

Assessment Schema for Problem-Based Science Unit of Study: Loggerhead Sea Turtles (*Caretta caretta*)

Essential Questions:

    I. What is happening to loggerhead sea turtles, and what can be done to prevent their extinction?

    II. What are the effects of the loggerhead sea turtle crisis on our local economy and the larger ecosystem of our coastline?

A. Objectives (Linked to State Curricula or Standards)

Upon completion of a unit about loggerhead sea turtles, students will be able to

- Describe at least 15 characteristics of loggerhead sea turtles, including but not limited to physical characteristics; habitats and food needs; migration patterns, including international interactions; reproductive processes; populations and population patterns; and destructive forces and extinction possibilities.
- Create a realistic plan to address the problems identified in an investigation of sea turtles.
- Describe the economic impact of plans and solutions.
- Write a cohesive, well-written persuasive letter.
- Describe the key components of teamwork in a scientific investigation.

B. Assessment Activities and Plans

Assessment questions:

- What products can students produce to demonstrate knowledge about loggerhead sea turtles?
- To what degree should products reflect knowledge and understanding?
- How will students be grouped to assure both individual accountability and team responsibilities?

C. Possible Student Products and Performances

- Posters delineating basic biological characteristics of loggerhead sea turtles.
- Maps depicting migration routes, feeding areas, and nesting areas.
- Spreadsheets and tables depicting rise and fall of populations and breeding statistics.
- PowerPoint and other presentations describing summary data.
- Skits and performances directed toward students in lower grades.
- Debates or discussions of possible solutions and costs associated with solutions.
- Written research reports.
- Letters and petitions to local, state, and national officials.
- Student self-ratings.
- Team self-ratings.

D. Summative and Traditional Assessments

- Teacher-created or text-available multiple-choice questions (related to state standards).
- Quizzes on vocabulary and contextual terms.

• Using hands-on activities, process skills, and strategies that enable young people to investigate, explore, discover, and reach conclusions about scientific phenomena.

• Using a science curriculum map that is closely aligned with state and national standards.

• Using a learning cycle or discrepant event lessons to challenge students' perceptions about science, scientific principles, and the natural world.

• Using collaborative, cooperative methods so that students can discuss scientific principles with others.

• Using activities and content that are naturally motivating for students and that look at science and scientific discoveries from different cultural perspectives.

• Using content and principles that naturally link and integrate subjects so that students can better understand how science is relevant to their lives.

• Using problem-based learning activities that link scientific concepts, principles, and content with relevant real-world problems.

• Using the available wealth of technology and network services to help students investigate and examine science and scientific principles.

Strategy 7.1:
Use a process skills approach to teaching science.

Discussion

Students should see science as a way to understand their world. Regardless of grade level, students bring their own experiences and knowledge to the classroom each day, and with those experiences they bring natural curiosity and wonder. Good science teachers take advantage of these qualities by providing well-designed instruction and activities that allow students to make sense of their experiences and learn basic science principles that affect everyday life.

Certain important process skills—observing, classifying, measuring, inferring, communicating, predicting, and experimenting—help students understand the nature of science. Note that these terms all imply *action*: *observing* involves using the primary senses to examine a phenomenon; *classifying* involves sorting, arranging, and identifying relationships; *measuring* involves gathering information about relative size; *inferring* involves making judgments or conjectures on the basis of gathered information or experiences; *communicating* involves sharing or disseminating information; *predicting* involves using known information to foretell what may take place; and *experimenting* involves developing and then testing a hypothesis. When students are actively immersed in process skills, they come to understand science facts as they should: as building blocks for understanding their world.

Classroom Examples

In Juanita Mendoza's 5th–6th grade classroom, students are actively involved in examining several life science concepts and principles. Mendoza has provided a variety of seeds that the students have germinated, planted, and grown in the classroom. Each student maintains a daily journal of observations for a specific plant, keeping careful records of the plant's measurements, colors, development, and growth, as well as predicting what the plant might do next on the basis of previous observations. Each student is also required to identify the plant by its proper name; as the plants grow, the students identify and properly classify their respective plants.

In addition, students conduct cellular examinations, taking small samples of each plant's leaves and examining them under a microscope, looking for various cellular structures and examples of cell division. Students record results of these examinations in their journals and share their findings by creating posters and drawings.

Students also use their plants to pose experimental questions, mostly about how the plants would react to external stimuli and other environmental factors. The students then set up experiments that help them answer their research questions.

Throughout the unit, Mendoza guides the students in their investigations and provides direct instruction on botanical processes, cellular structure, and related biological content.

Resources

Fredericks & Cheesebrough, 1993; Hassard, 1992.

Strategy 7.2:

Encourage content-rich, active exploration and use hands-on approaches that help students confront scientific misperceptions and understand scientific truths.

Discussion

Students of all ages hold many misperceptions about science and scientific concepts. Unfortunately, the paper-and-pencil tasks and textbook assignments so often used in science classrooms rarely offer students either a complete picture of a concept or an understanding of a concept's basic principles. Hands-on, active participation and manipulation of materials, on the other hand, help students reformulate their original ideas and build a sound foundation for acquiring science content, thinking about concepts creatively and critically, and correcting misperceptions.

Teachers should keep in mind that such science activities demand well-organized, thoughtful plans to assess students' prior knowledge of a concept, a carefully sequenced set of learning activities and assignments, a method to evaluate whether students have learned the content, and ways to link the activities and concepts to students' lives. Such activities are more successful if the teacher is well organized, possessing not only the specific materials and equipment for the activities but also other text-based materials. The room should be full to bursting with materials to support lessons or units.

For these types of lessons to be fully effective, teachers must also have a clear and deep understanding of the concepts to be taught. Often, teachers have had little recent experience with some of the science concepts they try to teach; it may have been some time since they took a science class, and what was once learned may have faded in the face of other responsibilities. Therefore, teachers who intend to use hands-on approaches must often spend considerable time refamiliarizing themselves with the appropriate concepts, using college and high school texts, association and conference materials, and the Internet to bring themselves up to speed.

Classroom Examples

Arlene Washington's 4th grade classroom walls are decorated with charts, diagrams, and pictures of electrical appliances, generators, and batteries. Her lessons incorporate a variety of different approaches, but they have one thing in common: during every lesson, students manipulate materials and equipment, exploring not only the uses of electricity but also how it is generated and transmitted. Washington also provides well-designed handouts and organizers for each lesson, introducing vocabulary words and key concepts with pictures and graphs.

In one lesson, students examine static electricity. In addition to balloons and other objects commonly used to demonstrate the properties of static electricity, Washington introduces an electrophorus (a device used to produce electric charges through the process of electrostatic induction) that she has made from a pizza pan, a large dowel, and a section of plastic pipe. With these materials, she leads the students toward an understanding of static electricity and the difference between voltage and amperage.

Washington also uses a neon wand and a small fluorescent bulb to demonstrate how the various atoms within these bulbs give off colored light when barraged by electrons. She uses a variety of other materials (including magnets, iron filings, batteries, bulbs, wires, switches, and electric bells) to explore types of currents and circuits as well as such sophisticated principles as resistance. She helps students overcome their misperceptions of how electricity works by setting up rows of marbles in a tray to show how electrical energy appears to move instantly along a conductor. Washington expertly guides students through an exciting array of activities and experiences, including building small electric motors.

Parents of Washington's students are consistently happy with their children's progress in learning science; they often remark that in her class, the students nearly always seem to be *doing* science.

Resources

Barba, 1998; Fredericks & Cheesebrough, 1993; Friedl, 2005; Martin, Sexton, Wagner, & Gerlovich, 1997; McBride, Bhatti, Hannan, & Feinberg, 2004; Ostlund, 1992; Singh, Granville, & Dika, 2002.

Strategy 7.3:

Use a learning cycle strategy of instruction.

Discussion

Since the 1960s, the learning cycle has evolved into an instructional model that is easy to use, extremely effective, and very engaging. The learning cycle uses exploration, discovery, experiences, questions, and examples to help students understand scientific principles and apply them to new situations or problems. The cycle consists of three phases: *exploration, concept introduction*, and *application*.

During the *exploration* phase, students explore various phenomena, principles, concepts, and problems, using materials and objects to discover how the concepts are related or interact. Students often form hypotheses and explore various perceptions and misperceptions regarding the concepts.

The second phase, *concept introduction*, involves a more direct form of instruction, as the teacher presents explanations and additional examples. This brief but crucial portion of the lesson helps students understand how the activities and concrete materials relate to a scientific principle. The teacher also explains how the principle relates to students' lives.

The last phase of the learning cycle is *application*. After they have explored a scientific principle and heard the teacher's explanation and examples, students use what they have learned to solve an additional problem or apply the principle to a new situation. This final phase

can allow students additional time to manipulate materials, or it can employ more traditional paper-and-pencil methods. This phase of the cycle not only reinforces students' understanding of a principle but also can serve as a form of assessment.

The learning cycle can be used with students of nearly all ages, ability levels, and cultures. Both young children and older students benefit from this model because the format resembles the discipline of science itself: students learn to construct knowledge from a series of explorations that lead to discoveries, predictions, and new knowledge. The model is especially effective in helping older students replace inaccurate thinking or erroneous knowledge with new, authentic understanding.

Classroom Examples

Maryann Watson's 6th grade students enter the room to find each table set up with a birthday candle, a canning jar, a Styrofoam plate, and a container of water. This is the exploration phase of the learning cycle. Using a small piece of clay to affix the candle to the jar's lid, they place the candle in the center of the Styrofoam plate. After lighting the candle and pouring a few milliliters of water onto the plate, the students predict what will happen to the candle when the jar is placed over the candle. Most predict that the candle will go out, and some even suggest that lack of oxygen is the reason. What they seldom foresee, however, is the movement of the water upward into the jar as the candle goes out. Several further attempts and explorations (for example, altering the amount of water or the number of candles) reveal some discrepancies in the students' predictions.

Next comes the concept introduction phase. After listing the various student-generated hypotheses on the board, Watson explains briefly the phenomenon that the class has just witnessed, delivering information about air, heat energy, air pressure, and molecular movement. Finally, the application phase: Watson asks students to predict what will happen when a hard-boiled egg is placed on the open top of a milk bottle after heat has been introduced into the bottle (the egg gets sucked into the bottle). Following this demonstration, she uses a relevant textbook selection and a handout to reinforce students' learning.

Resources
Beisenherz & Dantonio, 1996; Marek & Cavallo, 1997; Martin, Sexton, Wagner, & Gerlovich, 1997.

Strategy 7.4:
Use unexpected, discrepant events to facilitate science process skills, explain misunderstood science principles, and assess student knowledge.

Discussion
Discrepant events can be a very effective teaching strategy, particularly when they are planned and executed in a thoughtful, engaging manner. Discrepant events are simply events and activities that happen in a way that is counter to expectations; they create strong emotions in

students and provide strong motivation to solve the problems associated with the events.

Carefully planned lessons using discrepant events can be very important learning experiences for students; indeed, many older students describe such classroom incidents as some of their most memorable school experiences. More important, these unexpected events can lead students to true understanding of the scientific principles associated with them.

Classroom Examples
Janet Greenberg has given each pair of her 3rd grade students a beaker filled with ice, a thermometer, and a container of water. Students add the water to their beakers, and Greenberg displays a large chart on the overhead projector with a space for each pair to predict the temperature in their respective beakers of ice water. Greenberg listens carefully, gathering and recording the students' predictions. Most groups of students predict that the temperature of their ice water will be at or near zero.

Having recorded the students' predictions, Greenberg distributes small paper cups containing a few grams of common table salt. She then asks students to predict the temperature of their ice water after they add 15–20 grams of salt. Having seen salt used to melt ice on sidewalks, most students predict that the temperatures of their little systems will rise significantly after the introduction of the salt into the beakers. Greenberg again records all the predictions and then asks the students to add the salt to their beakers and record their observations. Most are quite surprised to see the temperature drop.

Greenberg then leads a discussion about melting and freezing points, heat of fusion, heat of vaporization, and other grade- and age-appropriate science concepts. Using an LCD projector, she also shows a number of Web sites that contain simulations of the actions of the salt and the water. Finally, she leads the class in a few more activities and discusses further examples of this phenomenon and how it relates to their everyday lives.

Resources

Friedl, 2005; Martin, Sexton, Wagner, & Gerlovich, 1998.

Strategy 7.5:

Use cooperative learning strategies to engage all students, especially culturally diverse students, in the social processes of learning science.

Discussion

When planned and implemented thoughtfully, cooperative learning improves most students' understanding of science concepts. It appears to improve concept and information retention, problem-solving skills, attitudes toward science (and toward teachers!), self-concept, and relations among different cultures and races. Students from some different cultures consistently prefer group activities to competitive, individual classroom tasks—but they also prefer reporting on their respective group work individually. Well-organized cooperative learning activities can blend group learning with individual accountability and group interdependence.

Cooperative learning needs to be distinguished from mere small-group work. Cooperative learning groups should be carefully formed, with thought given to individual student strengths, weaknesses, and behavior, as well as to the teacher's learning goals. Cooperative learning groups seem to work best when students are given specific responsibilities that combine learning the material with such roles as recording data, presenting data, using technology, managing materials, and managing cleanup.

Teachers proficient in cooperative learning strategies test and retest different arrangements and types of activities according to their changing student populations and the science content being taught at any given time. Implementing cooperative learning is not easy, nor is it something teachers are likely to master quickly; it will take time, attention to detail, and many rehearsals and trials before teachers grow comfortable with this valuable approach.

Classroom Examples

After introducing a lesson on animal adaptation with a six-minute video, Grace Martin asks her students to move into their prearranged cooperative groups. She has already examined the students' prior knowledge of adaptation, their ability to work together, and their reading, listening, and writing skills. She has formed today's groups on the basis of all these factors. She reminds students of the group-work procedures, emphasizing that everyone has a designated role and that it is important to work together.

The materials manager in each group gathers the needed equipment and materials, and the recorder prepares to record the lesson's events using an observation worksheet prepared by Martin. Once everything is in place, Martin gives a five-minute lecture covering some of the content in the video and then directs the students' attention to a sheet of directions for the work ahead, reading the directions aloud as the students follow along.

Martin reminds the students that they must depend on one another for ideas and that each group will receive a score that will be entered into a cooperative science learning gradebook. She also reminds students that they need to pay careful attention to their group's work to be able to complete the additional individual work required.

As the lesson proceeds, the students examine a variety of texts, pictures, and real animals (including a gerbil, a snake, and tropical fish), discussing and listing the ways in which certain parts of the animals are adaptations, and then following the teacher's written and oral instructions. Group members collaboratively reach conclusions that they present to the whole class. One student presents the group's conclusions while another displays the work on a bulletin board.

Near the end of the lesson, Martin again presents some direct instruction that pulls together the lesson's major points and helps students relate the content to their own lives. She finishes by assigning homework and reviewing what the class has learned.

Resources

Barba, 1998; Johnson & Johnson, 1986, 1987; Martin, Sexton, Wagner, & Gerlovich, 1998; Marzano, Pickering, & Pollock, 2001; Okebukola, 1985; Tobin, 1993; Watson, 1991.

Strategy 7.6:
Use motivating techniques, activities, and attitudes with students of all cultures and backgrounds.

Discussion

There are numerous ways for teachers to motivate students' interest in science. Students of all ages and cultures are naturally curious about the world they live in, and classrooms that link science with life outside school encourage students to act on this natural curiosity. Motivating, too, are those classrooms that recognize students' prior knowledge, regardless of their backgrounds or neighborhoods, and that contain culturally familiar reference points, role models, analogies, and experiences.

Motivation correlates directly to the level of success that students find in a classroom. The more students experience success, the more likely they are to expect success in the future and to persevere in their efforts to solve problems and complete tasks. In addition, students who experience success are less likely to misbehave; in fact, they will often help the teacher keep other students on task.

Conversely, students who consistently experience failure are more likely to cause problems in class, less likely to attempt new tasks or assignments, less likely to participate fully in cooperative groups and other learning activities, and less likely to set personal goals.

Therefore, science teachers need to be aware of students' cultural backgrounds, histories, and neighborhoods and to plan and deliver thoughtful lessons and activities that foster and build on student success.

Classroom Examples

Gerald Foster's 6th grade students are a diverse group; looking around his classroom, it is easy to spot black, Hispanic, Asian American, and white students. Foster consistently uses common cultural items and analogies to enliven his lessons. For example, he uses origami paper to demonstrate chemical relationships, automobile parts to illustrate systems and principles of chemical and physical science, and tortillas and bagels to illustrate types of chemical reactions. He also provides handouts with illustrations of important terms and ideas so that all students, regardless of language ability or cultural background, have an accurate understanding of science concepts.

Foster's classes are known for their absence of behavioral disruptions and for students' high level of motivation. Foster is flexible and accommodating in his use of cooperative learning and small-group work, realizing that some students' cultural backgrounds make it harder for them to answer questions in a large-group setting. And some of his students are made more comfortable by being allowed to simply observe a demonstration rather than being required to work with the materials. Foster is committed to differentiating assignments and allowing students to make informed and guided choices without diluting the quality of the work. For example, he often allows students to demonstrate their understanding by making presentations and completing projects that have cultural relevance for them; his classroom walls display rap lyrics, drawings, posters, and poetry illustrating scientific principles.

Foster favors short problem-solving segments that break tasks into small, student-centered objectives. He also breaks complex science principles into logical, easy-to-understand pieces. His lessons are consistently positive; he avoids focusing on students' mistakes and instead highlights the positive aspects of any given response while helping class members move toward a proper understanding of each principle. He emphasizes that scientists use failed experiments, errors, and other disappointments to gain understanding and solve problems.

Resources

Atkinson, 1964; Barba, 1998; Gay, 1988; McClelland, 1965; Ogbu, 1992; Suzuki, 1984.

Strategy 7.7:
Use multicultural perspectives when teaching science.

Discussion

Traditionally, U.S. science education has been grounded in theories and methods that were generated primarily by male European scientists. Regardless of its origins, this approach ends up omitting from the curriculum many important scientists and scientific discoveries and methods from other cultures.

U.S. classrooms increasingly contain students from diverse backgrounds. Global population shifts are affecting not only the methods teachers use but also the ways in which students understand content. Young people tend to be more interested in science content when they see how people from their own cultures have viewed the scientific principles and learn how those principles are now better understood because of a variety of multicultural contributions.

Perhaps one of the most important reasons to take a more diverse approach to teaching science is the fact that minorities and women are significantly underrepresented in most fields of scientific endeavor. Including the contributions and accomplishments that have been systematically omitted for so long sends students of all backgrounds a strong message that everyone is capable of doing science.

Classroom Examples

Hannah Wilkins's diverse class of 9th graders is beginning a short unit on space exploration and astronomy. Several students have limited proficiency in English, so Wilkins is careful to form balanced work teams. She is determined to include a wide range of activities and assignments that will allow her students to investigate how 20th century space exploration benefited from the contributions of female scientists and scientists from different cultures.

After several short discussions on some of the scientists included in the textbook, Wilkins constructs a bulletin board displaying brief biographies of some fairly well-known culturally diverse scientists. Another bulletin board provides space for students to post biographies and displays highlighting lesser-known female, Asian, South American, and Eastern European scientists and astronomers. Her students use the Internet and a host of other resources to gather data about these scientists. By the end of the unit, the bulletin board highlights the contributions of scientists from all over the world and from various periods of history.

Wilkins assigns several groups the task of developing an electronic database and making computer-generated presentations about these scientists to other middle school science classes. The database includes such astronomers as Caroline Herschel, who discovered eight comets during the 18th century; Williamina Fleming, who devised a system of classifying stars; Arzachel, who discovered the elliptical nature of planetary orbits in the 11th century; Subrahmanyan Chandrasekhar, who contributed much to the field of stellar evolution; Yusuke Hagihara, who was instrumental in the development of satellite systems; and Henrietta Leavitt, who discovered variable stars in the late 1800s. In addition, three times during the unit, Wilkins invites female and culturally diverse scientists from local laboratories, hospitals, and businesses to speak about their work.

Wilkins's efforts have reaped rewards. She has observed improved student attitudes about science and a higher quality of student work. She also makes good use of student research: at the end of the year, she finds that she herself is far more knowledgeable about the contributions of women scientists and scientists from other cultures.

Resources

Banks & McGee, 1993; Barba, 1998; Fathman, Quinn, & Kessler, 1992; National Science Teachers Association, 1991.

Strategy 7.8:

Use techniques that naturally integrate other content areas to help students understand how science relates to their own interests and lives.

Discussion

Teachers are finding that integrating different areas of the curriculum gives students a deeper and more meaningful understanding of concepts and results in higher standardized test scores. And no area of the curriculum is better suited to an interdisciplinary approach than science. When students learn scientific principles within a real-life context, they tend to remember them more clearly. In addition, students who successfully and regularly participate in interdisciplinary units generally have better attitudes toward a subject and improved relationships with teachers and are better able to work in cooperative groups.

Educators need to plan thematic or integrated approaches very carefully—whenever possible, with other teachers. When departments are not able to work together, individual science teachers can carefully incorporate other content areas into their lessons, especially mathematics and social studies, which often fit naturally. Science teachers can also weave English and language arts throughout a given topic by using a variety of trade books or supplemental texts. Thoughtful assessment is the most dependable means of ascertaining the depth and breadth of student learning. Students' products and assignments should be evaluated thoroughly using a well-developed set of grading guides and rubrics that focus clearly on the content and objectives.

Teachers should use caution in developing interdisciplinary science lessons. Curriculum integration is not automatically better than a more traditional approach; often, science content taught in this manner can take too much time to present and loses its meaning for students. Teachers need to ensure that the integrated approach will help students learn more than a more traditional approach would.

Classroom Examples

Mathew Chang, a science teacher, and Louise Richards, a history teacher, are fortunate to share a stable group of 9th grade students throughout their respective block schedules, and they are able to periodically link their two disciplines in fairly concrete ways. For example, when Richards was teaching the period covering the early to mid–20th century, including World War II, Chang developed several lessons about some of the scientific inventions that occurred as a result of the war.

In discussing their content objectives for the remainder of the year, the two teachers realized that they could link their content areas in several ways. During a month of joint planning after school, they created a series of lessons to help their students understand how scientific advancement, especially in space exploration and astronomy, connected with the period of the Cold War.

Chang created lessons on propulsion, gravity, inertia, energy transfer, ascending cones, Newton's laws, and other principles related to exploring space; Richards linked political events, national budgets, changes in education, and other historical topics to the space race and current space exploration efforts. Each teacher also created and distributed advance organizers and other pictorial representations illustrating and linking the concepts studied. Both teachers have reported significant gains in students' progress and test scores on these topics.

Resources

Beane, 1996; Friedl, 2005; George, 1996; Jacobs, 1989.

Strategy 7.9:

Use a thematic approach to connect big ideas, unifying theories, or other principles with broad implications.

Discussion

Educators who want to avoid teaching science as a set of discrete facts for students to memorize should make themes a key component of the science curriculum. Most students are familiar with the concept of themes; they often study themes of various kinds of literature, themes that give structure to music, or themes that provide guidance in understanding mathematical concepts.

Themes enable students to grasp the larger framework of science. Indeed, most states' science standards are organized around naturally occurring threads of science principles that logically form themes.

Common themes used in science classrooms at all levels include *energy*, as an underlying concept for physical, biological, and geological science; *systems*, as a way to look at patterns, interactions, and boundaries of science subject areas; *evolution*, as it applies to patterns, processes, and changes throughout time; *change*, as a way of examining systems, trends, cycles, ecology, and adaptation; and *structures*, as a way of viewing the natural world and its tremendous diversity.

Classroom Examples

The science department of Kennedy Middle School consists of eight teachers who have selected a six-week theme for 8th and 9th graders titled "Change—The Earth in Its Universe." Using a wide variety of exploratory and direct instructional strategies, the science teachers expect students to come to understand how the Earth, as part of a changing universe, changes constantly as it speeds through time. They use the sun as a central part of the unit: students examine atmospheric effects and weather, the effects of the sun and moon on the Earth, the Earth's place in the solar system, the solar system's place in the galaxy, and how galaxies form a tiny portion of the universe. Finally, the teachers introduce students to the idea of chaos theory and how it is related to change.

The teachers continually emphasize the interrelationships of different but connected systems, the evolutionary processes inherent in our ever-changing Earth, and how humankind has effected changes on the planet. They use the subtheme of *cycles* to help students understand the changing nature of life processes, the planets and the solar system, plate tectonics, and ecosystems.

Resources

Barba, 1998; Fredericks & Cheesebrough, 1993; Friedl, 2005; Gallagher, 1993; Hassard, 1992.

Strategy 7.10:
Use technology, the Internet, and multimedia for student work and for topical research, exploration, and instruction.

Discussion

Teachers are gaining significantly more access to and proficiency in computers and various electronic media. More schools are connected to the Internet than ever before, and the education market is flooded with instructional software of varying quality and usefulness. Although teachers are growing more comfortable with technology, the pace at which new materials are being introduced is staggering. CD-ROMs, DVDs, high-speed network access, and digital video technologies enable teachers to conduct simulations and experiments that were once far too complex for classroom use.

Students who use technology in a meaningful, well-planned manner appear to demonstrate higher achievement and improved attitudes toward science. Their retention of factual knowledge and basic skills also appears to improve when teachers accompany traditional instruction with short, effective, computer-based exercises. Some research suggests that the time needed to learn a concept is shortened when standard instruction is supplemented with computer-based activities (Edelson, Gordin, & Pea, 1998). However, science teachers should also be aware that higher-order thinking and problem solving are best achieved through lessons based on hands-on, experimental, real-life activities.

Much of the software commonly found in school classrooms is multipurpose, containing programs for word processing, graphics and graphing, statistical computation, spreadsheets, and database management. Most of these software packages have become fairly easy to use, and even elementary students are often quite proficient. The Internet also holds much promise for young science students in terms of interaction and mentoring. By using e-mail, digital cameras, Webcams, listservers, and newsgroups, teachers can connect students with working scientists who can assist students with projects and research.

Good planning is crucial. Teachers must not only know how to use technology in the science classroom but also be able to evaluate the quality of the software and the uses to which computers are put. It takes time for teachers to become comfortable with computer software and hardware; although most applications are far easier to use than they were just a few years ago, lesson rehearsal and debugging are still necessary.

Classroom Examples

Diane Rubin, a high school earth science teacher, has developed a sequence of topics to complement the state's mandated curriculum guidelines; the lessons feature outcomes that she believes will be both engaging and productive. Using a set of teacher-generated geology projects, each small group of students poses a question of interest and sets out to investigate various geological processes and events.

Besides using an assortment of texts and trade books, Rubin arranges for her students to contact a number of scientists and graduate students working in the field. She has also found several Web sites containing information and links to other sites in the general area of geology and geological processes. Her planning pays off as the students begin to generate well-developed, focused questions. In some cases, scientists use Webcams to broadcast answers and show actual geological sites—becoming guest speakers without leaving their work sites.

Throughout the series of lessons, Rubin guides the students toward her predetermined set of objectives by having them present their findings to the rest of the class. The students gather an extensive list of resources and become familiar with using a database to sort data and bibliographical information. In their Power-Point presentations, they incorporate photographs and graphic and video clips of various geological phenomena. Using a well-crafted set of evaluation items based on the teacher's learning objectives, students peer-evaluate each presentation. By e-mail, the students thank their scientist mentors and electronically send them copies of their projects and results.

These kinds of activities and strategies require extensive preparation. Many such activities and assignments evolve over a period of time as teachers implement additional activities, ideas, and content—but they all begin with good planning.

Resources

O'Neill, Wagner, & Gomez, 1996; Peters & Stout, 2006.

Strategy 7.11:

Use problem-based learning activities and investigations to teach scientific concepts and principles that have application to students' lives.

Discussion

Problem-based learning, with its focus on complex real-life problems, enables students to engage in higher-order thinking and problem solving. In science education, the problems are generally embedded with sound empirical and theoretical scientific principles, but the application, use, or impact of the principles may lead to difficult decisions and have serious social implications.

Developers of problem-based learning point out that the approach is generally not the best way to deliver large quantities of content; rather, it is an extremely useful strategy to use when teachers want students to collaborate, grapple with difficult problems, understand the links among different disciplines, produce constructive artifacts, perform authentic investigations and research, and use the language and vocabulary of science. In many cases, problem-based learning activities and their culminating products or performances result in action on the part of school communities or other officials. Indeed, it is generally these types of activities that are particularly interesting to the various media that cover schools and school events.

Teachers who are adept at problem-based learning are generally excellent planners; the planning that is required for this approach is

extensive and often difficult for the same reasons that the problems themselves are difficult: the problems have multiple scientific, social, or political dimensions; multiple points of access for investigation; and, in general, a great deal of background material for reading and understanding.

Classroom Examples

Simon Gutierrez's 7th grade class is preparing to take a field trip to a stretch of local beach that is a protected sea turtle nesting ground. One of Gutierrez's students read an article last year about how several of the loggerhead turtles' nests had been vandalized and destroyed and suggested that the class "do something about it."

Gutierrez decided to use this as an opportunity to teach about the species and its habits and history and to link the unit to the state standards, which contain large sections on conservation and responsible use of resources. In planning the unit, however, he discovered that there are a number of controversies regarding the topic, including conflicts with development plans, the impact of turtle protection on employment in the home construction industry, the impact of turtle protection on the fishing and shrimp industries, and how industrial and agricultural pollution contribute to the decrease in viable nests.

Gutierrez spent several months preparing for the unit. He read extensively about the topic, visited a number of local businesses and industries, spoke with numerous individuals whose livelihoods relied on fishing and tourism, and wrote to various federal and state government agencies to gather many free or inexpensive resources. He also made arrangements to check out more than 200 books from local libraries to use during the unit.

The unit begins with the formation of teams of students assigned to conduct extensive research not only on the loggerhead turtles but also on the factors that are contributing to the decline in the nests. The students use the library, the Internet, and other resources to develop sets of "issue papers" that are collected and read by all the students. In addition, speakers from the local area—including a businesswoman who owns a large land development firm, a local independent fisherman, a manager of a local processing plant, and an agent from the National Marine Fisheries Service—make presentations to the students over a period of several weeks.

As the unit progresses, students become deeply involved in the many issues surrounding the biology of sea turtles, including their physical characteristics and habitats as well as the ways in which the endangered turtles are related to the many social and economic factors in the students' community. For example, the turtles' protected status forced local fishermen to use costly equipment to prevent turtles' deaths in the nets. After about four weeks, Gutierrez's students are ready to present their findings and their recommendations to the community during a special meeting of county and city officials.

Resources

Barba, 1998; O'Neill, Wagner, & Gomez, 1996; Torp & Sage, 1998.

Bibliography

American Association for the Advancement of Science. (1990). *Science for all Americans.* New York: Oxford University Press.

American Association for the Advancement of Science. (1993). *Benchmarks for scientific literacy.* New York: Oxford University Press.

Atkinson, J. W. (1964). *An introduction to motivation.* Princeton, NJ: Van Nostrand.

Banks, J. A., & Banks, C. A. (1993). *Multicultural education: Issues and perspectives* (2nd ed.). Boston: Allyn and Bacon.

Banks, C. A., & Banks, J. A. (1993). Social studies teacher education, ethnic diversity, and academic achievement. *International Journal of Social Education, 7*(3), 24–25.

Barba, R. H. (1998). *Science in the multicultural classroom: A guide to teaching and learning* (2nd ed.). Boston: Allyn and Bacon.

Beane, J. (1996). On the shoulders of giants! The case for curriculum integration. *Middle School Journal, 28*(1), 6–11.

Beisenherz, P., & Dantonio, M. (1996). *Using the learning cycle to teach physical science.* Portsmouth, NH: Heinemann.

Cavaness, D. (2004). Exposing your students to science inquiry. *Science Scope, 27*(8), 12–17.

Edelson, D. C., Gordin, D. N., & Pea, R. D. (1998). Addressing the challenges of inquiry-based learning through technology and curriculum design. *Journal of the Learning Sciences, 8(3–4),* 391–450.

Fathman, A. K., Quinn, M. E., & Kessler, C. (1992). Teaching science to English learners, grades 4–8. In *NCBE program informational guide series* (Vol. 11). Washington, DC: National Clearinghouse for Bilingual Education.

Fensham, P., Gunstone, R., & White, R. (Eds.). (1994). *The content of science: A constructivist approach to its teaching and learning.* Washington, DC: Falmer Press.

Fort, D. C. (1993). Science shy, science savvy, science smart. *Phi Delta Kappan, 79*(9), 674–683.

Fredericks, A. D., & Cheesebrough, D. L. (1993). *Science for all children*. New York: HarperCollins.

Friedl, A. E. (2005). *Teaching science to children: An inquiry approach* (6th ed.). New York: McGraw-Hill.

Friedman, T. L. (2005). *The world is flat: A brief history of the twenty-first century*. New York: Farrar, Straus, and Giroux.

Gallagher, J. J. (1993). Ability grouping: A tool for educational excellence. *College Board Review, 168*(6), 21–27.

Gay, G. (1988). Designing relevant curricula for diverse students. *Education and Urban Society, 20*(4), 327–340.

Gega, P. C. (1994). *Science in elementary education*. New York: Macmillan.

George, P. S. (1996). The integrated curriculum: A reality check. *Middle School Journal, 28*(1), 12–19.

Harcombe, E. S. (2005). Science teachers, under construction. *Educational Leadership, 62*(6), 50–54.

Hassard, J. (1992). *Minds on science*. New York: HarperCollins.

Jacobs, H. H. (Ed.). (1989). *Interdisciplinary curriculum: Design and implementation*. Alexandria, VA: Association for Supervision and Curriculum Development.

Johnson, R. T., & Johnson, D. W. (1986). Action research: Cooperative learning in the science classroom. *Science and Children, 24*(2), 31–32.

Johnson, R. T., & Johnson, D. W. (1987). How can we put cooperative learning into practice? *Science Teacher, 54*(6), 46–48, 50.

Johnson, R. T., & Johnson, D. W. (1991). So what's new about cooperative learning in science? *Cooperative Learning, 11*(3), 2–3.

Kahle, J. B. (1996). Highlights of the National Research Council's national science education standards. *School Science and Mathematics, 96*(5), 274–275.

Katz, L. G., & Chard, S. C. (1989). *Engaging children's minds: The project approach*. Norwood, NJ: Ablex.

Lawton, M. (1997). Science proves a big mystery to U.S. pupils. *Education Week, 17*, 9.

Lemke, M., Calsyn, C., Lippman, L., Jocelyn, L., Kastberg, D., Liu, Y. Y., et al. (2001). *Outcomes of learning: Results from the 2000 Program for International Student Assessment of 15-year-olds in reading, mathematics, and science literacy* (NCES 2002-115). Washington, DC: National Center for Education Statistics.

Marek, E. A., & Cavallo, A. M. L. (1997). *The learning cycle: Elementary school science and beyond*. Portsmouth, NH: Heinemann.

Marek, E. A., & Methvan, S. B. (1991). Effects of the learning cycle upon student and classroom teacher performance. *Journal of Research in Science Teaching, 28*(1), 41–53.

Martin, R., Sexton, C., Wagner, K., & Gerlovich, J. (1997). *Teaching science for all children* (2nd ed.). Boston: Allyn and Bacon.

Martin, R., Sexton, C., Wagner, K., & Gerlovich, J. (1998). *Science for all children: Methods for constructing understanding*. Boston: Allyn and Bacon.

Martin-Hansen, L. (2004). What to toss and what to keep in your curriculum. *Science Scope, 28*(1), 22–24.

Marzano, R. J., Norford, J. S., Paynter, D. E., Pickering, D. J., & Gaddy, B. B. (2001). *A handbook for classroom instruction that works*. Alexandria, VA: Association for Supervision and Curriculum Development.

Marzano, R. J., Pickering, D. J., & Pollock, J. E. (2001). *Classroom instruction that works: Research-based strategies for increasing student achievement*. Alexandria, VA: Association for Supervision and Curriculum Development.

McBride, J. W., Bhatti, M. I., Hannan, M. A., & Feinberg, M. (2004). Using an inquiry approach to teach science to secondary school science teachers. *Physics Education, 39*(5), 434–439.

McClelland, D. C. (1965). Toward a theory of motive acquisition. *American Psychologist, 20*(5), 321–333.

McIntyre, M. (1984). *Early childhood and science*. Washington, DC: National Science Teachers Association.

National Center for Education Statistics. (2002). *NAEP 2000 science assessment results released.* Washington, DC: Author.

National Research Council. (1996). *National science education standards.* Washington, DC: National Academies Press.

National Research Council. (2000). *Inquiry and the national science education standards.* Washington, DC: National Academies Press.

National Research Council. (2001). *Educating teachers of science, mathematics, and technology.* Washington, DC: National Academies Press.

National Science Teachers Association. (1991). *An NSTA position statement: Multicultural science education.* Washington, DC: Author.

Ogbu, J. U. (1992). Understanding cultural diversity and learning. *Educational Researcher, 21*(8), 5–14.

Okebukola, P. A. (1985). The relative effectiveness of cooperative and competitive interaction techniques in strengthening students' performance in science classes. *Science Education, 69*(4), 501–509.

O'Neill, D. K., Wagner, R., & Gomez, L. M. (1996). Online mentoring: Experimenting in science class. *Educational Leadership, 54*(3), 39–43.

Ostlund, K. L. (1992). *Science process skills: Assessing hands-on student performance.* New York: Addison-Wesley.

Perrone, V. (Ed.). (1991). *Expanding student assessment.* Alexandria, VA: Association for Supervision and Curriculum Development.

Peters, J. M., & Stout, D. L. (2006). Methods for teaching elementary school science (5th ed.). Upper Saddle River, NJ: Pearson Merrill/Prentice-Hall.

Piaget, J. (1951). *The child's conception of the world.* New York: Humanities Press.

Singh, K., Granville, M., & Dika, S. (2002). Mathematics and science achievement: Effects of motivation, interest, and academic engagement. *Journal of Educational Research, 95*(6), 323–332.

Suter, L. E. (Ed.). (1996). *The learning curve: What we are discovering about U.S. science and mathematics education* (NSF 96-53). Washington, DC: National Science Foundation, Division of Research, Evaluation and Communication, Directorate for Education and Human Resources.

Suzuki, B. H. (1984). Curriculum transformation for multicultural education. *Education and Urban Society, 16*(3), 294–322.

Tobin, K. (Ed.). (1993). *The practice of constructivism in science education.* Hillsdale, NJ: Lawrence Erlbaum.

Torp, L., & Sage, R. (1998). *Problems as possibilities.* Alexandria, VA: Association for Supervision and Curriculum Development.

Watson, C. R. (1991). Common sense tips for cooperative learning. *NCLMLS Journal, 13*(1), 24–25.

Wiggins, G. P. (1993). *Assessing student performance.* San Francisco: Jossey-Bass.

Windschitl, M. (2006). Why we can't talk to one another about science education reform. *Phi Delta Kappan, 87*(5), 348–355.

8

Diverse Teaching Strategies for Immigrant and Refugee Children

JoAnn Crandall, Ann Jaramillo, Laurie Olsen,
Joy Kreeft Peyton, and Sarah Young

Adolescents entering the adult world in the 21st century will read and write more than at any other time in human history. They will need advanced levels of literacy to perform their jobs, run their households, act as citizens, and conduct their personal lives. They will need literacy to cope with the flood of information they will find everywhere they turn. They will need literacy to feed their imaginations so they can create the world of the future. In a complex and sometimes even dangerous world, their ability to read will be crucial. Continual instruction beyond the early grades is needed.

—International Reading Association (1999, p. 3)

This chapter addresses the challenges facing immigrant students as they make the transition to schooling in the United States. We also consider the qualities of schools and instructional approaches that support these students most effectively. Due in part to the struggles that many immigrant students have in graduating from high school, we place particular emphasis on the education of secondary school students. The older the students, the greater their difficulty in catching up with their peers and graduating from high school. Yet immigrant students can succeed in school if (1) they are immersed in academic content and strong literacy practices that are presented in interesting, understandable ways; (2) they are integrated into the school's social and academic life; and (3) they have coaching and support from teachers who understand second-language acquisition and are committed to their students' success.

In this chapter we describe instructional and assessment strategies intended to develop students' language and literacy skills and to make academic content challenging, interesting, and accessible. These strategies represent excellent educational practice for *all* students. We also describe the important qualities of a professional development system to support teachers using these strategies in their classes.

Immigration and Schools

The United States is experiencing an unprecedented wave of immigration, with people from every continent joining an already diverse population. In 2004, the number of foreign-born in the United States reached a record 34.2 million people, or 11.9 percent of the total U.S. population. School-age children make up a large part of this population; in 2000, almost 20 percent of the 58 million students in grades preK–12 were children of immigrants (Capps et al., 2005).

Public schools are at the heart of efforts to incorporate immigrants into U.S. society, and the number of immigrant students is growing rapidly. The diversity of these newcomers, the complexity of their needs, and the swiftness and magnitude of change require new programs, materials, and approaches. These swift changes also demand teachers who are knowledgeable, responsive, and prepared to work with students of diverse language, educational, and cultural backgrounds.

A Changing Population

Children who speak a language other than English, many of whom are immigrants, are the fastest-growing segment of the U.S. school-age population. "Definitions of Student Populations" shows the definitions of the terms used in this chapter to describe these diverse populations.

Between 2000 and 2004, the number of students designated as limited English proficient (LEP) increased by 46 percent in grades preK–5 and by 64 percent in grades 6–12 (Capps et al., 2005). In 2003–2004, states reported 4.3 million LEP students (Padolsky, 2005). Some of these students speak no English at all, and some have limited prior schooling. Most English language learners (ELLs) are not immigrants but were born in the United States: 77 percent of preK–5 students and 56 percent of ELLs in grades 6–12 are second- or third-generation citizens (U.S. Census of Population and Housing, 2000, cited in Capps et al., 2005). As discussed in "Generation 1.5 Students" (p. 222), these children are sometimes referred to as "Generation 1.5." (See

Definitions of Student Populations

The terms used in this chapter to describe student populations represent distinct but overlapping categories.

English language learners (ELLs) are students whose first language is not English and who are in the process of learning English. Not all English language learners are classified as limited-English-proficient or are receiving special language or educational services.

Immigrant students include those born outside of the United States of parents who are not originally from the United States. (This includes refugees, regardless of legal status.) The term does not include those born and raised in non-English-speaking homes in the United States.

Limited-English-proficient (LEP) is an official designation originating with Civil Rights law, which defines rights of access for students in terms of national origin and language. The term stems from the 14th Amendment to the U.S. Constitution, the Equal Educational Opportunity Act of 1974, and the 1964 Civil Rights Act. Schools are required to take affirmative steps to identify students who are limited-English-proficient and provide services that will overcome their language barriers.

Newcomers are recent arrivals to the United States. Programs for newcomers vary in their definitions of who is a newcomer. Some use the federal government's definition of three years or fewer in the United States, yet others restrict newcomer status to those who have been in the United States for one year or less (Short & Boyson, 2004).

McKay & Wong, 2000, and Park, 1999, for more information about Generation 1.5 students.)

ELL students live primarily in the western United States, in urban areas, and in large school districts. California, New York, and Texas enroll the majority of ELLs, but other states are gaining larger ELL populations. Nevada and Nebraska have both seen a 350 percent increase from 1990 to 2000 in ELL elementary school populations, and states like South Dakota, Georgia, Arkansas,

and Oregon are not far behind (Capps et al., 2005). Forty-three percent of all public school teachers have at least one ELL student in their classes (Zehler et al., 2003).

This wave of immigration shows no signs of abating. Demographers project that 42 to 43 million immigrants, or about 13.5 percent of the total population, will live in the United States by 2010 (Capps et al., 2005). Further, the situation is far from static. The number of immigrants in a

Generation 1.5 Students

Generation 1.5 students have been characterized as first-generation immigrants who arrived in the United States before the age of 10. Thus, they share many more characteristics with second-generation immigrants than with "true" first-generation immigrants (Pew Hispanic Center/Kaiser Family Foundation, 2004).

A survey conducted by the Pew Hispanic Center and the Kaiser Family Foundation found that characteristics of these students included

- Greater levels of bilingualism
- Greater financial security
- More high school diplomas, and
- More likely to self-identify as "American," rather than from the country of origin, than first-generation immigrants arriving after the age of 10. (This is often reflected in a lack of first-language literacy.)

Although Generation 1.5 students are usually much more integrated into the American school system than newly arrived immigrants, their academic needs often do not fit in with those of either native English speakers or ELLs. Thus, they require specially tailored work and attention that English or ESL teachers may not be prepared to offer (Harklau, Losey, & Siegal, 1999).

school district—and the languages and cultures they represent—can vary dramatically from year to year. Increasingly, immigrant students are settling in communities that do not have the social and educational infrastructures in place to meet their needs; others find themselves in already highly populated immigrant areas that have placed a heavy burden on community resources.

The majority of immigrant students enter school at the elementary school level. Approximately 53 percent of ELLs are enrolled in grades K–4, 26 percent in grades 5–8, and 20 percent in grades 9–12 (Zehler et al., 2003). These students represent more than 100 different language groups, but three out of every four students speak Spanish (Capps et al., 2005). The overwhelming majority of public school teachers are white, middle-class, English-speaking women. Thus, most teachers do not share the language, culture, or national background of their students (see Figure 8.1).

Immigration's Academic Challenges

All immigrant students face the challenge of learning English well enough to participate

FIGURE 8.1

LEP Students by Language Group, 2002–2003

The sheer numbers of students who are designated as LEP indicate our need to reach all children. The numbers of students in the following language groups have been identified as limited English proficient.

Language Groups	Number of LEP Students	Percentage of LEP Students
Spanish	2,963,256	76.9
Vietnamese	90,659	2.4
Hmong	68,892	1.8
Korean	47,427	1.2
Arabic	44,681	1.2
Haitian Creole	43,137	1.1
Cantonese	36,942	1.0
Tagalog	35,495	0.9
Russian	33,860	0.9
Navajo	33,622	0.9
Khmer	28,910	0.8
Portuguese	24,684	0.6
Urdu	24,092	0.6
Chinese (unspecified)	22,255	0.6
Mandarin	18,097	0.5
Japanese	14,950	0.4
Punjabi	14,502	0.4
Serbo-Croatian	14,220	0.4
Bengali	14,056	0.4
Lao	13,778	0.4

Source: National Clearinghouse for English Language Acquisition. *NCELA FAQ: What are the most common language groups for ELL students?* Washington, DC: Author, 2007. Available at: http://www.ncela.gwu.edu/expert/faq/05toplangs.html

fully in an English-speaking world. They also face the pressure of learning academic subjects *before* they are fully proficient in English. The U.S. Supreme Court—in *Lau* v. *Nichols* (1974) and the Civil Rights Act of 1964—addressed this problem, defining the school's obligation to take affirmative steps to overcome immigrant students' language barriers and provide access to education.

Specifically, immigrant children need to learn not only social English but also the academic English required to participate successfully in school (Cummins, 1979; Teachers of English to Speakers of Other Languages, 1997). They must learn to read in English; comprehend academic discourse; write coherently; and speak and produce English at cognitively complex, academic, abstract levels. And they need to do so *quickly*. Depending on the strength of students' language development in their native tongue, developing a mastery of academic English can take from four to seven years (Collier, 1989; Hakuta, Butler, & Witt, 2000).

While they are becoming able to participate fully in instruction presented in English, immigrant students need a comprehensive, comprehensible means of learning academic subjects. They also need an accelerated curriculum to catch up with their English-speaking peers, whose progress is a moving target. Each year, native English speakers improve both in English and academic content knowledge. To catch up, immigrants have to make more than a year's progress each year.

From 4th grade on, when the school's academic and cognitive demands begin to increase rapidly, students with little or no academic and cognitive development in their first language do less and less well. Catching up and maintaining gains become increasingly difficult as the curriculum grows more challenging. High-stakes assessments in grades K–12, which determine student promotion and graduation regardless of English proficiency, can also challenge ELL students—especially those who are required to pass an exit exam to receive a high school diploma (Abedi, 2004; Ruiz-de-Velasco & Fix, 2002). Nineteen states currently require exit exams for high school graduation, and seven others are planning to implement an exit exam by 2012. The initial pass rates on math and reading/language arts exit exams are often much lower for ELLs than for native English speakers, many times lagging behind by 30 percentage points or more (Center on Education Policy [CEP], 2005b).

Consequently, graduation rates for many ELL and minority populations fall behind those of native speakers and white students. Although graduation rates often are calculated using different methods, one source found that 75 percent of whites, 53 percent of Hispanics, 51 percent of Native Americans, and 50 percent of blacks graduated from high school in 2001. In districts with a 9 percent or higher population of ELLs, the overall graduation rate was only 60 percent (Orfield, Losen, Wald, & Swanson, 2004). Percentages of college-ready students—defined as those who graduated from high school, had basic literacy skills, and took the minimum high school courses required for admission to postsecondary education—were even lower: 40 percent of whites, 23 percent of blacks, and 20 percent of Hispanics (Alliance for Excellent Education, 2005a).

Certain provisions of the No Child Left Behind Act (NCLB) of 2001 are intended to improve the education and opportunities for success for ELL children, such as holding states accountable for providing services, curricula, qualified teachers, and assessments that support ELLs (CEP, 2005a). Other NCLB requirements may prove to be more detrimental to ELLs; this includes an emphasis on testing and accountability measures penalizing low-performing schools that often, by geographic segregation, have large populations of ELLs. The degree of concentration of these students, and the accompanying challenges, is high. One study found that nearly 70 percent of ELLs are enrolled in 10 percent of elementary schools (Consentino de Cohen, Deterding, & Clewell, 2005).

Immigration's Personal and Social Challenges

ELL students are tremendously diverse, with differing national backgrounds, languages, cultures, schooling experiences, and reasons for immigration (Zehler et al., 2003). Some come from rural, isolated parts of the world; others come from urban, industrialized areas. Some fled wars and political repression; others came to join family members or seek work in the United States (United Nations Population Fund, 2003). Although the majority of ELL children are, unlike their parents, born in the U.S., the strain of issues related to language, culture, and their parents' possible lack of legal documentation can result in further difficulties (Van Hook, Bean, & Passel, 2005). All must adjust to a new culture and language, but the size of the gaps they must bridge, the resources they bring, and their success in making the transition differ enormously. Some immigrant students achieve at high levels, adapt quickly, and learn English well; others do not. Some are far more at risk of school failure than others. Understanding the factors that place students at risk helps educators recognize when extra support is necessary. Immigrant students face many of the following issues (Olsen & Chen, 1988):

• *Living in Transnational Families.* Many immigrants, especially those from Mexico and the Caribbean, maintain a binational life and sustain strong relationships on both sides of the U.S. border. For students, however, moving between countries can result in missed curriculum, loss of credits, and attendance problems, unless the school aligns its calendar with migration patterns, provides independent study options, offers partial credit, or provides other support.

• *Acculturating.* Immigrant students arrive in the United States with a variety of backgrounds. Entering a new culture and making a place for oneself is a daunting task. Many young people must choose between cultures, which can create deep identity crises. The process of acculturation often involves painful decisions about what to save or sacrifice, what to adopt or reject (Aronowitz, 1984). Rifts can open within families as youth become "Americanized" and reject their family ways. Tension can erupt at school, too, as immigrant children seek to maintain key parts of their traditional or cultural identities. Few students find a middle ground where they can be bicultural and bilingual and not have to give up a part of themselves to become a part of the U.S. culture.

• *Arriving as an Adolescent.* Young children often have an easier time than older ones in making the transition to a new land. Some adolescents go directly to work and never enroll in school (Cornelius & Rumba, 1995). Those who do enroll must leap from one school system and curriculum to another, often numerous times. Those with solid schooling in their native land have greater success in U.S. schools. Unfortunately, the number of immigrants arriving in secondary schools with little prior schooling and little or no literacy in their home language is increasing (Zehler et al., 2003). For these students, accelerated basic literacy instruction is necessary, though few secondary schools are prepared to provide this instruction.

• *Learning a New, Very Different System.* Immigrant students have an immediate need to learn how U.S. schools work. Bells ring and people change rooms; lunch is served in cafeterias; students store materials in lockers. More profound are the differences in teaching approaches, relationships between and among students and teachers, and school structure and expectations. Students in the United States are expected to participate in discussions and voice opinions. Tests do not determine their whole future. Teachers often are not accorded respect and authority. To understand this environment, immigrant students need support and orientation that their parents usually cannot provide. Instead, many parents rely on their children to explain the system of schooling and to translate materials provided only in English.

• *Recovering from Trauma.* Some students arrive from war-torn nations or refugee camps, scarred by the disruptions and trauma of war, trauma that may have dispersed their families (Rumbaut, 1994). They may have had little or no schooling; they may well have suffered hunger and disease. Nightmares and violent memories haunt them, and many suffer from post-traumatic stress syndrome, which is often largely undiagnosed and unrecognized among children and their families. Resettled refugees in western countries are 10 times more likely to suffer from post-traumatic stress syndrome than the general population (Fazel, Wheeler, & Danesh, 2005).

• *Enduring Displacement Within the United States.* Similar to ELLs who arrive from other countries and are recovering from trauma are those students who have experienced trauma and stress due to crises and natural disasters in the United States, such as Hurricanes Katrina and Rita in 2005. U.S. Census records show 13,600 foreign-born children under the age of 18 living in the area affected by Katrina and 110,000 in the area affected by Rita (Batalova, 2005). Disasters such as these can cause interrupted schooling, loss of official records and documents, greater unemployment and poverty, and separated families.

• *Dealing with Isolation and Discrimination.* In recent years, anti-immigrant sentiment has swept the United States. Many immigrants find that they have entered a racially divided society. Immigrant students encounter unwelcoming, sometimes hostile or violent, attitudes at school. Hate crimes and anti-immigrant incidents are on the rise. This unsafe atmosphere seriously hampers immigrant students' willingness to participate in school. Unfortunately, a common aspect of the immigrant experience is isolation and marginalization, the shame of being teased or ostracized for imperfect English and foreign ways. This isolation adds yet another barrier to acquiring English.

What Schools Can Do

Schools face a major challenge in responding to the needs of immigrant students because most schools were designed (and most teachers prepared) for a more homogeneous environment.

Studies have analyzed the characteristics of effective schools for immigrant and language-minority students (August & Hakuta, 1997; Berman et al., 1995; Carter & Chatfield, 1986; Council of Chief State School Officers, 2004; Garcia, 1988; Genesee, 1998; Genesee, Lindholm-Leary, Saunders, & Christian, 2006; Lucas, Henze, & Donato, 1990; Mace-Matluck, Alexander-Kasparik, & Queen, 1998; National Association of Secondary School Principals, 2005; Olsen & Mullen, 1990; Short & Boyson, 2004), and some schools boast innovative programs. But few schools have the capacity to deliver effective, comprehensive programs for immigrant students that support full participation in school, provide access to the entire curriculum, encourage strong English-language development, *and* result in high achievement. Getting from where we are to where we need to be must begin with a vision of what a comprehensive program would include.

Comprehensive Programs

A comprehensive approach to schooling provides both a strong academic program and a support structure to facilitate full student participation (August & Hakuta, 1997; Crandall, 1994; Duff, 2005; Lucas, 1997; Olsen & Mullen, 1990). The academic program includes customized learning environments for students with varying levels of English fluency and academic achievement. Articulation and coordination within, between, and among schools is also strong. The curriculum incorporates a focus on English language and literacy development, is accompanied by pacing guides, and is aligned with state content standards and accountability systems. (See California State Board of Education, 1999, for an example of state standards for English language learners.) A curriculum balanced between basic and higher-order skills incorporates students' native languages and cultures and offers opportunities for student-directed instruction (Garcia, 1988; Olsen & Mullen, 1990; Wong Filmore & Valadez, 1986). Teaching methodologies and curricula draw on students' home and community cultures (Trumbull, Rothstein-Fisch, Greenfield, & Quiroz, 2001) to bridge the gap between home language and literacy experiences and those expected in school (Garcia, 1988; Heath, 1983).

A comprehensive program rests on a strong initial assessment process to ensure appropriate student placement and to inform classroom instruction. After this formal assessment, teachers use informal assessments such as observation, portfolios, competency checklists, rubrics, conferences, self-assessments, group projects, and questionnaires to monitor student progress and provide feedback; this enables students to move to new levels of curriculum as their fluency in English grows (Duff, 2005; Fisher, Frey, & Fehrenbacher, 2004a; Wiggins & McTighe, 1998). Common assessments and consensus scoring within academic departments provide opportunities for teacher professional development, ensure that student progress is monitored locally, and promote instructional decisions that are made in standardized, evidence-based ways (Fisher, Lapp, & Flood, 2005).

Full access to the curriculum is ensured through a combination of native language instruction, if possible and appropriate, and sheltered-content instruction in English. Teachers are well-prepared with strong training in the principles and practices of second-language acquisition (Crandall, 1994; Echevarria, Vogt, & Short, 2004; Zeichner, 1992). In providing a well-rounded, content-rich curriculum, schools consider the benefits of block scheduling, an alternative to the traditional six- or seven-period school day. This method of scheduling has been found to result in more time spent on task on academic content, a smaller teacher workload, less stress for teachers and students alike, better relationships among students and teachers, more active participation in richer learning processes, and fewer interruptions (Alliance for Excellent Education, 2005b; Freeman, 2001; Olsen, Jaramillo, McCall-Perez, & White, 1999).

Finally, a comprehensive program provides extended time to allow students the extra support needed to learn English and academics simultaneously. Support services addressing war trauma, acculturation, orientation to a new culture and school system, and other challenges are either provided directly by the school or through referral relationships with community agencies and organizations that can deliver such support bilingually and biculturally. After-school clubs, tutoring, and other extracurricular activities are available for students who need extra help and who might not have a safe place to go when the school day is over. ELL parent nights and parent centers provide a place for families to learn more about their children's education or even take some English as a second language (ESL) or parenting classes on their own.

A supportive climate sets the tone for an educational program that promotes high achievement for all students. Research shows that a supportive school climate that helps ELLs succeed includes the following components (August & Hakuta, 1997; Lucas, Henze, & Donato, 1990; Olsen & Mullen, 1990; Zeichner, 1992):

- Valuing students' primary languages and cultures.
- Making high expectations concrete.
- Having school leaders who make the education of ELLs a high priority.
- Having school staff members committed to empowering ELLs through education.
- Enacting policies and programs that promote positive intergroup relations, such as conflict resolution; community building; antiprejudice programs; and curriculum about scapegoating, racism, and exclusion.
- Building strong relationships to support parent and community involvement.
- Valuing diversity.

Responsive Habits

Immigration brings a constantly changing stream of cultures, languages, and national experiences to schools; therefore, effective schools have found that they cannot simply institute a good program and leave it alone. Instead, they build habits and mechanisms for responding to the continually changing mix of cultures and languages. Responsive schools demonstrate the following characteristics (Olsen & Jaramillo, 1999):

- They consciously and conscientiously build capacity to deliver an effective academic program by investing in sustained professional development in collaborative, inquiry-based, and individual formats. (See also Crandall, 1994; González & Darling-Hammond, 1997.)

- They create data systems and processes that support ongoing analysis of immigrant student achievement, participation, and progress. These data become the basis for program improvement and new interventions.

- They recognize the importance of learning about immigrants' cultures, experiences, and needs, and they build structures that support listening to and learning from immigrants.

- Their structures support optimal teaching and learning for immigrants, including time for teacher collaboration, reflection, data discussions, and inquiry.

- They create mechanisms that allow parents and advocates to come together, shaping a voice in the school and district on behalf of immigrant students.

Improved Teacher Preparation

While the number of immigrant students in U.S. schools continues to increase, the number of teachers from other countries and from non-English-language backgrounds is declining, as is the percentage of teachers who have special preparation for teaching ELLs. In 2001–2002, Zehler and colleagues (2003) found that 43 percent of public school teachers had ELLs in their classes, which is 3.5 times more than those teachers surveyed in 1991–1992; 60 percent of teachers with at least three ELL students

received relevant training in the previous five years, but they averaged only four training hours. Moreover, teachers in schools with high concentrations of ELL students are more likely to be new teachers, have less academic preparation, and hold provisional certification (Consentino de Cohen et al., 2005). Thus, many of the 4 million ELLs in U.S. classrooms spend most of their day with teachers who have not been trained to work with them.

Unless both preservice and inservice teacher education programs change, this situation is likely to become even worse, because the greatest population growth in the United States is expected to be among Hispanics, Asians, and Pacific Islanders. By 2050, the Hispanic population in the United States is expected to increase from 13 percent of the total population to 23 percent, and the Asian and Pacific Islander population from 4 percent to 10 percent. Demographics show that many of these students will not be native English speakers (Day, 2001).

Teachers need to be prepared to provide instruction that reflects an understanding of: (1) second-language acquisition and development, (2) integration of language and content instruction, and (3) cross-cultural communication (Crandall, 1994). Some states (California and Florida, for example) have changed their certification requirements to reflect changing school demographics and address these areas of need. Sixteen states currently require K–12 ESL teachers to pass the Praxis II: English to Speakers of Other Languages (ESOL) for certification (Educational Testing Service, 2005). Even where certification requirements have not changed, districts and schools have undertaken various approaches to provide professional development in these three areas.

Professional development includes programs of peer observation, mentoring and coaching, teacher inquiry and research groups, and college courses. Effective professional development models are driven by student assessment data, teacher reflection and conversation, and a staff development team led by teachers from different academic departments. Teacher collaboration should be horizontal (across departments) *and* vertical (across grade levels). To be truly effective, these techniques must be long-term, site-based, and both teacher-designed and teacher-directed; programs must be designed to improve student learning, and they must allow adequate time for teacher inquiry and reflection (Crandall, 1998; Darling-Hammond, 1996; Frey & Fisher, 2004a; González & Darling-Hammond, 1997; National Commission on Teaching and America's Future, 1996).

One way to ensure long-term commitment is to establish partnerships between universities and schools that simultaneously address needed changes in teacher preparation and inservice professional development. Such partnerships can be achieved through a professional development school or center. In the professional development school, teacher educators, experienced and novice teachers, administrators, and other stakeholders in public education work together to provide a program of teacher education, much of which is taught on site by teams of experienced teachers and university faculty

members (Alliance for Excellent Education, 2005b; Crandall, 1994, 1998; Fisher, 2001).

Teacher candidates work alongside expert teachers, experiencing the reality of schools by spending more time in them than is now standard. In the process, teacher candidates provide schools with an additional, knowledgeable adult working in the classroom and help refresh veteran teachers with their enthusiasm and new ideas. One result of this collaboration is that the gap between preservice and inservice teacher education and between theory and practice is partially bridged (Crandall, 1994, 1998; González & Darling-Hammond, 1997; Holmes Group, 1990).

In one such partnership, an ESL/bilingual teacher education program provided a series of courses, workshops, and ongoing research and curriculum development that has helped to better prepare current teachers to work with their increasingly diverse student populations. In turn, these experienced teachers helped both the teacher education program and current graduate students develop a far better understanding of the challenges and strengths these students represent (Crandall, 1994, 1998).

Resources

Abedi, 2004; Alliance for Excellent Education, 2005a, 2005b; Aronowitz, 1984; August & Hakuta, 1997; Batalova, 2005; Berman et al., 1995; California State Board of Education, 1999; Capps et al., 2005; Carter & Chatfield, 1986; CEP, 2005a, 2005b; Collier, 1989; Consentino de Cohen, Deterding, & Clewell, 2005; Cornelius & Rumba, 1995; Council of Chief State School Officers, 2004; Crandall, 1994; Cummins, 1979; Duff, 2005; Echevarria, Vogt, & Short, 2004; Fazel, Wheeler, & Danesh, 2005; Fisher, Frey, &

Fehrenbacher, 2004a; Fisher, Lapp, & Flood, 2005; Freeman, 2001; Garcia, 1988; Genesee, 1998; Genesee, Lindholm-Leary, Saunders, & Christian, 2006; Gonzàles & Darling-Hammond, 1997; Hakuta, Butler, & Witt, 2000; Heath, 1983; Henderson, Abbott, & Strang, 1993; Lucas, 1997; Lucas, Henze, & Donato, 1990; Mace-Matluck, Alexander-Kasparik, & Queen, 1998; McKay & Wong, 2000; Minicucci & Olsen, 1992; National Association of Secondary School Principals, 2005; Olsen & Chen, 1988; Olsen & Jaramillo, 1999; Olsen, Jaramillo, McCall-Perez, & White, 1999; Olsen & Mullen, 1990; Orfield, Losen, Wald, & Swanson, 2004; Padolsky, 2005; Park, 1999; Ruiz-de-Velasco & Fix, 2002; Rumbaut, 1994; Short & Boyson, 2000, 2004; Teachers of English to Speakers of Other Languages (TESOL), 1997; Trumbull, Rothstein-Fisch, Greenfield, & Quiroz, 2001; United Nations Population Fund, 2003; Van Hook, Bean, & Passel, 2005; Wiggins & McTighe, 1998; Wong Filmore & Valadez, 1986; Zehler et al., 2003; Zeichner, 1992.

Strategies for Immigrant Students

The following teaching and learning strategies are central to any program of teacher preparation or professional development for educators seeking to meet the needs of a multilingual, multicultural student population. Current pressures associated with a stronger emphasis on testing and accountability may make some teachers hesitant to incorporate strategies that don't directly link to the bottom line: student outcomes on state tests and other national measures of progress. However, this comprehensive collection of strategies supports students academically, emotionally, and socially, and these strategies can prepare them to meet the high expectations that schools have of them.

Each strategy includes a rationale followed by several classroom examples. References offer the opportunity for further exploration. Although actual classroom examples are used throughout, teacher names are pseudonyms.

Resources

Alliance for Excellent Education, 2005b; Consentino de Cohen et al., 2005; Crandall, 1994, 1998; Darling-Hammond, 1996; Day, 2001; Educational Testing Service, 2005; Fisher, 2001; Frey & Fisher, 2004a; González & Darling-Hammond, 1997; Holmes Group, 1990; National Commission on Teaching and America's Future, 1996; Zehler et al., 2003.

Strategy 8.1:

Help students with limited or interrupted prior schooling develop basic skills.

Discussion

Increasing numbers of ELLs come from countries where political or economic upheaval limited their opportunities for schooling. Significant gaps in their education resulted (Crandall, Bernache, & Prager, 1998). Others come from rural areas that either provided few opportunities for acquiring an education or didn't even promote literacy or formal schooling (Hamayan, 1994).

Many students enter U.S. schools with limited prior education and literacy, as well as limited English proficiency. They face the double challenge of compensating for years of lost education as they try to learn English (Crandall, 1995; Crandall & Greenblatt, 1999). Even if they do speak English, they may speak the language in a way that is substantially different from what is expected in school. Students who arrive in the United States in elementary grades face some difficulty catching up to their peers, but secondary students face a much more enormous challenge, requiring many years of assistance by bilingual, ESL, and content-area teachers (Short & Boyson, 2004).

Like all newcomers to U.S. schools, these students need help in becoming accustomed to an educational environment that may differ greatly from what they left behind. Classrooms that encourage discussion, promote interaction with students of both genders, and allow freedom for self-expression are likely to pose adjustment problems for students accustomed to classrooms where a dominant teacher expects rote learning and imposes strict punishments.

For students with limited schooling experience, the adjustment is even more difficult. They need to learn a complex set of policies and procedures, such as how to follow schedules and what is expected of them when they come to class. These students may be challenged by even basic requirements like staying seated for long periods of time, bringing books and materials to class, and raising their hands to ask or answer questions. In addition, students with no prior education or literacy experiences need to develop basic literacy skills, such as discriminating among letters and numbers and understanding sound and symbol correspondences; they also may need to develop fine motor skills. Children with two or three years of education may have developed some of these skills, but they also may have limited exposure to print and

little experience with reading and writing and the myriad uses of literacy that are expected in schools. Their exposure to the basic academic skills of sequencing, measuring, classifying, and comparing also may be limited.

Students with little prior schooling need sequenced literacy and academic instruction to enable them to move through the stages of English language, literacy, and academic development until they can participate in regular courses (Kamil, 2003). Ideally, they should first develop literacy and explore the uses of reading and writing in their own language; then they can transfer these skills to English. This approach allows students to use their cognitive and oral-language resources as a basis for developing and understanding the uses of written language. If a classroom contains only a few students who speak the same language, or if appropriate materials or bilingual teachers are not available, then students may need to develop literacy in English first. Again, acquiring literacy solely in English takes more time and more steps than acquiring literacy based on substantial oral-language development in a student's native language.

Literacy learners need different instruction from that of ELLs who have substantial education in their own language. Placing literacy learners and those with limited schooling in beginning ESL classes with no special attention to their literacy and cognitive needs is not sufficient, as many of their peers have first-language literacy and academic knowledge on which to build.

If the limited numbers of students prevent the formation of special first-language or ESL classes, then ESL and mainstream teachers need to explore ways to provide additional support. Peer tutoring, learning buddies, cooperative groups, or teacher aides all can help, as does understanding that learning to be a student and developing basic literacy and academic skills takes time. Other students have acquired basic skills throughout their elementary education, an advantage that may have been denied to some immigrant students.

Literacy instruction need not be thought of as sterile activities teaching basic skills. Although it is important to teach letter formation, basic sound and symbol relationships, and left-to-right reading and writing skills, it is possible to do so within a framework that validates students' prior experiences and uses those experiences to develop more school-related knowledge and skills. A holistic approach to reading and writing, incorporating the teaching of basic skills where these become relevant, helps students see a role for reading and writing in their lives and makes literacy instruction both interesting and functional.

Drills and worksheets can bore students, especially students who are new to formal schooling (Hamayan, 1994). Many ELLs come from cultures with strong traditions of storytelling and oral history. Family histories, traditional stories, and rich personal experiences provide a strong, engaging oral base on which to develop written language.

Linking students' life experiences to needed academic concepts and skills provides a sequence of instruction that enables them to experience success, develop confidence, and make an easier transition to content-area classes. This takes time, however, and is likely to demand after-school or weekend tutoring, summer school, or additional years of high school, all of which are difficult for students who work to help provide family income. Strategies within classes can include the assistance of peer or cross-age tutors who share the students' first language or who have participated in higher-level ESL classes.

Educators need to distinguish between students with delayed (though normal) literacy development and students with learning disabilities. Initially, the difference can be hard to assess, especially when students are experiencing separation from family and country, dependence on extended family or friends, frequent movement from one home to another, memories of traumatic experiences, or isolation in their new community. Over time, however, if a student is not recognizing and understanding sound and symbol relationships or has difficulty remembering vocabulary or concepts from one day to the next, an assessment for special education services may be necessary.

Classroom Examples

Ms. Thompson has taught only three years, but she is a masterful teacher of literacy learners. Her classes combine a predictable sequence of activities that also foster engagement and creativity. Her students keep journals, write stories about themselves and their families, and also focus on reading and writing conventions.

Ms. Thompson begins each class with a whole-class warm-up in which she establishes that each student has the necessary materials and supplies and is ready to learn. She also uses this time to engage in conversation with each student. Sometimes she finds out what students did over the weekend or the previous evening (which usually involves substantial time working outside the home, thus leaving limited time for homework). Other times she talks about school events. Ms. Thompson ends each class with journal writing and a writing workshop. She requires students to have a class notebook organized into categories that correspond to the various phases of the class (Tate, 1997).

The warm-up is often followed by the development of a language experience story, which students dictate while Ms. Thompson records the words on the chalkboard (Allen & Allen, 1982; Dixon & Nessel, 1983; Taylor, 1993). The story may stem from something that students have talked about during the warm-up, a school event, a sequence of pictures, a short story or text that Ms. Thompson has read aloud, or something that happened in class. She draws out the children's experiences, writes vocabulary on the board, and makes mental notes of grammar or other items to work on later.

Ms. Thompson may use a semantic web or other graphic organizer to capture students' ideas and to provide all students with access to the vocabulary that only some of them might know. She might ask students to work in pairs or small groups to fill out a storyboard identifying the setting, characters, and major events before trying to write a story together. Students build on that oral discussion as they dictate the story to Ms. Thompson. Together the students read what they have written and suggest changes. Ms.

Thompson also offers suggestions, providing a more appropriate word or tense, often seizing the opportunity for a minilesson on some aspect of English vocabulary or structure.

Students then copy the story into their notebooks; they may be asked to engage in additional writing, either at home or in the next class, perhaps adding an ending or describing a character. Ms. Thompson builds oral- and written-language activities around these stories, focused on developing specific language skills. She might, for example, give students a typed version of the story with key words omitted, listing them at the bottom for students to identify. Or she might develop vocabulary exercises such as word matching, fill-in-the-blank sentences, or synonyms and antonyms. She might focus on a specific aspect of spelling, perhaps encouraging students to find other words that exhibit the same spelling rule. She also might divide the story into sentences on strips and ask students to work in groups to put these sentences in an appropriate order. Eventually, she might ask them to try writing the story themselves, in their own words.

Students spend a great deal of time in this class writing. They write about themselves and their lives, their class, and their school. During writing time, they receive individual attention from Ms. Thompson or help one another to find appropriate vocabulary or verb forms. Their early writings may consist of collecting and labeling pictures and creating class bulletin boards or books. Or they might spend time illustrating a story they have heard in class and working in pairs to write captions.

Over time, their stories become longer and culminate in an "autophotography" (Moran-Ender & Ender, 1995), an autobiography using both photographs and words. Each student uses an inexpensive camera to take pictures of family members, friends, pets, home, job, or anything they feel helps to identify who they are. They use these pictures to write a story about themselves, which is reproduced for both the learning resource center and Ms. Thompson's collection. Along with magazines and other reading materials, these books serve as readers that students may choose during periods of sustained silent reading or in developing ideas for their own writing.

Through their writing, students see the value of developing literacy, which extends and reinforces literacy development. They come to understand that expressing oneself in writing is a process full of starts and stops; writing can be difficult and discouraging, but it can also be liberating. Students have the support of their teacher and each other in conferences and on review sheets. The review sheets begin simply by asking students to identify one thing they liked about their partner's story; the sheets then ask questions that help writers extend and revise their writing (Peyton, Jones, Vincent, & Greenblatt, 1994).

Students take turns using the computers, with priority given to those who are editing or in the final stages of publishing their work. Ms. Thompson finds that using computers encourages revisions and makes the task of writing less troublesome for students learning to read and write. The computer also reinforces alphabetization and supports reading and writing development. Students may illustrate their stories, produce a cover and title page, and even write a brief description of the author for the back cover. These activities build students' pride in their newly acquired literacy.

Dialogue journals are central to Ms. Thompson's class. These written conversations between student and teacher offer private places where meaningful written dialogue can take place and students can receive immediate feedback on both their thoughts and their English (Peyton & Reed, 1990). In these journals, students are free to write about their concerns and their experiences, at whatever level they are able to or are comfortable with expressing. Ms. Thompson responds to each journal, modeling appropriate English but never correcting the writing. Instead, she responds to thoughts, concerns, and questions, validating the importance of literacy in authentic communication. She provides something for students to read that is at their level of literacy and is interesting and important to them.

Resources

Allen & Allen, 1982; Crandall, 1995; Crandall, Bernache, & Prager, 1998; Crandall & Greenblatt, 1999; Dixon & Nessel, 1983; Hamayan, 1994; Kamil, 2003; Moran-Ender & Ender, 1995; Peyton, Jones, Vincent, & Greenblatt, 1994; Peyton & Reed, 1990; Short & Boyson, 2004; Tate, 1997; Taylor, 1993.

Strategy 8.2:

Organize instruction around themes to integrate English language skills with academic concepts across the curriculum.

Discussion

The importance of teaching reading and writing across the curriculum is now well established. Science teachers are also reading and writing teachers when they help students perform experiments and write their findings in lab reports. Mathematics teachers teach reading and writing when they ask students to read word problems and explain, in writing, how they solved them. Not surprisingly, recently established standards in the content areas now include communication standards involving reading and writing as well as speaking, as students are unlikely to learn these skills in isolation, devoid of content.

The need to integrate reading and writing into content-area instruction is even greater when students are learning English. Students cannot be prepared for the academic language skills required for content-area classes or assessments without integrating these tasks, texts, and tests into their English language instruction. Furthermore, students are unlikely to learn academic English unless they are provided with meaningful contexts and content in which to do so (Crandall & Tucker, 1990; Kessler & Hayes, 1989). Thematic units that complement regular classroom instruction allow learners of English to integrate their language skills in a variety

of content areas. Studying relevant, meaningful topics increases student motivation and enhances learning.

The use of thematic units may be schoolwide (such as middle schools organized into instructional teams), or the units may be developed by pairs of teachers for use within a single classroom on any grade level that integrates language and content instruction (such as social studies and ESL). Teachers can choose (sometimes with student input) interesting topics or themes around which to build activities that link the content to be taught with corresponding language items from the areas of listening, speaking, reading, and writing (Enright & McCloskey, 1988).

As one teacher wrote in a reflective journal, "The approach that seems to be most successful is the approach that gets the most out of a lesson by stretching it across the curriculum." Thematic instruction helps students to see connections and relate what they are learning in one content area with content in another. Without thematic links, learning can seem fragmented and unrelated, especially for students who are new to U.S. classrooms.

The following steps are helpful in developing a thematic unit:

1. Identify a theme or topic.
2. Identify appropriate texts to use or adapt.
3. Identify needed language, especially new vocabulary.
4. Identify academic concept objectives.
5. Identify critical thinking and study skills objectives.

6. Develop activities that draw on students' experience and are relevant to their lives.

7. Choose activities that are appropriate for a variety of learning styles.

8. Consider activities that develop learning strategies (thinking and study skills) and use a variety of grouping strategies.

9. Ensure that activities involve oral and written language.

10. Sequence the activities.

11. Determine responsibility for each objective and activity (if more than one teacher is involved).

In an ideal thematic unit, all ways of learning are addressed: bodily-kinesthetic, spatial, linguistic, musical, logical-mathematical, and interpersonal (Gardner, 1993). The ideal unit also uses Gardner's intrapersonal and natural intelligences to appeal to learners.

Classroom Examples

Mr. Garcia recognized that his students' interest in the 1998 Winter Olympic Games in Nagano, Japan, could provide a unifying theme for an ESL and social studies unit. He began by asking students what they knew about Japan, webbing their responses, and organizing their answers into categories for further investigation by student groups (e.g., food, homes, sports, government, and families). Students presented their findings and used the information in a writing assignment that mirrored the functional writing test the state required for high school graduation. In this assignment, students wrote a letter describing what they had learned about

Japan to a cousin who had just won a trip to Nagano to attend the Olympics.

During the two weeks of the Olympics, students added to their knowledge of Japan, filling the original web and keeping a tally of the medals that each country won. They also completed a daily chart of these medals and converted the information to line and bar graphs. They used these graphs and charts to help them learn English comparatives and superlatives, such as better and best, more than and less than, and worse and worst.

Mr. Garcia brought the daily newspaper to class for students to use in determining when their favorite sports would be televised. They used that information and the results to report on the events as journalists. To summarize the events as a journalist would, they completed a 5-W Chart (who, what, when, where, and why) (Chamot & O'Malley, 1994). As a culminating activity, students worked in cooperative groups to prepare Olympic posters, taking roles such as poster designer and computer title creator. Social studies, mathematics, art, and English-language skills all were integrated into the project. The unit also was used to prepare for their science fair projects in the spring.

Environmental and social issues provide particularly rich possibilities for thematic instruction. One high school used the rain forest as the focus of instruction for all students for eight weeks. A middle school team focused on endangered species for a similar period. After reading *Brother Eagle, Sister Sky* (Jeffers, 1991), in which a Native American laments humans' destruction of the environment, students worked in groups to investigate the status of specific animals, focusing on distribution, habitat, food, speed and mode of travel, interactions with humans, and causes of endangerment. The students used the five themes of geography—location, place, region, movement, and interaction with the environment—as the basis for their investigations.

The middle school students presented their research results in a poster session, similar to what would be required in a science fair. They used latitude and longitude to allow others to locate specific places where the animals live, illustrated and identified specific landforms in the animals' habitats, and explained why some animals are endangered. As a whole class, students brainstormed ways they might help reverse human destruction of the environment and move animals off the list of endangered species.

Even something as simple as popcorn can unify concepts and language across the curriculum. Ms. Unger engaged her middle school students in a "Pop, Pop or Flop, Flop" unit that integrated mathematics, science, social studies, and language skills. To raise funds, students decided to sell popcorn. Ms. Unger suggested that they investigate which popcorn would provide the greatest return on investment, and she designed an experiment to compare various brands of popcorn. Students hypothesized that the most expensive popcorn would produce the fewest unpopped kernels. Each of Ms. Unger's five classes tested one brand. They ran six trials for their brand, counting the number of kernels in a cup before popping and comparing that

number with the number of unpopped kernels after popping. They converted that to a percentage of popped corn and then averaged the six trials. Each class contributed to a graph that enabled them to identify which popcorn produced the fewest unpopped kernels. To their surprise, the most expensive popcorn was not the best buy.

Other themes for secondary schools to use when integrating content and language instruction include immigration, nutrition, the solar system, the world family, pollution, and peace.

Resources

Chamot & O'Malley, 1994; Crandall & Tucker, 1990; Enright & McCloskey, 1988; Gardner, 1993; Jeffers, 1991; Kessler & Hayes, 1989.

Strategy 8.3:

Shelter instruction in content classes by using sequences of tasks designed to ensure that ELLs comprehend and master cognitively demanding subject matter.

Discussion

Content classes designed for students who are acquiring English have been given several different names. The term "sheltered English" has been used frequently, most recently within the context of the Sheltered Instruction Observation Protocol (SIOP). The SIOP model is a research-based instructional approach to sheltering content for ELLs. The eight components of SIOP (lesson preparation, building background, comprehensible input, strategies, interaction, practice/application, lesson delivery, and review/assessment) are used by math, science, social studies, and other teachers to support content instruction for all ELLs, regardless of grade level or subject area (Echevarria & Short, 2004; Echevarria, Vogt, & Short, 2004; Hudec & Short, 2002). Whatever name is used, these classes serve an important function in a comprehensive program for students learning English.

Whenever possible, offering content classes in students' primary language is the most efficient, direct means of ensuring students equal access to difficult content, especially those students for whom even a sheltered content class would be incomprehensible. When there are not enough students of a single primary language, or when students reach an intermediate level of fluency in English, creating sheltered content classes that are taught in English makes perfect sense. Many of the strategies described in the sections that follow this one work equally well in native-language content classrooms, in English language development classrooms, and in sheltered content classrooms. In fact, students benefit even more when teachers use a consistent array of strategies across content areas (Fisher & Frey, 2004; Fisher, Frey, & Williams, 2002).

Teachers of sheltered content classes need to master a repertoire of strategies to effectively teach a topic such as U.S. history, algebra, or biology in English to learners who have been in the United States for less than two years (Jameson, 1999). "Scaffolding" is the term used most frequently to refer to the tasks that teachers design to support their students as they encounter new

concepts and complex language (Bruner, 1986). Just as the name implies, scaffolds should be used as long as students need them. As students become more capable and autonomous, use of the scaffolds decreases. For example, graphic organizers (charts that organize information) of various types can help students understand confusing content. Once it is clear that the students have gained control over the concepts, the graphic organizers may not be necessary.

Although all students obviously profit from good instruction, what might be sufficient to enable a native English-speaking student to understand an idea may not provide a second-language learner with enough scaffolding to succeed. For example, a quick brainstorming session before starting a unit might be adequate for native English-speaking students in terms of assessing and activating prior knowledge. Second-language learners, on the other hand, usually need more investigation into what they know and do not know about the same topic. For these students, a brainstorming session might be followed by an anticipatory guide (see Strategy 8.6) and a journal entry on the topic. Each task approaches the subject from a slightly different perspective, giving students multiple opportunities to grapple with the ideas and language to be studied.

Thoughtful teachers in sheltered content classes spend substantial time considering what to teach. Approaching topics from different perspectives, using multiple tasks to ensure comprehension and mastery, and providing students with the tools to learn how to learn all require the teacher to filter out unimportant or extraneous pieces of the curriculum to get to the most essential, substantial concepts (Wiggins & McTighe, 1998).

Teachers often feel uneasy at first about not "teaching the whole book." Once they have successfully taught a sheltered class, however, they become advocates for teaching with depth rather than breadth—for *all* students. These teachers carefully examine their curriculum with an eye toward what their students need to know most. They concentrate on foundation concepts in their subject matter and ensure that they teach ideas critical to students' success.

The following strategies outline different types of scaffolding that can help teachers organize effective sheltered lessons. Designing an individual sheltered lesson involves a complex orchestration of many elements. Teachers might ask themselves the following questions as they plan:

• What will I do to assess and activate my students' prior knowledge? Can I relate course content to their personal lives?

• What are the big ideas, and how can I build my students' conceptual frameworks so they can comprehend and work with these big ideas?

• How will I incorporate explicit teaching of learning strategies into the lesson? How will these strategies promote my students' metacognitive development so that, over time, they become increasingly independent learners? As I teach the lesson, how will I check for understanding and make sure the students are actively engaged? What kinds of pictures,

graphics, and other contextual cues will help my students understand more?

• What kind of task can I give students at the end of the lesson to offer them a chance to attack the material in new or different ways?

• At the end of the lesson, how will we all assess the learning?

Classroom Examples

Mrs. Simons is a skilled teacher of sheltered content. Her primary responsibility is teaching literature to her advanced ESL students—the same literature that her students' native English-speaking peers are studying. After five or six years, she has become adept at incorporating a wide range of tasks into her sheltered language arts lessons. She is sensitive to the fact that students need extra instructional supports (or scaffolds) as they study difficult content. She is also keenly aware that most of her students will be studying in mainstream classrooms the following year, sitting next to native English speakers and expected to compete with them. Thus, she is committed to making sure that her students not only learn the content of the literature class but also are as prepared as possible for all of their classes.

This week, Mrs. Simons and her students in 8th grade sheltered language arts are finishing Laurence Yep's novel *Dragonwings* (1975), the story of a young Chinese boy's immigration to California at the turn of the century. Students' work folders for the novel are on their desks. An examination of several folders shows the various kinds of scaffolds that Mrs. Simons has used to ensure that her students understand the book. A reciprocal teaching chart and an active reading chart are stapled to the front of each student's folder.

Right now, students are working in groups of four, using reciprocal teaching to read four pages of the last chapter: One student reads a paragraph and summarizes it, another asks for clarification, the third asks two questions, and the fourth makes a prediction (Jones, Palincsar, Ogle, & Carr, 1987; Palincsar & Brown, 1984; Palincsar, David, & Brown, 1989). After each paragraph, the students change roles.

The folders reveal that Mrs. Simons has used various tasks to assess and activate her students' prior knowledge throughout the reading of the book. There are two anticipatory guides (see Strategy 8.6)—one on Chinese immigration and one on earthquakes—with follow-up activities to show changes in students' ideas. Several journal topics relate the story to students' personal lives (for example, "Write about when you, or a member of your family, came to this country").

For several chapters of the book, students have found important quotes, written them in a reading log, and responded to the quotes using the active reading chart. They have made several storyboards for other chapters, using a graphic organizer to summarize and relate important events. All of these activities will lead to essays in which students will write about whether the main character, Windrider, will fulfill his dream of becoming a dragon again. Students must provide evidence from the story to support any claims. The folders show that students already have experience with characterization through

exercises in charting what Windrider says, what he does, what other characters say about him, and how the author describes him. Next to these direct quotes from the book, the students have written what this tells us about Windrider. It seems clear that though the students' English is far from perfect, they are engaged in studying and mastering difficult content. They complain a little about "having to write an essay," but the complaints are tinged with pride.

Resources

Bruner, 1986; Echevarria & Short, 2004; Echevarria, Vogt, & Short, 2004; Fisher & Frey, 2004; Fisher, Frey, & Williams, 2002; Hudec & Short, 2002; Jameson, 1999; Jones, Palincsar, Ogle, & Carr, 1987; Palincsar & Brown, 1984; Palincsar, David, & Brown, 1989; Wiggins & McTighe, 1998.

Strategy 8.4:

Choose instructional behaviors that promote equity, comprehension, and active participation.

Discussion

Teaching cognitively demanding subject matter to students learning in a second language requires tremendous skill. Teachers must develop a wide repertoire of behaviors that assist student comprehension. One effective strategy is to develop routines for structuring the daily lesson and weekly plan.

When students know the classroom routines, they are better able to tolerate ambiguities naturally encountered in learning a new language. For example, students are better able to concentrate getting their thoughts on paper if they know that the routine for the beginning of class every Monday, Wednesday, and Friday is to check the overhead for the day's journal-writing topic. Because they also know the routine for passing out and collecting the journals, they can focus solely on their writing.

Increasing wait time (the time the teacher waits between asking a question and getting a response) gives second-language learners the extra seconds they sometimes need to construct a response in English. When teachers increase their wait time to a total of five to seven seconds, they see student responses grow longer, a wider variety of students participating in discussions, and even an increase in student questioning.

In sheltered content and ESL classrooms, teachers need to be sensitive to the range of language proficiency levels. For students in the earlier stages of acquiring English, focusing on the meaning of their contributions rather than on grammatical accuracy lowers anxiety. When the teacher repeats, rephrases, and uses many examples throughout instruction, students understand more.

Calling on students in a systematic way raises performance, especially among students who are considered low achievers. Attention to how students are seated in the classroom and in cooperative groups can also reap benefits (Johnson & Johnson, 1987; Johnson, Johnson, & Holubec, 1993; Kagan, 1994; Slavin, 1989-90, 1990; see also Strategy 8.5). Teachers who promote equity in the classroom carefully plan cooperative groups and other activities so that "low status" students have equal opportunities to perform "high status" jobs.

Skillful teachers of sheltered content employ a variety of methods to check for comprehension. A simple "thumbs up, thumbs down" (indicating yes, no, I understand, or I don't understand) gives the teacher immediate feedback. Using all kinds of visuals (pictures, snippets of video, graphics, models, and even body language) provides a rich, contextualized experience and greatly increases the possibility of student understanding.

Finally, the best teachers model *everything* for students, including procedures and processes. They show students, step by step, how to accomplish a task, including what each step looks and sounds like. They also teach and model how to ask for clarification if students don't understand. A teacher might even post possible clarification statements on the wall for students to see and use: "I need help with _____, please." "I don't understand this word (or sentence or paragraph)." "I am confused about _____."

Classroom Examples

Watching Mr. Jimenez and his students at work is a joy. As the students enter, the procedures for free voluntary reading are displayed on the overhead. The students get their books, sit down, and are reading when the bell rings. When the 15-minute reading period concludes, Mr. Jimenez moves to instruction. He is teaching the class how to use a compare-and-contrast chart. He speaks in a natural way and at an even pace, but his speech is sprinkled with such phrases as, "Let me say that another way" and *"Compare* means to show how things are the same" (and "how things are equal" and "how things are similar"). Mr. Jimenez not only uses extensive paraphrasing and rephrasing in his instruction, he also repeats key words and phrases that are crucial to understanding. Several times he repeats the phrase, "*Contrast* means to show how things are different."

Each student is assigned a number, which is written on a small card and placed in a box. Mr. Jimenez randomly draws numbers as a means of calling on students, but he also appears to target several who are not his top students. He consciously selects students who are struggling in class so they have equal opportunities to respond. He also uses a mix of lower- and higher-order questions. Some center on ensuring that students are "with him" in the instruction, such as, "What does the word *contrast* mean?" Other questions ask students to think in new ways and to stretch their understanding of the topic: "What two characters in the story we're reading would make an interesting compare-and-contrast diagram? Why?" Or, "When would this *not* be a good chart to use?"

Mr. Jimenez uses wait time to good effect. He understands the value of giving second-language learners extra time to construct an answer in their heads before responding. He tells everyone to think before answering, and he waits many seconds before calling on a student. He checks frequently for comprehension, asking students to respond nonverbally to such questions as, "*Contrast* means to show how things are different. Show me thumbs up if you say yes, thumbs down if you say no." Mr.

Jimenez models explicitly how to fill out the first two parts of the compare-and-contrast chart. He says, for instance, "This is how I think about a comparison," or "This is not a comparison." Then he explains why. When the students move to work in preassigned pairs to complete the task, Mr. Jimenez refers to a poster on the wall that spells out the norms for working in pairs, asking several students to say what each pair should do and why.

Resources
Johnson & Johnson, 1987; Johnson, Johnson, & Holubec, 1993; Kagan, 1994; Slavin, 1989–90, 1990.

Strategy 8.5:
Use cooperative learning strategies to encourage interaction and interethnic tolerance and acceptance among students of different ethnic groups.

Discussion
All classrooms are heterogeneous, with students of different backgrounds, expectations, strengths, and needs. But when students are from different countries and speak many different languages, the degree of heterogeneity increases dramatically. Students who have lived for years in African refugee camps join those whose entire lives have been spent in a large Asian city. Rural Haitian or Jamaican children who have attended school sporadically join Russian or Chilean children with extensive education. In other instances, students whose families have fought one another sit next to

243

each other, as do members of rival gangs. Students accustomed to wearing modest clothing in segregated classes find themselves placed in mixed-gender classes where some students wear shorts or other revealing clothes. Factor in differences in English language proficiency, educational backgrounds, academic expectations, and socioeconomic status and the mixture can be volatile. These differences, however, can also be the source of rich educational experiences *if* students can be helped to work together and learn from each other.

Cooperative learning offers one means for students to learn from and help each other (Crandall, 1999). In cooperative activities, small groups of heterogeneous students work together to accomplish tasks and share rewards. When teachers structure these groups carefully, students from dramatically different backgrounds can maximize their strengths while learning from others. Each member of the group plays an important role. For example, a self-confident student who likes to talk in class may be given the role of reporting the group's accomplishments while a quiet student who is a good reader might be responsible for leading the group through the assigned reading. Students with limited English proficiency may take on the roles of timekeeper or illustrator.

Cooperative learning promotes positive social interaction and communication, builds teamwork and a sense of community in the classroom, provides multiple opportunities for students to rehearse their contributions and receive feedback from peers before giving a presentation to the teacher or the whole class, and allows everyone to be both a teacher and a learner (Johnson & Johnson, 1987; Johnson, Johnson, & Holubec, 1993; Kagan, 1994; Slavin, 1990). Peer teaching helps students develop a deeper understanding of content and enables them to learn from others. As Tighe (1971) states, "Real learning ... is not a solitary task. One person cannot be expected to discover five different interpretations of a piece of literature. But five people can. This is where the real dialogue begins. Each student can examine his ideas in relationship to those of his peer group" (p. 23).

Cooperative learning has been found to accomplish the following:

• Reduce anxiety by giving students time to practice and learn from each other in small groups.

• Increase motivation and promote authentic use of English as students communicate with each other to complete their tasks.

• Provide more opportunities for students to listen and speak than is possible in teacher-centered classrooms.

• Allow students to receive support from and provide support to others in attempting to understand new concepts or differing points of view.

• Increase students' self-confidence and sense of self-worth as they view themselves as valuable members of their team.

• Offer opportunities for students to develop cross-cultural understanding, respect, and friendships. (Crandall, 1999; Crandall & Tucker, 1990; Jacob, Rottenberg, Patrick, & Wheeler, 1996; Johnson, Johnson, & Holubec, 1993; Kagan, 1994; Slavin, 1990)

Sometimes teachers must assign students to groups on the basis of their strengths and needs; at other times, groups can be formed randomly. When groups do not work out, reassignment of some students may be necessary, and students who prefer to work individually may need time to adjust to group efforts. But cooperative learning can benefit all students: those who are academically successful, those who have more difficulty, those who are English-speaking, those who are just learning the language, those who are outgoing, and those who are less so. Cooperative learning addresses different learning styles while helping students become comfortable with new ones. And cooperative learning can help students develop much-needed autonomy as learners.

Among the many cooperative activities available, some of the most effective for multi-ethnic and multilingual classes are: think/pair/share, jigsaw, roundtable or round robin, and numbered heads together.

Classroom Examples

Mr. Li's biology class brings together 36 students from diverse backgrounds, many of whom are still enrolled in ESL classes. Some of these students have substantial prior education; others have much less. Some of them clearly enjoy science; others do not. Mr. Li recognizes this diversity and organizes his course around thematic units that he hopes will motivate and interest students by focusing on issues relevant to their lives.

One unit centers on the rain forest and its potential destruction. Selecting a variety of readings that might interest different students, Mr. Li divides the class into groups of four, each group responsible for teaching the rest of the class about their particular article. Each group reads and discusses the article and then answers a set of questions.

Mr. Li circulates among the groups to answer questions and stimulate discussion. When the students are comfortable explaining the article to the other members of their group, they return to the whole class to teach their peers. Mr. Li uses this jigsaw reading technique frequently. He assigns shorter and less difficult articles and chapter sections to students with limited reading or English skills and complex articles to those students prepared to read them. He finds that this approach helps students to think through and understand smaller portions of material. When students are responsible for reading an entire chapter, they may feel overwhelmed and either give up or resort to reading without understanding.

Sometimes Mr. Li checks to see how well students have taught each other; he may ask a group to answer questions about the article read by another group. His aim is to build a sense of responsibility among students to make sure that they and their peers truly understand the material.

To introduce a new history chapter to her middle school students, Ms. Patterson asks them to write down what they know about that era and then to share it with a partner. After the two have shared, she asks them to join another pair of students, and together they combine what they know and develop a list of questions to be answered. This think/pair/share activity allows students to learn from each other in a nonthreatening way; it also establishes the beginnings of a set of objectives for the next unit. Ms. Patterson may use a K-W-L graphic organizer, in which students record what they know and what they want to learn. Later, they add what they have learned in the unit.

Ms. Ramirez, who teaches a sheltered chemistry course to ELLs at various levels of proficiency, groups her students by language background and encourages them to help each other using their common primary language when necessary. Her class focuses on chemistry in the community, helping students to see the value of chemistry in dealing with community issues and problems. When students first arrive in class, they find a sign on the door warning them not to drink the water. They spend the next few weeks trying to find the source of the problem. As they learn the scientific method, they work in small groups to create bilingual posters illustrating their findings. Sometimes Ms. Ramirez has the help of a graduate student who is preparing to become an ESL teacher; at other times, she has a bilingual student aide. Even when she is alone, however, she finds that students help and learn from each other through their cooperative tasks.

Before a new unit, and again after the unit when students are preparing for the unit test, Ms. Ramirez uses a version of roundtable or round robin, assigning students to small groups and asking everyone to contribute to the overall task. For example, prior to a unit on petroleum, she asks students to identify as many sources of energy as possible. Each group passes a piece of paper and a pencil to its members until all ideas are exhausted. Then they share their ideas with the other groups while Ms. Ramirez writes a master list on the board.

Mr. Winter routinely assigns students in his ESL class to form teams for project work, bringing in topics and concepts from across the curriculum. Sometimes he places students who share a common language in the same group, so that they can use both languages in their projects. At other times, he requires all members of a group to use English to communicate. Students function as reader, recorder (writer), facilitator, timekeeper, materials organizer, reporter and speaker, or illustrator as they produce country reports, career posters, or science projects. After groups have been together for some time, he changes assignments to encourage a greater sense of community in the class and enable students to learn from a larger number of peers. Mr. Winter reports that cooperative group work has helped students from different ethnic groups recognize that they have things in common and can become friends.

Resources

Crandall, 1999; Crandall & Tucker, 1990; Jacob, Rottenberg, Patrick, & Wheeler, 1996; Johnson & Johnson, 1987; Johnson, Johnson, & Holubec, 1993; Kagan, 1994; Slavin, 1990; Tighe, 1971.

Strategy 8.6:

Assess and activate students' prior knowledge.

Discussion

The work that teachers do with students at the beginning of a lesson can reap benefits for everyone in the class. Tasks designed to assess and activate students' prior knowledge serve many purposes. A well-designed task shows teachers immediately what their students know or don't know about a topic. Other tasks provide immediate links to the theme or topic by showing students that what they're studying connects directly to their own lives, thus establishing personal relevance and interest.

Teachers can ask themselves a series of questions before they decide which activity or task to use:

• What prior student knowledge do I want to try to activate that ties to the content most directly or powerfully?

• How can I show my students explicitly how the activity links to the theme or content?

• How can I show my students that they can use what they already know to understand something new?

• How can I best elicit my students' opinions, thoughts, or ideas about what they already know?

• What experiences can I provide for my students that will allow them to see and feel that what we are studying connects to their personal lives?

Most teachers have a repertoire of tasks for finding out what students already know. A journal activity allows students to write about personal topics that relate to something soon to be studied. For example, "Write about a time when you moved and had to leave something behind."

Brainstorming is another useful tool, and it can be done in many ways, from a standard list format to more complicated semantic webbing. The K-W-L format (Chamot & O'Malley, 1994) provides a structured way for students to chart what they already know about a topic (K), what they want to know (W), and then, at the end of the lesson, what they learned (L).

Students who are second-language learners can profit from the use of not just one activity, but several activities that allow them to uncover what they already know about a topic and see how it relates to their own lives, before they begin to study the lesson content.

Classroom Examples

One valuable tool designed to assess and activate prior knowledge is an anticipation and prediction guide, also known as an anticipatory guide (Chamot & O'Malley, 1994). Anticipatory guides are especially useful for science teachers, as they can reveal students' scientific misconceptions. Teachers can then structure their lesson so that students experience the scientific phenomena in a new way, giving them a chance to confront their misconceptions and restructure their thinking (Bruer, 1993).

In constructing an anticipatory guide, teachers select key concepts (or a key reading passage) and then create a short series of true-or-false statements encompassing the ideas they want the class to consider. The students respond to each statement individually, in pairs, or in groups. At this point, the teacher tells students that they don't need to know the correct answer—they should just make their best guess—but that they'll be responsible for knowing the correct answer by the end of the lesson.

Anticipatory guides are an effective addition to a language arts or literature class. Here, the goal of the guide is to enable students to interact personally with the ideas or values expressed. In this version, there is no correct response, for students are dealing with individual feelings. For example, before studying a thematic unit on courage, students might be asked to respond with "yes" or "no" to the following statements or ideas they'll encounter in the readings:

- It is important to act brave even if you don't feel brave.
- Physical courage is more important than moral courage.
- I have acted courageously at least once in my life.
- A person always knows what courage is when he or she sees it.
- A person can learn to have courage.

The teacher may ask students to periodically review their responses to the anticipatory guides as they progress through the unit, or to repeat the exercise at the end to see if their ideas have changed. In that case, students might be asked to supply evidence from the text that convinced them either to change their mind or to stick with their initial response.

Students in a physics class for second-language learners were given an anticipatory guide before studying Newton's Third Law. The teacher in that class systematically assesses his students' prior knowledge and possible misconceptions through the use of anticipatory guides. A key to understanding is in the "later" activity at the end of the lesson, in which students are asked to examine their prior beliefs by redoing the anticipatory guide and explaining why their first answer was either right or wrong.

Resources
Bruer, 1993; Chamot & O'Malley, 1994.

Strategy 8.7:
Build conceptual frameworks for new knowledge to ensure that students see how ideas or concepts relate to one another.

Discussion

For many students, especially those working in their second language, the content presented from lesson to lesson, unit to unit, or class to class often seems unconnected, unrelated, or even irrelevant. Students usually can repeat facts from U.S. history, earth science, or language arts; only rarely can they chart major historical trends and show how they are related, explain how the study of the Earth's surface connects to the study of the moon and the solar system, or compare and contrast two characters in a novel.

Schemas are interpretive frames that allow us to make sense of information by relating it to previous experiences (Schank & Abelson, 1977). Providing students with graphic organizers such as a story map, which explicitly displays the different chunks of information to be studied, helps alleviate the anxiety students naturally feel when they encounter new material in their second language.

Using a story map repeatedly while studying various short stories or novels provides a schema for the study of literature. All fiction is built by using characters, setting, and dialogue in a series of events or conflicts leading to some sort of resolution. The use of various graphic organizers showing the key ideas in a lesson or unit depicts what the teacher is teaching and what the students are responsible for learning. Graphic organizers can help teachers clarify their teaching goals, especially in sheltered content classrooms where depth rather than breadth of content provides the most linguistically rich experiences. Teachers can ask themselves, "What do I really want my students to learn here, and how can I display it to them graphically in a way that makes sense?" (See also Echevarria & Graves, 1998, pp. 313–333, and Short, 1991, for a discussion of graphic organizers with ELLs.)

Classroom Examples

Before launching a semester's work on the biosphere, the science teacher displays a large concept map showing the connections among ideas and concepts to be studied, placed in a hierarchical fashion. She gives each student a map and shows an identical map on the overhead projector. Listed are ideas such as matter, living things, nonliving things, heat, energy, water, animals, and plants.

The teacher briefly explains what will be studied, in what order, how the ideas are related, and the importance of each. She pauses after each idea to give students time to draw something that will help them remember the concept. Later, she uses the same concept map to test the students, leaving parts blank. She refers to the map frequently throughout the semester. At the end, she asks students to construct their own concept maps that show their understanding of the biosphere.

The social studies class is about to study several civilizations from various perspectives. The students and the teacher construct a concept map of what they want to discover about each civilization or culture and what they believe all cultures and peoples have in common. Their list of big ideas includes language, clothing, family structure, food, and religion. Through questioning and discussion with the teacher, the students decide to add "important values and beliefs" and "government" to the list. The list serves as a frame for the study of each civilization. Throughout the unit, the teacher uses various graphic organizers, such as Venn diagrams, to show how cultures are the same or different.

In a math classroom, after studying various geometric shapes, the teacher asks cooperative groups to create a concept map showing the connections among a parallelogram, a quadrilateral, a rectangle, a rhombus, a square, a trapezoid, and a triangle. The teacher instructs the students to "put the biggest or most general mathematical idea at the top" and to "make sure you draw, not just write the name of, the shapes so you are sure that you put them where they belong." Animated discussions ensue as students clarify the connections, clear up misconceptions, and struggle to reach consensus on the map's structure.

Resources

Echevarria & Graves, 1998; Schank & Abelson, 1977; Short, 1991.

Strategy 8.8:

Teach learning strategies to help students autonomously accelerate their acquisition of English and content knowledge.

Discussion

Research shows that instruction in learning strategies profits all students. Chamot and O'Malley's (1994) work with second-language learners reinforces the notion that students who learn to consciously monitor their own comprehension and have a storehouse of strategies to use when comprehension is a problem fare better than students who stumble along, hoping that somehow they will eventually "get it."

Explicit instruction in how to learn empowers students in ways that almost no other instruction does (Greenleaf, Schoenback, Cziko, & Mueller, 2001). Second-language learners often feel anxious and powerless in their new culture, new school, and new language. Like other students who experience challenges at school, they may attribute their success on a task to luck and their failure to their own lack of abilities or to forces outside their control (Borkowski, Johnston, & Reid, 1987). When students learn to use strategies, they begin to see the relationship between using strategies and success.

Effective instruction in the use of learning strategies is characterized by several features that help ensure students eventually gain the skills and autonomy necessary for self-monitoring. Research has shown that teachers should identify the strategy, explain why it is being taught (including its usefulness), demonstrate its use, give students abundant practice in applying it to real learning, show how to evaluate the effectiveness of using the strategy, and explore what to do if the strategy doesn't work (Duffy et al., 1986).

Skillful teachers of learning strategies value explicit instruction and teach in a way that reflects what they believe. A classroom that focuses on learning how to learn is full of language (from both teacher and students) such as

- This is how I think about this kind of problem.
- Before you read, you need to think about what you already know about the topic.
- Teresa, can you tell us what strategies you used to understand those two pages?
- I want you to write in your learning log what we learned yesterday, look at the picture up here, and predict how the lesson from yesterday is connected to the lesson today.
- I'm finished reading this section. Now I'm going to summarize. That's one thing that good readers do.

Classroom Examples

Students in an intermediate ESL class have just finished reading a chapter of John Reynolds Gardiner's short novel *Stone Fox* (1983). The teacher tells the class, "I'm going to model for you again today how to ask questions about a story. When I finish modeling, you and your partner are going to make some questions about this chapter. Take a minute and think, 'Why are we learning to make questions about stories?'" Hands pop up all over the classroom. The teacher calls on several students who answer, "To understand more," "A good reader makes questions," and "I get smart."

The teacher then says, "First I'm going to make one 'on the surface' question. Remember, that's a question that has an answer right in the story. You can point to the answer. Here's my 'on the surface' question: What kind of farm do Willie and Grandfather have?" The teacher tells the class to copy the question from the overhead onto their papers. She then asks them to give the answer and say why the question is "on the surface." Together, the class then constructs two more similar questions.

Next the teacher says, "Now I want you to think about the other kind of questions we know how to make. We also make 'under the surface' questions. Remember, those are questions that you have to think hard about. Those are questions where you cannot point to the answer on the page. Who remembers what words 'under the surface' questions begin with?" Students respond with "why," "how," "should," or "could." As the lesson continues, the teacher models "under the surface" questions, including, "Why

is Grandfather not speaking?" and "How should Willy help Grandfather?" The teacher asks the class to construct some questions with her, and then sets the pairs to work on making their own questions.

Resources

Borkowski, Johnston, & Reid, 1987; Chamot & O'Malley, 1994; Duffy et al., 1986; Greenleaf, Schoenback, Cziko, & Mueller, 2001.

Strategy 8.9:

Focus on reading and writing in all subject areas to ensure that students are actively engaged in literacy.

Discussion

Academic and cognitive demands increase with every grade level, yet literacy instruction decreases (International Reading Association, 1999). The need to concentrate on increasing every student's literacy becomes especially urgent for teachers of students who are struggling to close the achievement gap with their native English-speaking peers.

Collier (1989) has shown that some ELLs may need to gain as many as 14 months in reading comprehension for every year in school for several consecutive years to reach the 50th percentile on standardized achievement tests. Students who arrive in the United States with limited prior schooling and low literacy skills can take even longer—and require even more attention. With that challenge in mind, it is clear that the responsibility for teaching reading and writing can no longer be vested solely in the

English or ESL teacher. Teachers in all content areas need to know how to accelerate their students' literacy (Moje, Dillon, & O'Brien, 2000). Literacy coaches for school staff provide a system of long-term professional development that guides teachers in using appropriate literacy instruction strategies in all areas (Sturtevant, 2003).

Several methods promise to increase the literacy of second-language students. Reciprocal teaching (Fisher, Frey, & Fehrenbacher, 2004b; Palincsar & Brown, 1984) can dramatically improve reading comprehension scores. When using reciprocal teaching, teachers explicitly instruct students in four distinct strategy areas: questioning, predicting, clarifying, and summarizing. The teacher models how to create questions about what is happening, how to hypothesize about what might happen next, how to ask for clarification, how to know what to do when you don't understand, and how to state the most important ideas in what was just read. Teachers and students can practice reciprocal teaching dialogues in a whole-class setting. When students gain sufficient skill, they can then work in groups of four on selected portions of text.

As they work in groups, students take turns with each of the four strategies. Reciprocal teaching makes it very clear to students what good readers do. Literature circles use similar approaches to engage and instruct students in effective reading and comprehension skills (Ruby, 2003). Poor readers often believe that good reading consists of pronouncing all the words correctly (Crandall, 1981) or of being able to say the color of the main character's hair and eyes. When students understand the reading process thoroughly, they can begin to monitor their own comprehension and see the connection between application of the process and increased comprehension.

Teachers in all content areas can incorporate explicit instruction in reading strategies into their classrooms (Biancarosa & Snow, 2004; Kamil, 2003). A well-designed unit might include practice in the four skill areas of reciprocal teaching: On one day, students practice predicting by looking at pictures instead of text; in another session, they create questions based on reading the first paragraph of a text; they learn how to summarize by looking at a series of statements and deciding which are absolutely necessary for the summary and which can be omitted.

Teachers can also give students multiple opportunities to respond to text using various teacher-designed tasks: reading logs, in which students copy quotes from the text and then write their own response; first-response "writes," in which students read and then quickly write about what ideas came to them as they were reading; or graphic logs, in which students write quotes from the text and respond with a drawing or symbol that corresponds to the quote. Scaffolding student writing through a "gradual release model" will prepare students for more independent writing as their skills and confidence levels are built up (Fisher & Frey, 2003). The important idea is that teachers make sure that students are actively engaged with the text and that there is evidence of that engagement.

Classroom Examples

Ms. Salinas, who teaches Spanish for native speakers, shares students with four other teachers: a science teacher, a social studies teacher, a math teacher, and a language arts teacher. All the teachers have been working throughout the semester to teach their students how to respond to written text. When they began, most of the students had no idea that they could interact with the text—that they could hold a conversation with the text and have their own important ideas about it as they were reading. They had no experience with assuming responsibility for creating personal meaning from the text. Most of them struggled simply to get through one or two pages of any reading; at the end, they had little understanding of what they had read.

The teachers in Ms. Salinas's school have been working on reciprocal teaching strategies in their different content areas, and Ms. Salinas has just added elements of what the team calls "active reading strategies." Ms. Salinas found that she had to teach her students the different ways to respond to text.

For example, the students may read a short story and fill out a dialectical journal as they read. The prompts on the right side of the active reading chart provide sufficient scaffolding for the students in the beginning. In the left column, they write quotes or ideas from the story that they find interesting or provocative. In the right column, they then respond to the quote with a question, a speculation, a visualization, or some other response. The variety of responses shows that the students have internalized the notion that good readers are active constructors of meaning as they work their way through a text. Students have written responses such as

- Why did the character do that? That doesn't seem like what he would do!
- This story reminds me of the story we read last week. The two characters are very similar.
- In the next chapter, I predict that he will finally go visit his uncle because his uncle seems important to him.
- This part is just like my life. I have felt just like that before.

Resources

Biancarosa & Snow, 2004; Collier, 1989; Crandall, 1981; Fisher & Frey, 2003; Fisher, Frey, & Fehrenbacher, 2004b; International Reading Association, 1999; Kamil, 2003; Moje, Dillon, & O'Brien, 2000; Palincsar & Brown, 1984; Ruby, 2003; Sturtevant, 2003; Vacca & Vacca, 2004.

Strategy 8.10:

Give students multiple opportunities to read self-selected texts to build literacy and develop habits of reading that extend beyond the classroom.

Discussion

Getting students to read more of what they want to read is an often-overlooked strategy in teachers' attempts to raise reading scores and close the gap between second-language learners and native English speakers. Adding a voluntary reading program to the curriculum at any grade level provides what most second-language learners do not have at home or even at school: access to books.

Many advantages accrue for students who begin to read on their own. A compilation of research (Krashen, 2004) on voluntary reading shows that students involved in free reading programs do as well as or better than students involved in more traditional skills-based reading instruction. Second-language learners involved in free reading programs in school consistently outperformed those who received a more traditional language-teaching approach, with a mixture of grammar and oral exercises. Free reading also has positive effects on vocabulary acquisition, spelling, and writing accuracy and style—and thus the potential to dramatically increase the acquisition of English.

Frank Smith (1988) has written eloquently about the need to help students feel that they are part of the "literacy club," that they are members of this powerful "inside" group who expect to be able to read and write competently. But access to books is a problem for many poor and language-minority students. Spaces that abound with fiction and nonfiction books, magazines, newspapers, and comic books are often referred to as print-rich environments. Though it is understandable that many homes lack the economic resources to make such environments possible, many schools (especially secondary schools) have not made access to books a priority either. Many teachers committed to getting books into their students' hands comb secondhand bookstores, their own bookshelves, and garage sales to build a classroom library of engaging books. Other teachers work together to ensure that a portion of their school's discretionary money is allocated to the purchase of books for free reading programs, whether based in the school library or individual classrooms.

Schools that implement voluntary reading programs in classrooms use a variety of methods to heighten interest in reading and to ensure that reading happens regularly; schoolwide support of a voluntary reading program has been shown to change attitudes about reading in ways that one classroom teacher alone could not accomplish (Fisher, 2004). In schools using voluntary reading programs, teachers and students conduct research on what students would like to read. They ask other teachers, see what kinds of books students check out on their own, and ask the students themselves. Teenage romances, horror books, Newbery Medal winners, comic books, series—all qualify for inclusion if students want to read them (though paperbacks work better than hardbacks). The idea is to get students to read *something* so they will want to read more (Frey & Fisher, 2004b). High school teachers report that their ESL students even pick up a good children's book with no embarrassment if it is part of a classroom library that has many types of books from which to choose.

Most teachers set up some sort of system for voluntary reading. They want to make sure that the time for reading is extended and consistent. For example, reading may take place at the beginning of class every day for 15 minutes. Students are taught the process for selecting and checking out a book; they learn such strategies as perusing the back cover to see if it looks interesting. Teachers look for students who seem to be struggling to maintain focus and try to help them select a book more appropriate to their reading level or interest.

An open sharing of ideas and progress shows what others in the class are reading. As a means of sparking interest in a book, the teacher might conduct a talk on a selected book, giving a short description of the characters, plot, or setting. Recommended reading lists from fellow students can help to guide student selections. Teachers often incorporate some kind of accountability into the program, so they are better able to chart students' progress. For example, progress may be assessed during a conference in which teacher and student talk about what the student is reading. Or, students might keep a daily reading log tallying how many pages they have read and writing short summaries. A reading folder might include a list of books read over the course of the year, reflections on progress in reading, and book reviews to be passed on to next year's class.

Classroom Examples

When 12-year-old Juan entered his 7th grade advanced ESL class, he wrote in his reading portfolio, "I don't like to read." Asked what kinds of books he liked, he wrote, "None." In response to a question about when he reads, he said, "I read only when I have to." He spent the first two weeks of free reading staring at the pages of books he picked up at random from the revolving bookshelf in his English classroom. Juan made no progress in reading a book and tended to pick up a different book every other day. He was easily distracted during reading time and often attempted to disturb students around him who were trying to read.

Ms. Alvarez, Juan's teacher, had experience with such students. She knew it might take him a while to settle into the routine of reading. She also knew that she would have to help him. After the second week, Ms. Alvarez took Juan aside during free reading time and said, "Juan, I see you've had some trouble finding a book you want to read. Let me help you find something today." Together, they perused a variety of books on the shelf. Ms. Alvarez selected three that she thought he might like and told him to sit down with them, look at the back covers, read the first page, and then decide on one. When he had done that, she said, "Now, for this book you need to read the first two chapters. If, after that, you don't like it, we'll pick out another one together."

Over the next three weeks, Juan read the first two chapters of four different books. Finally, one day Ms. Alvarez noticed that Juan was one-third of the way through a short novel by Gary Soto—way beyond Chapter 2. When she asked him later if he wanted to try a different book, he replied, "No. I kind of like this one." Over the course of the semester, Ms. Alvarez saw subtle shifts in Juan's behavior toward reading. He came in, sat down, and usually began the task of reading. Though he read slowly, the summaries in his reading logs showed that he understood most of what he read. By the end of the semester, Juan had read two short novels (about 150 pages each) plus a short book on soccer stars. He wrote in his portfolio, "This is the first time in my life I ever read a whole book."

Resources

Fisher, 2004; Frey & Fisher, 2004b; Krashen, 2004; Smith, 1988.

Strategy 8.11:

Guide students beyond the text to reexamine, reconnect, and rethink the major ideas or concepts.

Discussion

The walls of many classrooms are filled with posters, drawings, and writings that students have created after studying a particular piece of literature, an historical era or figure, a scientific concept, or a thematic unit. The best culminating tasks in a sheltered content classroom exhibit several characteristics.

First, the task allows students to take ownership of the material and create meaning for themselves. A good end-of-study task builds on the strengths of different class members by giving them, over time, the chance to express themselves through an array of formats: poetry, drama, music, or fine arts.

A good "beyond-the-text" task also forces students to go back to the text to clarify, question, and reread with a different purpose in mind. In this way, the task gives second-language learners the chance to refocus on the overall meaning of the text (Walqui, 2000). Many excellent beyond-the-text tasks require students to transform one genre into another: a scientific text turned into a TV news item; a historical narrative turned into a live debate; a short story turned into an "open mind" task that displays, with graphics and

phrases, the main conflicts a character is facing, from that character's point of view.

Teachers may find that a combination of individual and group responses to content works best. At times, the best approach may be for each student to create a poem or graphic of the content; other lessons may more naturally call for a group-constructed product. If the purpose of the task is to solidify a particular concept, then the teacher may ask groups to create a "team word web" that shows their joint understanding of how the content fits together. In any case, if the task is a group activity, the teacher needs to ensure that all members contribute equally to reach shared accountability for the end product. For example, each student uses a different colored marker to write his or her part of a conversation or dialogue or is responsible for a different section of a storyboard. Constructing a rubric with students beforehand specifying the features of a good text and providing models from previous classes give students clear guidelines for performance expectations (Walqui-VanLier, 1991).

Classroom Examples

A quick tour of the sheltered content classrooms in one school hallway shows that the teachers ask their students to respond to their learning with a variety of creative, beyond-the-text tasks. In the social studies class, students have just finished studying the Renaissance. In groups, they are preparing to question classmates who will sit on the "hot seat" in front of the class. Students have volunteered to assume the personae of da Vinci, Sir Thomas More,

Cervantes, Machiavelli, and Shakespeare. The groups have been asked to design hard questions that will force the students in the hot seat to live in the shoes of the historical figure. Hot-seat students have been asked to prepare themselves to answer the questions as a Renaissance person would respond, with appropriate viewpoints, attitudes, and ideas.

One wall of the language arts classroom is covered with student-created journey maps for John Steinbeck's novel, *The Pearl* (1993). Each map shows "trigger events," or events chosen by the student as being most important. Displays of key learnings make clear what happened or what was learned as a result of the trigger events. Finally, each map contains detours or dead ends—events in the story that seemed to cause problems but in the end did not affect the resolution as much as it seemed they might. Each paper uses a combination of words, phrases, symbols, colors, and pictures to explain what the student learned. The borders of each map are filled with symbols that demonstrate the students' understandings of *The Pearl*.

Resources

Harvey & Goudvis, 2000; Walqui, 2000; Walqui-VanLier, 1991.

Strategy 8.12:
Restructure and maximize time to meet students' needs.

Discussion

Teachers and students alike often struggle with the traditional structure and scheduling of the typical secondary school, which results in strict departmentalization among content areas, teacher isolation, and lower status for ELL students and teachers (Ruiz-de-Velasco & Fix, 2000). Students come and go every 50 minutes or so, based on a rigid system of bells. Time for learning is sliced neatly into six or seven distinct subjects, each with its own slot. Teachers see a succession of groups of 25 to 35 students passing through each class—as many as 125 to 150 students each day.

Some schools are attempting to address the disconnectedness of this system by instituting such innovations as block scheduling, rotating schedules, career academies, and other strategies aimed at making education more cohesive and meaningful. Structural changes to the school day can play an important role by providing longer blocks of time (90 minutes or two hours) for in-depth methods of instruction that so many teachers wish they could use but cannot fit into the rigid traditional schedule (Olsen & Jaramillo, 2000).

Even a radical restructuring of time does not ensure that class time is well spent. Close examination of many secondary classrooms reveals wasted minutes, time ill spent on taking attendance, and a general lack of urgency about the preciousness of each moment. Newly arrived second-language learners often find themselves at odds with this kind of schooling, which is already less structured and formal than that of their homes. Thoughtful teachers (no matter what the schedule) seek ways to manage their classrooms so that every minute is used to maximum advantage.

Time-conscious teachers create clear classroom expectations about the use of time. They begin class as soon as the bell rings and do not stop until the last possible minute. They often begin class with the same procedure or routine, so that students always know what materials they need, where to look for instructions, and how long they have to complete each task. For example, a language arts teacher might routinely begin with a journal topic written on the overhead projector. Students know that they need to record the topic and date by the time the bell rings and that they have 10 minutes to complete this first task. Math teachers might begin with a set of problems that reviews a previous concept. Free reading is another way to open the period with an academic focus. (See also Strategy 8.10.)

Routines for retrieving and storing materials, moving from one activity to another, and moving from pair to group to individual work help reduce wasted time. Students do not have to wonder how to accomplish the routine, and they know they are expected to complete it promptly. Explicit teacher modeling of tasks also reduces the amount of time students must spend getting started. When teachers invest instructional time showing "This is what it looks like" and "This is

what it sounds like," students are more likely to get busy right away.

Careful attention to task assignments within cooperative groups helps all students work toward completion in a timely fashion. This means that each member of the group must have an important, carefully defined role to fill, reducing the possibility that one or more members will simply relax and let the others do all the work.

Another way of looking at time receives less attention and is often overlooked. Teachers need to anticipate ways of ensuring that students are actively engaged for as much of each period as possible. For example, a whole class might have their books open to the same page. The teacher calls on individual students to read, and it appears that just about everyone is following along in the text. But how does the teacher really know that the act of following is not merely mechanical? Without evidence of engagement, many students may simply be pretending to pay attention when they are really thinking about the upcoming dance, the fight they had this morning with their brother, or the fact that they're hungry.

Evidence of active student engagement is the most powerful tool that teachers have to maximize their use of time. That evidence can take many forms. During instructional time, teachers should encourage students to say and do many things, always with the idea that something specific can be pointed to as evidence of engagement. It can be as simple as, "Turn and tell your partner . . ." or as complex as "You have just taken notes on this minilecture (five minutes maximum). Now, in the right-hand column, write a few questions about what you have just heard."

Ensuring that students are actively engaged in any reading process can take the form of reciprocal teaching, responding to text through a reading log, or any method that forces students to periodically make public their understanding of what is being studied. Time-conscious teachers effectively manage not only the surface aspects of time use (such as in-class routines and starting and ending at the bell) but also student engagement during the class period.

Classroom Examples

Mr. Malabonga, a mentor teacher, has spent his preparation period observing various teachers to find some good models for managing classrooms. Several new teachers are struggling with issues of classroom management, especially the wise use of time and expectations for how students use time. Mr. Malabonga plans to conduct joint observations of the good teachers with the new teachers, knowing that they can profit from seeing specific behaviors of good teachers.

On this day, Mr. Malabonga stops to visit Ms. Bart, a teacher widely respected by teachers and students alike. As he watches her teach, he jots down what he will highlight when he returns to do the joint observations with the new teachers.

- Procedures for individual, pair, and group work are clearly posted. Ms. Bart refers to the posters frequently to remind students of her expectations.

- Class begins at the bell. Students are in their seats, already working on the warm-up assignment, when the bell rings. Ms. Bart spends this time explaining to a new student the expectations for beginning class, including where to keep his journal, how the journals are passed out, and how they are to be put away. She quietly monitors the progress of the class members as they work.

- When students move to a new kind of group project, she clearly directs them concerning where, how, and when to move. Each student in the group has a clearly defined role, and the group has a clearly defined time limit to complete the task.

- Ms. Bart uses a variety of methods to ensure that all students are actively engaged. She even uses such terms as, "I need to see that your brain is engaged."

- Part of the new group project requires that the group brainstorm a topic. As students brainstorm, each member is required to repeat what the other students say, and each is required to write it down.

- Ms. Bart and the students work until one minute before the bell rings.

Resources

Olsen & Jaramillo, 2000; Ruiz-de-Velasco & Fix, 2000.

259

Strategy 8.13:

Nurture a sense of community in the classroom.

Discussion

Many teachers today face classrooms that mirror the rapidly changing demographics of their states, communities, and school districts. Just a decade ago, a class might have included only one second-language or immigrant student; today, classrooms are filled with an unprecedented mixture of cultures, languages, national backgrounds, and ethnicities. Schoolwide efforts to address these pressing issues often center on the superficial aspects of building community—an assembly to honor Dr. Martin Luther King Jr., a dance for Cinco de Mayo, or a parade for Chinese New Year. Teachers are left searching for ways in which they and their students can find meaningful common ground within the four walls of the classroom.

Careful teachers find ways of avoiding divisions, aware that classrooms can splinter along invisible fault lines. When a class is made up of students from many different primary-language backgrounds, the teacher can ensure that work groups create interactions among students from different language groups. Even when a teacher must pair a proficient primary-language speaker with a less proficient one of the same language to provide peer assistance, the teacher sees that the pairing is merely a temporary arrangement.

Teachers also need to consider the range of language fluency in the classroom. Status often accrues to those who speak English more proficiently; structuring situations so that students of varying levels of proficiency must work together to complete a task helps break down barriers, especially if students less proficient in English contribute a meaningful, valued portion of the task in their native language.

Several well-researched, well-documented approaches to cooperative learning (Johnson & Johnson, 1987; Kagan, 1994; Slavin, 1989–1990, 1990) address some of these issues (see also Strategy 8.5). Each approach requires considerable skill and practice by the teacher to succeed. But teachers who invest the time notice improvements in intergroup relations as well as increased academic achievement (Crandall, 1999).

It is critical to distinguish between doing cooperative learning and simply putting students in groups to do some work. Although it is often called cooperative learning, group work can be a somewhat random collection of students completing some task together. In real cooperative groups, such as those Kagan (1994) describes, the teacher assigns students to groups; each group represents students with a range of abilities. True cooperative groups operate on the principle of positive interdependence: each student has a role and is accountable to the rest of the group. The groups incorporate clear individual accountability and an emphasis on students' use of collaborative skills.

Some teachers have been trained in complex instruction (Cohen & Lotan, 1997), an approach to cooperative learning that goes directly to the heart of status in the classroom. Teachers make explicit the kinds of skills and abilities needed for groups to solve intrinsically interesting problems or to complete group products (such as an investigation focused on the theme of social stratification in medieval Japanese society). Group norms govern expectations and behavior. For example, students who systematically engage in complex instruction projects know that at least one will be good at all of the tasks involved, and everyone will be good at some of them. Because the group tasks truly require the use of multiple abilities, not all of which relate to reading and writing, every student can contribute to the group product. The task structures in complex instruction units also break down the hierarchies that exist in classrooms, which reflect the larger school and community.

Other teachers employ a variety of methods to build group inclusion and class cohesiveness. Many such activities make up the team-building portion of cooperative learning approaches. A common activity gives teams a problem to solve, but team members may not speak or use nonverbal cues. Team members receive an envelope with parts from different broken squares. Their group task is to reassemble the pieces into squares, following the above rules. Another interactive method of building teams is a variation of Kagan's numbered heads together activity (see also Strategy 8.5). Students count off in groups of four or five, so that every student has a number. The teacher poses a question to the class and asks groups to put their heads together to discuss their response. After allowing a minute or two for group discussion, the teacher repeats the question and calls out a number. The teacher then calls randomly on one group

to answer, and the student with that number in the group answers.

Teachers who use methods of grouping and instruction to break down barriers find that their classrooms are significantly more equitable, lively, and happy for all students. Methods such as complex instruction, which directly address potential inequities and unequal status within the academic context, are powerful on multiple levels.

Classroom Examples

Ms. Tan is dedicated to creating a classroom governed by mutual respect and understanding. The 32 students in her 7th grade social studies class represent a mix of cultures, languages, national backgrounds, ethnicities, and races. Seven students are black, 5 are Euro-American, 2 are newly arrived from Russia, 10 are from Central America and Mexico, and 7 are Southeast Asian—2 from Thailand, 1 from the Philippines, and 4 from Vietnam.

Recently, racial tensions have been rising in the surrounding community and spilling over into the school. Ms. Tan notices that students are increasingly segregating themselves by groups and sticking together more. Even though her classroom has been relatively calm, she has redoubled her efforts to promote inclusion and cooperation.

Today, students are seated in their cooperative groups working on a jigsaw project. On the surface, there is no way to tell how they are grouped, though it is obviously not by ethnicity, language, or race. Some examples of group team-building projects are displayed on one wall—in one case, the groups have created a group identity and drawn a picture or symbol to match. The teams are reading short historical pieces related to different immigrant groups. Seated in topic-specific "expert" teams, the team members will soon return to their home teams with information on the immigrant experience they have read about—when it took place, why the person came, how the person felt on arriving, what conditions and attitudes greeted him or her, and whether the immigration was voluntary or involuntary.

The work in home teams is productive and focused. Students are responsible for filling out a grid outlining what other team members are providing from their reading in the expert groups. Each team member will then choose an immigrant experience unlike their own or their family's. Their job will be to stand in the shoes of that person and write a diary-like account of that experience. Ms. Tan will spend considerable time making sure that students know and appreciate the differences between voluntary and involuntary immigration. She has planned several activities to help them process the hard feelings that are bound to come up as the unit proceeds, but she knows that avoiding the issues would be worse.

Resources

Cohen & Lotan, 1997; Crandall, 1999; Johnson & Johnson, 1987; Kagan, 1994; Slavin, 1989–1990, 1990.

Strategy 8.14:
Foster students' self-esteem and leadership skills.

Discussion

Bilingual and bicultural students are valuable resources. Unfortunately, these students are often viewed in terms of what they *lack* (especially English language proficiency) rather than what they can contribute. The value of bilingualism in cognitive and economic terms is well established. Bilingualism promotes cognitive flexibility and creativity, enabling bilingual individuals to view issues from multiple perspectives. In addition, bilingual workers bring much-needed skills to an increasingly global economy (Hakuta, 1987; Tucker, 1990).

Not all schools recognize the value of knowing more than one language. Although schools may recognize the importance of foreign languages for English-speaking students, they often neglect the languages that immigrant students bring to school, relegating students' primary languages to the home or the community, rather than gradually adding English to that primary language.

This deficit model can have a profound impact on immigrant students, as well as on the teachers and administrators who work with them. Bilingual students may be overlooked when others are encouraged to run for student government, apply to honor societies, participate in Advanced Placement courses, or receive training as peer mediators. They may not receive equal consideration for college or career counseling. Their immigrant status may also limit their participation in government-funded work-study programs or college financial aid programs.

Marginalization often causes these students to internalize others' perceptions of them. Rather than taking pride in themselves and their backgrounds and recognizing the value of their bilingualism and biculturalism, they doubt their self-worth or seek to prove it outside of school. Some students must contribute to their family income, and the low-skilled jobs available to them may further diminish their sense of self-worth. Conflicting expectations of family, friends, and school can create incredible pressures.

Students need opportunities to identify and celebrate their strengths, not focus on their weaknesses. Fortunately, there are many ways to accomplish this. Perhaps the most important is to have high expectations of these students and to provide opportunities that allow them to live up to those expectations. Teachers can be trained in specific mentoring techniques that focus on communicating with students about dropout prevention, career exploration, decision making, transitioning to postsecondary or vocational education, conflict resolution, and community participation (Rumptz, Lucas, & McEmrys, 2001).

For example, ELLs, or those who have recently exited from ESL or bilingual programs, may be ideal tutors for peers still enrolled in these courses. Older ELLs may be ideal tutors for younger children who are just learning to read. These tutors play an especially important role when they assist students at risk of failure in overcrowded elementary schools (Cook & Urzúa, 1993; Heath & Mangiola, 1991). Peer tutoring by older or more proficient students works nearly as well as teacher tutoring (Cohen, Kulik, & Kulik, 1982), and the benefits to the tutor are substantial.

Teachers have long known that one of the best ways to learn something is to teach it. The act of tutoring increases students' confidence in themselves as learners, improves their academic skills, and increases the likelihood that they will stay in school. In addition, tutoring helps develop interpersonal and leadership skills. Cross-age tutoring programs have the additional benefit of encouraging young people to consider teaching as a career—a critically important possibility, because the declining percentage of Hispanic, Asian, and other minority teachers creates an absence of role models in schools.

Additional activities that celebrate students' languages and cultures are also important. International clubs and festivals, extracurricular activities involving sports or music in which students excel, and opportunities to learn one another's dances can help students develop pride in their heritage. When newly arrived immigrants help a school win the state soccer championship, everyone recognizes and celebrates their accomplishments. Similarly, the publication of student stories or poems in school journals or newsletters validates student efforts and offers a valuable outlet for self-expression. Simple banners or hall exhibits reflecting students' diverse backgrounds help establish a positive multicultural environment.

Teachers can provide opportunities for students to demonstrate special linguistic and cultural knowledge, such as asking students to teach a short lesson on their language or to relate a local proverb to one from their native country. Working cooperatively on class projects helps students recognize one another's strengths. Former students with successful careers may be invited to class to discuss their careers and the role that bilingualism has played in their achievement; current students can serve as experts in teacher development courses and workshops, helping teachers and administrators to understand their countries and cultural backgrounds. The important point is to emphasize students' strengths while addressing their linguistic and academic needs.

Classroom Examples

Ms. Hernandez, a high school Spanish teacher, recognized that many of her Spanish-speaking students were having difficulties in regular Spanish classes, as their spoken language differed from the textbook variety, and formal instruction in their own language was limited. Rather than underscoring students' strengths, the classes were further eroding their self-confidence.

Ms. Hernandez decided to develop a sequence of Spanish courses for native speakers, building on their oral language and developing their formal (especially written) language skills to further their ability to use the language in academic and professional contexts. After taking this course sequence, students transitioned into advanced placement Spanish classes with mainstream students, where they were able to earn college credit. Ms. Hernandez also developed a cross-age tutoring program in which Spanish-speaking and English-speaking high school students tutored ELLs in a nearby elementary school. Some of the Spanish-speaking students found themselves helping the English-speaking high school students with their Spanish. After this experience, several students indicated an interest in becoming teachers.

Teachers at one high school developed a weekend cross-cultural leadership institute at an environmental education center, where students from many different backgrounds were encouraged to develop confidence, leadership, and cooperative skills. For many students, this was their first weekend away from home. One activity required students to help each other negotiate an obstacle course, which required teamwork, confidence, physical and mental agility, and determination. Other activities engaged students in creating a banner for the school, participating in a talent show, and working with a variety of arts and crafts. In addition, two student government leaders (formerly in ESL classes) led an evening session, providing a forum for students to articulate their concerns about the school and to act on them by developing resolutions, which were subsequently presented to the student government and the principal for action.

Through these activities, friendships developed among students who had previously viewed each other with suspicion. Several of the participants became volunteers, guides, and interpreters for parents and new students at the international student guidance office during registration week. In doing so, they gained community service credits required for graduation. Another source of community service credits grew out of a field trip to a local nursing home, where students found senior citizens eager to talk with younger people who spoke their languages. Several students began visiting seniors regularly.

Another teacher, Mr. Wu, initiated a writing workshop by asking students to list things they liked about themselves, things they could do well, and things others liked about them. Students expanded their lists to serve as a means of introducing themselves to the class. As a follow-up activity, students brought personal items to school, including photographs and other pictures explaining who they were. In small groups, they elaborated on why these things were important to them. They wrote captions for the photographs and pictures, in both English and their primary language, and combined them with other items in a collage that was later displayed in the classroom.

Ms. Johnson routinely uses cooperative learning to integrate diverse learners into her middle school social studies classes. She groups ELLs with English speakers who are sensitive to the needs of these students and assigns roles that allow them to demonstrate special skills, such as designing and illustrating group posters. In the same middle school, a science teacher and a graduate student serving an internship helped immigrant students develop science fair projects. One project, by a 7th grade Somali student, won first place in chemistry. This student, who had only recently arrived from a refugee camp, learned to use the computer to enter the findings for her project poster.

Resources

Cohen, Kulik, & Kulik, 1982; Cook & Urzua, 1993; Hakuta, 1987; Heath & Mangiola, 1991; Rumptz, Lucas, & McEmrys, 2001; Tucker, 1990.

Strategy 8.15:
Facilitate students' participation in college and career planning.

Discussion

Immigrant students often dream of going to college, but even those who succeed academically may have little understanding of how to achieve that dream. They may even believe college is impossible for them. High school exit exam requirements may hinder or discourage altogether immigrants' desire to attend college. Their experiences in their home countries may have led them to think that college is available only to the wealthy or that options for women are restricted. They may be unaware of the variety of colleges available, the possibility of combining work with school, or the many sources of financial assistance. They may be expected to work to help support their families, or even to increase the number of hours they work after graduation. If they are the first in their family to consider college, they are quite likely to have a limited awareness of college requirements and the application process (Crandall & Greenblatt, 1999; Hadlock, 1994; Hutner, 1996). Federal law requires K–12 enrollment for all children, regardless of legal status. However, undocumented students may encounter residency, tuition, or financial aid-related requirements when applying to college that they were unprepared for (Biswas, 2005). An estimated 7,000 to 13,000 undocumented students graduate from U.S. high schools and enroll in college each year (Passel, 2003).

It is easy to forget the difficulty of the college application process. Horn and Carroll (1997) found that only a few of the students considered at risk in their study completed all of the steps necessary for college participation: aspiring to a college degree, taking appropriate courses, passing entrance exams, completing an application, and enrolling in college. English-speaking students born in the United States find this process difficult to negotiate; it is even more difficult for ELLs who may not even be aware of the steps involved.

Teachers and guidance counselors often overlook students who are still receiving ESL instruction as possible candidates for college, confusing limited English proficiency with limited academic ability. In addition, teachers and administrators are seldom aware of the test requirements for immigrant students seeking higher education; these tests and policies governing entrance examinations vary widely (Bunch, 1995). Changing federal policies concerning immigration status further complicate the situation because these policies determine who is eligible for federal financial aid (federally funded scholarships).

Students need support structures to complete the application process and role models to help them envision themselves as potential college students; they also need to have information presented in language they can understand. Role models can help students sort through the many types of colleges available: two-year or four-year, public or private, coeducational or single gender, large or small, and liberal arts, technical, or trade. Students' choices are often limited to schools where friends or older siblings have enrolled or colleges in the immediate vicinity. Without visits to other colleges or opportunities to discuss options with peers or alumni, students are likely to rely on those institutions with which they're most familiar.

Support structures and modeling are also important in career planning. Students may not understand the economic value of postsecondary education or the fact that higher education correlates with higher earnings and more stable employment. Without opportunities to talk with or shadow potential role models, or to visit workplaces with diverse employees, they may focus on areas of work limited by their experiences. Most secondary schools have career planning facilities, often involving sophisticated job-interest surveys or computer-assisted career planning programs; however, these instruments are not usually available in languages other than English, and the level of English may be beyond the proficiency of English learners. Even when appropriate materials are available, immigrant students may not be aware of them or know how to access them.

It is possible to address both college preparation and career planning through specific courses for immigrant students. In college preparation classes, focus on selecting colleges, filling out applications, developing a résumé, crafting the student essay required in the application, and preparing for the variety of tests that will be required—the SAT, Test of English as a Foreign Language (TOEFL), or American College Testing Program (ACT). Financial planning, including identifying and accessing sources of financial assistance, is also an important consideration. In a career preparation class, the focus might be on identifying personal interests and strengths, analyzing potential jobs that use these strengths, reviewing required coursework and ensuring that students' schedules are appropriate, identifying postsecondary education that might be needed, and helping identify potential postsecondary institutions.

It is not sufficient, however, to relegate career and college planning to separate courses. As one teacher put it, "We need *every* teacher to help with the college and career process." Teachers across the curriculum need to relate their coursework to the world outside the classroom and help students to see the interrelationships between what is taught in class and further education and employment. Classroom activities can be augmented by guest speakers who can serve as role models and motivators and provide information on how they chose their own college or career. Inviting prominent bilingual community members communicates the importance of bilingualism and biculturalism as a job asset to all students, not just ELLs. Former students who attend local colleges or are home on vacation can also be invited to talk to classes or to dialogue with students through e-mail or letters,

serving as valuable sources of encouragement and information.

Classroom Examples

Mr. Elson (an ESL teacher) and Ms. Sing (a social studies teacher) are on the same middle school team, including ELLs and native English speakers. They coordinate their instruction, sometimes including the math or science teachers. They routinely weave career and college information into their teaching.

For example, a unit on U.S. history dealing with slavery and the Civil War also included a visit to a former slave home (the site was an archaeological dig in the middle of an apartment complex). Students visited the dig, saw archaeologists at work, and interviewed college students at the site about their work. Though the middle schoolers may be too young to choose a career, they became aware of career possibilities and of the role that postsecondary education plays in these careers. Units emphasizing the importance of college and career planning are also developed for students to take with them when they are called back to their home countries for extended periods of time, which helps students maintain their English proficiency.

At the high school level, Ms. Vaznaugh teaches college and career planning in her intermediate ESL classes; she incorporates job-interest surveys, college and career field trips, and test preparation. The latter is especially important, as students will have to demonstrate their proficiency in English for admission to college and successfully complete standardized tests.

Using a variety of test-preparation materials, students analyze individual items for test-taking strategies. Students also take simulated tests, analyze the results, and share their experiences with students who have taken the test. These activities help reduce students' anxiety about the tests and reinforce the importance of planning for the experience. As Ms. Vaznaugh says, "Kids know less about college than we think they do. They need direct information, guidance, and support."

Another teacher incorporates college applications into her English class, focusing on the personal essay in the application form. Yet another teacher, Ms. Haynes, includes an introduction to keyboarding and word processing, using résumé development and essay writing for college and career planning as the basis of instruction. These classes introduce students to the college and financial assistance available through the Internet or local software. Students usually work in pairs or small groups when using the Internet or the software programs, freeing Ms. Haynes to answer specific questions or to provide assistance to groups of students.

Special career and college visits are planned for ELLs and those who have recently exited the ESL program. During these visits, students can meet with other immigrant students to see what kinds of career paths they are pursuing. Some teachers pair career visits with planning as a means of meeting the school's community service requirement. Thus, a visit to a nursing home or hospital not only makes students aware of the wide array of jobs available in the health and nursing care fields but also provides potential sites at which students can perform community service required for graduation.

Much of what is introduced in these classes is reinforced through after-school programs or clubs such as the Honors Council, an extracurricular activity focused on college and career planning (Hadlock, 1994). When the council began, only high-achieving senior students (those with a 3.0 grade-point average or above) were included; over time, however, students with a 2.0 or above have been added, and a second council—for freshmen, sophomores, and juniors—has also been initiated (Hutner, 1996). The councils encourage an earlier focus on postsecondary planning and provide for the development of peer mentors; students in the upper-level council can earn community service credits by helping those in the lower council. A similar set of courses, one for juniors and another for seniors, has been added to the school's curriculum, though the after-school activities and the emphasis on postsecondary options in ESL and other courses continue.

Resources

Biswas, 2005; Bunch, 1995; Crandall & Greenblatt, 1999; Hadlock, 1994; Horn & Carroll, 1997; Hutner, 1996; Passel, 2003.

Success for All Learners

English language learners have much more in common with native English speakers than many educators might expect. As children grow into adolescence and prepare for adulthood, they need to develop the linguistic, cultural, and cognitive skills necessary to succeed in the

United States and the world of the 21st century. The older students are, the harder it becomes to catch up to the expected levels of academic achievement, technological skills, critical thinking, and literacy required to succeed in the adult world. High school dropout rates across the nation are disturbingly high: 7,000 students drop out of high school every day (Alliance for Excellent Education, 2005a). The majority of these dropouts are minority students and ELLs—and these populations are expected to outnumber the majority-white, native English-speaking students in the future.

All students need teachers who are not only content specialists but also literacy specialists. All students need the opportunity to participate in college preparatory classes. All students need to become versed in both social and academic language in English, and they must be able to integrate knowledge across disciplines. In addition, ELLs, who may not be first-generation immigrants, need teachers who understand principles of second-language acquisition and who are able to shelter content materials that are embedded in thematic units. Some ELLs may need orientation to the U.S. school system before they are able to learn English.

The strategies presented in this chapter provide clear rationales and classroom examples of what works for ELLs. As many ESL teachers know, these strategies are good instructional practices that will benefit native English speakers and ELLs alike. Working with ELLs requires an understanding of their backgrounds and personal stories, their academic strengths and challenges, and their potential and goals for the future. Consider the following students, some of whom might already be in your classroom today.

The Immigrant with a College Dream

When Marco was a boy, his father and older brothers moved to the United States, leaving Marco and his younger sisters to help their mother with the small family farm in rural Mexico. Though Marco was needed on the farm, his mother demanded that he attend school as often as possible. When Marco was 15, the rest of the family was able to move to the United States. Although Marco's parents completed only a few years of schooling, his mother was determined that her children would receive a good education. Marco often talked about his mother's dream that her children attend college.

Shortly after his arrival in the United States, Marco began working as a cook in his brother's restaurant. Though he worked 30 hours a week, Marco was able to maintain more than a 3.5 grade point average. He wanted to attend college so that he could learn accounting or business management to help his brother manage the restaurant (and some day possibly have a business of his own), but neither he nor his family knew much about the college application process. His family couldn't afford to help pay for college, either. In fact, they needed Marco's help just to keep the restaurant open.

Fortunately, during his junior year, one of Marco's teachers suggested that he participate in his school's Honors Council, where he received help in choosing a college and filling out the necessary forms for admission and financial aid. He learned that he was eligible for a state-guaranteed access grant for disadvantaged students with good grades, as well as a federal Pell Grant. He took a course to prepare him for both the SAT and the TOEFL and applied for and received both grants.

Unfortunately, Marco's scores on the SAT and TOEFL were lower than he had hoped; he feared that his dream of a college education would not come true. However, during one of the field trips he took with the council, Marco learned about the local community college, where he could earn an associate degree in accounting and perhaps be able to transfer to a four-year college. He also discovered that his grants would pay for all his expenses. Marco is now in his second year at the college—majoring in accounting and still working at his brother's restaurant. He plans eventually to transfer to a four-year college.

The Literacy Student

Patricia was 14 when she left her mother in El Salvador to come to the United States to live with her father and stepmother. In El Salvador, Patricia lived in a rural area, where she had little need to attend school. When she arrived in the United States, it was almost the end of the school year, and Patricia was placed in 8th grade, though she needed to learn English as well as the basic academic concepts that others in her grade had already learned.

When she moved on to high school, she was fortunate to be placed in a special literacy and basic skills course for ELLs, as well as in a beginning ESL class. Though she had to overcome many obstacles, her determination and the support of her teachers and family enabled her to make steady progress. In just a year, she achieved a 2.25 grade point average; after another year of a special academic skills class, she was able to pass two of the four required state examinations as well as raise her grades substantially.

Much of Patricia's success was due to the highly structured, although flexible, approach of her literacy and basic skills teachers, who taught her the importance of attending class and being prepared to learn. They convinced her that she would succeed. In her class, she learned how to organize a notebook, work with other students, and ask for help when she needed it. Family problems (her father and stepmother separated, and her brother was injured on the job) have forced Patricia to work both at home and in a part-time job. Though these demands are taking their toll and Patricia's grades are falling, she is determined to finish school. Her ESL teacher has suggested that she enter the school's work-study program next year and finish the last two tests. If she does, she will be one of the proudest seniors when she graduates next year.

The Elementary School Newcomer

Yesenia arrived from Mexico two months before beginning 3rd grade in a Title I school in inner-city Phoenix. Prior to her arrival, Arizona had voted to approve Proposition 203, which changed the system of bilingual education in Arizona schools. Proposition 203 required that school instruction in Arizona be implemented in

English only, with a one-year English immersion program for monolingual Spanish speakers. Yesenia began the 3rd grade in a classroom where she could not communicate with her teacher.

Although every student in her classroom was also Hispanic, she was one of the very few who could not speak English at all. Moving to a new school would be difficult for any student at such a young age, but Yesenia had come from a different country and found herself in a new and unfamiliar setting. As a result, she appeared withdrawn and painfully shy, rarely speaking to any of her classmates. She found school frustrating. Though she possessed basic literacy and numeracy skills in Spanish, her lack of English fluency kept her far behind her classmates in school achievement.

Mathematics appeared to be the area she most excelled in, although she continued to interact with numbers in Spanish. She quickly grasped concepts common to the 3rd grade curriculum, such as money, telling time, place value, basic mathematical functions, and fractions, experiencing the most success when working with hands-on activities that incorporated manipulatives and pictures, along with small-group discussion. One of her greatest strengths was her ability to think conceptually, applying mathematic concepts to real-life problems. As might be expected, Yesenia continued to struggle with story problems and with following directions. However, she developed keen observation skills that enabled her to watch and listen to others in her small group, ultimately increasing her understanding of the activity.

Yesenia's shyness was itself a barrier to her English-language acquisition. However, as the school year continued, she gradually gained the confidence to ask for help in Spanish, rather than waiting for her blank stares to indicate her lack of comprehension. By the end of the year, Yesenia had adjusted to classroom activities and began to speak up for herself in both Spanish and English. She continued to be one of the strongest math students, and she began to transfer her learning strategies for numeracy and apply them to English literacy.

Bibliography

Abedi, J. (2004). The No Child Left Behind Act and English language learners: Assessment and accountability issues. *Educational Researcher, 33*(1), 4–14.

Allen, R. V., & Allen, C. (1982). *Language experience activities* (2nd ed.). Boston: Houghton Mifflin.

Alliance for Excellent Education. (2005a, February). *High schools in the United States* (Fact sheet). Washington, DC: Alliance for Excellent Education. Available: http://www.all4ed.org/publications/NationalEducationSummitOnHighSchools/National.pdf

Alliance for Excellent Education. (2005b, September). *Case study: University Park Campus School in Worcester, Massachusetts*. Washington, DC: Alliance for Excellent Education. Available: http://www.all4ed.org/publications/University%20Park%20Campus%20School.pdf

Aronowitz, M. (1984). The social and emotional adjustment of immigrant children: A review of the literature. *International Migration Review, 18*(2), 237–257.

August, D., & Hakuta, K. (1997). *Improving schooling for language minority children: A research agenda*. Washington, DC: National Academies Press.

Batalova, J. (2005, October 1). *Spotlight on foreign born in areas affected by Hurricanes Katrina and Rita*.

Washington, DC: Migration Information Source. Available: http://www.migrationinformation.org/USfocus/display.cfm?id=343

Berman, P., McLaughlin, B., McLeod, B., Minicucci, C., Nelson, B., & Woodsworth, K. (1995). *School reform and student diversity: Case studies of exemplary practices for LEP students* (Draft report). Berkeley, CA: National Center for Research on Cultural Diversity and Second Language Learning and BW Associates.

Biancarosa, G., & Snow, C. (2004). *Reading next: A vision for action and research in middle and high school literacy.* (Report to Carnegie Corporation of New York). Washington, DC: Alliance for Excellent Education.

Biswas, R. (2005). *Access to community college for undocumented immigrants: A guide for state policymakers.* Boston: Jobs for the Future.

Borkowski, J. G., Johnston, M. B., & Reid, M. K. (1987). Metacognition, motivation, and controlled performance. In S. J. Ceci (Ed.), *Handbook of cognitive, social, and neuropsychological aspects of learning disabilities* (Vol. 2, pp. 147–174). Hillsdale, NJ: Lawrence Erlbaum.

Bruer, J. T. (1993). The mind's journey from novice to expert: If we know the route, we can help students negotiate the way. *American Educator, 17*(2), 6–15, 38–46.

Bruner, J. (1986). *Actual minds, possible worlds.* Cambridge, MA: Harvard University Press.

Bunch, G. (1995). Five tests and five schools: Information for international students (and their teachers!) about entrance exams for higher education. In E. Holden (Ed.), *College-bound immigrants and international students: A manual for setting up a support network.* Baltimore: Project WE TEACH, University of Maryland Baltimore County and Prince George's County (MD) Public Schools.

California State Board of Education. (1999, July). *English-language development standards for California public schools, kindergarten through grade twelve.* Sacramento: Author.

Capps, R., Fix, M., Murray, J., Ost, J., Passel, J., & Herwantoro, S. (2005). *The new demography of America's schools: Immigration and the No Child Left Behind Act.* Washington, DC: Urban Institute.

Carter, T. P., & Chatfield, M. L. (1986). Effective bilingual schools: Implications for policy and practice. *American Journal of Education, 95*(1), 200–232.

Center on Education Policy. (2005a). *From the capital to the classroom: Year 3 of the No Child Left Behind Act.* Washington, DC: Center on Education Policy.

Center on Education Policy. (2005b). *States try harder, but gaps persist: High school exit exams 2005.* Washington, DC: Center on Education Policy.

Chamot, A., & O'Malley, J. M. (1994). *The CALLA handbook: Implementing the cognitive academic language learning approach.* New York: Addison-Wesley.

Cohen, E. A., & Lotan, R. A. (1997). *Working for equity in heterogeneous classrooms: Sociological theory in practice.* New York: Teachers College Press.

Cohen, P. A., Kulik, J. A., & Kulik, C. L. (1982). Educational outcomes of tutoring: A meta-analysis of findings. *American Educational Research Journal, 19*(2), 237–248.

Collier, V. P. (1989). How long: A synthesis of research on academic achievement in a second language. *TESOL Quarterly, 23*(3), 509–531.

Consentino de Cohen, C., Deterding, N., & Clewell, B. (2005). *Who's left behind? Immigrant children in high and low LEP schools.* Washington, DC: Urban Institute.

Cook, B., & Urzua, C. (1993). *The literacy club: A cross-age tutoring/paired reading project.* Washington, DC: National Clearinghouse for Bilingual Education.

Cornelius, W. A., & Rumba, R. G. (Eds.). (1995). *California's immigrant children: Theory, research, and implications for educational policy.* San Diego: San Diego Center for U.S.-Mexican Studies, University of California.

Council of Chief State School Officers. (2004). *Immigrant students and secondary school reform: Compendium of best practices.* Washington, DC: Author.

Crandall, J. A. (1981). *A sociolinguistic analysis of the literacy demands of clerical workers.* Unpublished doctoral dissertation, Georgetown University, Washington, DC.

Crandall, J. A. (1987). *ESL through content-area instruction: Mathematics, science, social studies.* Washington, DC and Englewood Cliffs, NJ: Center for Applied Linguistics and Prentice-Hall Regents.

Crandall, J. A. (1994). Strategic integration: Preparing language and content teachers for linguistically and culturally diverse classrooms. In J. E. Alatis (Ed.), *Strategic interaction and language acquisition: Theory, practice, and research* (pp. 255–274). Washington, DC: Georgetown University Press.

Crandall, J. A. (1995). Reinventing (America's) schools: The role of the applied linguist. In J. E. Alatis, C. A. Straehle, B. Gallenberger, & M. Ronkin (Eds.), *Linguistics and the education of language teachers: Ethnolinguistic, psycholinguistic, and sociolinguistic aspects* (pp. 412–427). Washington, DC: Georgetown University Press.

Crandall, J. A. (1998). Collaborate and cooperate: Preparing language and content teachers. *English Teaching Forum, 36*(1), 2–9.

Crandall, J. A. (1999). Cooperative language learning and affective factors. In J. Arnold (Ed.), *Affective factors in language learning* (pp. 226–245). Cambridge, UK: Cambridge University Press.

Crandall, J. A., Bernache, C., & Prager, S. (1998). New frontiers in educational policy and program development: The challenge of the underschooled immigrant secondary school student. *Educational Policy, 12*(6), 719–734.

Crandall, J. A., & Greenblatt, L. (1999). Teaching beyond the middle: Meeting the needs of underschooled and high-achieving immigrant students. In M. R. Basterra (Ed.), *Excellence and equity for language minority students: Critical issues and promising practices* (pp. 43–80). Washington, DC: American University, Mid-Atlantic Equity Center.

Crandall, J. A., & Tucker, G. R. (1990). Content-based language instruction in second and foreign languages. In A. Sanivan (Ed.), *Language teaching methodology for the nineties* (pp. 83–96). Singapore: SEAMEO Regional Language Centre.

Cummins, J. (1979). Cognitive/academic language proficiency, linguistic interdependence, the optimal age question, and some other matters. *Working Papers on Bilingualism, 19*, 197–205.

Curtain, H., & Haas, M. (1995). *Integrating foreign language and content instruction in grades K–8.* Washington, DC: ERIC Clearinghouse on Languages and Linguistics.

Darling-Hammond, L. (1996). The quiet revolution: Rethinking teacher development. *Educational Leadership, 53*(6), 4–10.

Day, J. C. (2001). *U.S. Census Bureau national population projections.* Washington, DC: U. S. Census Bureau, Population Division and Housing and Household Economic Statistics Division. Available: http://www.census.gov/population/www/pop-profile/natproj.html

Dixon, C. N., & Nessel, D. (1983). *Language experience approach to reading (and writing).* Hayward, CA: Aleman Press.

Duff, P. (2005). ESL in secondary schools: Programs, problematics, and possibilities. In E. Hinkel (Ed.), *Handbook of research in second language teaching and learning.* Mahwah, NJ: Erlbaum.

Duffy, J. L., Roehler, M., Meloth, M., Vavrus, L., Book, C., Putnam, J., & Wesselman, R. (1986). The relationship between explicit verbal explanation during reading skill instruction and student awareness and achievement: A study of reading teacher effects. *Reading Research Quarterly, 21*(2), 237–252.

Echevarria, J., & Graves, A. (1998). *Sheltered content instruction: Teaching English-language learners with diverse abilities.* Boston: Allyn and Bacon.

Echevarria, J., & Short, D. (2004). Using multiple perspectives in observations of diverse classrooms: The sheltered instruction observation protocol (SIOP). In H. Waxman, R. Tharp, & S. Hilberg (Eds.), *Observational research in U.S. classrooms: New approaches for understanding cultural and linguistic diversity* (pp. 21–47). Boston: Cambridge University Press.

Echevarria, J., Vogt, M., & Short, D. (2004). *Making content comprehensible for English language learners: The SIOP Model*. Boston: Allyn and Bacon.

Educational Testing Service. (2005, September). *The Praxis Series passing scores by test and state*. Princeton, NJ: Author.

Enright, D. S., & McCloskey, M. L. (1988). *Integrating English: Developing English language and literacy in the multilingual classroom*. Reading, MA: Addison-Wesley.

Fathman, A. K., & Quinn, M. E. (1989). *Science for language learners*. Englewood Cliffs, NJ: Prentice-Hall Regents.

Fazel, M., Wheeler, J., & Danesh, J. (2005, April 9). Prevalence of serious mental disorder in 7000 refugees resettled in western countries: A systematic review [Online article]. *The Lancet, 365*(9467). Available: http://www.thelancet.com/journals/lancet

First, J., & Carrera, J. W. (1988). *New voices: Immigrant students in the U.S. public schools*. Boston: National Coalition of Advocates for Students.

Fisher, D. (2001, December). Trust the process: Increasing student achievement via professional development and process accountability. *National Association of Secondary School Principals Bulletin, 85*(12), 67–71.

Fisher, D. (2004). Setting the 'opportunity to read' standard: Resuscitating the SSR program in an urban high school. *Journal of Adolescent and Adult Literacy, 48*(2), 138–150.

Fisher, D., & Frey, N. (2003). Writing instruction for struggling adolescent readers: A gradual release model. *Journal of Adolescent and Adult Literacy, 48*(2), 396–405.

Fisher, D., & Frey, N. (2004). *Improving adolescent literacy: Content area strategies at work*. Upper Saddle River, NJ: Pearson.

Fisher, D., Frey, N., & Fehrenbacher, T. (2004a). And in the center ring, high-stakes tests. In D. Fisher & N. Frey (Eds.), *Improving adolescent literacy: Content area strategies at work* (pp. 169–181). Upper Saddle River, NJ: Pearson.

Fisher, D., Frey, N., & Fehrenbacher, T. (2004b). Reciprocal teaching: Giving responsibility to students. In D. Fisher & N. Frey (Eds.), *Improving adolescent literacy: Content area strategies at work* (pp. 153–168). Upper Saddle River, NJ: Pearson.

Fisher, D., Frey, N., & Williams, D. (2002, November). Seven literacy strategies that work. *Educational Leadership, 60*(3), 70–73.

Fisher, D., Lapp, D., & Flood, J. (2005). Consensus scoring and peer planning: Meeting literacy accountability demands one school at a time. *International Reading Association, 58*(7), 656–666.

Freeman, D. (2001, November). Blocking the school schedule: Potential for instructional change. Paper presented at annual meeting of the University Council for Educational Administration, Cincinnati, Ohio.

Frey, N., & Fisher, D. (2004a). Teachers matter, and what they do matters most: Using literacy strategies, grouping, and texts to promote learning. In D. Fisher & N. Frey (Eds.), *Improving adolescent literacy: Content area strategies at work* (pp. 1–14). Upper Saddle River, NJ: Pearson.

Frey, N., & Fisher, D. (2004b). Using graphic novels, anime, and the Internet in an urban high school. *English Journal, 93*(3), 19–25.

Garcia, E. (1988). *The education of linguistically and culturally diverse students: Effective instructional practices*. Washington, DC, and Santa Cruz, CA: National Center for Research on Cultural Diversity and Second Language Learning/Center for Applied Linguistics.

Gardiner, J. (1983). *Stone fox*. New York: HarperCollins.

Gardner, H. (1993). *Multiple intelligences: The theory in practice*. New York: BasicBooks.

Genesee, F. (Ed.). (1998). *Program alternatives for linguistically diverse students* (Educational Practice Report No. 1). Santa Cruz, CA: Center for Research on Education, Diversity & Excellence.

Genesee, F., Lindholm-Leary, K., Saunders, W., & Christian, D. (2006). *Educating English language learners: A synthesis of research evidence*. New York: Cambridge University Press.

González, J. M., & Darling-Hammond, L. (1997). *New concepts for new challenges: Professional development for teachers of immigrant youth.* Washington, DC, and McHenry, IL: Center for Applied Linguistics and Delta Systems.

Greenleaf, C., Schoenback, R., Cziko, C., & Mueller, F. (2001). Apprenticing adolescent readers to academic literacy. *Harvard Educational Review, 71*(1), 79–129.

Hadlock, C. (1994). College-bound immigrant and international students: A manual for setting up a support network. In J. A. Crandall & E. Holden (Eds.), *Raising college and career expectations and helping immigrant students to achieve them.* Baltimore: Project WE TEACH, University of Maryland Baltimore County and Prince George's County (MD) Public Schools.

Hakuta, K. (1987). *Mirror of language: The debate on bilingualism.* New York: BasicBooks.

Hakuta, K., Butler, Y. G., & Witt, D. (2000). *How long does it take English learners to attain proficiency?* University of California Linguistic Minority Research Institute Policy Report 2000-1. Stanford University, Palo Alto.

Hamayan, E. (1994). Language development of low-literacy students. In F. Genesee (Ed.), *Educating second language children: The whole child, the whole curriculum, the whole community* (pp. 278–300). Cambridge, UK: Cambridge University Press.

Han, M., & Baker, D. (1997). *A profile of policies and practices for limited English proficient students: Screening methods, program support, and teacher training: SASS 1993–1994 (NCES 97-472).* Washington, DC: National Center for Education Statistics.

Harklau, L., Losey, K. M., & Siegal, M. (Eds.). (1999). *Generation 1.5 meets college composition: Issues in the teaching of writing to U.S.-educated learners of ESL.* Mahwah, NJ: Erlbaum.

Harvey, S., & Goudvis, A. (2000). *Strategies that work.* New York: Stenhouse.

Heath, S. B. (1983). *Ways with words: Language, life, and work in communities and classrooms.* Cambridge, UK: Cambridge University Press.

Heath, S. B., & Mangiola, L. (1991). *Children of promise: Literate activity in linguistically and culturally diverse classrooms.* Washington, DC: National Education Association/American Educational Research Association.

Henderson, A., Abbott, C., & Strang, W. (1993). *Summary of the bilingual education State Educational Agency program survey of states' limited English proficient persons and available educational services, 1991–1992.* Arlington, VA: Development Associates. (ERIC Document Reproduction Service No. ED 369 292)

Henke, R. R., Choy, S. P., Chen, X., Geis, S., Alt, M. N., & Broughman, S. P. (1997). *America's teachers: Profile of a profession, 1993–94.* Washington, DC: U.S. Department of Education, National Center for Education Statistics.

Holmes Group. (1990). *Tomorrow's schools.* East Lansing, MI: Author.

Horn, L. J., & Carroll, C. D. (1997). *Confronting the odds: Students at risk and the pipeline to higher education.* Washington, DC: U.S. Department of Education, National Center for Education Statistics.

Hudec, J., & Short, D. (Eds.). (2002). *Helping English learners succeed: An overview of the SIOP model* [Video]. Washington, DC: Center for Applied Linguistics.

Hutner, J. G. (1996). Preparing freshman, sophomore, and junior immigrant and international students for entrance into college. In E. Holden (Ed.), *College bound immigrants and international students: A manual for setting up a support network.* Baltimore: Project WE TEACH, University of Maryland Baltimore County and Prince George's County (MD) Public Schools.

International Reading Association. (1999). *Summary of adolescent literacy: A position statement for the commission on adolescent literacy of the International Reading Association.* Washington, DC: Author. Available: http://ira.org/resources/issues/positions_adolescent.html

Jacob, E., Rottenberg, L., Patrick, S., & Wheeler, E. (1996). Cooperative learning: Context and opportunities for acquiring academic English. *TESOL Quarterly, 30*(2), 253–280.

Jameson, J. (1999). *Enriching content classes for secondary ESOL students.* McHenry, IL, and Washington, DC: Delta Systems and Center for Applied Linguistics.

Jeffers, S. (1991). *Brother eagle, sister sky: A message from Chief Seattle.* New York: Dial Books.

Joftus, S. (2002). *Every child a graduate: A framework for an excellent education for all middle and high school students.* Washington, DC: Alliance for Excellent Education. Available: http://www.all4ed.org

Johnson, D. W., & Johnson, R. (1987). *Learning together and alone: Cooperative, competitive, and individualistic learning.* Englewood Cliffs, NJ: Prentice-Hall.

Johnson, D. W., Johnson, R. T., & Holubec, E. J. (1993). *Circles of learning* (4th ed.). Edina, MN: Interaction.

Jones, B. F., Palincsar, A. S., Ogle, D. S., & Carr, E. G. (1987). *Strategic teaching and learning: Cognitive instruction in the content areas.* Alexandria, VA: Association for Supervision and Curriculum Development.

Kagan, S. (1994). *Cooperative learning resources for teachers.* San Juan Capistrano, CA: Kagan Cooperative Learning.

Kamil, M. L. (2003). *Adolescents and literacy: Reading for the 21st century.* Washington, DC: Alliance for Excellent Education.

Kessler, C., & Hayes, C. (1989). Foreword. In A. K. Fatham & M. E. Quinn (Eds.), *Science for language learners.* Englewood Cliffs, NJ: Prentice-Hall Regents.

Krashen, S. (2004). *The power of reading: Insights from the research* (2nd ed.). Portsmouth, NH: Heinemann.

Lucas, T. (1997). *Into, through, and beyond secondary school: Critical transitions for immigrant youths.* Washington, DC, and McHenry, IL: Center for Applied Linguistics and Delta Systems.

Lucas, T., Henze, R., & Donato, R. (1990). Promoting the success of Latino language minority students: An exploratory study of six high schools. *Harvard Educational Review, 60*(3), 315–340.

Mace-Matluck, B., Alexander-Kasparik, R., & Queen, R. (1998). *Through the golden door: Educational approaches for immigrant adolescents with limited schooling.* McHenry, IL, and Washington, DC: Delta Systems and Center for Applied Linguistics.

Maroney, O. H. (1998). Who is teaching the children? More trained bilingual teachers are needed for excellent education. *IDRA Newsletter, 25*(1), 6–8.

McKay, S. L., & Wong, S. C. (2000). *New immigrants in the United States: Readings for second language educators.* Cambridge, UK: Cambridge University Press.

Minicucci, C., & Olsen, L. (1992). An exploratory study of secondary LEP programs. In P. Berman (Ed.), *Meeting the challenges of diversity: An evaluation of programs for pupils with limited proficiency in English* (Vol. 5). Berkeley, CA: BW Associates.

Moje, E., Dillon, D., & O'Brien, D. (2000, January/February). Reexamining roles of learner, text, and context in secondary literacy. *Journal of Educational Research, 93*(3), 165–181.

Moll, L. C., Amanti, C., Neff, D., & Gonzalez, N. (1992). Funds of knowledge for teaching: Using a qualitative approach to connect homes and classroom. *Theory into Practice, 31*(2), 132–141.

Moran-Ender, C., & Ender, M. G. (1995, March). A picture and a thousand words: Autophotography in the ESOL classroom and beyond. Presentation at the TESOL Annual Convention, Long Beach, California.

National Association of Secondary School Principals. (2005). *Creating a culture of literacy: A guide for middle and high school principals.* Reston, VA: Author.

National Center for Education Statistics. (1997). *Findings from the condition of education 1997: The social context of education.* Washington, DC: Author.

National Clearinghouse for English Language Acquisition. (2007). *NCELA FAQ: What are the most common language groups for ELL students?* Washington, DC: Author.

National Commission on Teaching and America's Future. (1996). *What matters most: Teaching for America's future.* New York: Author.

Olsen, L., & Chen, M. (1988). *Crossing the schoolhouse border: Immigrant children in California schools.* San Francisco: California Tomorrow.

Olsen, L., & Jaramillo, A. (1999). *Turning the tides of exclusion: A guide for educators and advocates for immigrant students.* Oakland, CA: California Tomorrow.

Olsen, L., & Jaramillo, A. (2000). When time is on our side: Redesigning schools to meet the needs of immigrant students. In P. Gándara (Ed.), *The dimension of time and the challenge of school reform* (pp. 225–250). Albany, NY: State University of New York Press.

Olsen, L., Jaramillo, A., McCall-Perez, Z., & White, J. (1999). *Igniting change for immigrant students: Portraits of three high schools.* Oakland, CA: California Tomorrow.

Olsen, L., & Mullen, N. (1990). *Embracing diversity: Teachers' voices from California schools.* San Francisco: California Tomorrow.

Orfield, G., Losen, D., Wald, J., & Swanson, C. (2004). *Losing our future: How minority youth are being left behind by the graduation rate crisis.* Cambridge, MA: Civil Rights Project at Harvard University.

Padolsky, D. (2005, May). How many school-aged English language learners (ELLs) are there in the U.S.? Message post to http://www.ncela.gwu.edu/expert/faq/01leps.html

Palincsar, A. S., & Brown, A. L. (1984). Reciprocal teaching of comprehension-fostering and comprehension-monitoring activities. *Cognition and Instruction, 1*(2), 117–175.

Palincsar, A. S., David, Y., & Brown, A. L. (1989). *Using reciprocal teaching in the classroom: A guide for teachers.* Berkeley, CA: Campion Group.

Park, K. (1999). 'I really do feel I'm 1.5': The construction of self and community by young Korean Americans. *Amerasia Journal, 25*(1), 139–163.

Passel, J. (October 2003). *Further demographic information relating to the DREAM Act.* Washington, DC: Urban Institute.

Pew Hispanic Center/Kaiser Family Foundation. (2004).

Peyton, J. K., Jones, C., Vincent, A., & Greenblatt, L. (1994). Implementing writing workshops with ESOL students: Visions and realities. *TESOL Quarterly, 28*(3), 469–487.

Peyton, J. K., & Reed, L. (1990). *Dialogue journal writing with nonnative English speakers: A handbook for teachers.* Alexandria, VA: Teachers of English to Speakers of Other Languages (TESOL).

Richard-Amato, P., & Snow, M. A. (1992). *The multicultural classroom: Readings for content-area teachers.* White Plains, NY: Longman.

Ruby, J. (2003). Fostering multilayered literacy through literature circles. *TESOL Journal, 12*(3), 47–48.

Ruiz-de-Velasco, J., & Fix, M. (2000). *Overlooked and underserved: Immigrant students in U.S. secondary schools.* Washington, DC: Urban Institute.

Ruiz-de-Velasco, J., & Fix, M. (2002). Limited English proficient students and high-stakes accountability systems. In D. Piché, W. Taylor, & R. Reed (Eds.), *Rights at risk: Equality in an age of terrorism* (pp. 245–261). Washington, DC: Citizens' Commission on Civil Rights.

Rumbaut, R. (1994). The crucible within: Ethnic identity, self-esteem and segmented assimilation among children of immigrants. *International Migration Review, 28*(4), 748–794.

Rumptz, M., Lucas, L., & McEmrys, A. (2001). *Teens in transition: Best practices in mentoring adolescents.* Portland, OR: NPC Research. Available: http://www.npcresearch.com/Files/Teens%20in%20Transition.pdf

Schank, R., & Abelson, R. (1977). *Scripts, plans, goals, and understanding.* Hillsdale, NJ: Erlbaum.

Short, D. J. (1991). *How to integrate language and content instruction: A training manual.* Washington, DC: Center for Applied Linguistics.

Short, D. J., & Boyson, B. (2000). *Directory of secondary newcomer programs in the United States: Revised*

2000. Washington, DC: Center for Applied Linguistics.

Short, D., & Boyson, B. (2004). *Creating access: Language and academic programs for secondary school newcomers.* McHenry, IL, and Washington, DC: Delta Systems and Center for Applied Linguistics.

Slavin, R. E. (1989, December/1990, January). Research on cooperative learning: Consensus and controversy. *Educational Leadership, 47*(4), 52–54.

Slavin, R. E. (1990). *Cooperative learning: Theory, research, and practice.* Englewood Cliffs, NJ: Prentice-Hall.

Smith, F. (1988). *Joining the literacy club.* Portsmouth, NH: Heinemann.

Steinbeck, J. (1993). *The pearl.* New York: Penguin.

Sturtevant, E. (2003). *The literacy coach: A key to improving teaching and learning in secondary schools.* Washington, DC: Alliance for Excellent Education.

Tate, O. (1997, May). Teaching literacy-level ESOL students. Presentation at Mid-Atlantic Equity Conference, College Park, Maryland.

Taylor, M. (1993). The language experience approach. In J. A. Crandall & J. K. Peyton (Eds.), *Approaches to adult ESL literacy instruction* (pp. 47–58). Washington, DC, and McHenry, IL: Center for Applied Linguistics and Delta Systems.

Teachers of English to Speakers of Other Languages. (1997). *ESL standards for pre-K–12 students.* Alexandria, VA: Author.

Tighe, M. J. (1971). Creative dialogue: Teaching students to teach themselves. *New Directions in Teaching, 2*(4), 21–25.

Tucker, G. R. (1990). Cognitive and social correlates of additive bilinguality. In J. E. Alatis (Ed.), *Georgetown University Round Table on Languages and Linguistics 1990.* Washington, DC: Georgetown University Press.

Trumbull, E., Rothstein-Fisch, C., Greenfield, P., & Quiroz, B. (2001). *Bridging cultures between home and school: A guide for teachers.* Mahwah, NJ, and San Francisco: Lawrence Erlbaum and WestEd.

United Nations Population Fund. (2003). *The state of world population 2003. Making one billion count: Investing in adolescents' health and rights.* New York: United Nations Population Fund. Available: http://www.unfpa.org/swp/2003/pdf/english/swp2003_eng.pdf

Vacca, R., & Vacca, J. (2004). *Content area reading: Literacy and learning across the curriculum.* Boston: Allyn and Bacon.

Van Hook, J., Bean, F., & Passel, J. (2005, September 1). *Unauthorized migrants living in the United States: A mid-decade portrait.* Washington, DC: Migration Information Source. Available: http://www.migrationinformation.org/Feature/display.cfm?id=329

Walqui, A. (2000). *Access and engagement: Program design and instructional approaches for immigrant students in secondary school.* McHenry, IL, and Washington, DC: Delta Systems and Center for Applied Linguistics.

Walqui-VanLier, A. (1991). *Sheltered instruction: Doing it right.* Unpublished manuscript.

Wiggins, G., & McTighe, J. (1998). *Understanding by design.* Alexandria, VA: Association for Supervision and Curriculum Development.

Wong Fillmore, L., & Valadez, C. (1986). Teaching bilingual learners. In M. C. Wittrock (Ed.), *Handbook of research on teaching.* New York: Macmillan.

Yep, L. (1975). *Dragonwings.* New York: Harper & Row.

Zehler, A. M., Fleischman, H. L., Hopstock, P. J., Stephenson, T. G., Pendzick, M. L., & Sapru, S. (2003). *Descriptive study of services to LEP students and LEP students with disabilities. Policy Report: Summary of findings related to LEP and SpEd-LEP students.* Submitted to U.S. Department of Education, OELA. Arlington, VA: Development Associates.

Zeichner, K. (1992). *Educating teachers for cultural diversity.* East Lansing, MI: National Center for Research on Teacher Learning.

Index

Note: Information presented in figures and tables is represented by *f* and *t* respectively.

About the Authors

Beverly J. Armento is Research Professor Emerita at Georgia State University. She has taught elementary and middle school social studies and language arts in New Jersey, Florida, and Maryland, and has prepared K–12 social studies educators for more than 40 years. She also directed the Georgia State University Center for Business and Economic Education for more than a decade. Her major interests are in learner-centered, learning-centered classrooms in diverse school settings and in the preparation of empowering educators. She continues to teach in the teacher education program at Oglethorpe University in Atlanta, Georgia, and she serves as an active volunteer with the Youth Services Programs at Refugee Family Services in Atlanta. Phone: 770-310-1231. E-mail: Barmento@aol.com.

Marie Carbo is Executive Director of the National Reading Styles Institute (NRSI) and an international reading consultant. Author of the Reading Style Inventory and originator of the Carbo Recorded-Book Method, she has published more than 100 articles and books for children, parents, and teachers. Her latest book is *Becoming a Great Teacher of Reading*, published by Corwin Press. She may be contacted at NRSI, P.O. Box 737, Syosset, NY 11791. Phone: 516-921-5500. E-mail: marie@nrsi.com.

Robert W. Cole, proprietor of Edu-Data, is a writer, editor, and consultant in Louisville, Kentucky. His credentials include 14 years at *Phi Delta Kappan* magazine, seven of them as Editor-in-Chief; 10 years as President of the Educational Press Association of America and member of the EdPress Board of Directors; four years as Founding Vice President of the Schlechty Center for Leadership in School Reform; 11 years as Senior Consultant to the National Reading Styles Institute; Creative Director of the Power Reading Program; and Editor of *The Lens*, published online by the Center for Empowered Leadership. He has presented workshops, master classes, and lectures at universities nationwide, including Harvard University, Stanford University, and Indiana University. He has also served as a special consultant to college and university deans in working with faculties on writing for professional publication. Phone: 502-767-7220. E-mail: cole@edu-data.org.

JoAnn (Jodi) Crandall is Professor of Education, with a focus on ESOL/bilingual education, and Director of the Interdisciplinary Doctoral Program in Language, Literacy, and Culture at the University of Maryland, Baltimore County. She is the author or editor of several books and articles focused on curriculum and instruction for English language learners, including *Content-Based Instruction in Elementary and Secondary Settings* and *Content-Based Instruction in Higher Education Settings*, both published by TESOL. For five years, Crandall directed Project WE TEACH to improve the academic achievement and postsecondary options of immigrant secondary school students. She may be contacted at UMBC, Education Department, 1000 Hilltop Circle, Baltimore, MD 21250. Phone: 410-455-2313. E-mail: Crandall@umbc.edu.

Beatriz S. D'Ambrosio is Professor of Mathematics Education at Miami University in Oxford, Ohio. Her research interests lie in bridging the gap between research and practice in mathematics education. With the intent of empowering teachers, she has focused on building preservice and inservice experiences that develop the teacher researcher. Her goal in working with teachers is to help them attend to the mathematics of children, hence empowering the children as young mathematicians. Phone: 513-529-2546. E-mail: dambrobs@muohio.edu.

Sally Hampton is a Senior Fellow for the National Center on Education and the Economy (NCEE). Most recently, she was a Senior Scholar at the Carnegie Foundation for the Advancement of Teaching. Formerly, she served as Director of English Language Arts for NCEE, as well as Deputy Director of Research and Development. She has taught in both urban and rural classrooms, directed a National Writing Project site, and developed a K–12 research-based writing program and the staff development materials to support this program. E-mail: shampton@ncee.org.

Ann Jaramillo is an English language development teacher at La Paz Middle School in Salinas, California. While at California Tomorrow, she was Senior Project Associate in the program on immigrant education, helping to create immigrant-responsive secondary schools. Jaramillo also conducts professional development on sheltered content instruction and English language development strategies throughout California. Jaramillo may be contacted at California Tomorrow, 436 14th St., Suite 820, Oakland, CA 94612. Phone: 510-496-0220. E-mail: annj@californiatomorrow.org.

Signe E. Kastberg is Assistant Professor of Mathematics Education at Indiana University–Purdue University at Indianapolis. Her research interests lie in understanding the development and application of knowledge in mathematics teacher practice. She has focused on exploring and articulating the creative mathematical and pedagogical acts of students and teachers. Phone: 317-274-6829. E-mail: skastber@iupui.edu.

Laurie Olsen is Executive Director of California Tomorrow, a nonprofit research and technical assistance organization in Oakland, California. She has developed a national reputation as a researcher, speaker, and consultant to schools on issues of equity and achievement in public schools. She is the author of several publications on immigrant education, including *Made in America: Immigrant Students in Public Schools* (The New Press, 1997). For five years, she directed a successful demonstration project in restructuring secondary schools to respond to the needs of immigrant students. She is lead partner in the PROMISE Initiative—a six-county collaborative to develop model schools preschool through high school that lead to high-achieving English learners—and works with leadership teams from secondary schools on strengthening English learner programs throughout California. She may be contacted at California Tomorrow, 1904 Franklin St., Suite 300, Oakland, CA 94612. Phone: 510- 496-0220. E-mail: laurieo@californiatomorrow.org.

Joy Kreeft Peyton is Vice President of the Center for Applied Linguistics in Washington, D.C. She served as Associate Director of the Program in Immigrant Education, which focused on developing excellent secondary school programs for immigrant students. She is coeditor of the series *Topics in Immigrant Education* and has authored, coauthored, and edited several publications on educational approaches for immigrant students. She may be contacted at Center for Applied Linguistics, 4646 40th St. NW, Washington, DC 20016-1859. Phone: 202-362-0700, ext. 545. E-mail: jpeyton@cal.org. Web site: www.cal.org.

Marietta Saravia-Shore is Associate Professor, Lehman College, City University of New York (CUNY). She received her Ph.D. in Anthropology and Education from Columbia University. She is coeditor of *Cross-Cultural Literacy: Ethnographies of Communication in Multiethnic Classrooms* (Garland). She previously directed the Bilingual Education Applied Research Unit at Hunter College (CUNY) and was Associate Director of the Institute for Urban and Minority Education (IUME) for Professional Development and Educational Programs at Teachers College, Columbia University. She founded and directed the IUME Cross-Cultural Literacy Center prior to coming to Lehman College, where she served as Executive Director of the Bronx Educational Alliance for seven years.

Charles Watson has been a classroom science teacher, an administrator, and a teacher educator. He has published several articles and books about science education and middle-level education and is the Chair of the School of Education at the University of Evansville in Evansville, Indiana. Phone: 812-488-2004. E-mail: cw73@evansvill.edu.

Sarah Young is an ESL Specialist at the Center for Applied Linguistics in Washington, DC. Her current focus is on adolescent and adult English language learner instruction, language assessment, and teacher training. She has taught high school ESL overseas and adult ESL in the United States. She may be contacted at the Center for Applied Linguistics, 4646 40th St. NW, Washington, DC 20016-1859. Phone: 202-362-0700, ext. 529. E-mail: syoung@cal.org. Web site: www.cal.org.